MW01259818

Our Friends the Enemies

Our Friends the Enemies

THE OCCUPATION OF FRANCE AFTER NAPOLEON

Christine Haynes

Harvard University Press
Cambridge, Massachusetts
London, England
2018

Printed in the United States of America

First printing

Library of Congress Cataloging-in-Publication Data

Names: Haynes, Christine, 1970– author.
Title: Our friends the enemies : the occupation of France after Napoleon/Christine Haynes.
Description: Cambridge, Massachusetts : Harvard University Press, 2018. |
Includes bibliographical references and index.
Identifiers: LCCN 2018006849 | ISBN 9780674972315 (hardcover : alk. paper)
Subjects: LCSH: France—History—Restoration, 1814–1830. |
France—History—Louis XVIII, 1814–1824. | France—Foreign relations—1814–1830. |
Napoleonic Wars, 1800–1815—Peace. | Military occupation.
Classification: LCC DC256.8 .H39 2018 | DDC 944.06/1—dc23
LC record available at https://lccn.loc.gov/2018006849

To my parents,

David and Marilyn Haynes,

and to my sons,

Oliver and Simon Wilson

Contents

There were no more enemies;

there were neither victors

nor vanquished, but only

liberators and good friends!

—François-Simon Cazin, remembering how Allied troops and French inhabitants danced together during the occupation of France, 1815–1818

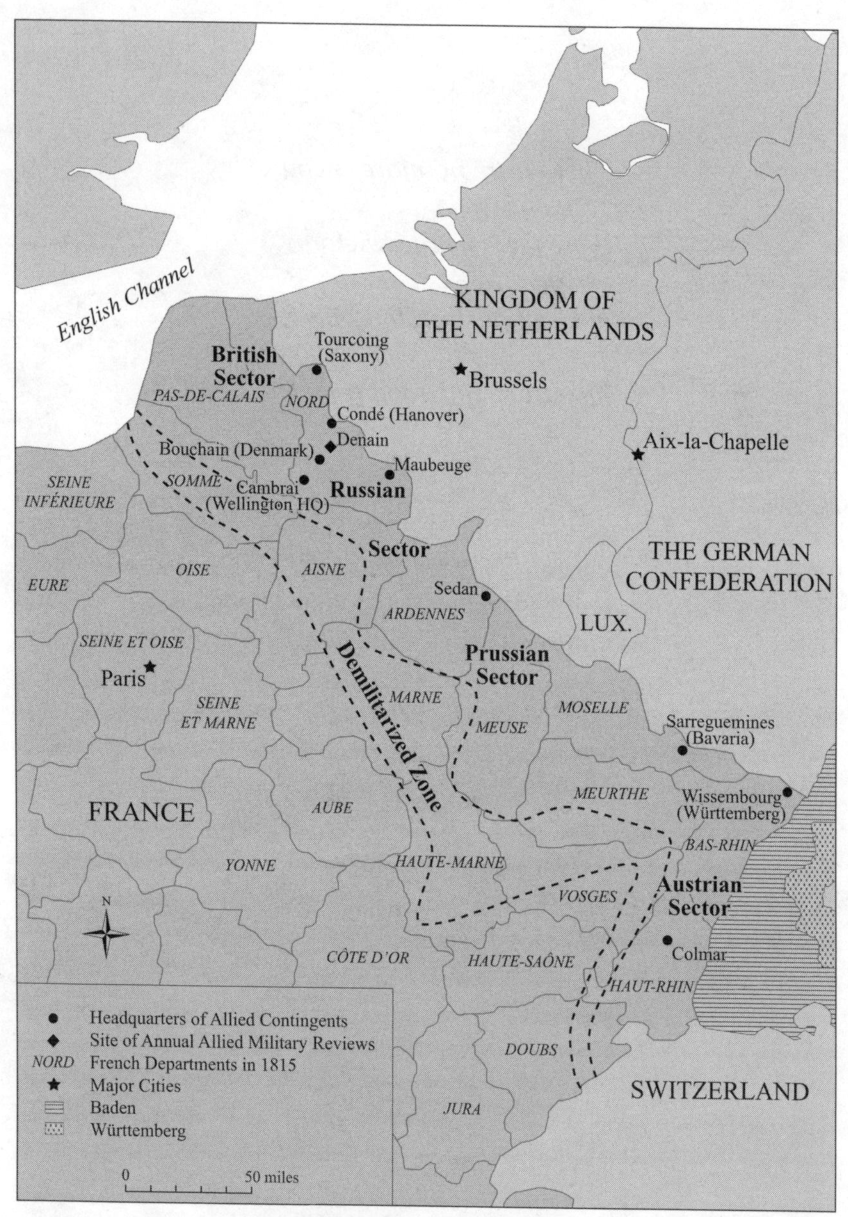

Occupation of Guarantee, November 1815–November 1818. Allied sectors and demilitarized zone overlaid on French departments.

Introduction

In May 1815, as troops from the Allied powers of Europe remobilized to fight Napoleon Bonaparte, who had returned from exile to France two months earlier, popular songwriter Pierre-Jean de Béranger penned a *chanson* about the "demoiselles," or prostitutes, of the Palais-Royal in Paris. Remembering how these damsels had experienced a boom in business when the Prussians and Russians first invaded Paris in March 1814, the song predicted that if "the enemy was going to turn everything upside down again at our house," their homeland of the Palais-Royal would "rejoice." Noting that the previous year honest as well as fallen women had taken lovers among the foreign troops, it concluded, "Business wi' soon be booming,/If I believe an old libertine/of a sacristan./Even if there are a few burned houses,/A few people slain,/That's the least of our worries./But I'll laugh well if I'm violated./Long live our friends,/Our friends the enemies!"[1]

Facetious as it is, the refrain encapsulates the main challenge facing Europe at the close of the Napoleonic Wars: how to turn enemies into "friends." In 1815 the Allied powers were confronted again with the problem of how to restore order not just in France but throughout Europe. Across the Continent and much of the rest of the world, the transition from war to peace was long and protracted. Contrary to the standard narrative, the Napoleonic Wars did not end on the battlefield at Waterloo, but continued with a massive invasion of much of France by over a million men. It took considerable time and effort by both sides—beyond just the wiles of the demoiselles of the Palais-Royal—to transform the former enemies into anything approaching "friends."

The challenge of restoring order in the aftermath of war had been faced by the European powers before, in the Peace of Westphalia of 1648 and, more recently, the Congress of Aix-la-Chapelle in 1748, both of which aimed to reestablish a balance of power between sovereign states. In the aftermath of Waterloo, however, the Allied leaders developed a new method for ensuring peace: occupation for the purpose not of conquest but of reconstruction, and not just of a sovereign state but of an entire people, to reconcile them with the community of nations.

In addition to negotiating a settlement at Vienna and maintaining their coalition as a Concert of Europe, the Allies instituted an "occupation of guarantee" against political instability in the defeated country. According to the peace treaty signed on November 20, 1815, the Allies would station 150,000 troops under the command of British field marshal Arthur Wellesley, Duke of Wellington, in seven departments along the northeastern frontier. The occupation, projected to last up to five years, was to be financed by the French, who were also responsible for paying reparations, totaling 700 million francs, plus still-to-be-calculated claims by Allied nationals. In early 1817, after the restored king Louis XVIII dissolved the ultraroyalist legislature, the so-called Chambre Introuvable, the Allies deemed the government stable enough to reduce this force and the accompanying maintenance burden by thirty thousand troops. The remaining troops stayed another year and a half, until November 1818, when, with the help of foreign financiers, the French paid off their reparations. Ultimately lasting three years, the occupation of guarantee was the first modern "peacekeeping mission." It played a pivotal role in the reconstruction of France and Europe after twenty-five years of revolution and war.

Despite its significance, this first modern occupation has been overlooked by historians. To the extent it has been included in surveys of the post-Napoleonic era, the story has usually been told from above, with an emphasis on high diplomacy between such "great men" as the Duke of Wellington, Tsar Alexander I of Russia, Austrian foreign minister Klemens von Metternich, and French foreign minister Armand-Emmanuel du Plessis, Duc de Richelieu.[2] Historians have focused on the Congress of Vienna and Concert of Europe at the expense of other key institutional strategies for restoring order, including the occupation of guarantee and accompanying reparations.[3] There has been no comprehensive examination of this episode as experienced by both the occupiers and the occupied.[4]

The aftermath of war, including military occupation, has drawn more attention from scholars of later conflicts—in the second half of the nineteenth and, especially, the twentieth century. A new wave of scholarship has explored what the French call *sortie de guerre,* or exiting from war. Many of these studies emphasize the novelty of both the problems of and the solutions for ending conflict seen in these later "total" wars, beginning with the American Civil War (1861–1865) and Franco-Prussian War (1870–1871) and, especially, the two world wars. In the accounts of most political scientists as well as historians, the use of pacific as opposed to belligerent occupation as a means of reconstructing a nation after war developed in the mid-nineteenth century, at the earliest. In particular, the restriction of occupation to protect noncombatants and private property is generally dated to the Lieber Code of the American Civil War, followed by the Hague Convention of 1899.[5]

But these developments originated at least a half-century earlier, in the aftermath of the Napoleonic Wars. In particular, the use of occupation for the purpose of peacemaking and political reconstruction was pioneered in the occupation of guarantee. One of the most important, if neglected, legacies of the Napoleonic Wars, this peacetime occupation inaugurated a new approach to the age-old problem of how to end war. The Revolutionary and Napoleonic Wars (1792–1815, with the brief Peace of Amiens in between in 1802–1803) have been characterized by historians as the first "total war."[6] Extending this logic into the postwar period, the occupation of guarantee represented a novel attempt at "total" peace. Redefining the enemy to exclude the noncombatant people of the defeated state, it constituted a key—if heretofore unrecognized—transitional step between the early modern aim of "just war" (*jus ad bellum*) and the more modern goal of humanity in warfare (*jus in bello*), to limit the brutality of a conflict and to speed its resolution.[7]

Like the notion of "total war" with which it was inextricably linked, the aim of "total peace" originated long before the twentieth century, in the Enlightenment and French Revolution. Until the eighteenth century, the end of war was usually conquest. In international law as codified by Hugo Grotius (*jus gentium*), occupation remained defined by appropriation of the defeated territory and its resources. Under the influence of the Enlightenment, victors shifted toward more systematic requisitions and contributions and, if necessary, reprisals against resisters. In the political cauldron of the French Revolution, as total war was used to effect ideological transformation, occupation became a tool of regime change. Despite their official renunciation of war for conquest, successive revolutionary governments often imposed oppressive occupations on neighboring countries under the guise of "liberation." If the defeated proved malleable enough, they were designated a "friend" or "ally" and annexed to France or made a "sister republic." Increasingly, though, these ostensibly pacifist arrangements reassumed the Old Regime form of conquests, especially under Napoleon, who did not bother to disguise his imperialist designs.[8]

Out of the struggle against Napoleon, however, emerged a novel approach to peacemaking. Recognizing that ending total war required transforming the political culture of the defeated nation, the Allies adopted a multilateral, positivist, and pacifist strategy for reintegrating the French people into the international community. Overcoming their own significant divisions, they focused on two related goals: security and order. Continuing the cooperative approach first manifest in the Central Administration (*Zentralverwaltung*) instituted by Prussian Baron vom Stein in 1813 to manage public affairs in French-occupied territories as they were "liberated" by Allied armies, they defined their mission as guaranteeing a successful regime change. Although British prime minister Robert Jenkinson, Second Earl of Liverpool, along with most of the Prussian leadership, initially demanded more traditional conquest—including cession of territory—the Allies ultimately agreed to the temporary occupation of guarantee as the best means of ensuring political stability. Explicitly distinguishing this sort of occupation from the "plunder and war" undertaken by the Revolutionary and Napoleonic armies, they aimed, in the words of the Duke of Wellington, "to continue to keep our great object, the genuine peace and tranquillity of the world, in our view, and shape our arrangement so as to provide for it."[9] Insisting that their enemy was not the French people but only Napoleon himself, they positioned themselves (paradoxically, in terms similar to the French revolutionaries before them) as "liberators," "allies," and "friends" of the defeated nation. Concerned less with the restored monarchy's legitimacy per se than with its stability, they assumed a tutelary role vis-à-vis the new regime in order to block the threat of both counterrevolution and revolution. Although the terms of this occupation were no less harsh than those of many more traditional conquests, they were designed as an incentive for the defeated nation to reform itself politically: in lieu of territorial losses, the monetary burdens would force the country to put its financial—and political—house in order, to rejoin the community of nations. In its concern for noncombatants, protection of private as well as public property, respect for civilian authority, and commitment to the rule of law, the occupation of guarantee also represented a new way of making peace.

In the end, due to its multilateral and cooperative nature, the occupation of guarantee was remarkably successful. Focused on restabilizing the French polity, it instituted positivist limits on the powers of the occupiers, including in requisitioning and policing. In practice, the occupation did involve considerable violence. Long after the transition from military invasion to peacekeeping operation at the end of 1815, occupying troops continued to behave as "enemies," plundering, insulting, attacking, and raping French inhabitants, especially in the northeast. However, as a result of concerted efforts by Allied officers and French authorities at all levels, this violence was kept in check—and subject to prosecution—on both sides. Under the occupation of guarantee, there was thus considerable accommodation, and even fraternization or friendship, between occupiers and occupied, particularly among the upper classes, but also further down the social scale. Especially in Paris, but also in the northeast, the occupation provided the context for significant cross-cultural exchange—of language, food, fashion, literature, and more. Such exchange sometimes fueled nationalism, but it also revived cosmopolitanism. By bringing together peoples from across the Continent for a relatively extended period, the occupation of guarantee cultivated a new idea of "Europe" as a political entity.

In addition to promoting reconciliation between the French and their former enemies, the occupation played no small part in the reconstruction of the economy and government of France—and, by extension, the rest of Europe. Although the role of the occupation has been overlooked in most histories of this period, it was no mere backdrop to the economic and political history of the new regime, which was really less a "Restoration" than a "Regeneration," a transitional hybridization of Old Regime and Revolution. In order to pay the occupation costs and war reparations, as well as the debts left by its predecessor, the restored monarchy introduced a number of measures that finally resolved the financial crisis—which dated from the outbreak of the French Revolution—and put the French economy on a more stable footing. In addition, under the tutelage of a Council of Allied Ambassadors, the Restoration government resisted the influence of its most reactionary supporters to institute a number of relatively revolutionary reforms, thereby promoting a wave of liberalism, both within France and (via the occupying troops) beyond. Paradoxically, this window of liberalism closed with the end of occupation, when French as well as foreign leaders feared that without Allied military force they could not suppress revolution.

Focusing on the three years of occupation, this book paints a picture of daily life on the ground, for both occupiers and occupied, in Paris as well as in the provinces, especially the occupied zone of the northeast. To recover the experiences of occupation, it relies on military, diplomatic, and police records from dozens of departmental and municipal repositories in northeastern France as well as national archives in France, Great Britain, and Germany. In particular, it makes heavy use of reports from stagecoach drivers to the French ministry of police regarding public opinion in the provinces. Supplementing these official sources with private letters and memoirs, it also draws on contemporary pamphlets, periodicals, guidebooks, travelogues, plays, songs, paintings, and prints to provide a sense of popular culture and everyday life under occupation.

The book is divided into three parts. The first part explicates the ways in which the occupation of guarantee perpetuated a state of war between Allied troops and French inhabitants. By the summer of 1815, the French (along with most of the other nations of Europe) were exhausted by over two decades of war. In addition to a second foreign invasion, which dwarfed that of 1814 not just in sheer numbers of troops but also in territorial extent and overall brutality, the country was also suffering from a violent civil war between partisans of Napoleon Bonaparte and supporters of Louis XVIII. This time around, the foreign invaders, who had been forced to remobilize just as the peace settlement negotiated at Vienna was being signed, were in no hurry to leave France. For months, Allied sovereigns and diplomats quarreled over how to punish and stabilize France after the return of Napoleon. Finally, in the treaty of November 20, 1815, they settled on the "occupation of guarantee" as the main instrument for ensuring that the French indemnify the Allies and create a secure government. Following this treaty, those troops not slated to participate in the occupation of guarantee evacuated French territory; the remaining 150,000 soldiers marched to their garrisons in the northeast, where they would remain from late 1815 or early 1816—with only a small amount of movement—until November 1818. Despite its peaceful intention, the occupation of guarantee continued to make local inhabitants and Allied troops into "enemies." The requisitions demanded by the occupying forces placed a heavy material burden on the subjects of Louis XVIII, especially in the northeast zone, where inhabitants often had to provide officers and soldiers with lodging, in addition to provisions and services. Moreover, the occupation was accompanied by significant violence—verbal as well as physical—committed by both sides, ranging from theft and destruction of property, to insults and rumors, to assaults, murders, and rapes, including the metaphorical "rape" of the Louvre and other cultural institutions by Allied troops in the fall of 1815.

Despite numerous offenses on both sides, however, the occupation provided a context for more amicable relations between the former enemies. The second part of the book analyzes the ways in which the occupation of guarantee promoted accommodation and exchange, if not always true "friendship," between occupiers and occupied. The state of war between occupiers and occupied was kept in check by the regulations and institutions of the occupation of guarantee. Both sides worked to maintain strict discipline, and even to cooperate in policing. When those efforts failed to prevent violence, they routinely charged, tried, and punished crimes, in accordance with an agreement between the Allied command and the French ministry of justice that foreign offenders be judged by a court-martial of their own army while French ones be judged by the civilian judiciary. This process helped to keep the peace between former enemies. In the northeast as well as the capital, these enemies became reconciled to each other in a number of other ways. Via not just law and order, but mutual aid, official courtesies, regular fraternization, and even romance, at virtually all social levels, the two sides cultivated a remarkable amount of what contemporaries termed "good intelligence" and "harmony." The occupation also promoted a surge in cross-cultural contact between French and foreigners. Following the peace first in 1814 and again in 1815, the country was inundated not just with troops but also with tourists from most of the states of Europe, especially Great Britain. Eager to see—and taste—the wonders of France for the first time in over twenty years, these visitors brought new foods, fashions, ideas, and amusements of their own. Contrary to urban legend, Russian soldiers did not bequeath the term "bistrot" to French restaurateurs during the occupation. However, they did inspire another cultural phenomenon, the so-called *montagnes russes*, or "Russian mountains"—early roller coasters. While the presence of so many different peoples on French territory generated a clear sense of national difference, it also promoted a renewed spirit of cosmopolitanism, on all sides.

In addition to promoting cross-cultural exchange and reconciliation, the occupation of guarantee contributed to the reconstruction of France, economically, politically, and internationally. These reconstructions are analyzed in the third part of the book. In the wake of the Battle of Waterloo, France faced numerous economic challenges, including not just the requisitions and reparations demanded by the Allies but also the commercial disruption resulting from the collapse of the Napoleonic Empire. On top of that, France suffered (along with most of the northern hemisphere) from a severe subsistence crisis after a volcanic explosion in Indonesia in April 1815 caused two of the coldest and wettest growing seasons on record. To address these various challenges, the French government employed a combination of taxation and borrowing, while also adopting an approach to political economy that mixed liberalism and protectionism. This mixed approach proved remarkably successful in jump-starting commerce and industry by the late 1810s. At the same time, the occupation provided the context for the political regeneration of France. Under the watch of the Council of Allied Ambassadors, the government introduced reforms in a number of domains, including electoral procedure, military recruitment, and the press. Although they did not prevent another revolution in 1830, these reforms, like the new measures in the realm of political economy, ensured the survival of revolutionary liberalism into the nineteenth century.

Satisfied with these efforts at regeneration, the Allied powers agreed to negotiate the end of the occupation of guarantee two years ahead of schedule. Meeting at the spa town of Aix-la-Chapelle (Aachen), in what was then Prussian territory, at the beginning of October 1818, they acceded not only to the liberation of France by the end of the next month but also to France's readmittance into the Concert of Europe. By the end of November, the Allied contingents had evacuated their encampments and set off for home. The French celebrated their liberation with banquets, festivals, plays, and songs.

Outside of the occupied zone of the northeast, this historical episode soon faded from public memory. However, as this book suggests, the occupation of guarantee shaped the history of modern Europe. Building on Enlightenment and revolutionary ideas about how to end war, it instituted a new approach to peacemaking, one that focused on the political reconstruction of the defeated nation. The occupation was key to the establishment of a new postwar order that succeeded in maintaining relative peace across the Continent for almost a century, until the outbreak of the Great War in 1914. In the end, the occupation of 1815–1818 went a long way toward transforming the "enemies" of Béranger's song into allies, if not true "friends."

Part One

Enemies

Chapter One

Exiting War, Twice

When Pierre-Jean De Béranger penned his song "Our Friends, the Enemies," it had been little more than a year since the Allied powers of Europe first invaded France to overthrow the empire of Napoleon Bonaparte, who was dethroned on April 2, 1814. The invasion of 1814 seemed to mark the end of over two decades of almost continuous coalition—and global—warfare between partisans and opponents of the French Revolution of 1789. However, it proved to be only the prelude to another, more brutal invasion and occupation of the country, due to yet another regime change in France. As noted by numerous observers at the time, the twenty-three months between the first invasion of France beginning in January 1814 and the Second Treaty of Paris toward the end of November 1815 were some of the most eventful and costly in French—and European—history. Béranger, who witnessed the invasion of 1814 firsthand, when the house where he resided near the Rochechouart barrier on the edge of Paris was "saluted" with several Allied shells, was not alone in experiencing a "painful impression" from both invasions.[1]

By 1814, France had experienced almost twenty-five years of upheaval as a result of the Revolution. Beyond issuing the "Declaration of the Rights of Man and of the Citizen," the Revolutionaries completely restructured society and eventually abolished the monarchy. The Revolution destabilized not just France but also the continent of Europe for decades. Within France, the Revolution provoked a civil war, the Terror.

Internationally, it unleashed what one historian has labeled the first "total" war between France and much of Europe, whose monarchs feared the spread of revolutionary ideas.[2] Beginning in 1792, when the Revolutionary government declared war on Prussia and Austria, the French army campaigned from one end of the Continent to the other, as well as in the Middle East, South Asia, and the Caribbean.

It was in this context that Napoleon Bonaparte, a minor nobleman from the Mediterranean island of Corsica who became a military hero, rose to power. Overthrowing the Revolutionary government in a coup in 1799, Napoleon crowned himself emperor in 1804. Fueled by his ambition to rule a "Grand Empire" on the Continent, Napoleon continued the Revolutionary Wars, defeating Prussia (1806), invading Portugal and Spain (1807 and 1808), and subjugating Austria (1809). At the hands of his Grande Armée, these countries all endured military occupation. Prussia suffered the loss of half of its territory and population, a reduction of its military forces, and a war indemnity totaling 120 million francs, not including expenses for the Grande Armée as it mobilized for a campaign against Russia. In 1806, Napoleon also dissolved the Holy Roman Empire, incorporating (more or less forcibly) into his empire as satellites or allies many of the minor powers of the "Third Germany," including Baden, Württemberg, Bavaria, Saxony, the Hanseatic cities, and the newly created Westphalia. At the height of the Grand Empire in 1812, only Great Britain and Russia had resisted conquest.[3]

However, that year marked the beginning of the end for Napoleon. In one of the most famous miscalculations in military history, in late June he launched an invasion of the Russian Empire, ruled since 1801 by the young and dashing Tsar Alexander I. After a series of inconclusive battles, in mid-September the French army reached Moscow, which had been deserted—and burned—by its inhabitants. After a month of indecision, during which Alexander refused to negotiate, Napoleon ordered a retreat just as the brutal Russian winter was beginning. The invasion of Russia was a complete disaster. Of the more than six hundred thousand soldiers who participated, almost half from outside France proper, less than thirty thousand returned, a result less of battle than of cold, hunger, and disease; over a hundred thousand were captured. Following this debacle, Austria and Prussia and, one by one, the other German powers allied with France, joined the coalition with Russia and

Great Britain. Financed by subsidies from the British, this multinational coalition handed Napoleon a series of defeats, most famously in the Battle of Nations at Leipzig, Saxony, in October 1813.[4]

The Invasion of 1814

In the wake of this defeat, France was invaded from both east and west. After Napoleon rejected a peace proposal negotiated by the Allies in late 1813, on the first day of the new year from across the Rhine marched three coalition armies composed of Russians, Poles, Austrians, and Germans, including a number of states that had switched sides after Leipzig: the Army of the North, under Swedish king (and former Napoleonic marshal) Jean-Baptiste Bernadotte; the Army of Bohemia, under Austrian field marshal Karl Philipp von Schwarzenberg; and the Army of Silesia, under Prussian field marshal Gebhard Leberecht von Blücher, a fearless but erratic, and now white-haired, military strategist dubbed somewhat erroneously "Marshal Forward." From the southwest came a mix of British and Iberian forces under the command of Arthur Wellesley, soon to be named Duke of Wellington, a native of Ireland who, after obtaining a commission as an army officer, had served mostly in India before taking leadership of the Peninsular Campaign in 1809. In the east, the Allies marshaled 375,000 troops, plus another 300,000 reserves; in secondary theaters in Italy and Spain, they claimed another 267,500, including 68,000 under Wellington alone. Despite incessant intrigues between Allied diplomats and conflicts between civilian and military leaders, the anti-Napoleon coalition was vastly superior to the French force both in size and preparation. Devastated by the campaigns of 1812 and 1813, the French army—an underequipped mix of young conscripts and recalled pensioners—now numbered only 442,000 effective troops. In spite of some last-ditch victories by Napoleon, culminating in a final stand at Arsis-sur-Aube on March 21, the collapse of the empire was quick. By this point, the regime retained little support among the French population, who were weary of heavy conscription and taxation. Although there were pockets of resistance, mainly in the east, most French surrendered—and even fled—at the sight of the foreign troops, especially the Cossacks of the Russian Empire, who had developed a reputation for brutality during the Russian campaign of 1812.

In the southwest, where royalism remained strong through the Revolution and Empire, inhabitants welcomed the British, accompanied by the Bourbon Duc d'Angoulême, nephew and son-in-law of the executed Louis XVI.[5]

After signing the Pact of Chaumont to remain united against French aggression for the next twenty years, the Allied coalition pushed across eastern France to the gates of Paris. On March 31, 120,000 Allied troops entered the capital from the northeast, led by Alexander I, who proclaimed himself the "liberator" and "protector" of the French. Following a last defense by Marshal Moncey at the Clichy barrier, the French laid down their arms. According to eyewitness Sir Hudson Lowe, a British officer who would later guard Napoleon on Saint Helena,

> The Cossacks of the guard preceded [Alexander's] Entrance into the Capital. These are mostly from the Don, men with whom Nature has been lavish of her Proportions & all selected from their height. The Austrians, Russian & Prussian Guards & Cuirassiers, forming together a Corps of about 40,000 men, followed. The Grand Cortege entered at the Barrier of the Faubourg St. Martin. The Population of Paris was pouring as a stream upon it from every Channel. At first Populace alone was observable, but as the March approached the Boulevards, these were soon mixed with & almost outnumbered by Persons of the better classes. The cries of Vive l'Empereur Alexandre—Le Libérateur—La Paix almost rent the air.

As the troops paraded into the center of Paris, they were even offered drinks by some inhabitants. Responding to this enthusiasm, four days later, at the instigation of the turncoat foreign minister Charles-Maurice de Talleyrand, the Senate voted to overthrow Napoleon.[6]

However, not all French viewed the Allies as liberators. Contrary to later histories that characterize the conquest of 1814 as "gentle" in comparison to that of the following year, this invasion was traumatic and humiliating for inhabitants. For the first five months of 1814, the northeast (and, to a lesser extent, the southwest) was inundated with foreign troops, appropriating—often by force—lodging, food, drink, forage, equipment, and virtually anything else they desired. Already suffering from the last years of the Napoleonic Wars, when they had endured endless movements of troops and requisitions of supplies, as well as epidemics of typhus and dysentery, these regions were crushed by the invasion of 1814. In the area around Avesnes in the Nord alone, more than two hundred thousand Russian and Prussian troops passed back and forth, wreaking havoc in small villages. In addition to exacting scarce resources, such troops inflicted considerable violence on the local population, including assault, murder, and rape. In the spring of 1814, Allied troops burned numerous villages in northeastern France. In response to such "excesses," as they were termed by contemporaries, many French peasants abandoned their homes and went into hiding. The aftermath of the invasion was vividly described in a June 10, 1814, letter from the prefect of the Doubs region around Besançon to the interior minister:

> In spite of all of my efforts to maintain order during the passage of the Austrian troops, I receive every day from each commune where they lodge reports on the excesses of every type that they commit. All the habitations are delivered to pillage, the inhabitants beaten, the women insulted, finally the majority of the villages are deserted, which renders almost impossible the supply of vehicles necessary for the transport of baggage. . . . Although I cannot be held responsible, I am no less painfully afflicted to see the department I had been rather lucky to preserve (during the four months of war) from pillage and all exactions, be devastated in the era of peace, and at the moment when I would most desire that it was flourishing, to offer resources to the King, instead of soliciting aid.

The French state would spend years trying to compensate victims for damages incurred in 1814.[7]

Conditions were not much better in Paris, whose inhabitants suffered shock at seeing their city occupied by foreigners for the first time since the Hundred Years' War four centuries earlier. Russian officers such as Prince Golitsyn relished the "numerous and marvelous wonders" that had occurred in such a short span, bringing Allied troops through hundreds of combats from Moscow all the way to Saint-Cloud, where they played "God Save the King" on a piano left by the fleeing Empress Marie-Louise. But other observers were more circumspect about the dramatic reversal for the French. Following Alexander I's entry into Paris, the city became a "garrison town," according to English observer J. W. Ward: "[W]hat a matter of greater interest and greater surprise it is to see France—to see the great nation that only a few months ago seemed so near realizing its old plan of universal dominion—not only beaten, but delivered over bound hand and foot to foreign masters." In similar language, the Frenchman Alfred Nettement later remembered,

> For the first time in centuries, the foreigner entered Paris as a victor. . . . This time, this city, which had seen erected the scaffold of Louis XVI, witnessed, twenty-one years later, the Tartars enter its walls. The emperor of Russia and the king of Prussia, marching at the head of their columns, followed along the boulevard the painful path that Louis XVI had followed to go to his torture, and the Tsar entered at the head of his guard into the city from which had departed the phalanxes that had watched his Kremlin collapse in flames.[8]

The Allied powers endorsed the revival of monarchy under Louis XVIII, who had been living in exile in England since 1807. Such a restoration was not foreordained. In France, the royal family had been largely forgotten over a generation of revolution and war, and Louis XVIII, now an obese, awkward, fifty-nine-year-old man, was by no means beloved. Until close to the end of the war, a number of Allied leaders, especially Metternich, remained willing to negotiate with Napoleon. However, when Napoleon refused to agree to Allied peace terms, England and Russia ultimately opted for a Bourbon Restoration, which they viewed as more in line with the wishes of the French people than a regency under Napoleon's queen, Marie-Louise, or an alternative ruler, such as Bernadotte. Taking the boat from Dover to Calais, the new king entered Paris for the first time in over two decades on May 3. Acknowledging the new ideas that had germinated in France in his absence, Louis XVIII "granted" a Charter of constitutional rights to the French people, which among other things protected the purchasers of nationalized lands and amnestied all citizens for past political opinions.[9]

After this regime change, the French were able to obtain a relatively mild settlement from their conquerors. According to a treaty signed in Paris on May 30, they were allowed to keep territorial gains up to 1792 and to recover colonies lost during the wars, including the sugar islands of Guadeloupe and Martinique. They did not have to pay indemnities, and they were granted a delegation at the Congress of Vienna, which was to convene later in the year to reconfigure the political geography of Europe. Napoleon, who had abdicated on April 11, was exiled to the island of Elba, off the west coast of Italy. Although there was some talk of a military occupation to protect the restored monarchy, the coalition decided against it.[10]

Beginning on June 5, Allied leaders evacuated France, and soldiers returned home to be discharged or reassigned. Some twenty thousand

British troops, including many veterans of the Peninsular War, were transported across the Atlantic to fight in the War of 1812, arriving just in time to participate in the burning of Washington, D.C., in August 1814. Meanwhile, Allied officers and statesmen proceeded from Paris to London, where they were fêted by the prince regent, the future George IV. On the road from Dover, adorned with flags and illuminations, the emperor of Russia and the king of Prussia, as well as the Duke of Wellington, were mobbed by enthusiastic crowds. In London, they attended endless dinners, spectacles, and balls in their honor, along with the Prussian princes, Metternich, Russian general Matvei Platov, and Blücher, the last of whom gained a reputation for drinking to excess. All of England—and much of the Continent—celebrated the peace with public banquets, parades, bonfires, and thanksgiving sermons and hymns. Later that summer, Allied diplomats moved on to Vienna for the opening of the Congress. By early fall, when Ludwig von Beethoven conducted his "Chorus in Honor of the Allied Princes" for the dignitaries at the Congress of Vienna, it seemed that these princes—and their militaries—had finally put an end to the conflicts that had plagued Europe for a generation.[11]

Invasion, Again

However, the hope for peace was short-lived. As a country vicar in western France later remembered, "Eighteen hundred fifteen was rung in at our home by the trumpet of foreigners. Our countrysides, so joyous, were saddened by the presence of new guests, who would long torment their inhabitants." During their second visit, these "guests" would call themselves "allies" of the restored king, but, to many French, they often seemed more like enemies.[12]

Following the departure of the coalition troops in May 1814, it did not take long for tensions to flare again, both within France and without. Domestically, the restored Bourbon monarchy struggled to reestablish itself. Already by late 1814, the monarchy provoked popular opposition with some early measures, particularly the disbanding of the army, the reinstitution of the *droits réunis* (excise taxes on products such as alcohol and tobacco), and the introduction of a law enforcing the observance of Sundays and religious holidays. Dissatisfaction with the regime was exacerbated by the émigrés, who demanded indemnification for property lost during the Revolution.[13]

The dissatisfaction was fueled by events outside France, including rumors from abroad about Spanish refugees, Italian revolutionaries, and Prussian territorial ambitions in Lorraine. By the fall, the Allies at Vienna were already squabbling over territory, especially in the German lands. In exchange for concessions in Poland, Prussia demanded land from Saxony or, barring that, from the frontier with France.[14] Such saber rattling increased the sense of instability in France, fueling opposition to the monarchy among ex-soldiers and other partisans of Napoleon. By early 1815, there was again talk of war between France and the rest of Europe.

Encouraged by reports of discontent, in late February Napoleon escaped from Elba and disembarked on the southern coast of France. Rallying support on the way to Paris, on March 20 he took back the throne of France, forcing Louis XVIII to flee to Ghent, in the Netherlands, and the Allied powers to rearm. After what would come to be called his Hundred Days in power, Napoleon was defeated by the British and the Prussians in the Battle of Waterloo on June 18. Forced to abdicate, the former emperor departed France on July 15 aboard the British ship *Bellerophon*, bound for exile on the distant island of Saint Helena, in the South Atlantic, where he would die six years later.[15]

Meanwhile, Louis XVIII returned to Paris. Encouraged by the Duke of Wellington, who had served briefly as ambassador to France before leading the British army at Waterloo, he followed the Allied troops in their "baggage train," as critics complained. In a proclamation dated June 25, Louis threatened to punish the soldiers who had fought for Napoleon. At Talleyrand's suggestion, however, he soon adopted a more conciliatory stance. In another proclamation three days later, Louis placed himself "between the allied armies and the French, in order to soften the pains that he had not been able to prevent." Admitting he had made mistakes, he pardoned those French who had been "misled" by Napoleon, excepting those who had directly aided "the usurper." By the time he reached Paris on July 8, the twice-restored king had formed a new, more liberal government. Given that this government was established with foreign help, however, the Second Restoration was already tainted for many French.[16]

The association of the returning king with the foreign enemy was not helped by the behavior of the invading armies. Despite a general order from Wellington on June 20 reminding his troops that they were "allies" of France, there were soon widespread reports of extensive pillaging by British and Prussian, as well as Hanoverian and Belgian, troops. Around Maubeuge, as a British lieutenant remarked in his journal, one inhabitant complained that although he had anticipated being protected by the English army, "he found us on the contrary worse than the Cossacks, who had visited during the last war." The Prussians were even worse. At Compiègne, where troops under the command of Blücher looted the château, the same British lieutenant denounced the "rapacity of the Prussians, our brave allies." According to another English observer, Private Wheeler, encamped near a château belonging to French marshal Michel Ney on June 30, "The Prussian army passed our camp on its march to go into position on the other side of the canal, they did not forget to destroy everything they could as they moved on. . . . [E]verything they could lay their hands on was knocked to pieces. A small town about two miles from us which we marched through was completely sacked, it reminded me of some of the doings of the French in Portugal." When French inhabitants complained about the pillaging, Blücher, recalling the damage wrought by French troops around Berlin in 1806, replied sarcastically, "They did only that? They could have done much worse."[17]

Within two weeks of the Battle of Waterloo, the Prussians and British had reached Paris, which capitulated on July 3. As a banker in the city reported, "Since three days ago, the allied armies are masters of the Capital and occupy it in a manner much less courteous even than last year. All the bridges, the public places, without excepting the Carouzal [Place du Carrousel at the Louvre], and some streets and Boulevards are armed with cannons with the Wick lighted as if it were a question of repressing or containing an entire population." In the capital, where the flags of the Allies flew over the Chamber of Deputies, the Duke of Wellington arrived just in time to prevent Blücher from blowing up the Pont d'Iéna, a bridge named for the French victory over Prussia in 1806. Placed under the governship of a Prussian officer, General Müffling, Paris was crowded with Prussian and British soldiers, soon joined by Austrians and Russians. By mid-July, when Tsar Alexander reviewed the Allied troops, close

Revue des troupes alliées passée à Paris, au Pont de Neuilly, le 17 juillet 1815, par les souverains étrangers. Engraving, 1815. BNF.

to two hundred thousand soldiers were encamped in the environs of the capital, whose population at the time was a little over seven hundred thousand. Unlike in 1814, when Parisians were exempted from housing the invaders, in 1815 they were required to lodge at least ten soldiers per household. To accommodate the excess, wooden barracks were built in the center of Paris, including on the Champs-Élysées and the Champ de Mars. The British also set up camp just outside the city, in the Bois de Boulogne, whose trees were decimated for firewood. In addition to lodging, the occupiers demanded considerable quantities of food, forage, clothing, furniture, and subsidies for the troops. Beyond such requisitions, which averaged some 600,000 francs per day, the city was asked to pay a war "contribution" of 100 million francs—later reduced, thanks to Tsar Alexander, to 10 million. Until it was paid, General Müffling camped with a hundred soldiers at city hall. This second invasion was summarized by British observer Helen Maria Williams: "Thus, in the short space of fifteen months, was the capital of France twice besieged, and twice compelled to open its gates and receive the law of the conqueror,—Paris, the triumphant city; Paris, which the revolutionary orator had surnamed the 'Chef lieu du globe!' How are the mighty fallen!"[18]

Bivouac prussien, dans l'allée du Champs de Mars. Print by Martinet, ca. 1815. Fondation Dosne-Bibliothèque Thiers (Collection Frédéric Masson), Paris.

By the time of the capitulation of Paris, the terms of which required the French army to move beyond the Loire River, much of the rest of the country was already being invaded by hundreds of thousands of soldiers from almost every nation in Europe. Within a week of the Battle of Waterloo, a municipal register in Wissembourg noted the arrival, amidst a terrible rain, of "enemy allied" troops from small German states "on foot and on horse . . . in such great number that one must wonder from where they came so quickly, into a town that the French army had left only the night before." Four days later, this town had the "honor" of welcoming the Russian and Austrian emperors and the Prussian king, all of whom stayed overnight. Greeted by crowds who only a week before had shouted "Vive l'Empereur!" at Napoleon, these sovereigns were followed by their armies.[19] From across Europe, soldiers continued to pour into France, in part to provision themselves after mobilizing for war so far from home. In the words of justice minister Étienne-Denis Pasquier:

> It seemed that all of Europe thirsted to crowd the soil of France; even though the deployment of so many forces had become completely useless [since the surrender of Napoleon], one judged it nevertheless appropriate to give the French nation the spectacle of the irresistible power under which it was commanded to bend. In spite of the rapid success of the duke of Wellington and general Blücher, in spite of the occupation of the capital, not a single corps had suspended its march; everyone who, from the frontier to the banks of the Rhine, carried a gun, everyone who was not indispensable to the guarding of states and fortified towns, seemed to have given himself a rendez-vous on the territory of France.[20]

In the six weeks between the Battle of Waterloo and the end of July, the Prussian contingent alone increased from 100,000 to 280,000. By early September, some 1.2 million soldiers—the largest force ever gathered to date—were spread over the country: approximately 320,000 Austrians, 310,000 Prussians and allies, 128,000 English and allies, 250,000 Russians, 60,000 Bavarians, 20,000 Würtembergers, 16,000 Badois, 8,000 Hessians, 15,000 Piedmontese, and 8,000 Saxons. Even the Spanish, apparently provoked by French deserters and returning émigrés, made incursions across the frontier.[21]

As they moved into France, the invaders wreaked havoc, seizing weapons, plundering supplies, destroying fields, raiding treasuries, levying contributions, burning villages, raping women, and threatening local authorities. The second time around, they were motivated not just by greed but by revenge. Following the lead of Blücher, who had yearned since 1806 to inflict vengeance on the French for their occupation of Prussia, they subjected the country to the sort of "military punishment" traditionally inflicted by occupying armies. The "rapacity" of the Allies was chronicled in declarations made by stagecoach drivers to the ministry of police. Following the capitulation of Landrecies in late July, Prussians and Saxons covered the countryside, sacking vineyards, trampling crops, slaughtering livestock, and demanding liquor, under threat of violence. Around Chalon-sur-Saône, where peasants went without food to meet the continual requisitions of Allied troops, the Austrians "devastated everything and even killed several individuals in three villages in the region of this town under the pretext that during the war of 1814 seven or eight of their soldiers had been killed by the peasants." Recognizing that such violence might be justified, an anti-Bonapartist farmer in the region around Belfort noted in his family record book during

Gräuelscenen aus dem Elsass ("Scenes of Horror in Alsace"). Hand-colored engraving, probably 1815. Cabinet des Estampes et des Dessins de Strasbourg; Photo Musées de Strasbourg, M. Bertola.

the invasion of 1815, "[W]e found it absolutely impossible to supply the needs of an enemy army, which was anyway irritated with reason against we who, of our own action, had constrained them to come back a second time to punish us. Thus they fulfilled amply this commission, not limiting the kinds of excesses to which they delivered themselves, pillaging churches, burning villages, devastating countrysides, etc." The Comtesse de Boigne, daughter of a French ambassador about to be stationed in London, later remembered her return to Paris from Piedmont in summer 1815: "However disposed I was to share the joy caused by the return of the king, it was empoisoned by the presence of the foreigners. Their attitude was even more hostile than the year before." Only eleven months after Allied troops had departed France, they returned in an even more extensive and vengeful manner, provoking more than one inhabitant to wish for deliverance from such "allies."[22]

The Military Occupation of July–November 1815

Contrary to the year before, however, in 1815 the Allied invaders were in no hurry to leave. Piqued at the French for having forced them to rearm against Napoleon, they insisted on occupying most of the country until the nation relinquished its weapons and offered substantial guarantees against further revolution and war. Ignoring French pleas to be treated as an allied people (on the ground that they had cooperated in the defeat of Napoleon), foreign leaders condoned and even encouraged punitive behavior by their troops. As the British ambassador to Portugal, George Canning, wrote in a letter to Madame Germaine de Staël, "We have conquered France, France is our conquest, and we want to exhaust her so that she will no longer budge for ten years." Between early July and early August, this "conquest" was regulated in a series of agreements between Allied and French authorities. But until the two sides could agree on a final peace settlement, France remained under a more or less arbitrary military occupation.[23]

This was especially true in the first month or so after the invasion. As foreign troops advanced into a region, their first order of business was usually to disarm local inhabitants, sometimes by force. They then proceeded to demand—or simply pillage—contributions in money and kind. In contravention of the treaty of capitulation, which stipulated that foreign forces were to respect local authorities as well as private and public properties, Allied invaders imposed endless requisitions and taxes. During July 1815, reports from informants in the provinces reveal the extent of these demands. In Dijon, some twenty thousand Austrian troops levied enormous requisitions of wine, eau de vie, and beef, as well as lodging. Around Nancy, where large quantities of fabric and sheets were requisitioned for the Russian army, "all the peasants and bourgeois of the villages have abandoned their houses," where its troops had committed "the greatest horrors." From Lyon, a stagecoach driver reported, "The roads of Bourgogne are all covered with allied troops; They continue their ravages; All the postmasters' horses, as well as forage, are appropriated or requisitioned. If these vexations are not repressed, it will be impossible to continue this public service." If their demands were not satisfied, the Allies punished local citizens with monetary fines, prison sentences, or worse. Harkening back to the brutality of the Thirty Years' War, the Austrians, among others, even employed the system of "collective responsibility," whereby if a village did not provide the requisitions demanded, it was subjected to a heavy fine. The least incident became a pretext for a monetary exaction. For instance, when a crowd yelled "Vive l'Empereur!" (referring to the defeated Napoleon) at a visiting Italian cardinal in Bourg, the town was fined 60,000 francs.[24] In addition to appropriating supplies and revenues, the invaders asserted authority over local government, intervening in policing, justice, border patrol, customs regulation, and management of public lands and state monopolies. Through the summer, they seized municipal treasuries, tax rolls, official stamps, and public stores of tobacco, salt, oil, and wood.[25]

On July 24, the Allies standardized their *occupation de guerre* in a formal memorandum. They tried to divide the burden of occupation across as much of the country as possible by assigning each Allied contingent a defined zone. Covering sixty departments, this "war occupation" extended across almost all of the north and east of France, from the English Channel down to the Riviera. North of the Loire, beyond which river all French troops were to remain, the only areas excluded from occupation were parts of Brittany and Cotentin. The memorandum also proposed to systematize Allied requisitioning. When this failed to prevent abuses, the Allies agreed, on August 6, to prohibit any further direct requisitions and contributions. In exchange, they required 50 million francs for the maintenance of their armies, to be paid in installments on August 25 and September 25, as well as a clothing and equipment allowance of 120 francs per man, the exact amount of which remained in dispute but ultimately totaled at least 135 million francs.[26]

To meet these financial demands, on August 16, 1815, the French government imposed a *contribution extraordinaire,* or exceptional tax, of 100 million francs on all departments. To be collected from the principal taxpaying landowners and capitalists of the realm, this tax varied with the resources of departments. Those that had suffered the most from the invasion and occupation were asked to pay less than those that had remained relatively unscathed. While some prefects effected this additional imposition by means of a proportional increase in the existing tax rate, the *contribution extraordinaire* was essentially a forced loan from the richest subjects, whom the government promised to repay at a later date.[27]

Despite the agreement of August 6, abuses continued into the fall. In the region around Lyon, Austrian authorities barraged the prefect with demands for uniforms—including for 54,000 shirts and undergarments,

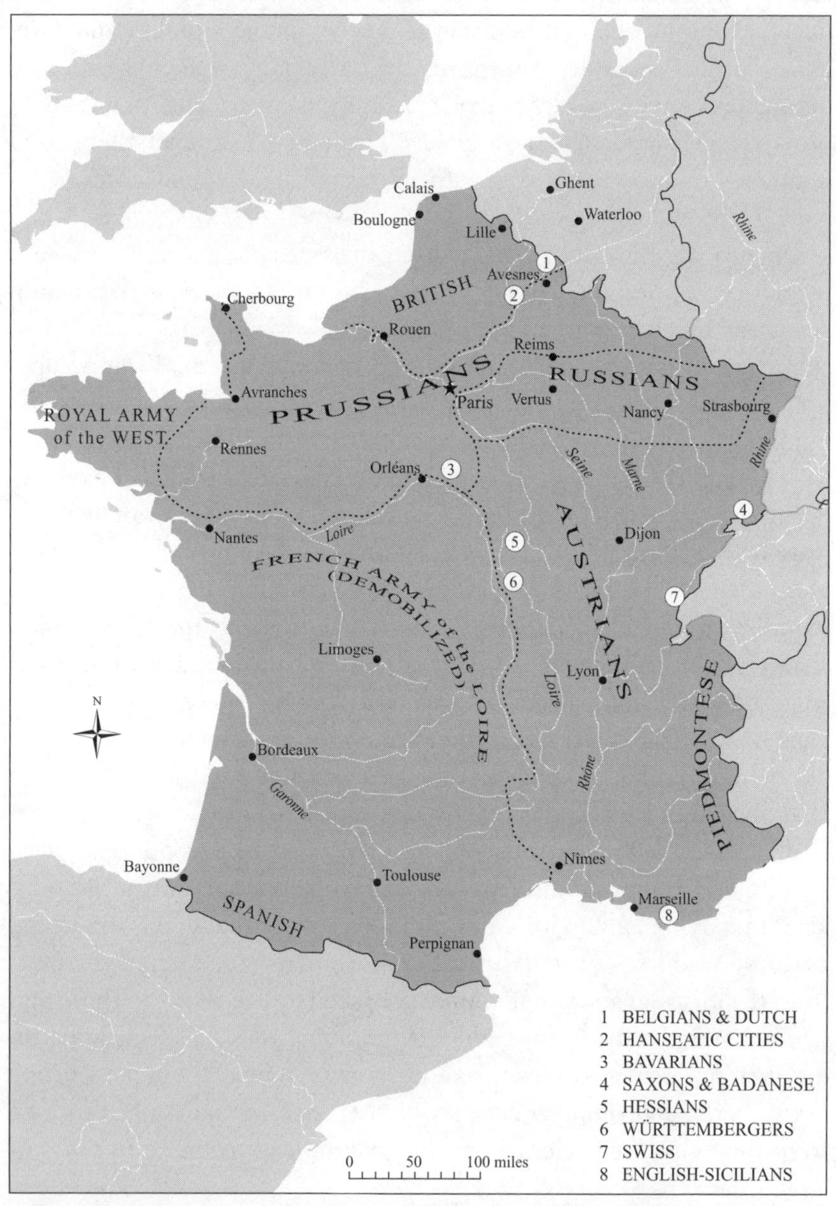

Military occupation, July–November 1815. Adapted from Roger André, *L'occupation de la France par les Alliés en 1815: juillet-novembre* (Paris: Boccard, 1924), 56–57.

20,000 shakos (ornamented military caps with visors) and "German" boots, and 10,000 gaiters and "ordinary" pants, plus 4,000 "Hungarian" pants, in addition to tens of thousands of yards of cloth—mostly for a camp at Verpillière, where troops were gathering for a review. Recognizing that this was a "game" to circumvent the prohibition on monetary contributions, the prefect complained to a subordinate,

> As one says, Monsieur, with each day comes its pain; but still it is necessary that it is singular and not greater than one can bear. I do not know when ours will end; but what I know only too well, is that it is aggravated and modified at each instant. I had barely provided for the needs demanded by the arrival of *our friends* the enemies, when suddenly there fell on my shoulders a [Austrian] governor, then a commissary . . . then a requisition of food, then a requisition of shirts and undergarments, then other requisitions of all kinds and colors, up to taffetas, cock feathers, and stocks of bread.[28]

In Normandy, where forty thousand Prussian troops were stationed, a two-week visit by Blücher in late August cost the department of the Orne approximately 18,000 francs in table expenses for luncheons and dinners.[29] In Alsace, occupied by about 150,000 troops through the end of 1815, the mayor of Issenheim complained that the commander of a Württemberger regiment was demanding payments for repairs of clothing and equipment. When the mayor, "tired of being the toy of every soldier," refused to pay, the commander garrisoned in his house eighteen men, who helped themselves to whatever they could find, including his stock of wine. By mid-November, the Allied troops in France had reportedly drunk three hundred million bottles of wine.[30] As one local historian said of Austrian forces in the Haute-Loire, such excesses constituted a thinly "disguised pillage, because accomplished under cover of legality due to the system of receipts [for requisitions]."[31] Between July and November 1815, historian Roger André estimates, the war occupation cost the French a minimum of 495,664,833 francs, averaging over 2.5 million francs per day.[32]

In violation of the agreement of early August, the occupying forces also continued to seize arms, carriages and wagons, tobacco, salt, stamped paper, postal mail, natural resources (including oil and wood), art, and public monies. Despite official proclamations forbidding them from interfering with local administration, they raided municipal treasuries and tax offices, and even arrested local officials. Between July 1815 and early 1816, a French Commission on Requisitions, established to coordinate supplies with a parallel Allied commission, received hundreds of complaints from provincial authorities about such abuses by Allied forces, especially by contingents from Austria, Bavaria, and Württemberg. By 1816, the Austrians alone had seized from public storehouses over nine hundred thousand francs' worth of tobacco. The Austrians were also notorious for appropriating excise taxes, not just on tobacco but also on stamped paper, salt, and wine. But they were not alone in pilfering French public coffers. Prussians, Württembergers, Russians, and Bavarians—who during the initial invasion appropriated public transports and treasuries around Meaux and Auxerre—sequestered tax monies totaling 1.8 million francs by the end of 1815. Allied troops also removed thousands of works of art from French libraries, churches, and museums, including the Louvre.[33]

When French administrators objected, they were threatened with arrest and even deportation. Even the prefect of Paris was menaced with arrest by the Prussian governor, "under pretext that he did not show enough deference toward him." Between August 20 and September 10 alone, twenty prefects and subprefects, and an even greater number of mayors, were imprisoned, many in Prussia, for resisting Allied demands for monetary contributions and material supplies. Many of these officials, including Jules Pasquier and Alexandre de Talleyrand, were relatives of cabinet ministers, suggesting that the Allied leadership intended to use them as pawns in negotiations with the French government. Under pressure from the Allies, a number of these officials resigned their posts; some even committed suicide.[34] In short, well after the military occupation had been systematized by early August 1815, it retained its arbitrary character. By mid-September, when Tsar Alexander orchestrated a spectacular display of Allied power at a review of 150,000 troops at a camp near Vertus in the Marne, most of France was in a state of despondency.[35]

Resistance and Terror

The military occupation exacerbated political tension within France, already rife after three regime changes in fifteen months. As the Allies conquered France for the second time, much of the country degenerated into civil war. In some parts of the country, particularly the east, partisans of the empire continued to fight foreign troops for weeks and even months. Where the return of Napoleon had been less welcome, royalists launched a "White Terror" against supporters of the "usurper."

As Allied troops invaded the north and east, a number of communities put up fierce resistance. Foreshadowing the *francs tireurs* who defended France in subsequent invasions, Bonapartist *fédérés* fought against the invading forces, even under blockade or siege. France's second-biggest city, Lyon, resisted until July 12, when it surrendered to the Austrians. Along the northeastern frontier, Maubeuge and Landrecies did not capitulate until July 14 and 20 respectively, for which they paid dearly to Prussian and Saxon troops. Strasbourg, where General Jean Rapp barricaded himself on his retreat from Waterloo with the Army of the Rhine, did not surrender until July 22. A number of other towns, including Huningue, Belfort, and Neuf-Brisach in Alsace and Laon and Rocroi farther north, held out for six weeks or more. Moreover, even after the French army had been pushed beyond the Loire, it continued to generate unrest, for instance in Limoges, where the "devastations" caused by French soldiers provoked several families to flee to the neighboring regions of Bordeaux and Angoulême.[36]

On the other hand, in the south and west, where royalists had already begun to oppose Napoleon in early 1815, supporters of the monarchy engaged in brutal reprisals against associates of the emperor. Within a week of the Battle of Waterloo, there was an explosion of terror in the south, beginning in Marseille, now guarded by the British fleet. Beginning on the night of June 24, the city erupted in violence against residents connected to the Bonapartist cause, particularly the so-called Mamelukes—the Arabs who had migrated there in the wake of the Egyptian Campaign of 1798—leaving some fifty dead, two hundred wounded, and eighty burned buildings. Two days later, as the royalist Marseillaise socialite Julie Pellizonne noted in her journal, "The morning of the twenty-sixth, the commotion was extreme, the people supported by the *compagnies franches* came in a crowd to all the houses of individuals known to be of the party of Buonaparte (the day before, there had been several devastated) but this day, there were a lot more. They threw furniture out of the windows, they broke, shattered, or burned everything found and left only the walls. . . . The majority of these individuals had fled, but those whom they managed to catch had a bad fate," including two "unfortunate negresses." Over the next month, the terror spread across the south, from Toulon, which Napoleonic marshal Guillaume Brune refused to surrender until July 24; to Avignon, where the general was murdered as he attempted finally to flee; to Nîmes, where, in a revival of the religious wars of the sixteenth century, Catholic royalists persecuted Protestant liberals, causing the flight of some 2,500, mostly prominent manufacturers. In Nîmes, according to André Jardin and André-Jean Tudesq, not only were dozens of homes ransacked and people killed, but Protestant bourgeois women were forced to endure the humiliation of having their drawers pulled down and buttocks beaten with nail-studded paddles that marked them with bloody fleurs-de-lys. Against all the violence, the regime in Paris did little.[37]

In fact, over the next few months, spontaneous terror was accompanied by "legal" terror, fueled by a new Chamber of Deputies elected in mid-August, the so-called Chambre Introuvable, or Unobtainable Chamber, said to be "more royalist than the king." Following the return of Louis XVIII, Bonapartists were purged and replaced by royalists, from the level of the ministerial cabinet down through prefects to mayors, and even to local councilmen and civil functionaries, such as notaries and contractors. In the end, somewhere between fifty thousand and eighty thousand officials were dismissed. The new government also reorganized the military, from the ministry of war down to the rank-and-file, including the national guard. Following the submission of a number of generals to the king, on August 11 the minister of war, Laurent de Gouvion Saint-Cyr, cashiered most of the army, including 70 percent of the royal guard, leaving a force of only fifty-five thousand. The reorganized regime punished those who had betrayed the monarchy during the Hundred Days. Following a decree of July 24 banishing Napoleon's accomplices, the minister of police, Joseph Fouché, drafted a list of *proscrits,* or outlaws, who had supported the "usurper" or betrayed the monarchy in 1793. Whittled down to fifty-four generals and "regicides," many of these *proscrits*—with some famous exceptions, such as Marshal Ney, who was executed on December 8—were permitted to escape. Following passage of the so-called amnesty law by the ultraroyalist Chamber in January of the next year, however, they were prosecuted or exiled. Beginning in the fall of 1815, the new chamber also passed a number of measures against revolutionary political activity, including prevotal courts to judge "exceptional" crimes against the government, such as rioting and brigandage. These special courts convicted about nine thousand (mostly poor) inhabitants, one-third of whom were sentenced to capital punishment, before they were discontinued two years later.[38]

Such measures amplified the sense of political instability in France. As Jules Michelet later remembered, "The double fall of the Empire, and the double restoration of the Bourbons, succeeded each other with the rapidity of a theater scene change." Such "scene change" generated considerable bitterness and anxiety, which was aggravated—even if it was also contained—by the presence of a foreign army. As Michelet, a republican, described the White Terror, "A foolish and insolent minority, seeing itself under foreign protection, insulted a France still bound by her defeat, and played among the sparks which could, from one moment to the other, ignite a big fire."[39]

"How Terrible Are the Scourges of War"

By late 1815, most of the country was in a state of disaster. Already depleted from years of massive mobilization, heavy taxation, and economic dislocation, as well as disease, many French had little left to give the hordes of occupying troops. In the midst of yet another regime change, they now faced further requisitions and taxes, not to mention violence and destruction, with no end in sight. Threatened with hunger, some hid their property, including livestock and food, as well as money, or simply abandoned their homes, fleeing to neighboring forests, marshes, caves, and even as far away as Spain. Others fell into complete despair.

In Paris, in addition to massive requisitions and random abuses, the population suffered the trauma of seeing the capital occupied by hundreds of thousands of troops. As English observer Helen Maria Williams described the city in 1815:

> Paris itself, though spared the worst evils of war, wears still the aspect of a conquered city,—guarded by foreign troops at all its gates, foreign troops posted at every bridge, and cannon which seemed as if it were pointed at the palace of the Tuileries. The Bois de Boulogne, the Hyde Park of Paris, may

> now be termed rather a desert than a royal domain. We might almost imagine ourselves in the wilds of America, amidst huts framed of logs and branches, with the ground cleared around them, and nothing left but the stumps of trees marking where they once grew. The walks, formerly crowded with splendid equipages of the gay and great, have lost their shade and their visitors, and are transformed into streets of tents.

The Bonapartist Laure Junot, Duchesse d'Abrantès, later recalled the "terrible humiliation of seeing the foreigner inside our walls [in Paris]." Recalling the Allied cannons in the public squares of the capital, she bemoaned, "[W]e were in the end between the sword and the cannon; and whether it was or was not our fault we were no less unhappy."[40]

As traumatic as the occupation was for the capital, it was far worse for the countryside, especially in the northeast, which had already endured the Allied invasion and evacuation of 1814, as well as the passage of tens of thousands of troops, French and foreign, to and from Belgium during the Hundred Days. In one of many similar reports from the region after the invasion of 1815, a traveler arriving from Bar-sur-Aube described the town as "entirely devastated; the inhabitants reduced to the most frightening misery, have been forced to cut the wheat before its maturity in order to feed themselves and the allied troops with which they are crushed. . . . [A] large village about a mile from the town . . . was entirely burned by the Bavarians; the inhabitants, who had attempted to resist, were massacred by a detachment sent by a commandant at Vendoeuvre, under pretext of suppressing the revolters." This report claimed that between six thousand and seven thousand French "partisans" who had taken refuge in the forest between Bar-sur-Aube and Troyes were waging war against the Allied troops. In the region around Avesnes, which was traversed by some 240,000 troops in a single year, "All of these movements brought desolation to the country," according to historian Marc Blancpain. "[T]hefts, rapes, fires, trampling on fields that had not all been harvested. The population, often, hid as in 1814 in the depths of the brush and forest and in the obscurity of grottoes."[41]

Most devastated of all was the Ardennes, along the border with the new Kingdom of the Netherlands. Sometimes labeled the "Siberia" of France, this region was swarming with Prussian and Russian troops. By the end of 1815, local authorities were reporting to the central administration that the department was "in complete despair." In early November, the prefect reported, "The movements of foreign troops cause the most acute worries. The old ones leave after having exhausted all the resources, and then arrive new ones in such great number that it is impossible to satisfy them. In this situation, we predict excessive misery for this winter. The administration fears the effects." The next month, he wrote, "For the last six months, the Prussians have occupied this Department. The Russians have established themselves here in equal number. Several communes are almost ruined, and will soon be abandoned by all inhabitants, if these troops stay any longer." By early the next year, the Twenty-Third Legion of the Royal Gendarmerie reported: "The inhabitants there are in despair, one sees there only tears. Prussians and Russians all contribute to the total ruin of this important part of the Realm." Describing the incessant thefts and rapes committed by the occupying troops, the report continued, "The inhabitants are fleeing everywhere; soon it will be a vast desert."[42]

But no region was spared the burden of the military occupation. In the Bas-Rhin, which between September and December 1815 housed 288,634 soldiers and 93,938 horses on a population of about half a million, Madame de Montbrison wrote to her friend, "We desired the Allies, we waited for them as liberators. . . . But, alas! The conduct of these Allies (I except the Russians and the English) has not been what we expected from them." In Colmar, which received troops from Baden and Bavaria as well as Austria, a Madame de Berckheim complained, "The requisitions take from us our very last *sou;* the troops change, but not our misfortunes." Farther west, in the Maine, where inhabitants were terrorized by Prussian troops, the country vicar bewailed, "How terrible are the scourges of war!"[43]

In an effort to hasten a settlement with the Allies, Joseph Fouché, a revolutionary who had survived all the regime changes of the last two years and was now interior minister, submitted a formal report to the king, "On the Situation of France and Its Relations with the Foreign Armies," on August 15. Concerned that the military occupation was exacerbating civil conflict within France, Fouché concluded:

> The ravages of France are at their height; one ruins, one devastates, one destroys, as if there were for us no hope of either peace or reconstruction. The inhabitants take flight before undisciplined soldiers; the forests are filled with

> unfortunates who seek there a last asylum. The harvests are going to perish in the fields; soon despair will no longer hear the voice of any authority, and this war, undertaken to ensure the triumph of moderation and of justice, will equal the barbarism of those most deplorable and too famous invasions of which history recalls the memory only with horror.

Privy to this report, even the Duke of Wellington became concerned about the state of France. Anxious not to provoke further unrest, he wrote, "If the system followed by the Prussians and now imitated by the Bavarians is not rejected, the allies will soon find themselves in the same situation as the French were in Spain"—in other words, in a state of guerrilla warfare.[44]

Negotiating Peace

Under pressure of the "war" occupation, the French government was eager to reach a definitive peace settlement. Since July, Talleyrand had been unsuccessful in obtaining such a settlement with his counterparts among the Allies, who would not negotiate with the French until they disarmed. Following the reorganization of the French army on August 11, they began to discuss a peace treaty, but they could not agree on terms. While most Allied leaders agreed that this time around the nation needed to provide additional security against future aggression, they differed on a number of other questions, including how long the French should remain under occupation, how much financial reparation they should pay, and whether they should concede additional territory beyond the frontiers of 1792 imposed on them by the treaty of 1814. Some members of the coalition, particularly Prussia and Austria but also British prime minister Lord Liverpool, thought France needed to be punished for having backed Napoleon in his return to power. They wanted to exact heavy financial indemnities—as much as 1.2 billion francs—as well as significant territorial concessions, particularly in Alsace and Lorraine, which were to be transferred to Prussia and Austria. Pushed by its military commissioner, Karl Friedrich von dem Knesebeck, the Prussian civilian leadership, including Karl, Freiherr vom Stein, and Karl August, Fürst von Hardenberg, even circulated a map of these proposed dismemberments, which would have taken from France most of the fortresses built under Louis XIV along the northern and eastern frontiers. However, such a punitive approach was resisted by other Allied leaders, including Tsar Alexander and, especially, Robert Stewart, Lord Castlereagh and the Duke of Wellington, who maintained that it would destabilize France. As the Russian ambassador, Carlo Andrea Pozzo di Borgo, a Corsican who was an archenemy of Napoleon, is said to have acknowledged: "If France consents to such an arrangement, she will be erased from the political map of Europe. . . . [This proposal] is a master-work of destruction."[45]

According to the more moderate Allied leaders, the main goal of any settlement was to ensure durable peace—as well as financial indemnification—for the nations of Europe. As Wellington wrote to Castlereagh on August 11, 1815, the object of the Allies in their campaigns against Napoleon "has been to put an end to the French Revolution, to obtain peace for themselves and their people, to have the power of reducing their overgrown military establishments, and the leisure to attend to the internal concerns of their several nations, and to improve the situation of their people." In contrast to a permanent cession of territory, Wellington advised a temporary occupation, at the expense of the French, which he saw as the best means of helping the monarchy to secure its authority, as well as of enabling the Allied coalition to obtain recompense for past suffering. Informed by his past experiences with the British army in India and Spain, the duke argued: "These measures will not only give us, during the period of occupation, all the military security which could be expected from the permanent cession, but, if carried into execution in the spirit in which they are conceived, they are in themselves the bond of peace."[46] In a memorandum dated August 31, Wellington outlined what he saw as the goals of a temporary occupation:

> First, to give security to the government of the King, and to afford him time to form a force of his own with which he can carry on his government, and take his fair share in the concerns of Europe; secondly, to give the Allies some security against a second revolutionary convulsion and reaction; and, thirdly, to enable the Allies to enforce the payment of those contributions which they deem it just towards their own subjects to lay on France in payment of the expenses of the war.[47]

This gentler approach to the defeated power was endorsed by the Russian diplomatic corps, after Alexander I received an appeal from Louis

XVIII, who said he would resign his throne rather than accept the dismemberment of his country.

Under pressure from Wellington and Alexander, the other Allies eventually agreed to lighten their terms, resulting in an ultimatum of September 20, which listed six bases for continued negotiations: (1) the Treaty of Paris of May 30, 1814, was reaffirmed; (2) some territory would be taken from France along the Dutch, German, and Italian borders, including Philippeville, Marienbourg, Givet, Charlemont, Saarlouis, and Landau; (3) fortifications at Huningue would be destroyed; (4) the French would have to pay 800 million francs to indemnify the Allies for the costs of the recent war; (5) another 200 million francs would be required to pay for the construction of new fortifications along the frontier; and (6) the northern and eastern departments of France would be occupied by an Allied army of 150,000, at French expense, for seven years. But even this ultimatum was viewed as too harsh by the French government, which rejected it as unprecedented under international law. The French cabinet insisted that because the war had been fought against Napoleon, not the French people, it should not have to make such territorial and financial concessions. Given the stalemate, Talleyrand, no longer trusted by either the king or the Allied leadership, was forced to resign on September 25.[48]

Negotiations were left to a new minister of foreign affairs, Armand-Emmanuel du Plessis, Duc de Richelieu. A distant nephew of the more famous Cardinal Richelieu and a former émigré who had spent most of the revolutionary and imperial era in Odessa, Russia, where he served as governor of the Caucasus region, Richelieu had the confidence and sympathy of the Russian tsar as well as the royalist faction in France. Although he felt unprepared for this responsibility and had been left little room for maneuver by Talleyrand, Richelieu proved himself a skilled defender of French interests. Arguing that the only way to strengthen the monarchy was to maintain the territorial integrity of France, he countered the Allied ultimatum, insisting on no loss of territory but offering an indemnity of 600 million francs and an occupation of five years. By early October, when a preliminary protocol was signed, Richelieu had obtained a number of concessions from the Allies, including the retention of Alsace and Lorraine plus northern Flanders, and the fortresses of Joux, Écluse, and Charlemont, as well as reduced burdens for the indemnity and occupation. This protocol formed the basis for the Second Treaty of Paris, of November 20, 1815, which ended the initial wartime occupation and, following Wellington's proposal, instituted a more limited, peaceful "occupation of guarantee."[49]

A New Approach to War Termination

The Second Treaty of Paris was really a series of treaties between France and the individual powers of the coalition that had defeated Napoleon. Its main goals were to ensure "proper indemnities for the past and solid guarantees for the future," including protection of the king's authority and constitutional Charter. France was essentially placed under the oversight of the Allies until they were satisfied it was no longer a threat to Europe. The settlement reduced the territory of France to its frontiers of 1790 and required a ring of fortresses outside these borders. In addition to a temporary occupation at French expense, the treaty required the payment of a still substantial war indemnity. Maintaining a Council of Allied Ambassadors to monitor political developments in Paris, the treaty also formalized a Quadruple Alliance (of Britain, Russia, Prussia, and Austria) to protect "order" against revolution, thereby promoting international political cooperation in Europe. Unprecedented in the law of war, this settlement, especially the "occupation of guarantee," marked a new approach to peacekeeping.[50]

To promote security, the Second Treaty of Paris included a range of provisions, beginning with the return of all war prisoners and deserters to their home nations. France lost a number of strategic territories along its northeastern frontier, including Philippeville, Marienbourg, and the duchy of Bouillon to the Netherlands; Saarlouis and Saarbrücken to Prussia; Landau (which had so fiercely resisted the invasion) and the territory north of the Lauter to Austria, which in turn ceded them to Bavaria and Hesse; and Savoy to Sardinia. Together, this represented some five thousand square kilometers and three hundred thousand inhabitants. In addition, the fortress of Huningue, deemed threatening to Swiss neutrality, was destroyed. To defend the border against any aggression by the French, the treaty required the reconstruction of a number of old fortresses in the Netherlands, overseen by the British, with some financial contributions from the Dutch and the French.[51]

But the key to guaranteeing security in France was the occupation force. Placed under the integrated command of the Duke of Wellington, the multinational occupation force was the first of its kind. Going beyond the loose coalition forged in the last years of the Napoleonic Wars, it constituted a "unique advance in the annals of military command," in the words of Thomas Dwight Veve. Prohibited from interfering in civilian administration, it was designed as a peacekeeping force. Stationed in and around eighteen garrisons in seven departments along the northeastern frontier between the English Channel and Switzerland, the occupation army totaled 150,000 men: 30,000 from each of the four main powers—Britain, Russia, Prussia, and Austria—plus another 30,000 from the minor powers. The Austrians, under the command of general Johann Maria Philipp, Baron de Frimont, had their headquarters in Colmar; the Prussians, under lieutenant general Hans Ernst Karl, soon to be named Count von Zieten, in Sedan; and the Russians, under field marshal Mikhail Semenovich, Count Vorontsov, in Maubeuge. The British, under Wellington and his chief of staff and quartermaster general, Sir George Murray, had their field quarters in Cambrai. From the minor powers, there were ten thousand Bavarians, centered in Sarreguemines; five thousand Saxons, in Tourcoing; five thousand Hanoverians, in Condé; five thousand Danes, in Bouchain; and (after some debate over their number and placement) five thousand Württembergers, in Wissembourg. Before January 1, 1816, the rest of the Allied forces were to leave France. Each national contingent was to include a mix of infantry, cavalry, and artillery units. In addition to training regularly throughout the year and undergoing biannual inspections, the troops were invited to participate in joint exercises each fall, on the plains of Denain, near Valenciennes. Within the occupation zone, the French army was allowed to maintain small contingents of five hundred to three thousand men in twenty-four garrisons, including Calais, Lille, Metz, and Strasbourg. To prevent conflict between Allied and French armies, a demilitarized zone was established along the southwestern edge of the occupation zone. Reduced from the proposed term of seven years, the occupation of guarantee was slated to last up to five years, until the French had fulfilled their obligations, including financial payments, to the Allies.[52]

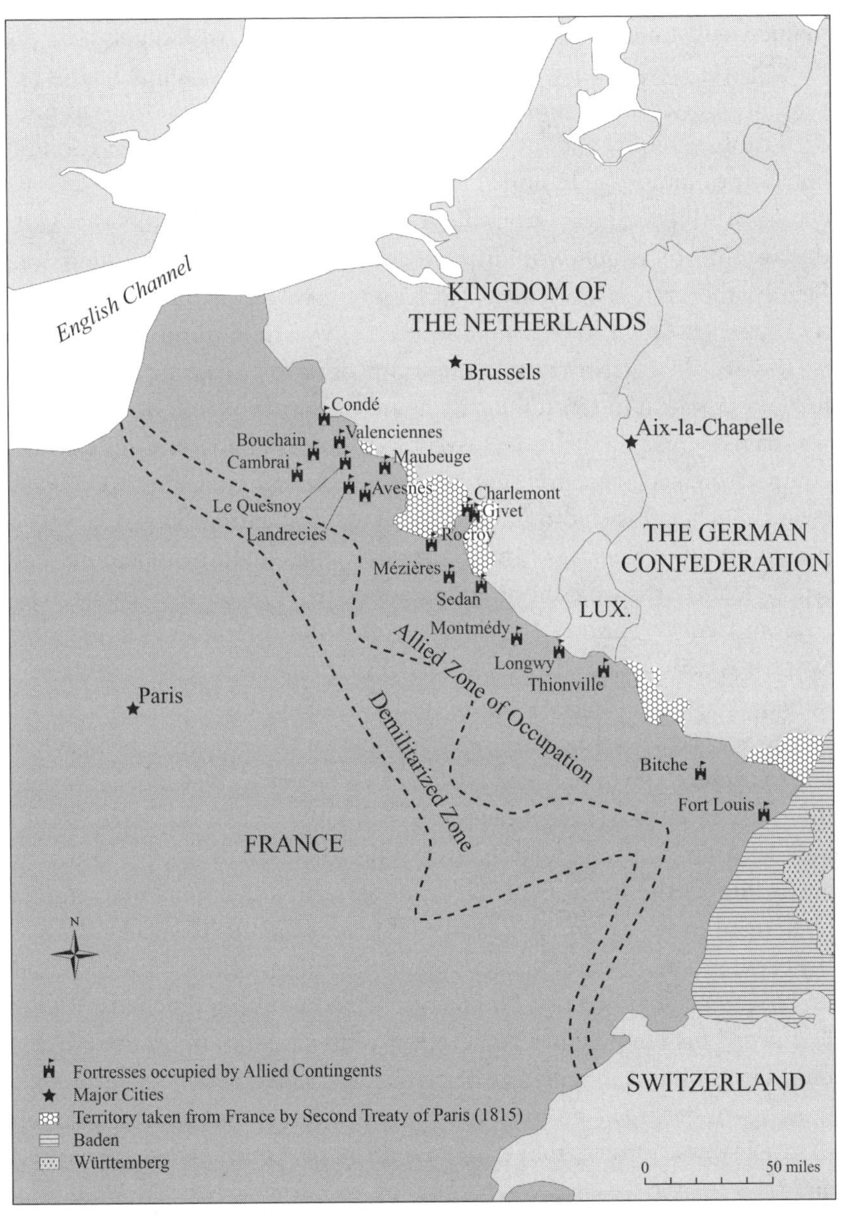

France after the Second Treaty of Paris, November 1815. Territories lost and fortresses occupied.

Although they had been negotiated down from the most punitive amounts proposed by some of the Allies, the financial requirements remained substantial. To pay and equip the army of occupation, the French were required to make "contributions" of 50 million francs per year, in quarterly installments, plus provide daily rations for two hundred thousand men and fifty thousand horses, totaling another 100 million francs annually. In addition, they were required to reimburse the claims of Allied subjects from the Revolutionary and Napoleonic Wars, the amount of which would be determined by an Allied commission. Finally, the French were required to pay a war indemnity, negotiated by Richelieu down to 700 million francs, 137 million of which would go toward the fortress reconstruction program. Following the first defeat of Napoleon in 1814, the only financial burden placed on the French was to recognize the debts incurred by the imperial government through contracts signed with private entities outside of France. In 1815, however, the Allies insisted on additional indemnification. Payment was a precondition of the end of the occupation. Although the indemnity had antecedents in the contributions demanded by France from Prussia, Austria, and other countries during the Revolutionary and Napoleonic Wars, it was designed as a "reparation," in the modern sense of repairing damage to rejoin the community of nations.[53]

The Second Treaty of Paris was difficult for the French to bear. When it was presented by the Allied coalition, Richelieu at first refused to sign it and threatened to resign his post, until Louis XVIII implored him to accede. After finally signing the treaty, he collapsed in distress and said, according to the memoir of Baron de Barante, "A Frenchman should be hanged for signing such a treaty."[54] Just as painful for Richelieu was the presentation of the settlement to the Chambers of Peers and Deputies on November 25. Blaming Napoleon for necessitating the treaty, Richelieu urged his countrymen to accept it with resignation, in the interest of international reconciliation: "In spite of the evil that the usurper has done to all nations," he concluded his speech, "let us give them reason to grieve those wrongs that they now do to us. Let us give these nations and their peoples reason to rely upon us, to know us better, so that they will reconcile themselves freely and forever with us." Responding with stony silence, the two Chambers did approve the treaty.[55]

Outside the halls of government, the treaty was met with anger but also relief. In Paris, according to police reports, there were some complaints about the war indemnity, directed especially against those who had backed Napoleon, but nonetheless "the promulgation of the peace Treaty had generally wrought Pleasure." In the provinces, reports from stagecoach drivers suggest that most French, especially those outside the departments subject to the "occupation of guarantee," welcomed the departure of a large part of the Allied force and expressed at least superficial support for the monarchy. In some locales, there was concern over the financial burden imposed by the treaty. In the Aveyron, for instance, the publication of the treaty engendered alarm, even among workers and peasants, who feared that if France were unable to fulfill its engagements toward the foreigners, it would be forced to cede more territory. Elsewhere, however, inhabitants were more resigned to the settlement. From the Dordogne, a police informant reported, "People shuddered at the peace treaty; but everywhere confidence is expressed in a better future."[56]

Evacuation and Encampment

Even as the treaty was being finalized, Allied troops were on the march to their home countries or new encampments. The troops ordered to leave France were not always happy to return home. In his memoir, the Comte de Haussonville recounted how the Russian colonel quartered in his grandmother's château at Gurcy begged her, unsuccessfully, to retain him in place of her old *maître d'hôtel,* lamenting, "Well, here I am, to my misfortune, recalled with my regiment to Russia. How can I leave such a lodging without regret." This reluctance on the part of Allied troops to leave their relatively comfortable assignment in France is manifest in numerous prints from the time depicting Allied and especially Russian troops exhibiting regrets—and even shedding tears—as they bid adieu to French women.[57]

Meanwhile, to staff the new occupation of guarantee, Allied authorities rushed to decide which troops to leave—or move—into the occupation zone, which officers to place in command, and where to station them all. In late 1815, the Duke of Wellington implored the British secretary of state for war and the colonies, Henry, Third Earl of Bathurst, against the opposition of Parliament, to obtain fresh contingents of British as opposed to Hanoverian troops for the occupation of guarantee. (Apparently, not all recruits were excited about their new assignment. A popular poem bewailed: "Quartered in the mud villages in French Flanders/Where the men caught cold, the horses glanders.")[58] The numbers and locations of troops were then conveyed to local military and civilian authorities by the French ministry of war. Before occupying their assigned garrisons, the Allied armies were required, in conjunction with French military commissioners, to conduct formal inspections, to ensure they would be returned in the same state, with no loss of equipment or weaponry, at the end of the occupation.

Despite considerable planning, the movement of hundreds of thousands of troops was often disruptive. By late November, the roads leading out of the country were crowded with foreign soldiers. From the Meurthe, a police informant wrote, "We are astonished that this department, excepted by the treaty from those that the foreign troops are supposed to occupy, still has ten thousand Bavarians who are making no preparation to leave. It is also traversed by five thousand Saxons and some Russian corps. From this result all the inevitable disorders; destructions in the forests, thefts on the Roads." The region between Calais and Boulogne was overrun with British troops awaiting transport across the Channel. Between December 14, 1815, and February 4, 1816, through the port of Calais alone embarked 19,414 men and 4,043 horses, plus 164 servants, 1,792 women, and 1,067 children. The evacuation of all these troops affected neighboring countries, too. From Brussels a police informant wrote, "It is remarked that on their passage these soldiers [from Prussia], treat the Belgians no better than they treated the French; everywhere one hears only complaints from the inhabitants against the Prussians." The troops often took with them food and materiel expropriated from the communes where they had been stationed. From Laon in late November, a police informant reported that the prefect of the Aisne had been forced by a Prussian commander to accede to a massive requisition of provisions of all sorts, which his troops planned not to consume en route but to ship back home.[59]

In Paris, the evacuation was delayed temporarily at the request of the French government, which wanted to ensure that the capital was calm before it relinquished the additional security provided by the presence of tens of thousands of foreign troops. In mid-November, a police agent at the Invalides station reported that there were still 1,100 Prussian and English troops quartered at the École Militaire, "destroying the barracks as much as they can[;] they steal the sheets, make themselves vests with the covers; burn their cots to save wood to sell. They break the iron ramps, the stairs: They engage in such devastations especially at night. They also take the locks from the doors and sell them to people who prowl around the École. . . . One hopes that the Prussians will leave tomorrow." But by the end of January 1816, the Duc de Richelieu reported to the French ambassador in London that all British troops had left the city, leaving behind some supplies, such as biscuits and cannons, which they donated to the French war ministry. Although Richelieu would have preferred that he stay in Paris, even the Duke of Wellington moved his headquarters to Cambrai, in the new British occupation zone, returning to the capital only for occasional meetings.[60]

As the foreign troops departed, residents of cities outside the occupation zone such as Marseille, Rouen, Dijon, and Lyon heaved a sigh of relief. In these areas, stagecoach drivers reported, the "public spirit" was improving. From the Ain, a police informant noted in mid-December, the peace treaty had been received "with resignation" where there were no foreigners, but "with joy" in territories that had been occupied but were now liberated. In the area around Grenoble, news of the upcoming departure of the Allied troops "much diminished the fermentation reigning in the majority of Communes," and in the Haute-Saône, "The public spirit improves in proportion as the foreign troops retreat."[61] In the northeast, however, the "evacuation" of one contingent just meant the arrival of another, sometimes even more brutal, force. In the Ardennes, where three arrondissements were assigned Russian troops coming from around Nancy, their reputation remained so terrifying that the inhabitants of Landrecies, among others, "came to regret the Prussians" who had occupied the town in 1815.[62]

By January 1816, the various Allied contingents were more or less settled in the zones they would occupy for the next thirty-five months. In the north, the British divided their forty thousand troops, ten thousand of which were Hanoverians, between the departments of the Pas-de-Calais and the Nord. Commanded per Wellington's request by veterans

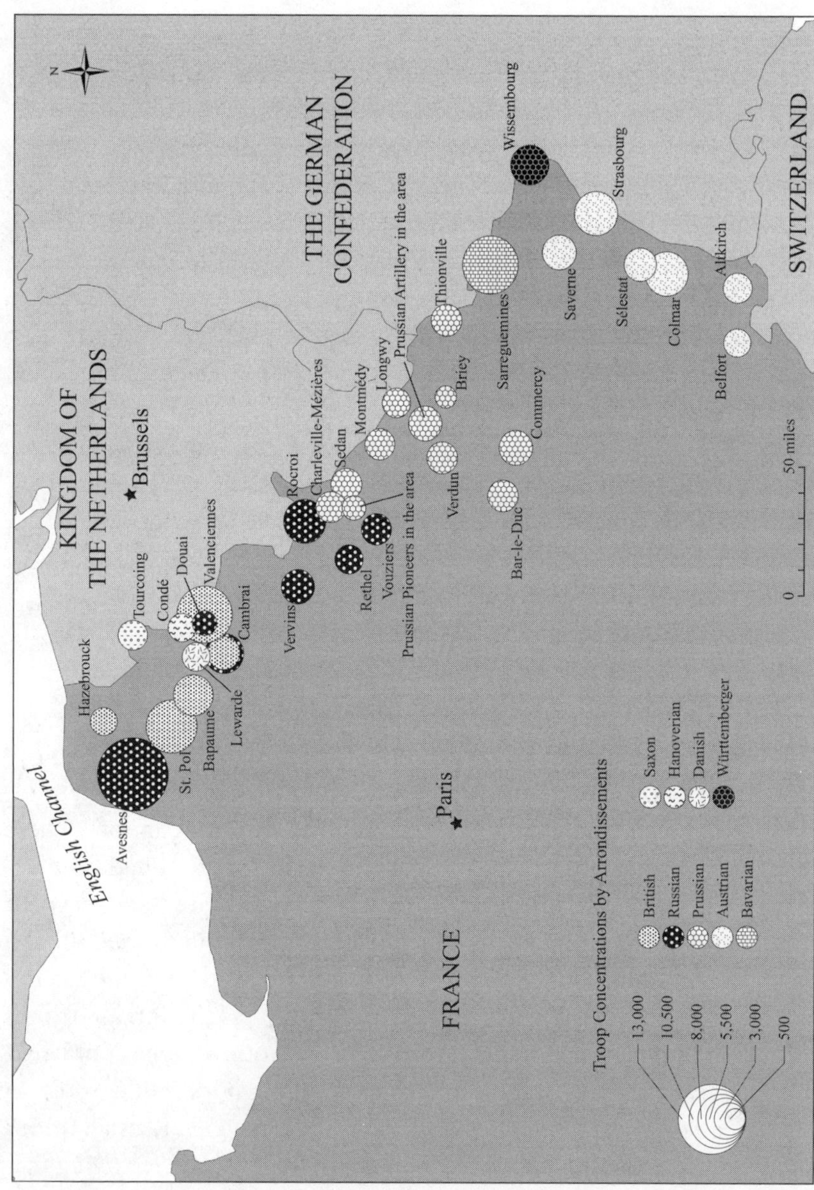

Allied troop concentrations by arrondissements. These numbers, based on troop returns at the height of the occupation of guarantee between mid-1816 and early 1817, were compiled from: "État d'effectif et d'emplacement de l'armée anglaise et de ses contingens, à l'époque du 1er Mars 1817" and "Commission mixte près l'armée russe: Situation générale des troupes du Corps d'armée russe à l'époque du 1er Avril 1817," SHD 3D/134; "State of Prussian Contingent, June 1816," in *WSD,* 11:414; "Tableau de l'armée d'occupation autrichienne," AN, F7/9899; and Sir George Murray Papers, NLS, 46.7.18 A & B and 46.7.19. In the Austrian sector, no troops were stationed in Strasbourg, which remained a French garrison, only in the surrounding arrondissement.

of the Peninsular War, the British force in France comprised three brigades of two squadrons each of cavalry and three divisions of three brigades of infantry, plus artillery. Headquartered in Cambrai, it also had a large garrison in Valenciennes, where Sir Charles Colville commanded the third infantry division. Another division of infantry, under Sir Henry Clinton, was stationed at Saint-Pol.[63]

Also in the department of the Nord, which received about one-third of the total occupation force, were the Saxon and Danish contingents, with five thousand each. The Saxons, who since the summer of 1815 had been stationed in Alsace around Sélestat and Colmar, marched via Nancy, Reims, and Laon to Quesnoy by mid-January 1816. Regrouped at Béthune, they were assigned a headquarters at Tourcoing. Under the command of General von Gablenz, the Saxon force comprised a regiment of hussars, a battalion of chasseurs, a battery of six-pound cannons, and four battalions of infantry, under Colonel von Seydewitz, divided between the communes surrounding the citadel of Lille, including Armentières, Comines, Seclin, La Bassée, Saint-Amand, Roubaix, and Quesnoy (until 1817), but with Tourcoing bearing most of the burden.[64] The Danish contingent, which had not taken part in the invasion, was formed at the request of the Allies in mid-October and did not depart from home until November 20. Including five battalions of infantry, two batteries of artillery, four squadrons of cavalry, an equipment train for baggage and ammunition, and a campaign hospital with four hundred beds, this contingent did not reach the French frontier until January 11, 1816. Commanded by Prince Frederick of Hesse, cousin of the king of Denmark, it occupied a line running from Bouchain, where it was headquartered, to Lens. Prince Frederick, accompanied by two aides-de-camp and some women, installed himself near the middle of this line, at Lewarde.[65]

Moving south, the Russian contingent of thirty thousand men, with its headquarters in Maubeuge, occupied a territory 120 kilometers long by 20–60 kilometers wide, extending from Valenciennes in the north to Givet in the south, and from the frontier with the new Kingdom of the Netherlands in the east to the arrondissement of Vervins in the west. In the department of the Nord, it included the area around Cambrai, Le Cateau, and Avesnes. In the Ardennes, it comprised the arrondissements of Rocroi, Rethel, and Vouziers as well as the *chef-lieu* of Mézières. Although none of these towns contained more than a few thousand inhabitants, together they received some fourteen thousand Russian troops and their horses. The Russian zone also reached into a few cantons in the departments of the Aisne and Moselle. Commanded by Count Vorontsov, son of the Russian ambassador to London, this contingent included four regiments of dragoons (named Courland, Kinburn, Smolensk, and Tver); seven regiments of infantry; seven companies of artillery; some Cossacks and chasseurs; and a company of pioneers. More than the other Allied contingents, these Russian regiments, with the exception of those named Riajsk and Yakoutie, rotated frequently among locations in and outside of France.[66]

In addition to fourteen thousand Russians, the department of the Ardennes housed twelve thousand Prussians, for a total of twenty-six thousand men, plus twelve thousand horses. Headquartered in the fortified city of Sedan, the rest of the Prussian contingent was stationed in the departments of Moselle and Meuse.[67] During the initial invasion of 1815, the Moselle had been occupied by 82,000 soldiers and 3,280 officers, plus 28,000 horses from Prussia, under the command of Generals von Bülow and von Thielmann in Metz, as well as 40,000 soldiers and 1,600 officers from Russia and some additional troops from smaller German states. For the occupation of guarantee, these forces were reduced, first to fifteen thousand men together and then, after the spring of 1817, to even fewer, with the Prussians stationed around Longwy and Thionville and the Russians around Courcelles-Chaussy and Briey. Also in the Moselle was the Bavarian contingent, with 6,359 soldiers and noncommissioned officers—3,372 of which were lodged with inhabitants—and 250 officers, with 2,009 horses. Over one thousand of these men were quartered in the town of Sarreguemines, on a local population of only 3,608 (almost 2,300 of whom were children). The rest were divided between all but twelve of the ninety-three communes in the arrondissement, with half of these taking small groups of between six and fifty. The remainder of the Prussian contingent was stationed in the Meuse, around Bar-le-Duc, where 14,342 men, 174 officers, and 4,360 horses were due to receive rations in a canton of about 16,000 inhabitants.[68]

Along the Rhine River, the region of Alsace was occupied by troops from Austria and Württemberg. The Austrian contingent of thirty thousand troops, commanded by Baron de Frimont, an émigré from Lorraine who had switched allegiance to the Habsburg army, was split more or less evenly between the two departments of the Bas-Rhin and Haut-Rhin, with its headquarters in the city of Colmar. In Colmar itself, along with the officer corps were stationed six companies of Kerpen infantry, totaling 1,300 men, with 120 horses. Mulhouse, a center of industry to the south, housed three thousand, as did Altkirch, whose population was little more than two thousand at the time. The rest of the total of 17,750 "mouths" and 1,961 horses stationed in the department of the Haut-Rhin were quartered—mostly in barracks—in smaller towns and villages such as Dannemarie, Ribeauvillé, Soultz, and Thann. The other half of the Austrian contingent was stationed in the Bas-Rhin, in the region around Strasbourg, which remained a French garrison. In the Bas-Rhin were also encamped some five thousand troops from the small German state of Württemberg, across the Rhine. Under the command of Baron von Woellwarth, who developed a reputation for bad humor, these forces were headquartered in Wissembourg, on a permanent population of little more than four thousand, with smaller numbers scattered in surrounding villages such as Niederbronn, Oberbronn, and Lauterbourg.[69]

Yearning for Liberation

Even as these foreign troops moved into their new positions, the French were already yearning for liberation. From the beginning of the occupation of guarantee, the new government made fulfillment of its obligations to the Allies one of its primary missions, in order to expedite their departure. In particular, the Duc de Richelieu worked tirelessly, first to alleviate the burden of occupation, and then to end it. Within six months, he was already pressing Allied leaders to reduce the number of troops—and required requisitions—in the occupied zone.

Until the Allies agreed first to reduce their troops, in the spring of 1817, and then to evacuate them altogether, in late 1818, the occupation of guarantee remained nothing less than a humiliating reversal of fortune for France. Little more than three years earlier, Napoleon's Grand Empire had stretched across the Continent. Since the beginning of 1814, France had borne the psychological and financial costs of this ambition, experiencing two invasions in quick succession. During the war occupation of July to November 1815 alone, the material costs had totaled close to 500 million francs. Now constrained to the territory it had held at the beginning of the French Revolution, it was occupied by 150,000 foreign soldiers, for whose maintenance it was responsible. Already financially devastated by the wars of Napoleon, France now faced the additional burden of indemnifying its former enemies. Totaling some 1.4 billion francs, the costs of occupation and indemnification would take years to pay. In addition, the repeated regime changes had only aggravated internal political tensions.[70] The disillusionment with the postwar settlement is encapsulated by a poignant letter from a royalist nobleman in Burgundy to his nephew in the Seine-et-Marne in mid-1816, regarding damages to the latter's estate: "The good for which the allies made us hope has ruined you. For the French, there remains only time, for those who are young, deprivation for several more years, and hope and, from this moment, the consolation of no longer being under a regime like that of Buonaparte. What is worth more than that?"[71] In this situation, many French continued to view the "Allies" as enemies.

Chapter Two

A Burden So Onerous

BETWEEN LATE 1815 and early 1816, as Allied troops began to move to their assigned garrisons, local administrators in the northeast scrambled to receive them, often with little notice. In the department of the Nord, the prefect alerted the mayor of Tourcoing on January 28, 1816: "I have just learned and I hasten to inform you that a detachment of Saxon troops, composed of 686 men and 300 horses, is due to arrive tomorrow in your commune, to be stationed there, according to the conventions of 20 November 1815. I bid you to take right away the measures necessary to ensure their lodging. I also bid you to require the inhabitants to supply their subsistence." In Hazebrouck, where an advance guard of English cavalry, including 480 men and 500 horses, arrived on January 11, the subprefect responsible for providing them with lodging and subsistence complained that he had not been warned of the troop movement and insisted that the department, which already had some fifty thousand men in garrison, not be overburdened. When the prefect passed this complaint on to the ministry of war, he was told that local authorities needed to get used to handling such details on their own. Farther south, in the Ardennes, the burden of providing for the army of occupation was movingly evoked in a brief from the mayors of the rural communes of the canton of Givet. The mayors argued that the canton, considerably diminished in size by the peace treaty, had suffered more than any other from the recent invasion. Detailing the burdens inflicted by the initial occupation of the region by thirty thousand

Prussian troops, they lamented that these troops were now to be replaced by Russian ones: "What was the despair of these communes? When suddenly they found themselves encumbered with such a large number of men and especially of horses, that it was physically impossible to contain them." The mayors demanded that the occupying troops be stationed not in small villages already devastated by the initial invasion, but in larger towns, such as Givet and Charlemont, where they could be lodged in barracks.[1]

As these frantic missives from local authorities suggest, requisitioning was one of the biggest sources of tension between Allied troops and French inhabitants. As Allied troops moved into their regions, French men and women were faced with the immense task of feeding, housing, and equipping them, as well as their entourages of sutlers, laundresses, and other camp followers and family members, whose numbers totaled as much as 10 percent of the troop contingent in the British case. Even after the occupation force was reduced in December 1815 to 150,000, it required enormous quantities of foodstuffs, forage, wood, candles, beds, tables and chairs, linens, dishes, silverware, and wagons and horses, as well as lodging. To build and repair barracks, hospitals, officer quarters, and meeting rooms, as well as to transport personnel and equipment, required countless hours of corvée by local tradesmen and porters. As the municipal council of Ligny in the Meuse complained, as it scrambled to house passing soldiers in the town's 145 homes (of which only 107 were at all suitable for lodging), such demands constituted "a burden so onerous and really exceeding our forces."[2]

Such a burden had long been imposed on communities occupied by foreign armies, including the French army throughout the Revolutionary and Napoleonic Wars. In many ways, it was continuous with previous military practice, whereby mobile armies relied on the local countryside for their provisioning. Despite a number of developments in logistics under early modern states, including quartermasters, convoys, and magazines, Napoleon still supplied his armies via controlled foraging and enforced taxation on the local population. However, such "contributions," as they were labeled, were systematized under the occupation of guarantee. After the initial invasion in 1815, when foreign troops often pillaged out of vengeance or anxiety, the Allies regularized the supply process. In contrast to previous contributions exacted by conquering armies, their requisitions were regulated by treaty and coordinated by joint commissions of French and Allied supply officers. Moreover, they were paid by the defeated French state, which also committed itself to indemnifying inhabitants for expenses incurred as a result of the invasions of 1814 and 1815. The occupation of guarantee thus played an important, if unacknowledged, role in the shift toward modern logistics. Following this transitional period, modern states became more concerned to supply their armies via regular contracts with suppliers, protecting private property even in contexts of invasion and occupation.[3]

Despite the efforts of Allied and French authorities to systematize requisitioning, however, the burden still weighed heavily on ordinary French, especially in the countryside, where living conditions remained austere at best. Well into the nineteenth century, peasant families typically lived together—often with their livestock—in a one-room cottage, centered around a hearth. Furnished with little more than a bed and a table, this abode, lit only by candles and heated only by wood or peat, was often dark and cold. To sustain themselves for their strenuous work, peasants relied mainly on bread, as much as a kilogram per person per day, baked at home. This staple was supplemented with boiled porridge, vegetable soup (seasoned with lard), greens and roots, and (only after the late eighteenth century or so) potatoes; meat, especially beef, was a rarity reserved for illness and holidays. To drink, peasants had only water—which they usually had to haul from a fountain—or cider, rarely wine or even coffee. This dearth, which had been exacerbated by the last years of the Napoleonic Wars and would be again by the grain crisis of 1816–1817, made the requisitions of the occupiers—especially the daily rations of meat, alcohol, and fuel—all the more onerous. The table rations demanded by officers, on the scale of the menus of Parisian restaurants, seemed utterly extravagant. In small communities in the northeast, where occupiers often outnumbered residents, the occupation was experienced as an intrusion of space and a waste of resources. It also constituted a drain on the time and energy of local inhabitants, who were required to assist in transporting supplies—including scarce water—for the occupiers, at a time when roads and waterways were still primitive. These burdens would cause considerable resentment among the occupied.[4]

Requisitioning

Before the Allied armies even entered France in 1815, the Duke of Wellington issued a general order against requisitioning without payment. From Nivelles, on June 20, he commanded:

> The Commissaries of the army will provide for the wants of the troops in the usual manner, and it is not permitted either to soldiers or officers to extort contributions. The Commissaries will be authorised, either by the Field Marshal or by the Generals who command the troops of the respective nations, in cases where their provisions are not supplied by an English Commissary, to make the proper requisitions, for which regular receipts will be given; and it must be strictly understood that they will themselves be held responsible for whatever they obtain in way of requisition from the inhabitants of France, in the same manner in which they would be esteemed accountable for purchases made for their own Government in the several dominions to which they belong.[5]

During the initial military occupation, this order was honored mostly in the breach. Before the signature of the Second Treaty of Paris, in the absence of clear procedures and rates for requisitions, the supply process was chaotic and arbitrary, and pillaging by troops remained widespread. By the time of the transition to the occupation of guarantee in January 1816, local authorities were struggling to meet the demands of the Allies. As one representative plea to the war ministry from the hard-hit department of the Ardennes described the situation, while the promise of indemnities "sustains patience, close to giving way to despair, if the exaggerated demands of the troops for their subsistence do not cease. . . . it is imperative that such promises are followed closely by actions; in the interest of the inhabitants who are at wit's end and threaten to desert their countries, as well as in the interest of the King, whose name will be unanimously praised as soon as the promised aid arrives."[6]

To alleviate conflicts over supplies between Allied military governors and local administrators, the French government created a centralized Commission on Requisitions to coordinate the supply process. Established by royal decree on July 9, this commission was composed of four members, all former imperial officials; its president was a Jacobin from Genoa, Louis-Emmanuel Corvetto, named count by Napoleon, who would soon be named finance minister. The Commission on Requisitions worked with local prefects and subprefects, on the one hand, and national cabinet ministers, on the other, to respond to the demands of the Allies, centralized in their own joint Administrative Council of the Allied Armies. In late July, the commission acceded to the request by the Allies for 50 million francs over the next two months for the upkeep of their troops, plus an additional allowance for clothing and equipment of 120 francs per soldier. In exchange, according to a circular to the Allied governors of occupied departments dated August 15, 1815, Allied troops were to abstain from intervening in the financial administration of the departments. To fund the payments to the Allies, in mid-August the Commission on Requisitions levied an "extraordinary contribution" on each department, proportional to its resources. However, these measures did not take into account the sums already paid by various communities. Nor did they stop the Allies from making additional exactions. Receiving numerous reports of exorbitant demands by the Allies, the commission could do little but urge departments that still had provisions to share them with neighboring ones. The Pas-de-Calais, for instance, was asked to contribute 250,000 rations of food and 30,000 of forage toward a demand for 400,000 rations of food and 120,000 of forage from the town of Valenciennes in the Nord. In fact, the Commission on Requisitions proved to be ineffective at centralizing the supply process. As a report by the minister of war concluded already on July 24, the commission did not have the means to execute its functions. Noting that it lacked timely information on troop demands, accurate knowledge of government supplies, or adequate agents on the ground, the report argued that the commission required the assistance of the French ministry of war. Much less powerful than its Allied counterpart, the Commission on Requisitions could do little more than transmit complaints from local officials to cabinet ministers, who alone had the authority to present them to the Allied leadership. By early 1816, this commission ceased to operate.[7]

With the transition to the occupation of guarantee, the French ministry of war was given responsibility for provisioning the Allied armies, who nonetheless retained their own supply officers, coordinated by the Allied chief of staff, British quartermaster general Sir George Murray, a Scottish gentleman who had served the Duke of Wellington since the Peninsular Campaign. According to the second article of a "Military

Convention" annexed to the treaty, the pay, equipment, and clothing of the Allied troops were to be covered by an annual payment of 50 million francs, in specie on a monthly basis, by the French government. But the government was to supply in kind food and forage, as well as lodging, fuel, and lighting, sufficient for two hundred thousand men and fifty thousand horses. Beginning in late 1815, the war ministry began to centralize the supply process. While it asked some local authorities to maintain their contracts with individual entrepreneurs for certain requisitions into the new year, it began to charge its own quartermasters with managing the supply to Allied troops. Assisted by local *commissions mixtes* of French and Allied supply officers, which operated throughout the occupation of guarantee—and even for several months afterward—to coordinate requisitioning and verify accounting, the quartermasters in turn relied on big military suppliers to procure and distribute the provisions stipulated by treaty. Beginning in late November, at prefectures throughout the occupation zone, military officers organized public auctions at which suppliers bid for contracts for the provisioning of foodstuffs, meat, drink, heating and lighting, and forage.[8] These contracts, initially issued for eighteen months, were awarded to some of the biggest entrepreneurs in France, most of whom had supplied provisions and transports to the army during the Napoleonic Wars. Often, these suppliers subcontracted with local (especially Jewish) entrepreneurs, including the firms of Cerf Beer, as well as Beer's son-in-law, Auguste Ratisbonne, who provided thousands of francs worth of food, drink, and forage to Bavarian and Württemberger troops in the Bas-Rhin.[9] Throughout the occupation, commentators in and outside of the military debated the best approach to supply, with some supporting this centralized system and others advocating a more liberal approach of direct contracts between local authorities and entrepreneurs.[10] But, from the beginning of 1816 through the end of the occupation in November 1818, responsibility for requisitioning remained in the hands of the French war ministry.

Under the occupation of guarantee, the supply process was governed by a *tarif,* or ration table, negotiated between the French ministers of war and foreign affairs and the Allied ambassadors, along with a Military Convention appended to the treaty of November 20, 1815. In addition to specifying the daily portion—and quality—of bread, meat, forage, heating, and lighting to Allied troops, this *tarif* regulated such related matters as lodging, hospitals, transports, postal service, and customs. Outside of the necessary items provided in daily rations, it specified that troops could not demand additional supplies such as soap, butter, or chalk, which they were obliged to purchase themselves. While communes were charged with financing guard duty, including heating and lighting day and night, as well as postage of official mail among Allied and French authorities, private correspondence and travel were at the expense of the troops. Regarding customs, materials destined for clothing the troops could enter freely if they bore the proper certification, and troops entering or leaving France did not have to pay duties on objects for use by their army. However, all other imports and exports were subject to normal customs regulations—a stipulation that would provoke much conflict between French customs officers and Allied troops.[11]

Subsistence

Throughout the occupation, the most onerous burden on the occupied French was the subsistence of the Allied army. According to the *tarif,* the daily ration for each Allied soldier was: two pounds of bread (or one and two-thirds of flour or one and one-sixth of biscuit); one-half pound of fresh meat (or one-fourth of lard); some form of grain or vegetable (one-fourth pound of *gruau,* a sort of gruel; three-sixteenths of rice; one-half of fine flour of wheat, peas, or lentils; or one-half of potatoes, carrots, turnips, or other fresh vegetables); a ration of alcohol (one-twelfth of a litre of eau-de-vie, one-half litre of wine, or one litre of beer); and one-thirtieth of a pound of salt, all supplied by the French ministry of war. For each of these foodstuffs, the quality was stipulated in detail: the flour was to contain three-fourths wheat and one-fourth rye and, if not already baked into bread, was to be supplied with the ovens and wood necessary for baking it. The meat, three-fourths from steers and one-fourth from cows (or pork, if the *commission mixte* judged it suitable), was to be butchered, unless otherwise requested by the army, which then retained the hide of the animal. The liquid rations were to be those ordinarily consumed in the region, with the alcoholic content of eau-de-vie regulated down to the degree. And the grains and vegetables, dried whenever possible, were to be of a "loyal quality, marketable and clean." To ensure adequate supplies, the *tarif* stipulated that there should always be at least a two-week reserve of food and forage.[12]

This basic ration was modified for particular contingents or ranks. Finding the ration of meat too small for British troops, the Duke of Wellington arranged to have them receive an extra three-eighths of a pound of meat but a half-pound less of bread and no vegetables or salt, with the difference in cost of about one halfpenny per ration to be paid by the British government. Wellington advised that Russian soldiers, who collected less pay than the other contingents, should receive an extra third or fourth of a pound of flour to make their traditional drink of kvass, as well as at least 50 percent more salt and one-thirtieth of a pound of soap per day, which was indispensable but otherwise unaffordable to them. In all contingents, officers received additional table allowances, proportional to their rank: generals were allotted twelve rations; majors, three; and noncommissioned officers, one. Following the military convention, the French agreed to convert the portions for officers into an average price per day (at the rate of 2.61 francs per ration), to be paid in money rather than in kind. These payments totaled over 925,000 francs per month; British officers alone received some 235,000 francs per month. When the army of occupation was reduced in early 1817, these monetary payments were decreased by only one-seventh, so that the remaining officers could maintain their lifestyle. According to the convention, servants received the same rations as soldiers, up to the number allotted for each army, while administrative employees and health officers were assimilated to officers of their rank. Wellington also approved partial rations for women and children accompanying the troops, as well as associated storekeepers and civil administrators.[13]

Limited as they were, these rations were still more generous than the normal intake of most French peasants and workers. The table allowances for officers such as Murray, who received 250 francs per month throughout the occupation, permitted elite urban dining practices never before seen by most rural inhabitants. These monthly allowances equaled as much as nine months' salary for an ordinary worker. Even the soldier's ration was quite liberal compared to the daily diet of an ordinary Frenchman. Although the amount of bread allotted was similar, the ration of meat, amounting to about ninety kilograms per year, far exceeded the annual consumption of even the relatively well-off Parisians, who ate less than sixty-five kilograms per year.[14]

To supply these rations, the war ministry relied on three main entrepreneurs: Sieur Dominique-César Leleu, formerly in charge of the provisioning of Paris, for bread, biscuit, gruel, rice, dried legumes, and salt; Sieur Cassabois, for meat; and Eugène Rouffio, for liquids, including wine, beer, and eau-de-vie. According to their contracts, in exchange for a payment per ration, these entrepreneurs were charged with financing the purchase, manufacture, delivery, storage, and distribution of the stipulated provisions—of "good and loyal" quality and enough quantity to last at least two weeks—to Allied troops in garrison, including in hospital and on march. This provisioning process was to be monitored by the mixed commissions in the locality, who would in turn issue receipts. Although the suppliers were granted use of government warehouses, they were responsible for paying all maintenance costs, losses, taxes, and customs duties. According to their contracts, they were to purchase all supplies within France, unless they received special permission from the war ministry. Such permission was granted to Leleu, who during the subsistence crisis of 1816–1817 arranged shipments of grain not just from the west of France but also from Danzig, Amsterdam, Louvain, Bremen, and Cologne. Similarly, all substitutions for stipulated rations required approval from the mixed commissions. To ensure that they would fulfill these contracts, the suppliers were required to provide the names of two guarantors and to pay a security deposit, ranging from 800,000 to 1,500,000 francs, in cash, property, bonds, shares of the Bank of France, or credits from the war ministry.[15]

Despite the size of their enterprises, these contractors struggled to supply provisions of the required quantity and quality, especially during the grain crisis of 1816–1817. In addition to having to arrange shipments from overseas, Leleu claimed thousands of francs of losses from the increases in prices caused by the crisis. During this same period, the drink supplier Rouffio asked to shift from supplying grain alcohol, which was prohibited by many localities to conserve grain for food, to grape-based spirits—to the chagrin of the occupying troops.[16]

The Allies often complained about their provisions, sometimes demanding a different type or better quality of food or, especially, drink.

Early in 1816, the mayor of Ligny reported to the war ministry that, in spite of a decree from the prefect that the liquid ration be eau-de-vie, the commanding officer of the Prussian garrison insisted on beer for his troops.[17] In the Russian zone, troops complained relentlessly about the "inadequate" grain alcohol, beer, and wine provided by the military entrepreneurs, pushing their leadership to designate one officer per regiment to verify the quality of such provisions. Even after the systematization of requisitioning, according to a study of the occupation of the Nord, "[I]t would be an error to believe that the inhabitant was going to escape completely from the demands of the troops. The poor quality of the provisions furnished by the entrepreneurs often provided a pretext for resorting once again to local requisitions."[18]

Occupying troops were also entitled by the military convention of November 1815 to a daily ration of tobacco. This provision was resisted by local authorities, who chafed at supplying a product that was a state monopoly and hence a source of revenue. In late 1815, a tax administrator in the Meuse vehemently protested the sequestering of tobacco by the occupying Prussians: "In the moment of exhaustion in which the taxpayers of this department find themselves," he wrote to the department prefect, "the sale of tobacco is so to speak the only branch of revenue that remains to the Government. It is thus of the greatest concern that it receive no violation." Although in this case the Prussians backed down, other Allied commanders persisted in demanding a supply of cheap tobacco for their troops, insisting that it was a matter of "primary necessity," like a foodstuff or medicine. The *tarif* of November 1815 thus stipulated that Allied troops could obtain, at a discounted price of 60 centimes, a half-kilogram of tobacco per man per month. This discount was subsidized by the war ministry to the state tobacco monopoly.[19]

Lodging

Beyond the considerable burden of filling the stomachs—and lungs—of the Allied troops, inhabitants of the occupied territories faced the herculean challenge of putting roofs over their heads. Difficult enough in the main garrison towns, where the occupation was centered, this challenge was all the more daunting in rural areas, where the local population was often no bigger—and was sometimes smaller—than the size of the contingent stationed there. To facilitate the process of installing the Allied troops, the minister of war sent commissioners to the areas they were to occupy to help local authorities arrange lodging, and these local authorities in turn often delegated power to military commissaries to contract with suppliers for the necessary facilities, repairs, and furnishings.

Initially, troops were housed with individual townspeople, as they usually had been during the invasions of 1814 and 1815. In response to billets from Allied authorities, requesting lodging for a certain number of officers, soldiers, and horses, local officials would assign them to particular households. In the small town of Rocroi (population under ten thousand) in the Russian sector, for instance, at first soldiers were lodged with inhabitants, who, according to their means, housed two, four, six, and sometimes eight, which was for them an "extremely heavy burden," according to a nineteenth-century history of the town.[20]

However, to mitigate the tensions that inevitably arose between former enemies in such close quarters over the longer term of the occupation of guarantee, the French war minister soon ordered that as many troops as possible be placed in barracks. Insisting this was the only way to reduce burdens on individual households, the minister pledged money to communities that needed, in the absence of suitable public buildings, to rent or furnish spaces for troops.[21] Prefects asked local authorities to provide them with lists of buildings in their communities that might serve as barracks. The response was often disheartening. As the mayor of Longeville in Lorraine replied to the prefect of the Meuse, "Monsieur, I have received the circular which you did me the honor of addressing me on the 24th of this month [January] regarding locations appropriate for housing the Foreign troops, [but] there are none in this commune[;] not only are all the houses occupied but nineteen-twentieths of them can be considered only cottages."[22] Other communities, recognizing the importance of easing the burden on their residents, set to work to prepare collective barracks. In Lille, for example, keen to avoid "the presence of little disciplined men" having everything at their disposal while the local peasants were away at work, local authorities insisted on the urgency of collective lodging: "The excesses of all kinds have pushed the inhabitants to a state of distress, so close to despair, that several have abandoned their residences, and a greater number will flee to the interior, if one does not succeed in quartering the occupying troops."[23] Given that such quarters did not exist or were not in a habitable state in many towns, this approach forced numerous communes to scramble to identify, construct, and repurpose buildings that could be used for communal housing, including churches, schools, factories, hospitals, and châteaux. In the village of Oberbronn in the Bas-Rhin, for example, the estimate for renovating the local château and surrounding buildings to lodge some 1,060 Württemberger troops exceeded 30,000 francs.[24]

Only when such communal barracks were not possible—or were not tolerated by a particular regiment—were soldiers to be lodged with local inhabitants. In Tourcoing, a town of only twelve thousand that did not possess any barracks, Saxon troops, numbering six hundred at their height, had to be lodged mostly with landowners and merchants but also with workers in the local textile industry. By mid-1817, the inhabitants of the town were so overburdened by the cost of billeting these troops, even after their reduction by one-fifth, that they begged the central administration for financial assistance.[25] Elsewhere in the Nord, some superior officers refused to house their troops in barracks, leaving inhabitants "to do battle with soldiers."[26] Officers and their servants continued to be quartered in rooms of their own, either with notable families or, when possible, in private houses or public facilities that had been vacated for the purpose. In Cambrai, where the Duke of Wellington had his field headquarters, some thirty vacant houses were renovated and furnished for officers and their entourages.[27] In the Bas-Rhin, sixteen officers of the Württemberger contingent, ranging from a major and quartermaster down to lieutenants and sublieutenants, had to be housed in proximity to the barracks in the château, in Oberbronn and nearby Niederbronn.[28] On occasion, local authorities granted exemptions from billets to certain householders—for instance, a national guardsman whose living quarters contained a store of tobacco, which he could not leave to perform his guard duty if foreign troops were present, and a midwife who claimed she could not host troops when she was often absent from home, delivering babies in the countryside.[29] But, in general, inhabitants could refuse to house the troops assigned to them only if they paid the cost of lodging them in an auberge.

Recognizing that billeting burdened individual householders, in April 1816 the war ministry promised to reimburse those who lodged foreign troops, according to a sliding scale, from 3 francs per day for a lieutenant general down to between 9 and 15 centimes (depending on the season) per day for noncommissioned officers and soldiers. To administer these indemnities in conjunction with the mixed commissions, local mayors and subprefects were charged with preparing quarterly reports of lodgings of foreign troops in their communities. But, based on complaints by local authorities, the indemnities often went unpaid for months, or even years. In Tourcoing, where such indemnities totaled 90,000 francs, the repayment process continued until 1822. These indemnities required a massive accounting effort and, in the end, were mostly relinquished to the municipal treasury, which used them to build public facilities.[30]

To avoid paying the indemnities, the state continued to push communities to house as many troops as possible in barracks. In March 1816, responding to reports of excessive demands for furnishings by Allied troops, the minister of war issued a memorandum to the occupied departments instructing them to do everything in their power to keep troops from evacuating barracks for private lodgings. While he admitted that such demands violated the terms of the treaty of November 20, 1815, he urged local administrators to make new sacrifices, increasing taxes if necessary to enable purchases not covered by the funds of the ministry.[31] Over a year later, in response to still more complaints about the difficulties of outfitting barracks, the minister once again defended this approach:

> We have rented buildings at state expense to make barracks; we have placed there available beds. A lodging indemnity has been accorded to inhabitants, which may be applied to the expenses for barracks. After that, it belongs to the local authorities to obtain the most useful results by a judicious employment of the means put at their disposal. The Prefects who have applied care and zeal to the effort have succeeded in ridding their administratees

from the burden of lodgings. That of the Bas-Rhin, for example, has quartered all the troops [in his department] in barracks. But the Prefect of Calais has done nothing. With the resources they have, others have made an unequal use, which has relieved only the towns while aggravating the burdens on the countryside.[32]

Indeed, some departments were more successful than others at lodging occupying soldiers, if not officers, in barracks. Most successful were the Bas- and Haut-Rhin, where Austrian and Württemberger troops were stationed. By the end of 1816, the Bas-Rhin had already placed over half its contingent of 21,000 troops in barracks; by August 1818, the department had housed 16,370 out of 18,580 occupiers in barracks. By the end of 1816, the Haut-Rhin had already lodged 5,450 in barracks and was quickly readying facilities for 4,635 more. To accomplish this, these departments expended considerable sums. The Bas-Rhin alone spent some 700,000 francs to renovate and furnish communal buildings, 250,000 francs to rent private buildings, 1.3 million francs to rent beds, and 936,000 francs on heating and lighting—still about 544,000 francs less than the ministry of war would have paid in lodging indemnities to individual householders. And, as the secretary of the prefecture noted in January 1817, these sums fueled the local economy, which needed all the help it could get in the current context: the barracks constituted, "at numerous places in the department, veritable workshops." Moreover, this approach had the advantage of leaving government-funded buildings and furnishings to communes after the occupation.[33]

Despite these efforts, Allied troops were not always satisfied with their living quarters. In violation of the terms of the convention, they still appropriated or changed their own lodgings without authorization from the French authorities. In Tourcoing, the municipality was barraged with endless complaints about damp courtyards, insufficient mirrors, unlit street lamps, and badly constructed stables. When their lodgings were found to be infected with disease or vermin, some Saxon troops stationed there insisted on new ones. According to a police report in March 1817, the six hundred Saxon troops, along with some forty accompanying women and children, lodged with local inhabitants, who paid for "harmony" with them by making numerous sacrifices of drink, supplementary foodstuffs, and even coffee, at an approximate cost of 15 sols per soldier per day, over and above the requisitions required by the 1815 treaty. Of these troops, the local police wrote, "They show themselves to be very demanding about everything."[34]

Furnishings

To furnish both communal barracks and individual quarters, especially for officers, the inhabitants of occupied communities had to provide a long list of household items, beginning with many thousands of beds. Alongside food and lodging, the supply and maintenance of bedding constituted one of the most burdensome requisitions. First, communities had to obtain enough beds to accommodate their assigned contingent of officers and soldiers (usually assigned two to a bed). In most cases, these were "military beds," which were already in barracks or were provided by the war ministry, but for which the local authorities were supposed to pay maintenance. As indicated by a printed letter from the minister of interior to prefects on August 3, 1816, asking for help in collecting this money, most towns delayed in paying the maintenance fees. As late as 1820, Charleville still owed over 4,700 francs; Sedan, 7,500.[35] Sometimes, these beds had to be moved by the ministry of war, for example from the fortress at Verdun to the town of Saint Mihiel in Lorraine, for an incoming contingent of about seven hundred Prussians.[36] Other times, they had to be purchased from local merchants by the local government, which then submitted its expenses to the central state. For the barracks in the château at Oberbronn, the Maison Herrenschmidt and Schwartz of Strasbourg supplied 645 wooden beds, 764 mattresses, 793 straw mattresses, 760 sacks of straw, 642 bolsters, 2,778 bedsheets of coarse linen, and 664 wool blankets.[37]

As this list suggests, supplying the Allied troops with clean bedding was a challenge for military quartermasters. Early in the occupation, conflict arose between French and Allied authorities, particularly the Russians around Maubeuge, over the timetable for changing bedsheets: according to a letter from a French military quartermaster in February 1816, the Russian commander in the town of Givet refused to conform to the French practice of changing sheets once per month in winter and once every twenty days in summer, threatening to lodge his soldiers on inhabitants if the sheets were not changed every three weeks even in winter. But, insisting that any deviation from the French system would wreak havoc with its finances, the war ministry held firm. As the occupation wore on, another conflict arose over responsibility for damages to bedding. In August 1816, the war ministry ordered that these should be paid by the Allied forces who caused them.[38] Disputes also arose over the quantity and frequency of the supply of straw, for bedding men and horses. Not until February 1817 was this process systematized by the minister of war so that, in Oberbronn, for example, the barracks were supplied by a local entrepreneur with eighteen kilograms of fresh straw for bedding at the beginning of each year and renewed by half that amount at quarterly intervals.[39] By May 1816, in the town of Valenciennes, the annual expense for bedding—augmented by the large number of married British soldiers—was estimated to be about 50,000 francs. In addition, the town had to pay a share of the expense of sanitizing 3,400 of these beds, which were infected with scabies, at a cost of 2.2 francs per bed.[40]

Once they had a place to sleep, soldiers, and especially officers, demanded a host of other furnishings, including tables and chairs, armoires, desks, cookware, dishes, silverware, linens, and office supplies. To take one egregious example, the Saxon chief of staff in Tourcoing, Colonel von Zerschwitz, requisitioned the following items to furnish five rooms, including one for his daughter: a table with twelve chairs; another table with six chairs; a buffet; some twelve additional chairs; at least six side tables; three beds; four heating stoves; at least two wardrobes; two mirrors; a desk; a chamber pot; and a baking oven; plus, curtains for five rooms.[41] Similar demands were presented by Allied officers to local authorities throughout the occupied zone. In the arrondissement of Wissembourg, each Württemberger officer disposed of an average of seventy household items, including such luxuries as foot warmers and salad colanders, as well as cribs for their children. Many of these items were acquired, at the expense of the French government, from local Jewish merchants.[42] In an era when most peasant households still possessed only one bed and a few other modest furnishings and utensils, these demands seemed outrageous.[43]

Heating and Lighting

Whether military barracks or private quarters, Allied lodgings also necessitated heating and lighting. For these purposes, they required not just countless heating stoves, lanterns, and candles but also enormous quantities of fuel, in the form of wood, charcoal, and oil. As thousands of Allied troops arrived in the area in late 1815, the town of Valenciennes negotiated with various entrepreneurs for the supply and maintenance of six hundred stoves. Although they remained rare among French peasants, who still relied on open fireplaces for heating as well as cooking, such stoves constituted one of the most common demands by Allied troops.[44] For fuel, they initially helped themselves to wood, provoking widespread complaints of deforestation. To systematize the demands for such items, a convention was passed in August 1816 between the war ministry and the Duke of Wellington, fixing the winter ration of a simple soldier at one cubic meter of wood per 120 men; two and a half pounds of charcoal per man; two and a half briquettes per man; or twelve and a half peats of bog, with double for noncommissioned officers, but half in summer.[45] Despite this agreement, however, Russian and Prussian officers continued to demand greater quantities of fuel, which locals often struggled to supply. In December 1816, a colonel commanding a Prussian brigade in the Meuse reported to the prefect that his soldiers could not yet occupy the barracks established for them in the former *hôtel* of the prefecture, because of the "total lack of wood for heating." In the same department early the next year, some towns were reported to be withholding provisions for heating the workshops of troops.[46]

The French also struggled to provide adequate lighting. In an era when most peasants still relied on candles and a limited number of oil lamps, Allied officers and soldiers demanded large quantities of oil to illuminate their quarters, especially during long winter nights. In addition, the Allies required great quantities of lanterns, wicks, and candles. In the arrondissement of Colmar, each company of Austrian troops in barracks was entitled to receive, per year, in addition to 641 cubic meters of wood or 776 cubic meters of pine (plus 90 pieces of peat for the guard outside), 750 pounds of candles and 150 pounds of oil for lighting. Given the scarcity of such lighting and heating supplies, any extra demands—such as were made by six Prussian hussards in the town of Autrécourt, who wanted a candle and a fire to be burned all day and night—caused bitter complaints by local inhabitants.[47]

Horses and Transports

In addition to feeding, housing, and equipping 150,000 men, the French were charged with the care of 50,000 horses. As during the Revolutionary and Napoleonic Wars, when the provisioning of mounts and forage had been one of the greatest logistical challenges for all sides, horses remained a massive burden on the local population. Like the troops themselves, horses were billeted on individual householders (often, the owners of hotels, who had larger stables) or housed in public buildings. In many cases, communities had to build or renovate stables for them, according to the specifications of the *tarif,* which required for each horse a stall at least four feet wide and eight feet long, furnished with a rack and manger. The French had to supply three pounds of straw per horse per day. To feed the animals, whose daily ration was ten pounds of hay plus five-eighths of a Paris-standard *boisseau* (a measure equivalent to about twelve and a half liters) of oats for light horses and a full *boisseau* for cavalry and officer horses, they also had to furnish immense quantities of forage. Given the heavy demand from local peasants along with Allied troops, as well as the poor harvests in 1816 and 1817, these requisitions were often difficult to fulfill, let alone with good quality grain. Beginning in March 1816, when the war ministry signed a contract with the Boubée Company of Paris for the provision of forage for the occupying army, the requisitions were generally furnished by military warehouses. However, if straw was furnished by an individual inhabitant, he or she was permitted to keep the manure produced by the animal—a stipulation that became cause for dispute between occupiers and occupied, given its value for agriculture. In addition to forage, horses required a variety of equipment and pharmaceuticals, including not just saddles and horseshoes but also nitrate salt, sulfur, tincture of aloe, pulverized crocus, soap, bandages, and various oils, aromatics, and medicines.[48]

Although they had their own horses, the Allied forces still requisitioned mounts—and wagons—from locals to help them transport supplies, baggage, and sick and wounded soldiers. Initially, such requisitions were levied via mandates by local mayors on individual wagoners and farmers, when beasts and equipment were not just appropriated outright by the occupying troops. Gradually, according to regulations issued by French authorities in mid-1816, these requisitions were centralized under the war ministry, which organized a system of "military convoys" for use by Allied troops. All orders for transports had to be issued to local suppliers via French military quartermasters. In some cases, French authorities even demanded that the troops use their own horses and wagons for transports, for which the war ministry would reimburse them. Despite these reforms, requisitions for transports remained one of the most onerous burdens on French peasants, who needed wagons and animals especially during the growing season. In February 1816, in an otherwise glowing report on the Prussian contingent stationed in his arrondissement, the subprefect of Verdun complained,

> The inhabitants of the countryside would endure even more patiently the presence of the Prussians, if daily, they and their horses were not exhausted by the numerous transports of food and forage, from the diverse supply depots to the encampments; and if, especially, obliged to fulfill this extremely difficult service, they were promptly and exactly paid, at the prices fixed by the decrees of M. the prefect. . . . A great benefit for this country, especially in the season of March [when planting was to occur], would be for the heads of each service to do [their own transports] themselves.

However, such pleas often went unsatisfied. In the village of Oberbronn, where over 1,000 Württemberger troops were stationed among 1,500 inhabitants, as late as the summer of 1818 locals were providing as many as 50 transports a month.[49]

"Pretentions without End"

Beyond basic necessities, the occupying forces demanded a wide variety of facilities, goods, and services. They continued to present local authorities with requests for everything from restaurants for officers, exercise fields, classrooms, separate kitchens and dining halls, bathhouses, cemeteries, forges and workshops, down to laundry services and extra dishtowels. In a number of communities, local authorities had to provide occupying forces with terrains, plans, and supplies for field maneuvers or shooting ranges. For the appropriation of local fields, the arrondissements of Dunkirk, Hazebrouck, Lille, Avesnes, Cambrai, and Douai in the Nord claimed damages of almost 17,000 francs, of which they were reimbursed 12,000 francs by the war ministry in October 1817. In the Moselle, expenses for such terrains for the daily exercises of Prussian and Bavarian troops totaled over 14,000 francs. Similar amounts were spent on warehouses. In late 1818, one of the biggest suppliers in the Bas-Rhin, Ratisbonne, demanded that the prefect reimburse him nearly 11,000 francs for constructing a hangar for forage over a year earlier. In several communities, local authorities had to find suitable facilities for the practice of religion by (often non-Catholic) Allied troops, even though the treaty of November 20, 1815, had said nothing about furnishing religious facilities. The British insisted on separate kitchens outside their barracks. Viewing indoor kitchens as dirty and unhealthy, they complained that, in the barracks at Valenciennes, the troops "were less certain of their meals at the present time than they often are on an active Campaign." The Russians, who could forgo beds but not baths, demanded steam, even in winter. In the Austrian zone, though the officer of the mixed commission decreed that women accompanying the occupying troops had no right to demand wood, soap, or utensils for washing, they were entitled to a locale for laundry, "the cleaning of clothing being a necessity for the soldier." Such demands often highlighted differing national standards, as in Longwy in March 1818, when a Prussian commandant, complaining of the lack of hygiene among local inhabitants, who used to wait for snow to clean the streets, insisted that local authorities assume responsibility for cleaning the latrines, which he claimed were in a "lamentable condition."[50]

For most occupying contingents, the most pressing and expensive request was a hospital. Although formal medical care was inaccessible to most ordinary peasants and workers, it had become common in military contexts with the rise of the mobile "ambulance" that accompanied troops on the battlefield during the Napoleonic Wars. Housing as many as several hundred soldiers at a time, each Allied military hospital required huge quantities of beds, tables, bathtubs, linens, bandages, medicines, and food and drink, including clean water and wine, in addition to personnel, such as pharmacists. (The Allied forces generally supplied their own doctors.) Already in late 1815, the Prussian quartermaster-in-chief ordered the prefect of the Ardennes to prepare for the arrival of two mobile "ambulances" in Mézières and Sedan, by supplying food and drink to the accompanying surgeons. Around the same time, Russian general Baron V. I. Loewenstern requisitioned the following supplies for a military hospital in Givet, to serve 200 men: 486 pillow covers, 150 mattresses, 22 straw mats, 58 covers, 368 chamber robes, 10 towels, 500 stockings, 45 wooden bed frames, 200 black trays for the doctors, and 100 spittoons. In the military hospital at Mézières, where the Prussian contingent routinely exceeded its allotment of two hundred beds, generating expenses of over 5,000 francs per month, the local authorities complained of their "pretentions without end," including menaces against the French pharmacist on duty. Realizing the expense of such hospitals, the subprefect of Wissembourg pleaded with the prefect of the Bas-Rhin to arrange for the transfer of a large facility for the Austrian contingent back across the Rhine to Baden.[51]

Exasperation and Despair

The requisitions levied by Allied troops placed a heavy material burden on the inhabitants of France, especially in the northeast, for more than three years. In Tourcoing alone, the Saxon occupation cost the municipality 99,752 francs, most of which was for lodging. In Colmar, headquarters for the Austrian army, occupation expenses totaled 256,585 francs, of which 162,212 were for lodging and 94,373 for diverse furnishing and maintenance costs. According to an estimate by the reporter of the finance committee of the Chamber of Deputies in 1821, the occupation cost as much as 2.416 billion francs, of which the department of the Nord bore the greatest part.[52] Following the initial invasion, these costs were nationalized by the restored monarchy, which also pledged to indemnify its subjects for the expenses they had incurred before the systematization of requisitioning. To meet these expenses, the monarchy relied on new taxes, such as an extra 25 centimes per franc of principal imposed on property owners by the finance law of March 19, 1817, as well as bond issues. The settlement process, which would require massive accounting, would continue for years beyond the end of the occupation. In the end, it provided only partial compensation for the material burden endured by millions of French.[53]

Moreover, such cold accounting fails to represent the true experience of requisitioning. For inhabitants of the occupation zone, requisitioning constituted a physical intrusion and psychological trauma, every day. In addition to consuming scarce resources, it completely upset traditional routines and habits. Even outside of the occupation zone, it threatened incomes and savings. For the French nation, the burden of requisitioning was experienced as a natural, even meteorological event, a sort of "parasite" or "plague."[54]

This "plague" was especially acute due to the real meteorological event that hit France, along with the rest of the northern hemisphere, in 1816, the "year without a summer." As a result of the ensuing subsistence crisis, French suppliers struggled to procure enough grain to provision soldiers and horses, provoking complaints among the Allied armies. In the Ardennes, Russian troops complained of delays of as much as four or five days in shipments of bread and meat. By 1817, the shortages were so severe that Russian commander Vorontsov protested that the bread distributed to his troops contained sand.[55] Given the extra demand and poor weather during these years, local authorities insisted there was little they could do. As a report to the minister of police from the Pas-de-Calais explained in spring 1817, "The Services for subsistence are assured, those for bread and forage have occasioned some demands which the Sub-Prefect has fulfilled right away, the poor quality of the wheat that arrives by sea hardly permits us to make a Bread as good as desirable, and the scarcity of hay obliges us to use one of bad quality."[56] From Hazebrouck, the subprefect reported that, while the service of bread, meat, liquids, and heating was assured, that of forage was "suffering" and had occasioned a lot of trouble for the civil administration, which, in spite of changing contractors, was still having difficulty obtaining a sufficient supply of oats.[57] Despite the military convention's stipulation that smaller quantities of barley or rye could be substituted for the ration of oats, the lack of forage in the area around Sedan prompted Prussian authorities to "employ the most severe measures," such as visiting private homes to locate hidden supplies.[58] These shortages prodded the Duke of Wellington to agree to a reduction in size of the occupying army in early 1817.

In the meantime, the burden of requisitioning proved too much for some communities to bear. Already in January 1816, in response to incessant demands from Prussian officers for eau-de-vie rather than beer, as well as for military transports, the prefect of the Meuse reported, "I cannot hide that the exasperation and despair [here] have reached their final term, that several inhabitants have abandoned their houses, and that a traveler little susceptible to let himself be swayed, reported to me yesterday that, having stopped a few minutes in Beauzée, where a squadron of [Prussian] hussards is encamped, he heard the inhabitants say if their situation did not change promptly, they would burn their own village and abandon their fields. Things are at such a point that the littlest accident could bring the greatest misfortunes."[59] Such exasperation and despair persisted throughout the three-year occupation, provoking considerable resentment and, often, violence between the former enemies.

Chapter Three

Violation

In June 1816, one year after the definitive defeat of Napoleon, inhabitants of France protested that the Allied forces were still treating them as enemies. The residents of Sedan complained that the Prussian troops garrisoned there had "let themselves go to the point that they mistreat the citizens as if they were *in enemy territory.*" Another report indicated that the English garrison at Valenciennes was detested for its "indiscipline" and "bad treatment" of the inhabitants. The Russians, garrisoned in Rethel, Rocroi, and Vouziers, "vex the inhabitants, subject them to various contributions, and often threaten to burn their villages." According to a police informant, the authority of the subprefects was "frequently powerless and unknown by these foreign soldiers, who behave absolutely as if *in enemy territory.*" Even the Saxons, who had one of the smallest contingents in the occupation, provoked the French with various "excesses." In mid-June, in Blamont in the Meurthe-et-Moselle, several brawls broke out between locals and a detachment of about 150 Saxons escorting a convoy. According to a report, "These [soldiers] presented themselves in the town with the impudence and the audacity of a victor *in a conquered territory.*" Before the national guard and gendarmerie could reestablish order, several people were assaulted and injured.[1]

Such tension was certainly exacerbated by the first anniversary of the Battle of Waterloo on June 18, whose celebration by British and Prussian contingents humiliated the French. But the sense that the occupation was merely a continuation of war persisted across the years the Allied forces remained on French soil. In spite of their claim to be there as "friends" of the French people, they continued to behave as enemies, pillaging, imprisoning, requisitioning, insulting, assaulting, murdering, and raping. Contemporary documents are full of accounts of "excesses," "vexations," "bad treatments," and "abuses" committed by troops. Whether motivated by material need, insecurity, or vengeance on the part of foreign occupiers, many of whom had previously experienced occupation by French armies, the violence took a variety of forms, against property and people, from verbal to physical, and from psychological to cultural. It was particularly acute in regions where partisans had resisted invasion in 1814 and 1815. While violence was committed by all of the contingents involved in the occupation of guarantee, it was most severe among the German-speaking forces, especially the Prussians and the Württembergers, in part because the latter spoke the same dialect of German as the peasants in the Bas-Rhin where they were stationed. Rather than declining over time, violence between occupiers and occupied actually peaked in early 1817, around the time of the announcement of the reduction of the occupation force by thirty thousand and the second anniversary of the Battle of Waterloo. It spiked again in the second half of 1818, before the final liberation of France. For the French, one of the most humiliating "excesses" was the reappropriation of artwork seized by Napoleon on his campaigns. Like many of the other offenses, this cultural pillaging was interpreted as a "rape" of France.

The French responded in a variety of ways, ranging from terror and flight, through resignation and accommodation, to resistance and provocation. Viewing Allied troops through the lens of the last campaigns of the Napoleonic Wars as "Cossacks" or "Teutons," they often met violence with violence. Throughout the occupation, they engaged in a sort of *petite guerre,* frequently assaulting and even assassinating foreign soldiers. Sometimes, they provoked such violence, for instance by reminding Allied soldiers of their earlier defeats at the hands of Napoleon. Varying in motivation, their violence took diverse forms, sometimes overtly political, sometimes more gratuitous or accidental. However, until the liberation of France in November 1818, it is safe to say that many inhabitants of the occupied zone treated their "allies" as enemies, as well as vice versa.

In many ways, the story of the Allied occupation of France between 1815 and 1818 is a universal tale of military conquest. In its physical and psychological effects, it was similar to earlier military occupations, including the French occupations of neighboring territories during the Revolutionary and Napoleonic Wars, as well as later ones, including the Allied occupations of Germany and Japan after World War II. During the occupation of guarantee a foreign force imposed its will on the local population, often violently, provoking feelings of anxiety, shame, and resentment. Continuing the cycle of violence initiated by French armies over the previous two decades, this "postwar" occupation prolonged the brutality of the Revolutionary and Napoleonic Wars, especially between French and Germans. However, the occupation was multinational, including small as well as large powers, and relations between occupied and occupiers varied with the national identity of the troops and their past relationship with the French. Moreover, in this case, the violence between occupiers and occupied spurred both sides to cooperate in regulating occupation, generating new developments in the international law of war.

Excesses

At the height of the occupation, the publisher of the popular "Bon Ton" prints issued one entitled *L'envie réciproque,* or "Mutual Envy." The image depicted a scrawny Frenchman looking in the window of a house occupied by a fat British officer eating a copious meal, complete with bottles of wine and liquor. "I have eaten nothing since yesterday," says the caption under the Frenchman. "God-dam," replies the British officer, "it must be nice to feel hungry." Although this particular caricature featured the British contingent, renowned for its appetite for food, especially meat, it encapsulates a broader grievance against all the occupiers: lack of moderation or discipline. Termed *excès* (literally, "excesses") in reports by local authorities, this offense was defined by violation of a norm. Involving outrage against a person or property, it ranged from pillage and waste, to cheating and theft, to property destruction and gratuitous violence, often mixed with drunkenness. Such excesses, while offensive enough in their own right, often provoked a cycle of conflict that ended in more serious violence.

Of course, one of the most common excesses was pillaging and *gaspillage*, or wasting, of provisions. These offenses were particularly egre-

L'envie réciproque. Suprême Bon Ton, no. 6, ca. 1815. BNF.

gious during the initial invasion of 1815. In Bar-le-Duc, for instance, the subprefect complained that Russian troops invaded vineyards and appropriated basketloads of (often still unripe) grapes, forcing their own director of military police to issue an order and send a safeguard to protect communes from such excesses.[2] Farther west, in the Nièvre, a local judge reported that, perhaps out of animosity against his royalist politics, the Hessian cavalry officer billeted on him not only required lavish meals three times a day but also berated him about the quality of the meals. Detailing the extravagant dishes he had supplied—including *oeufs en chemise,* pears, peaches, apricots, cooked apples, prunes de Reine Claude, pâté, lamb, omelettes, cheese, soup, potatoes in cream, frisée salad, and roasted duck, plus copious amounts of wine, coffee, and liqueur—the judge reported that the officer had frightened his servant by smashing plates on the table and exclaiming that, if he were not better served in the future, he would send twelve fusiliers to the house.[3] In the Ardennes, a local authority complained of the excesses by Prussian troops: "If he refuses to satisfy these exaggerated demands, the inhabitant does not always succeed in escaping bad treatments, but it never happens that he can avoid delivering everything that one demands because the soldier by physical force or verbal abuse always finds the means to penetrate into his lofts and to take well beyond what is due to him. One may call that a veritable brigandage."[4] One of the "excesses" most resented by locals was the hoarding and export (or resale, at double expense to French producers) of supplies. During the partial evacuation at the end of 1815, Prussian troops, among others, requisitioned extra provisions to transport home. Thus loaded down, they still "indulged in all imaginable excesses in the villages on their route," according to a stagecoach driver departing from Brussels on December 1.[5]

Pillaging in excess of the allotted requisitions continued long after the treaty of November 20, 1815. Throughout the occupation, there were reports of Allied troops stealing bread, wine, vegetables, game, and other provisions in the areas where they were stationed. In March 1817, noting the exceptional discipline of the English, a police report suggested by contrast how widespread such pillaging was: "The [British] Chiefs maintain a rather severe discipline and one hears only rarely complaints of marauding, such as destruction of chickens, theft of cabbages, turnips, potatoes in the countryside, small offenses that it is almost impossible to prevent totally in a country occupied militarily."[6] Theft was a problem especially among Russian troops, whose officers did not always distribute their salaries and rations in a regular manner. In a report to the ministry of police that otherwise praised the conduct of the Russians, particularly their officers, a police commissioner in the Ardennes noted, "The Russian soldiers are naturally inclined to theft, and although in this case the least complaint submitted to their leaders suffices to have the guilty punished with a rigor almost without example, and without the least delay, they cede no less to their penchant and never let escape an occasion to fleece."[7]

In addition to stealing property, Allied troops damaged it, whether out of malevolence or carelessness. In April 1816, some Prussian soldiers lodged at Mouzay broke the windows of the homes of the mayor and priest after they forbade dancing in an effort to prevent disputes between young people and foreign soldiers. In another incident, a British soldier desecrated a cross from a church, outraging the local population and causing the interior minister to seek reparations. Routinely, Allied troops committed "degradations" to buildings and furnishings.

Following the announcement of the troop reduction in March 1817, a police commissioner reported that in Valenciennes some two hundred decommissioned English troops, "drunk with anger and with wine broke or burned all the objects composing the furniture" in their barracks, which were already in disrepair after only a few months. Around the same time, when a contingent of Bavarian troops moved from Sarreguemines, taking with them some equipment from the stables, they left their barracks with damages valued at 1,500 francs. Sometimes, Allied commanders reimbursed local authorities for such damages. In the case of Valenciennes, British authorities pledged to pay 700 to 800 francs. But, often, inhabitants were left to foot the bill themselves.[8]

In terms of property damage, one of the most common complaints by French inhabitants against Allied troops concerned the destruction of forests and fields as a result of encampments, maneuvers, or hunts. In fall 1816, there was unrest in the area around Lille after Saxon, Bavarian, and English troops "maneuvered on the plains without respecting the harvests which had not yet been completed, and trampled on stacks of grain." On a field near Cambrai alone, the loss of rapeseed and barley was estimated to be 150,000 francs.[9] Elsewhere, the amount of damage may have been less—for instance, just over 2,700 francs for one field trampled by Russian troops on maneuver in the Ardennes in October 1816.[10] But, in a context of shortage, any degradation of farmland was psychologically as well as materially damaging, and the archives are full of itemizations of damages, upon which Allied commanders often insisted before they would consider indemnifying inhabitants. French authorities also complained of the destruction wrought when Allied officers hunted in local fields and forests. In March 1817, the prefect of the Pas-de-Calais reported on recent troubles between occupiers and occupied, of which the principal cause was the "violation of the rights of property of which such a great number of English officers render themselves guilty by hunting, with horses and dogs, across planted fields." Explaining the effect, the prefect continued:

> Following a bad harvest [in 1816] and a year so difficult in every respect, hope rests in the next harvest which the poor regard as the end of their misery. The peasant is besides avid, interested, jealous of the fruit of his labors. How can he thus envisage with sang-froid the devastation of his field; and then, returning to his cottage, find again his foyer shared with those same men who just caused

> him such notable harm? It is there, there is no need to search for it elsewhere, the principle that could make explode a long contained resentment; it is in the dignity, the justice, the interest even of the Allied Generals to stop such reprehensible abuses.[11]

The destruction of fields became such a problem that by mid-1817 French authorities insisted that Allied leaders forbid their officers from hunting before the official end of the harvest. But this request was not always respected by the officers, who complained that the French themselves had already started hunting, as evidenced by the game displayed at local markets.[12]

An even more devastating "excess" was fire, whether accidental or not. In March 1816, in Ancemont, in the Meuse, flames damaged a room occupied by some Prussian soldiers who had kept a fire burning in the chimney day and night for six weeks.[13] In September 1817, in Amappes, near Lille, according to a report from the local justice of the peace, two farmsteads were burned due to the "imprudence" of the Saxon soldiers lodged at one of them.[14] Given how devastating fire could be, even the mere threat of burning was viewed by the French as a grievous "excess."[15]

Other excesses involved accidents or caprices against persons. In December 1815, violence broke out in Perouse, in the Haut-Rhin, after four drunken Austrian cannoneers made two children cry by taking the cakes they had received as Christmas gifts.[16] In spring 1816, in Châtillon-sous-les-Côtes, near Verdun, a Prussian soldier entered a house where a friend was lodging, took a rifle, and shot it into the street, killing a small girl. Remarkably, this "extraordinary event" was deemed an accident by the mayor, and, after being arrested and imprisoned by French authorities, the soldier was pardoned at the request of the girl's family.[17]

Excesses were often fueled by drink. Celebrating the first anniversary of the Battle of Waterloo on June 18, 1816, English troops in Mons "delivered themselves to the most disgusting orgies [of drink] and comported themselves toward the inhabitants in the most condemnable manner. Plunged into a furious drunkenness, they ran through the streets, scorning the French and insulting them crudely. The officers, beyond reason, as well as the soldiers, dirtied themselves in the mud, and offered a picture of the most foul behavior."[18] Although this is a particularly obnoxious example, public drunkenness was a common excess throughout the occupation, among all of the national contingents.

Insults and Rumors

Often under the influence of drink, Allied troops engaged in verbal abuse of French inhabitants. Sometimes, this took the form of personal *véxations,* or "insults." Other times, it took the form of a diffuse rumor, termed a *bruit,* meaning "noise" or "rumbling." In both cases, it contributed to what French authorities termed *mauvaise intelligence,* or bad relations, between occupiers and occupied. Particularly troublesome in regions where occupiers and occupied spoke the same dialect, such as the Bas-Rhin and Saar, where Württemberger and Bavarian troops were stationed, these *véxations* and *bruits* often sparked physical conflict.

One of the most routine complaints against the occupiers was their insults against locals. Sometimes labeled *mauvais propos* or *invectives,* such insults took a variety of forms. In early 1816, a merchant in Commercy, in the Meuse, complained that when he tried to remove two Prussian soldiers lodged with a woman who was sick, one of them spat in his face. This incident, which quickly degenerated into a fight, ended with the merchant fleeing to inform the soldier's superiors, while the soldier trampled on his clothes and threatened the woman's servant girl. Around the same time, in Stenay, also in the Meuse, Prussian dragoons left their barracks at night to insult patrols of gendarmes, chasing them with sticks.[19]

Other "vexations" were more pointed. In April 1816, in the Alsatian village of Dannemarie, a widowed innkeeper named Dame Brungard lodged a complaint against a chasseur of the Austrian Tenth Battalion who, after refusing to pay for the beer he had drunk, broke a glass panel on a door and "vomited a thousand insults" against her and her son. Exclaiming to the latter that he was "a better Frenchman than him and that, despite the fact he was in an Austrian regiment, he was a good Bonapartist, that he had served Napoleon for ten years," the chasseur then threatened to get his arms. When he was arrested by the mayor, who could not locate his superior, he then threatened to kill him, too. Once informed of this arrest, the officer, too, insulted the mayor by laughing at his official scarf, colored white in allegiance to the Bourbon regime, and disparaged his authority.[20] Such insults were often political in nature. On the anniversary of the Battle of Waterloo in 1816, inhabitants were humiliated by the "impudence" of the "foolish talk" of the Prussians in garrison around Sedan. Elsewhere, French authorities complained about occupying troops uttering—or singing—revolutionary phrases, such as "Vive Napoleon," or, in the case of Bavarian troops in Saint-Avold in 1816, "a thousand horrors against the King."[21]

Even more overtly political were the *bruits* spread by Allied troops. In the summer and fall of 1815, as the terms of the occupation of guarantee were being settled, common rumors were that France would lose additional territory, especially in the east, to the Austrians and Prussians, or that disagreements between the Allies were going to provoke another war. In November, a police informant around Strasbourg reported, "The Saxons and Austrians spread the most worrisome noises in the countryside: they insist that Alsace is ceded to Austria, and hold the most indecent propositions regarding the Royal family: they also say that an insurrection has erupted in Bretagne, and that more than fifty thousand men are gathered and armed there." Early the next year, two English without passports were arrested in Dieppe, where they were spreading a rumor that France was going to be divided. At this time, the police ministry received other reports of rumors of a new war involving Austria against Prussia and Russia.[22]

Once the treaty of November 20, 1815, was signed, such rumors began to give way to others, mostly regarding the return of Napoleon. Despite assurances by British commanders that they would stamp out Bonapartist sentiment to strengthen the restored monarchy, their troops persisted in spreading "noises" about the former emperor. In early 1816, from Pas-de-Calais, a police informant reported, "The foreign Troops occupying this department, and especially the English, engage in the most inappropriate talk: Continual praise for the usurper; affected hunts for his portrait; purchase of all kinds of objects on which he appears. The officers say in a loud voice that England will make alternate use of Bonaparte and the Bourbons to trouble France; that, moreover, its dismemberment is only postponed, and that it will be executed as soon as the payment of the sums demanded is suspended; which is inevitable, according to these foreigners." Around the same time, English civilians traveling in public coaches reportedly offered money to beggars on the condition that they cry "Vive l'Empereur!" Later the same year, according to a report from a police commissioner to the prefect of the Nord, in the cafés of Cambrai a military musician about to return to

England spread the rumor that Napoleon was in the United States, after having escaped "in a sack" from Saint Helena.[23]

From late 1815 through late 1818 and beyond, numerous such stories about the imminent arrival of Napoleon, or of his wife and son, or of his brother Joseph were also spread by Prussian, Austrian, Saxon, and, especially, Bavarian troops. In September 1818, Bavarian troops were suspected of disseminating writings with seditious statements such as "Vive l'Empereur!" in the streets of Forbach. In some cases, such talk may have been motivated by genuine sympathy for the former emperor, whom these troops—or their countrymen—had previously served. In others, it was intended only to rankle the defeated French, for instance on the anniversary of Bonaparte's escape from Elba in March, when they grew particularly loud. Such *bruits* did not decline over time but in fact spiked in the months leading up to the liberation of French territory in November 1818. During the partial evacuation in the spring of 1817, the Prussian contingent in the Moselle warned locals that they would return, implying that they expected to mobilize against France again.[24]

Coming to Blows

Verbal abuse was often accompanied by physical violence. Often under the influence of drink, Allied troops attacked French civilians and soldiers, with sticks, firearms, bayonets, swords, and bare hands. There are endless reports of *mauvais traitements* (literally, "bad treatments") and *voies de fait* ("assaults") committed by Allied soldiers. Often these assaults degenerated into larger *rixes,* or "brawls," between groups of foreign soldiers and French inhabitants. Sometimes they resulted in deaths.

Such violence between occupier and occupied had a variety of causes and took a range of forms. In some cases, especially among officers, the violence followed the formal conventions of an *affaire d'honneur*, or duel, usually over some sort of (perceived) insult. In April 1816, in Mézières, a duel between a French gentleman and a Prussian commander over the burdens placed on the town resulted in the injury of the Prussian and the flight of the Frenchman.[25] In other cases, Allied soldiers and French inhabitants fought over political or religious differences. In

December 1815, in the village of Rougement, in the Haut-Rhin, some Austrian Uhlans subjected local Anabaptists to *mauvais traitements*.[26]

But such violence was usually more spontaneous, resulting from a breakdown in relations between occupiers and occupied living in close quarters and competing for scarce resources. In Paris in December 1815, after his carriage crushed the hat of a French servant who demanded a reimbursement, an Austrian military quartermaster grabbed the servant by the hair and gave him such a violent punch to the nose that his whole face was bloodied.[27] In September 1816, in Tourcoing, two Saxon soldiers attacked the homeowner on whom they were billeted after he tried to make them go to bed at nine in the evening.[28] In December 1817 in the Pas-de-Calais, a soldier from the British Thirty-Ninth Regiment, invited to share a meal with the family with whom he was lodging, demanded a larger portion and, when refused, seized a stick, gave the master of the house a serious wound to the head, and chased him, striking his wife, too. According to the prefect, the soldier was so furious, it took over half an hour before the local guard managed to arrest him.[29]

Some *mauvais traitements* resulted in deaths. In September 1815 in Lyon, the *Journal de Paris* reported that "two Austrian soldiers had violently beaten the wife of their host, a printer named Cottard, who rushed to defend her, and was so severely injured by one of these soldiers that he died on the sixteenth of this month. His wife also received serious injuries, and their daughter who came to the rescue of her parents, lost two fingers on her right hand."[30] In fall 1816 in Tourcoing, after an altercation at a dance, a group of drunken Saxon soldiers, determined to avenge themselves on the first Frenchman they saw, attacked a local named Dutertre. Pierced in the ribs by a sword, Dutertre died instantly. After the broken sword was discovered in the sheath of the servant to the perpetrator's brother, the guilty soldier was imprisoned, first in Tourcoing and later back in Saxony.[31] In May 1817, the medical officer at Vicq was gravely wounded by a gunshot, attributed to a Cossack, according to the subprefect at Douai.[32]

Many other individual assaults degenerated into brawls. In May 1817, in the commune of Cassel, after a French *garde champêtre*, or rural policeman, chased a British soldier away from a pasture where he had been cutting hay without permission, a group of English troops "took out their rage" on the citizens of the town, singling out one individual, whom they mocked, shook, and boxed. After the French fought back, injuring one of the soldiers, the troops, armed with sabers and sticks, assembled outside the house of the pasture's owner, where the guard was hiding. Breaking a window and threatening to knock in the door, they were prevented from harming the inhabitants only by the arrival of the mayor.[33]

Much of the violence occurred in and around cabarets and dance halls. In the Pas-de-Calais in May 1817, five soldiers of the British Thirty-Ninth Regiment, exiting a cabaret where they were refused eau-de-vie because they were already drunk, attacked some young people playing the regional game of *billon;* when, to avoid a bloody scene, the young people retreated, they were followed by the soldiers, who failed to catch them. These soldiers then encountered a postal courier from Tincques, who, ignorant of what was happening, stepped aside to let them pass. They mistreated him, wounding his face, and would have knocked him out if not for the supplications of his wife, who rushed to his side. The same soldiers mistreated and wounded another inhabitant, too.[34] In December 1817, at a party in Scheibenhardt, where several soldiers were dancing with local young people, according to a report from the prefect, "all of a sudden, one of [the soldiers], taken with wine, it seems, wanted to demand that one play for him a certain waltz. This was the beginning of the affair. Several soldiers then entered the room with swords in hand and beat the attendees, several of whom they injured. Informed of the event, the mayor of the commune arrived at the scene, where order was already reestablished." After investigating the incident, local authorities asked the military commander to punish the guilty.[35]

Indeed, dancing was a common cause of brawling between local inhabitants and foreign soldiers. Many disputes were provoked over the type of step to be performed, with the French preferring the contredanse and foreigners, especially Germans, insisting on the newer waltz. In the wake of several incidents, the subprefect of Douai, among other French administrators, ordered that waltzes and contredanses be alternated—and that, once begun, no dance be interrupted. Similar disputes over dance steps occurred in the English zone, in communes around Montreuil, Valenciennes, and Lille. In fact, by 1818, they had become common enough that royal prosecutors, as well as British commanders, including Wellington himself, proposed to ban dancing for the duration of the occupation.[36]

Some of the most serious violence occurred between Allied troops and local police authorities, especially the gendarmes, *gardes champêtres,* tax collectors, and customs officials, who struggled to maintain law and order and, particularly, to collect excise taxes and customs duties. In early 1816, on several occasions when French customs officers tried to stop Russian troops in civilian clothes from smuggling foreign cloth, violence ensued, resulting in the death of at least one "Cossack" and provoking the Russian commander to issue a decree insisting that troops cross the frontier only in uniform. In November 1817, the subprefect of Hazebrouck complained of a "difficulty" between local tax employees and the colonel of the British Eleventh Regiment of Dragoons, who were reportedly defrauding the French tax administration of duties on drinks they were importing.[37]

Violence was most common in zones where occupier and occupied spoke the same language—for instance in Alsace and Lorraine, where the peasants were likely to speak not French but German, like the occupying troops from Prussia, Bavaria, Württemberg, and Austria. As a local history of the occupation of the Moselle suggests, "[I]f the written documents are rather silent on this subject, one may easily imagine that the cause of disputes between villagers and soldiers was the result of verbal provocations, or rather of discussions in auberges that ended badly. In sum, one may conclude that the possibility of understanding one another thus rendered both occupiers and occupied more quick to quarrel, while in the sectors where one did not understand one another, human relations were generally more distant."[38]

This correspondence between shared language and frequent conflict certainly held true in northern Alsace, where the Württemberger contingent was stationed. This region experienced some of the worst violence of the occupation. German, as well as French, records describe countless assaults and brawls, provoked by both sides. In April 1816, the subprefect of the arrondissement of Wissembourg reported to the prefect, as well as the Württemberger commander, Lieutenant General von Woellwarth, on recent fights in a number of communes. In Niederlauterbach, a week after a brawl between some inhabitants and some chasseurs garrisoned there, responsibility for which was still in dispute, drunk troops broke the windows of a house where the mayor and tax controller were meeting. Although the troops were punished by their officers, the mayor insisted that they needed to change garrisons. In the same report, the subprefect described a "lively altercation" in a cabaret between soldiers and young people in which the latter were mistreated to the point that several of them fell almost unconscious; rather than quieting the quarrel, the commanding officers joined in. After the subprefect complained, General von Woellwarth detained for four days the commander of the battalion, who had neglected to inform him of this affair. Insisting that the only solution to the troubles was to find new encampments for these troops, the subprefect concluded,

> [T]here remains a lot of bitterness between the inhabitants and the occupation corps, stemming in large part from the fact that this corps is the same which upon its entry in Alsace, excited general indignation with its behavior. Pillage, concussions, everything was then employed to ruin the inhabitants, and it is not rare that the soldier who was the author is the same person to whom one is obliged to give asylum. The bad spirit [*mauvais esprit*] of the Württemberger Troops, their indiscipline, contribute to aggravating the situation of this arrondissement, already very unhappy from everything that it has experienced in the way of losses.[39]

Most problematic for French, as well as Allied, authorities were the conflicts that occurred over customs violations by Württemberger troops, bringing contraband from their homeland on the other side of the border. In early 1816, in the arrondissement of Wissembourg, there occurred a series of altercations between a small number of customs officials and a band of about fifteen Württemberger soldiers suspected of smuggling coffee, sugar, and tobacco across the border, to sell to merchants (identified in the documentation as "Jews") in the region. In one incident, the customs officials shot dead one soldier and injured another. In response to complaints by the Württemberger authorities, which reached the Duke of Wellington and the Duc de Richelieu, the French interior minister launched an investigation. In their reports, local authorities blamed the "indiscipline" of the Württemberger officers, who performed only one roll call per day, in the morning, thereby allowing their troops to roam free the rest of the day and night. They also blamed the poverty of the local peasants, whose desperation for cheap foodstuffs—and fraternization with the foreign soldiers—drove them to protect and even abet the smugglers. In the view of the local authorities, the only solution was to quarter the troops in barracks or relocate them farther from the frontier. The interior minister, on the other hand, admitted that French customs officials, who were generally "badly disposed toward the Government that employs them, seek to foment these sorts of quarrels and abuse with bad intentions the force that is entrusted to them." Regardless of who was at fault, foreign occupiers and French officials continued to engage in a sort of petty war throughout the occupation.[40]

Sexual Violence

Like most instances of military intervention, the occupation of 1815 to 1818 was accompanied by sexual violence. Ranging in form from malicious seduction through unwanted attention to forced violation, sexual violence was widespread, perpetrated by Allied forces of all ranks and nations, against local women—and, presumably, men—of a wide range of ages and classes. Although it is impossible to quantify, in part because of a difference in terminology as well as a lack of reporting, rape pervades archives and memoirs of the event. Labeled *viol,* it was a symbolic act of possession, not just of the individual victim but of the entire nation. Whether motivated by desire, anxiety, or vengeance, rape became a trope for the subjugation of France as a whole.[41]

Under the occupation, Frenchwomen were seduced and even abducted by Allied troops, especially the British, whose removal of local girls across the Channel drew the attention of authorities of both nations. In an era when parental consent was still required for marriage, such *rapt,* as it was termed by contemporaries, constituted a criminal offense. In January 1817, a police bulletin in Paris reported that a rich bourgeois, Sieur Laforest, was threatening to kill a British colonel, Mackineen, who had "suborned" his daughter, now four months pregnant, and refused to marry her. Demanding justice from the Duke of Wellington, Laforest planned to press charges against the colonel before a French court or British court-martial. This kind of seduction was even more common in the north of France, where thirty thousand British troops were stationed. By 1817, as some British troops began to leave France, officials on both sides of the Channel became alarmed at the number of French women accompanying them. One typical report, from a police commissioner in Cambrai to the minister of police, complained that "a very large number of young peasant women have left their families, to follow their lovers" and that "paternal and municipal authority had to intervene against these voluntary abductions." He described one "funny" scene: "A young girl, between her father who wants to keep her, and who beats her rudely, and the hero who pulls her and blocks the blows while saying [in incorrect French for 'do not hit'], *pas batter Monsieur, Monsieur pas batter.* Without a doubt Calais will be the end of the trip for these modern Arianes; but the damage is done, and will be without remedy. Several [of these girls] who arrived yesterday in Cambrai following a Regiment were booed by the rabble." While some female victims of British soldiers were left in France, others were taken across the Channel, lured by the promise of marriage under English law, before being abandoned. In October 1818, the French consul in Liverpool reported that a pregnant French woman had come to him demanding assistance to return to France after being abandoned by the British sergeant to whom she claimed to be married.[42]

Such incidents became an issue of state between France and England. According to a letter from the minister of the interior to the prefect of the Nord in January 1818, the King's Council in London had informed the French minister of foreign affairs that British soldiers returning home often brought from France "young village women whom they seduced by promising to marry them and persuading them that, to be valid, the marriage could only be performed in England; once there these young girls did not delay in being abandoned by their seducers, so that deprived of any resource in a country where they did not even know the language the situation of these unfortunate things became atrocious." While the minister of foreign affairs had already asked the Duke of Wellington to take measures to address this problem, he also asked local authorities to do their part to prevent such abductions, by verifying at the frontier the papers of women accompanying British soldiers, to ensure they had a legitimate marriage certificate. By 1818, concerned that such abductions would become even more numerous as British soldiers were demobilized back home, the governments of both countries forbade the passage of Frenchwomen to England without proper documentation.[43]

Nonetheless, in late 1818, according to the British *Morning Chronicle,* some five thousand Frenchwomen followed British troops to Calais in hope of accompanying them across the Channel. Since most were unmarried, they were sent back home by army authorities. Another newspaper reported that 1,409 women and 1,829 children still managed to embark with these troops. According to the paper, this number would be much greater "if police measures had not been taken to retain a lot of French girls and women who followed the English troops" and who now filled the prisons of the town, before being returned by gendarmes to their birthplaces. Such estimates probably understate the problem of *rapt* during the occupation.[44]

Sexual violence was especially common during the initial invasion of 1815, as it had been in 1814. During the summer of 1815, as Jacques Hantraye has shown, Allied troops engaged in aggression that may be termed sexual, ranging from undressing women and men, to insulting their sexual honor, to touching their bodies without permission, to violating them by force.[45] Upon their arrival in Paris, Allied troops, particularly Prussians, terrorized local women. On July 13, 1815, the *Journal de Paris* reported that two days before, in broad daylight, two Prussian junior officers, exiting a café, had accosted three women, two of which were "*d'un certain âge*," meaning older. One of the officers put a hand on the youngest of the three, in the "most indecent manner in the world." Seeing her recoil, the officer took offense and slapped her, then moved to unsheathe his sword. Fortunately, the other officer stopped him from harming the woman any further.[46] Other victims of the invaders were not so fortunate. A report on the Austrian contingent in the area around Chalon-sur-Saône in August 1815 noted, among a number of "horrors," the gang rape of a girl, whom the Austrian troops proceeded to beat fifty times with sticks before rubbing her wounds with salt and "mistreating" her once again.[47] As Roger André has concluded, during the chaotic period of military occupation between July and November 1815, the number of rapes "cannot be counted."[48]

Incidents of sexual violence continued to occur throughout the three years of the occupation of guarantee. Given the reluctance of many victims to report such incidents, as well as the vagueness of the language used to describe them, it is impossible to compile precise statistics on rapes by occupying forces. But there are numerous recorded instances of "violences," "outrages," assaults, "bad treatments," and attempted rapes, as well as *viols,* against French women by foreign troops, some of which were brought to trial, usually by Allied courts-martial. For January 1816, the records include a report on two rapes, one of a girl of twenty years and the other of a girl of six, as well as an assault of a third woman, by Russian soldiers in the Ardennes.[49] In the Pas-de-Calais in April 1817, a servant girl declared that an infantryman of the British Third Regiment lodged in the house had attempted to rape her but was forced to abandon his "enterprise" when a female neighbor, hearing her cries, ran to her rescue.[50] In mid-1818, four Bavarian soldiers were condemned for "violences" against a woman from Obergaille whom they had attacked as she was returning from the fields to "satisfy their brutal passion." Fortunately, she escaped, but only after "suffering every sort of insult and bad treatment."[51] In another heartbreaking example, in September 1818, two Prussian soldiers approached a girl of seventeen gathering flax in a field in the commune of Cheppy, seized her by the throat, and raped her, under threat of bared sabers; according to a report from the gendarmerie, the girl was sick in bed as a result of the "violences of every kind" she had suffered.[52]

Based on the reports, sexual violence was indiscriminate of age, class, marital status, and location: troops of all ranks attacked women aged six to sixty, in a variety of settings, including homes, fields, forests, and streets. Even when foiled in the act of rape, Allied soldiers inflicted considerable violence, as in an incident involving two Prussian soldiers in the region around Bar-le-Duc, who assaulted a man of sixty named Genty when he came to the aid of two young girls they intended to violate, breaking his arm and crushing his chest and skull; he died the next night.[53] While some assailants were arrested and tried, many such incidents went unpunished, either because the perpetrators could not be found or because they were not pursued by the authorities.

As in other historical cases of military occupation, rape symbolized the whole event of the occupation of guarantee for the defeated French. As Jacques Hantraye has noted in the case of the occupations of 1814 and 1815, it was a means of emasculating the French population by demonstrating control over people as well as territory.[54] This symbolic meaning of sexual violence was recognized by contemporaries, who often depicted the occupation—in letters, pamphlets, plays, and

Le baiser forcé, ca. 1815. BNF.

images—as the "rape" of France. In one example from 1817, a print called *Les Meringues du Perron ou Milord la Gobe* ("The Meringues of the Balcony [implying Chest], or Milord the Grabber"), a British officer is depicted outside a pastry shop, offering a (sexualized) meringue to a young woman while ogling the female shopkeeper's large breasts. In another, called *The Allies in Paris,* two cavalrymen on horseback, holding an extra-long, clearly phallic, lance and saber, leer at two uninterested young women.[55] But perhaps the most explicit representation of the occupation as a sexual violation was a print, *The Forced Kiss,* in which a foreign officer, again with a very long sword, seizes a woman with an expression of fear on her face. Suggesting that such force could work both ways, in the background is a woman chasing a soldier, who pushes her away.

The "Rape" of the Louvre

Symbolically, the most humiliating "violation" to which the French were subjected by the Allies was the appropriation of cultural trophies—many of which had been acquired by the Revolutionary and Napoleonic armies on their campaigns in other countries—from museums, libraries, palaces, state workshops, and other institutions. During the initial military occupation in 1815, Prussian and Austrian forces seized paintings, sculptures, antiquities, manuscripts, maps, and other cultural objects, including the bronze horses from Saint Mark's Cathedral in Venice, which had been placed on the Arc du Carrousel between the Louvre and the Tuileries to commemorate the campaigns of Napoleon. Following their example, leaders of other Allied powers, including the Netherlands, Brunswick, Hesse, Spain, Venice, Sardinia, and the Papacy, began to demand the return of items. Although most of these items had originally been plundered by French armies, their removal by foreign troops was nonetheless viewed by the French as a "rape" of their cultural patrimony.[56]

The "rape" of the Louvre stunned the French. Their outrage was noted by a number of contemporaries, including the anonymous "vagabond" in the British army who later published memoirs of the occupation of Paris in 1815. Recounting how first the "old moustache" Blücher and then other Allied leaders had demanded the return of various objects, the author described the scene as, under British supervision, foreigners began to pack up their booty:

> Being in coloured clothes, I insinuated myself among the groups of Frenchmen that occupied the space in front of the Louvre, and its approaches, and was much edified at the expressions of mingled rage, shame, and grief; if we had partitioned France among the allies, and made all the inhabitants tributary serfs, there could have been scarcely greater consternation, despair, and anger, than was given vent to by every one,—the lowest order of people seeming rather to suffer the most. . . . [As a train of carriages with packages of statues departed] I shall never forget the aspect of the surrounding French, or the suppressed curses that were on their lips; *sacré tonnerre,* and many other *sacrés* not quite so respectable, came from their mouths, and some of their shoulders I hardly expected would return to their places again.[57]

The consternation caused by the desolation of the Louvre was represented in a print by British caricaturist George Cruikshank, *The Departure of Apollo and the Muses—or Farewell to Paris.* In this caricature, as Allied troops cart off the bronze horses and other treasures while the king and the foreign minister, Talleyrand, watch helplessly, the director of the museum, Vivant Denon, leaning out of a window, holding a handkerchief in one hand and appealing to Apollo and his train with the other, exclaims: "Don't go yet Ladies & Gentlemen/Pray stay with us a little longer. We could keep you for ever & shall always regret that we were forc'd to part with you."

In fact, Vivant Denon had himself provoked the Allies to reclaim cultural booty. Born in 1747, Denon was a writer, artist, and diplomat who served the royal, revolutionary, and imperial regimes. In 1802, he was appointed by Napoleon as director of the Imperial Museum at the Louvre. During the Napoleonic Wars, he had led missions, most famously in Egypt but also in Italy, Germany, Spain, and the Low Countries, to claim artistic and scientific treasures for museums in France. Justified by the imperial regime, like the revolutionary one before it, in the name of cultural "universalism," this war booty made France, especially Paris, the museum capital of the world. By 1815, Denon's museum was a source of envy among the other nations of Europe. As an official report to the head of the King's Household explained, "Museum-mania . . . has infected all of Europe. There is no sovereign who does not now want to have a Museum modeled after that of France; the Magnificence

The Departure of Apollo & the Muses, or Farewell to Paris. Print by George Cruikshank, 1815. The British Museum.

of that of Paris has dazzled them, and may have been the true cause of its ruin. This city with this Monument has constantly been the center of Europe, and *jealousy,* much more than the *specious pretext of restituting to each what belonged to him,* has presided over its destruction." As Denon himself boasted, as the museum was looted by the Allies, "I erected, I achieved the most beautiful, the most grand monument that ever existed, [but] at present I am here only to distribute it methodically and prove to assembled Europe that there is still an honest man in place."[58]

In 1814, demands by former proprietors for cultural trophies were successfully resisted by the restored monarchy on the grounds that France's ownership of the objects was guaranteed by various treaties signed by its former enemies. Absolved by the First Treaty of Paris from returning the trophies, the restored Louis XVIII was able to reassure the Chamber of Deputies on June 4, 1814: "The glory of the French armies has received no hit: the monuments to their value remain and the chefs-d'oeuvre of the arts hence belong to us by the most stable and the most sacred of rights, the right of victory." Respecting this settlement, most Allied sovereigns relinquished their claims to the hundreds of objects they had lost to France. During the spring of 1814, Allied officials visited the Louvre as "respectful guests," according to an early twentieth-century history, and "some even had the sad courage to congratulate Denon on his skillful exhibition of the masterpieces that once had belonged to them." Before leaving Paris, Emperor Francis I of Austria visited the Royal Library, where, according to the memoirs of the Vicomtesse de Chastenay, "He had shown to him several precious manuscripts, previously removed from Vienna, and, noticing some concern on the faces of the librarians, he added that these manuscripts no longer belonged to him and that he had no other intention than to take a few notes." Nonetheless, some powers, including Prussia and Spain, continued to demand the return of artwork, well into 1815.[59]

In the aftermath of the Hundred Days, royal officials proved powerless against the "museum-mania" of the Allies. On their march from Waterloo to Paris, the Prussians looted the châteaux of Saint-Cloud, Compiègne, Rambouillet, and Fontainebleau. Saying of Napoleon, "A man must be a fool to have run all the way to Moscow when he had all these beautiful things," Prussian commander Blücher ordered the removal of dozens of paintings, furnishings, and art objects from Saint-Cloud. Reporting in mid-July to the intendant of the *gardemeuble,* or "warehouse," of the Crown on the expropriation of a number of paintings, the concierge at Compiègne said of Blücher, "The Prussian Commander regards all of the furnishings as his property and he does not hide his intention to take the most precious objects." In this cultural expropriation, Blücher's right-hand man was Prussian intendant general Friedrich Wilhelm, Baron von Ribbentrop, forefather of the Nazi foreign minister. The Prussians threatened the collections of the Museum of Natural History, many of which had been seized from Dutch stadtholder William V of Orange. They were preserved for France only by the intervention of Alexander von Humboldt, naturalist and brother of Prussian diplomat Wilhelm von Humboldt. The Prussians claimed that most of these objects had been taken from Berlin during the campaigns of 1806–1807, though some came from their newly acquired territory along the Rhine in Cologne and Aix-la-Chapelle. The Prussian leadership also targeted objects symbolizing the Empire. Following a two-week pillage of the royal porcelain manufactory at Sèvres, for instance, Baron von Ribbentrop ordered the shipment to Berlin of all porcelain related to the history of Napoleon, valued at 53,000 francs, as well as the sale to a third party—or repurchase by the French state—of the remaining porcelain for the benefit of the Prussian army. Following the capitulation of Paris in July 1815, the Prussians sent their war commissioner, Friedrich Jacobi, with an officer and twenty-five soldiers, to raid the Louvre. When Denon insisted he would not relinquish any artwork without formal instructions from his own government, he was threatened with military punishment.[60]

The example of the Prussians was followed in quick succession by the Austrians. At the end of July, Emperor Francis I instructed Metternich to oversee the return of objects taken from the Austrian Empire by French armies. Eager to satisfy the Venetians, under Austrian rule again, the emperor insisted especially on the removal of the lion of Saint Mark from the esplanade of the Invalides and the horses of Saint Mark from the Carrousel arch outside the Louvre. When these demands were resisted, the Austrian leadership sent troops to take the objects by force. Under the eyes of the king, the monument of the Carrousel was dismembered. According to the British "vagabond":

> There was nothing remaining on the arch but a kind of scaffolding with a temporary crane, and the empty car, which, after the wood work was removed, looked as if it had dropped out of the clouds. The triumphal arch, at that time, bearing this solitary empty vehicle, would have made a good emblematical entrance to a rail-road. I saw afterwards these Corinthian-Venetian animals in a wagoner's yard, in the *Chaussée d'Antin*. The brazen brutes were lying on their sides in straw, each occupying a wagon, looking as if they were on their way to the kennel, or the *knacker* [sausage-maker]. There were Austrian sentries and a guard in the yard, and the passing Frenchmen were shrugging their shoulders out of joint. The Austrians tried to remove the Venetian winged lion that was placed on a fountain of *les Invalides,* but in doing so they broke its leg, and made some other fractures. All these affairs served to inflict the greatest wound the *morgue* of the Parisians had ever received, and the effects will scarce ever be effaced from their memories.[61]

Over the next month, the Austrians forced Denon to cede numerous other objects, including 362 paintings, 2 mosaics, and 69 Chinese figures, previously taken from the Belvedere Palace.

The claims to cultural booty did not stop with the Prussians and Austrians. In a sort of snowball effect, beginning in August, similar demands—for objects housed in museums and churches across France—were issued by commissioners of other states, including the Low Countries, Brunswick, Hesse, Bavaria, various Italian states, and the Papacy, whose commissioner was the sculptor Antonio Canova, nicknamed "the packager" by Talleyrand. Beginning with the Dutch, whose new king wanted to ingratiate himself with the Catholics in the south by retrieving artwork plundered from Belgian churches, Allied commissioners requested items and, when French officials dallied in delivering, removed them by force. Such demands came even from England, where the former secretary to Lord Elgin, William Hamilton, published a letter to the king of France, advocating the restoration of the works of art in the Gallery of the Louvre to their rightful owners. They were also endorsed by a petition signed by over fifty artists across Europe.[62]

Initially, such claims were opposed by a number of Allied leaders, including Castlereagh, Metternich, and Alexander I, who were concerned to distinguish what France had taken by conquest from what had been ceded to France by treaty. Under pressure from Allied commissioners, however, these leaders soon backed the claims of the smaller powers. In Paris, Wellington joined Prussian general Müffling in sending soldiers to force open the doors of the Louvre to reappropriate the paintings demanded by the king of the Low Countries. Adding insult to injury, the "Iron Duke" justified his use of force as necessary retribution for French conquests. In a letter to Castlereagh dated September 23, 1815, and published soon after in the *Journal des débats,* he wrote:

> The same feelings which induce the people of France to wish to retain the pictures and statues of other nations would naturally induce other nations to wish, now that success is on their side, that the property should be returned to their rightful owners, and the Allied Sovereigns must feel a desire to gratify them . . . Not only, then, would it, in my opinion, be unjust in the Sovereigns to gratify the people of France on this subject, at the expense of their own people, but the sacrifice they would make would be impolitic, as it would deprive them of the opportunity of giving the people of France a great moral lesson.[63]

Not surprisingly, this "moral lesson" was not well received by the French. In response to this letter, an anonymous pamphleteer (identified only by the name Hippolyte) published some "Observations of a Frenchman on the Removal of the Chefs-d'Oeuvre of the Museum of Paris," denouncing this loss for the arts. Defending France's right to the masterpieces claimed by the Allies, the French pamphleteer wrote,

> Since the noble lord had the pretention, to give to twenty-five million French a great moral lesson; what lesson more imposing, more sublime, more solemn, more worthy of Scipion, of Bayard or of Turenne, could His Excellence [the Duke of Wellington] offer to the world, in the high degree of power given to him by victory, than if His Grace had respected his own work, articles 11 and 15 of the capitulation of last July 3 [which recognized the property of the French], a capitulation signed and guaranteed in the very shadow of his laurels?

Wellington's intervention on behalf of Allied seizures of artworks angered the French, who thereafter nicknamed the British commander "General Vilain Ton" (Nasty Style).[64]

With the duke's approval, commissioners from Prussia, Austria, the Netherlands, and other countries began to pack up paintings, statues, prints, manuscripts, maps, and other objects for transport back home. In a letter to the Comte de Pradel, director of the King's Household, on October 1, Denon described a "scandalous scene" the day before when a painting by Jules Roman, which had supposedly been offered to the French government by the municipal corps of Genoa, was violently removed by the commissioner of the king of Sardinia, defended by two Prussian officers. "Thus," Denon complained, "a painting given voluntarily by a power in homage has just been taken with the most extreme violence from the Royal Museum." In protest against such violence, two days later, with the Louvre essentially occupied by the Allies, Denon resigned his post as director of the museum. As he wrote six months later, "I have no place, I have returned everything, it was the only way to live tranquilly, still is it not obvious that I am not envied to have been something." Retiring from public life to live among his personal collection of art, Denon remained bitter until his death a decade later.[65]

Over the next few months, the treasures taken from museums in France began to arrive in the other capitals of Europe. In November, the paintings claimed by Austria, packed in twenty-six large boxes on five wagons, arrived at the Belvedere Palace in Vienna. On December 13, the eighteenth anniversary of their removal by the French, the horses of Saint Mark were replaced with much solemnity on the portico of the cathedral in Venice. In late 1815, according to the *Journal de Paris,* crates of scientific objects also reached their destination in Vienna. Some works, such as the collection of majolica vases painted by Raphaël, transported to Brunswick, were damaged en route. In Berlin, the works taken from Paris were put on public exhibition, with proceeds from tickets donated to the families of soldiers killed or injured in war.[66]

Meanwhile, the cultural institutions of France, especially the Royal Museum, were devastated, as even foreign observers recognized. In its summary of the year 1815, the British *Annual Register* noted, "[A]t length, amidst the groans, exclamations, and execrations of the Parisians, the gallery of the Louvre was wholly stript of all its foreign spoils, and reduced to the productions of French artists, and the few other articles of legitimate acquisition." To his sister Charlotte, Prussian prince Wilhelm, future emperor of Germany, wrote, "The Museum has a frightful air; since the Dutch School has returned home and since Austria and Spain retook their visitors, only half the paintings are left. One can now see how many they stole; it seems that there was [at the Louvre] an exposition of the beaux-arts of Europe that, in truth, was very interesting to see." The despoliation was noted by guidebooks to Paris. In his two-volume guide *How to Enjoy Paris* (1816), Peter Hervé said of the Louvre, "The leading attraction of Paris exists no longer!"[67]

Closing the museum to repair the damages in mid-November, French administrators began to assess their losses. According to an initial list compiled by general secretary of the Louvre Louis-Antoine Lavallée, the number of works taken by the Allies amounted to 5,233, of which at least 2,000 were paintings and antique sculptures "of the highest order." A more comprehensive inventory compiled later by the same secretary concluded that from the Louvre alone had been removed some 2,065 paintings, 130 statues, 150 bas-reliefs and busts, 289 bronzes, 271 sketches, 105 ivory vases, 76 vases in precious materials, 16 Etruscan vases, 37 wooden sculptures, 471 cameos, and 1,199 enamels. Prussia and Austria were by no means the only beneficiaries of these works. Some 421 paintings went to the small state of Cassel, for example, and another 284 to Spain; many of the enamels went to Brunswick. From the Allies, Lavallée did manage to save works valued at over 4.5 million francs. Nonetheless, he was removed from his position by the new regime in May 1816, at the age of twenty-nine, and driven to an early death only two years later. Long after his dismissal, this cultural property continued to be disputed. Into the 1820s, foreigners continued to petition the French state for the return of artwork they claimed had been taken during the Revolutionary and Napoleonic Wars. In 1829, the elector of Hesse was still demanding a painting by Rubens from the museum of Caen.[68]

To repair the damage to its museum, the royal administration not only recalled existing works from provincial institutions and ordered new pieces from French painters, but also resorted to a curious tactic. In an effort to rid itself of Bonapartist propaganda, as well as to finance the restoration of the Louvre, it sold art objects associated with Napoleon's regime to foreign states, especially Britain and Prussia. Full-length portraits of Napoleon and Josephine were sent to Berlin, where they were displayed in the royal palace. Most famously, Hippolyte, Comte de Pradel arranged the cession to the British government of a colossal marble statue by Canova of a nude Napoleon as Mars the Peacemaker. After paying 66,000 francs, including transport from a warehouse in Rome to London, the British government in turn offered the statue to the Duke of Wellington in gratitude for his military service in the wars against the French emperor. Since 1817, this statue has graced the foyer of Wellington's mansion in London.[69]

The "rape" of the Louvre humiliated the French. Describing the desecration of the Place du Carrousel and the Louvre to a business partner in Rouen, one businessman in Paris wrote, "Our museum is at the mercy of the Foreigners and soon there will remain to us only the sad memory of these priceless trophies. . . . The friends of the arts and all good Frenchmen tremble at these *profanations.*"[70]

Nourishing Hatred

Among the French, the reaction to such violence varied considerably. During the initial invasion, although there were certainly incidents of complaints, insults, and assaults against Allied forces, most French were more or less submissive. But as the occupation wore on, their resentment grew. Following the troop reduction in April 1817, and especially after the announcement of liberation in 1818, this resentment threatened to boil over into revolt, to the chagrin of authorities on both sides.

During the initial military occupation, the predominant reaction among most French was fear. With memories of the invasion of the previous year still fresh, inhabitants of the countryside, especially in the northeast, cowered at the first rumor of the return of the Allies. In the summer and fall of 1815, reports from local authorities in occupied regions are full of references to "terror" and "despair." For many, the terror was associated with the figure of the "Cossack," who had been the main bogeyman during the first invasion of France the year before. A type of cavalryman from the Don region of Russia first encountered by the French during the ill-fated invasion of that country in 1812, the Cossack had come to symbolize—through Napoleonic propaganda as much as actual experience—the foreign enemy during the campaigns of 1813 and 1814. As a result of publications such as "Historical Tableau of the Atrocities Committed by the Cossacks in France" and "Notice on the Diverse Peoples Who Supply Russia with Undisciplined Troops, Known by the Name of 'Cossacks'" as well as a number of theater pieces featuring the "Cossack," by 1815 this figure had become a synonym for "Hun" and "barbarian," in short for any people from outside of "civilization."[71] This perception of the enemy may be seen in a number of images from the first and second invasions of France, for instance in a hand-sketched "portrait" of a Cossack lodged on an inhabitant of Colmar in 1814, stereotyped with bugging eyes, crazy hair, and an enormous sword. However, when in actuality these Russian cavalrymen proved less brutal than Prussian and other German-speaking troops, the image of the "barbarian" was transfigured: while the "Cossack" became a more genteel figure, the German "Uhlan" or "Teuton" (precursor of the "Boche") now constituted the prime enemy, outside the boundary of civilization.[72]

In the face of these enemies, many French hid or fled, seeking refuge in cellars, attics, forests, and caves. As British general Alexander Cavalié Mercier described the village of Chenevière, in the path of the Prussian army, "The place, I should think, has not been visited by the Prussians, for no pillage or destruction is to be seen; but it is deserted—not a soul except our soldiers to be seen." As late as January 1816, in the Meuse, where "exasperation and despair are at their final term," according to the prefect, the inhabitants were reported to say that if their situation did not promptly change they would burn their villages and abandon their

Portrait d'un Cosaque qui a logé chez Mr. Kohler à Colmar en 1814. Anon. sketch. Bibliothèque des Dominicains, Colmar.

fields. In similar terms, a French officer in the neighboring department of the Ardennes reported that around Mézières, despondent inhabitants were threatening to desert their homes and, in the arrondissement of Rocroi, the excesses of the Russians had caused to emigrate "243 households which have taken refuge, some in the Department of the Aisne, and some in Belgium." The inhabitants were in such despair, he wrote, that "when fire broke out in several houses, only the Russians worked to extinguish it: the peasants, whom they reproached for not helping them, responded: when our houses will have burned, we will no longer be obliged to lodge you."[73]

As the invaders became occupiers, fear evolved into resignation among most lower-class artisans and peasants. The subprefect of Verdun noted that the hardest hit often complained the least: "The people apparently most used to suffering complain the least, though they necessarily give much more than the privileged man, who is never, like the unfortunate inhabitant of the country, obliged to sacrifice his own subsistence to lodge one or two soldiers, and make up the daily insufficiency of their rations." However, not all French were so passive. Many inhabitants, especially higher up the social scale, complained openly about Allied exactions. The same subprefect remarked, "There are, unfortunately, Monseigneur, among us, some indiscreet persons who express themselves too openly about the Prussians; others, who at certain epochs would have given with good heart half of their fortune to see arrive some liberators, and who today murmur much too much against the portion of the burden that is apportioned to them."[74] Such complaints did not stop at the desks of local authorities but were presented to Allied officials, too. In the hamlet of Stain, outside Paris, where he commanded a contingent of British troops in 1815, General Cavalié Mercier was astonished that the villagers were presumptuous enough to complain about the occupiers: "The villagers . . . , after being scared from their dwellings by our advance, have returned to them, only to find everything ruined and destroyed. Of course they are not in charity with us, and full of complaining . . . It is inconceivable that a conquered people, and a people whose armies have shown no forbearance in foreign countries, should thus dare lift up their voice and complain that the conqueror disturbs them, and puts them to some inconvenience."[75]

But the French did more than just complain about Allied exactions. As foreign troops settled in their garrisons, local inhabitants resisted in a variety of ways. At the end of 1815, as the British contingent evacuated excess troops, in the Pas-de-Calais French navy officers obstructed the embarkation of English horses, prevented boats from leaving port, and insulted the British nation. In Tourcoing, townspeople routinely refused contributions, lodging, and supplies to the occupying Saxon troops.[76] Such resistance was often defended—when not spearheaded—by local authorities, particularly mayors, who sometimes countered Allied demands with the threat or act of resignation. After the mayor of the commune of Langensoulzbach, in northern Alsace, resigned following a quarrel with the captain he was lodging, the subprefect of Wissembourg concluded that he "had demonstrated a little passion and had maybe put himself in the wrong by making injurious statements against the officers."[77]

Throughout the occupation, French men, and sometimes women, provoked foreign troops in various ways. In Strasbourg in the fall of 1815, some young people, including returning soldiers, insulted foreign officers, forcing the mayor—an ultraroyalist who suggested the occupation was the fault of the French themselves—to post a printed warning in both French and German outlawing such provocation.[78] In April 1816, in Tourcoing, a crowd of inhabitants interrupted a Protestant religious service by Saxon troops in the courtyard of the hospital by shouting lewd insults. In response, the mayor was forced to issue a decree requiring his subjects to maintain "the greatest silence" whenever such a religious ceremony occurred, under threat of punishment, and to send the local national guard to maintain order at future services.[79] Many of the offenses by French inhabitants occurred in public spaces, particularly theaters. In Rethel, during a performance of *The Hunting Party of Henri IV*, a couplet that had been inserted in honor of the emperor of Russia was booed, provoking anger among Russian officers in attendance. Although the guilty party was arrested by the gendarmerie, the local tribunal refused to investigate, "saying that the law does not cover seditious cries against foreign sovereigns." In early 1818, a similar disturbance occurred as a result of "provocations" toward a Prussian officer at a theater performance in Mézières.[80]

Such provocations often sparked quarrels, brawls, or worse. Violence was particularly common during the initial invasion, when French civilians, as well as soldiers, attacked and even assassinated Allied troops. On their march toward Paris, according to a rumor reported by a stagecoach driver on August 1, "a detachment of Prussians was massacred by some Peasants who had revolted and could no longer support the vexations that daily overwhelmed them." Around the same time, it was reported from Lyon that when twenty-some Austrians appeared in a small village near Pouilly, "the inhabitants, indignant over the bad treatment that one had made them endure, revolted and killed two soldiers; when the inhabitants refused to turn over the guilty, the village was reduced to ashes."[81]

Such violence against the occupier continued long after the peace treaty of November 20, 1815. In August 1816, in Bar-le-Duc, an ex-soldier from Clermont, drunk on wine, entered the guardhouse of the Prussians, "vexed" the men on duty, and struck their corporal. In March 1817, in a report that otherwise emphasized the good relationship between the French and the British, the subprefect of Hazebrouck described how locals had ignited one of several brawls by performing in a cabaret a "song that the English troops did not want to hear." Meanwhile, in the capital, in the last year of the occupation, a number of fights erupted between Frenchmen and English speakers. In one case, at three o'clock in the morning on April 10, 1818, in the Jardin du Luxembourg, two young people, one of whom was a French officer, provoked two Englishmen by exclaiming "God-damn!" After the officer was injured, he was joined by a crowd of about a hundred young people outside the Hotel Windsor, where the Englishmen were staying. Prevented from challenging his opponent to a duel only by the intervention of a police officer, he was forced to go to the prefecture, where he was reprimanded for having troubled public order.[82]

While many of these incidents were gratuitous, others were a direct response to Allied "excesses." In the area around Boulogne, where in preceding years numerous French corsairs had been taken prisoner by the British, locals took out their frustration on the English dragoons stationed there. In mid-1816, the inhabitants of Cassel, resisting mistreatment by some English soldiers, "in a spontaneous movement armed themselves with pitchforks, sticks and all sorts of arms in such a show of force that the English were forced to back down shamefully, without daring to raise their hands." A similarly violent outburst occurred in the Meuse in mid-1818, following "attacks on the virtue and acts of violence" against the daughter of a landowner by Prussian soldiers. After local young people attacked the Prussian garrison with sticks, seriously injuring several soldiers, their commander lodged his troops in the commune until the responsible parties were delivered to him. As late as September 1818, amidst rumors of thefts by Russian troops in the region, inhabitants of the country around Rethel were reported to be shooting at Russians who attempted to enter houses; one farmer killed a Russian cavalier, seen emerging from an attic with a packet of linen, whose horse fled and whose body was recovered by fellow soldiers.[83]

Indeed, many of these attacks resulted in deaths. Especially in the beginning but throughout the occupation, French soldiers and civilians murdered a number of Allied soldiers and officers. In mid-1816, on the outskirts of Sedan, two Prussian soldiers were found dead in the street; the inhabitants of the town were "strongly suspected." In Valenciennes, where the "animosity" of inhabitants toward the British contingent was rising as a result of their exactions, an English deliveryman was killed during the night; while the person responsible for the murder was unknown, it was thought to be the result of frequent brawls between the inhabitants and English soldiers. Farther south, in Mézières, a Russian officer was assassinated by a Frenchman whose wife he had seduced.[84]

Directed at all of the Allied contingents more or less equally, such resistance was found in almost every area and among almost every class from 1815 to 1818. However, it was especially pervasive in the countryside, where Allied officers exercised less control over the local population—among the peasants and workers, who suffered more (and gained less) from the presence of foreign troops in their communities. Moreover, it did vary over time. After the violence of the initial invasion in 1815, resistance declined somewhat until the spring of 1817, when the announcement of the troop reduction paradoxically caused a spike in resentment among the French. This reaction was explained in a letter from Colonel von Zerschwitz, interim commander of the Saxon contingent at Tourcoing, in February 1817. Describing a number of incidents in which local peasants had insulted or attacked Saxon troops, the officer bemoaned the "bad spirit demonstrated by the inhabitants of the Saxon encampments, since the rumor spread that the troops stationed in this country would leave France, or at least would be considerably reduced. It seems that the hatred against the Allied troops was restrained until now only by the conviction of our force and superiority and explodes in a truly dangerous manner as soon as the least false news encourages the inferior class of people." This "bad spirit" mushroomed in 1818, as the French awaited official word of the end of the occupation. As the subprefect of Verdun concluded in February of that year, in spite of the tight discipline maintained by the Prussian contingent stationed there, as a result of the petty annoyances of the occupation, "Every day, I see increase the hatred that the inhabitants of this country hold toward this nation." Although he did not think the people of the country would stir against the occupiers, he observed, "[T]hey nourish their hatred; they conserve it for a long time still without letting it explode, hoping one day to be able to avenge it."[85]

Two years into the occupation, in late 1817, the prefect of the Nord received a response from Paris to a report he had submitted on the "discontent" and "bitterness" against the army of occupation among inhabitants of his department. Acknowledging the legitimacy of these sentiments, the minister nonetheless urged the prefect to do everything he could to prevent violence against the occupiers. Recommending patience, he wrote:

> It was easy to predict that it would be thus, and the Government has proven that it knows how to make good on sacrifices already made, to obtain a tangible decrease in those we must still make. Your situation is delicate; but it is forced. The favors that I could grant to you, are those that you have to make yourself, for your subjects. Prevent, as much as possible, dissensions, discussions and brawls. Isolate, especially, in such a circumstance, both incidents and men. It is a time to endure [*C'est un temps à passer*].[86]

For ordinary French men and women, the occupation was indeed a "time to endure." For those who endured it firsthand, the postwar occupation was little different from a state of war. They still perceived the Allied troops as enemies.

Given that the state of war between France and the Allied coalition had technically ended with the Second Treaty of Paris, however, violence could no longer be permitted officially. In its goal to "guarantee" the peace rather than just punish the defeated, the occupation was supposed to contain rather than perpetuate violence between former enemies. In fact, during the occupation, one of the biggest challenges for both Allied and French officials was how to prevent and punish offenses by both sides. Through tight discipline, Allied leaders managed to keep "excesses" and "vexations" by their troops in check. In turn, French administrators worked hard to ensure "good harmony" between their subjects and the Allies. Together, they also negotiated a new procedure for ensuring justice for both sides. Introducing new limits on occupiers as well as occupied, the occupation of guarantee marked a transition between the imperial conquests of the Old Regime and the Napoleonic Empire, and the peacekeeping missions of the modern era.

Part Two

Friends?

Chapter Four

Peacekeeping

IN THE EVENING OF February 29, 1816 (a leap year), the mayor of Dannemarie, a small town in southern Alsace, drafted a formal report on an incident that had occurred earlier that day between some troops of the Austrian Tenth Regiment of Chasseurs and two women from the nearby fortified town of Belfort: Agathe Leroux, daughter of a second-hand clothing dealer, and Ursule Greb, daughter of a deceased cobbler. About eleven o'clock in the morning, these women, who were ostensibly passing through town on their way to Gummerstorff to collect some debts, had entered a cabaret to order a beer. Around one o'clock, after they became "altered," they were stopped by the Austrian troops. At the order of an officer, they were conducted before the adjutant-commander of the place and then to the corps of guards, who gave them each twenty-five blows with a stick, "in the manner customary with them for military punishment," according to the mayor's report. Finally, the two women were delivered to the local gendarmerie, to be imprisoned as "vagabonds." After investigating this incident, the subprefect of Belfort wrote the next day to the prefect that, while these women indeed had a "suspect reputation," they had provided no cause for this "act of rigor." He argued: "One witnessed with the greatest displeasure not only French subjects submitted to a military and foreign police, but also the extension and the consequence that such abuse of authority could have, if one does not restore order there." Adding that this was not the only abuse of power by the Austrian commander, Cassassa, who was also reported to be assigning lodgings to troops without consulting the mayor as required, the subprefect implored the prefect to ask the commander in chief of the Austrian army, General Baron de Frimont, to remind Cassassa of the limits of his attributions, insisting, "These subjects of misunderstanding could trouble the good harmony that must reign and that it is so important to maintain between the inhabitants and the Allied troops." The prefect replied that, even though Cassassa insisted the two women had been trying to debauch Austrian soldiers, he was nonetheless reporting the commander's "guilty behavior" to the general, who in turn sentenced him to corporal punishment.[1]

Despite this punishment, Cassassa continued to provoke complaints from authorities in the region. After several more incidents involving the officer—including the one in which he publicly ridiculed the Dannemarie mayor, who had just arrested a belligerent drunken Austrian soldier, for his white municipal scarf—local officials demanded Cassassa's removal from the town. By early April, the subprefect was warning the prefect, "I cannot hide from you that the violations of the treaty [of November 1815] that this commander permits himself may have grave consequences in a canton where the inhabitants are very irascible and very brave."[2]

The case of Dannemarie illustrates one of the most difficult issues raised by the occupation of guarantee for occupiers and occupied alike: Who held the power to enforce law and order? In occupied territory, did this power accrue to foreign military authorities? Or did it remain with local civilian institutions? While many Allied leaders asserted policing power for their security, French officials defended their own sovereignty. As they grappled with these issues, Allied and French authorities worked out a new, albeit still temporary, approach to the law of occupation.

Prior to this occupation, when international law was still focused on how to ensure a "just war" (*jus ad bellum*), military conquest entitled a victor to impose its own law on a defeated people. While combatants might agree to limit this power for a particular conflict, there was no international regulation of war or its aftermath. Because it was designed not as a semipermanent conquest but as a provisional step between war and peace, however, the occupation of guarantee necessitated a different approach. While the civilian population was still expected not to endanger the security of the occupying force, this force was now required to limit its power, to respect the people and property in the occupied territory. In the occupation of guarantee, Allied and French leaders developed a new, positivist system for administering occupied territory. Ultimately cooperating on policing, discipline, and justice, they initiated a shift, which would come to fruition later in the nineteenth century, toward *jus in bello,* in other words toward using law less to avoid war than to regulate it.[3]

At the beginning of the occupation, Allied troops asserted their power to arrest and punish French subjects at will. French administrators, however, insisted that, according to the terms of the military convention appended to the treaty of November 20, 1815, they retained authority over policing and justice of their own subjects. As the case of Dannemarie indicates, even after the treaty, conflicts persisted over authority, especially regarding criminal justice. But by mid-1816 French and Allied authorities had begun to systematize policing and justice. In addition to instituting procedures for reporting complaints, authorities on both sides exercised strict discipline to prevent violence. When offenses occurred, they routinely indemnified the victims and punished the perpetrators. Following some initial confusion about who had jurisdiction over crimes committed, the two sides agreed that acts by local inhabitants would be tried by a French court, while those by foreign soldiers would be judged by a court-martial of their national army. Although there were some complaints about this system, in general it proved quite effective. While it was developed ad hoc for this particular occupation, this positivist approach to peacekeeping anticipated later, more permanent international agreements to make the practice of war—including its aftermath—more humane, such as the Geneva and Hague Conventions.

Law and Order

During the initial invasion of 1815, Allied forces often asserted authority over a wide variety of military and civilian functions, including the disarmament of civilians as well as soldiers, promulgation of laws, guarding of fields and forests, collection of taxes, patrolling of borders, arrest of offenders, and punishment of crimes. Appointing "general governors" and instituting military police or gendarmeries, they imposed martial law on the territory they occupied, often detaining and penalizing inhabitants who resisted their authority. This arbitrary "military rule" was supposed to end with the treaty of November 20, 1815, which guaranteed the sovereignty of the civilian administration in France. However, even after the transition to the occupation of guarantee, Allied troops continued to interfere in policing, often in violation of the treaty. Only gradually, through protracted negotiation, did French and Allied leaders develop a clear division of labor over law and order, which helped to strengthen civilian administration and contain political unrest in France.

Allied intervention in policing was particularly rampant during the military occupation of 1815. Before the settlement of November, occupying troops exercised "military police" throughout the country, seizing arms from civilian resisters and demobilized soldiers, requiring documentation from travelers (especially those returning from military service), collecting taxes for themselves, interfering in the reestablishment of customs boundaries, and arresting French inhabitants, including officials, at will. Such arbitrary policing was practiced by the German contingents in particular. From the area around Dijon, local officials complained that Austrian officers were assuming all government authority.[4] In Amiens, in the department of the Aisne, the royal court begged the minister of justice to restore its authority against the occupying Prussians, who were trying suspected criminals via their own military courts.[5] But other contingents exercised "military police," too. In the Meuse, the Russian imperial gendarmerie policed the occupied towns and surrounding roads, with the acquiescence of the French police administration. In some places, this "military police" became so egregious that some French functionaries—such as one mayor in the department of the Meuse, whose wife had been mistreated by the occupying Russians—threatened to resign.[6]

Against the assertion of such arbitrary police power by the occupying army, the peace treaty of November 20, 1815, specifically recognized the authority of French officials. According to Article V, "it has been judged indispensable to occupy, during a fixed time, by a Corps of Allied Troops, certain military positions along the frontiers of France, *under the express reserve, that such Occupation shall in no way prejudice the Sovereignty of His Most Christian Majesty, nor the state of possession, such as it is recognized and confirmed by the present Treaty.*" Moreover, the military convention annexed to the treaty further specified, in Article VI, that "[T]he Civil Administration, the Administration of Justice, and the collection of Taxes and Contributions of all sorts, shall remain in the hands of the agents of His Majesty the King of France." Customs, too, would remain under French authority: "They shall remain in their present state, and the Commanders of the Allied Troops shall throw no obstacle in the way of the measures to be taken by the officers employed in that service, to prevent frauds: they shall even give them, in case of need, succor and assistance." To prevent abuses by Allies, the next article stipulated that goods for occupying troops could enter the country duty-free, but only if accompanied by a certificate of origin and approved by the commander in chief. Finally, in Article VIII, the convention guaranteed the authority of the gendarmerie: "The service of the *Gendarmerie* being acknowledged as necessary to the maintenance of order and public tranquility, shall continue, as hitherto, in the Countries occupied by the Allied Troops." In no uncertain terms, the treaty of 1815 limited the authority of the occupying army over military as well as civilian administration in France.[7]

However, the Second Treaty of Paris by no means put a stop to "military policing" by Allied forces. Into the next year and beyond, the Allies continued not only to assert their authority over civilians but also to block the rebuilding of institutions—including the national guard and gendarmerie, as well as the army—that were supposed to assume the function of policing. In January 1816, the royal gendarmerie in the department of the Ardennes reported that the director of the Prussian military police, Count von Loucey, had asserted that his authority extended over French subjects and that French courts should involve themselves only to execute the punishments he decreed. While a note in the margin of one such report suggests that the war ministry accepted, at least temporarily, the right of occupying troops to police the arrondissement in which they were stationed, a gendarmerie official insisted that these police powers flouted the "natural judges" of the French: "I do not think that this intrusion of authority may be maintained, without inflicting a considerable prejudice either on the government of the King, or on those who by their station must enforce the laws."[8] Around the same time, the subprefect of Cambrai complained that, in addition to demanding provisions in excess of those stipulated by military convention, Russian troops were forcing civilian administrators to follow their orders and punishing "militarily" those officials and individuals against whom they had complaints.[9] While Russian commander in chief Vorontsov soon ordered that his troops could not arrest French inhabitants without delivering them immediately into the hands of French justice, along with a formal report on their offense, Allied troops continued to assert policing power. In a typical example, in the town of Remering in early 1817, a Bavarian officer arrested the local police sergeant for publicizing some announcements from the mayor without his approval. When the mayor sent him a letter of protest, insisting he did not have the authority to arrest a French civil servant, the officer ripped the letter to shreds.[10]

Well into 1816, the Allies persisted in disarming French officers and soldiers, even going so far as to require special paperwork from demobilized and deserting troops. In January, in the arrondissement of Verdun, a Prussian officer demanded a list of active troops who had served under Napoleon, in order to ensure that they not leave the area without his permission. Of this demand, the prefect of the Meuse concluded, "This is yet another proof that several foreign officers are not yet penetrated with the true principles which should in this moment direct their behavior in all parts of the Realm that they are called to occupy as friends." But the French ministry of war responded that one could not refuse the officer such a list.[11] In June 1816, an English general, upset about several murders committed against his soldiers, ordered the national guard in Cambrai to deposit their arms at city hall within three hours.[12] Elsewhere, Prussian and other Allied soldiers chased demobilized French officers and soldiers from their homes and obstructed the reformation of departmental army legions.

Gradually, Allied leaders began to cooperate with the French military establishment in policing. Already in January 1816, Vorontsov was reportedly insisting that, far from obstructing the formation of a new French army loyal to Louis XVIII, he was encouraging it "with all his heart." In March, in response to a request from the Duc de Richelieu, the Duke of Wellington agreed to admit to his headquarters the French commander of the gendarmerie in the occupied departments, to help investigate and remedy any disorders. At the same time, however, the commander in chief of the occupation insisted that, while the Allies could not require any extra paperwork from demobilized troops, they did have the right in occupied departments to verify passports. By 1817, French officials were better able to resist Allied efforts at "military police." But, as seen in a British order authorizing troops in the Pas-de-Calais to use arms against local inhabitants in the case of brawls, such "military police" remained a threat throughout the occupation of guarantee.[13]

Power struggles between Allied and French officials arose especially over control of public lands and revenues. Long after the initial invasion, Allied troops continued to hinder the policing of common lands, such as fields and forests. There are numerous records of conflicts between occupying forces and French rural policemen and forest wardens, who were charged with keeping gleaners and poachers off these lands. Even more frequent were disputes caused by Allied interference in the work of tax collectors and, especially, customs officers. During the invasion of 1815, the Commission on Requisitions received numerous complaints regarding the difficulty of reestablishing control over the collection of import and export duties vis-à-vis the occupying forces, especially the Prussians.[14] French officials struggled to reassert their authority over revenue, particularly along the frontiers with the Netherlands and the German Confederation. In November 1817, in the arrondissement of Béthune, in the Pas-de-Calais, four English soldiers were reported to be obstructing the work of excise tax employees, preventing the arrest of a cabaret owner found with counterfeit cards, and even freeing a smuggler caught importing prohibited tobacco; two of the soldiers were eventually arrested by their commanding officer.[15] Many such incidents turned violent. In Hazebrouck, a conflict erupted between officers of the British Eleventh Regiment of Dragoons and excise revenue employees who seized a wagon of meat and wine the dragoons wanted to import without paying the required taxes. The seizure so angered the regiment's officer that he threatened to impose new requisitions on the town, in complete violation of the treaty of 1815.[16]

Throughout the occupied zone, Allied troops routinely impeded and usurped the power of French civilian and military officials. Widespread during the invasion of 1815, such intervention continued at least sporadically, particularly in localities with difficult foreign commanders or weak French authorities, over the next few years. It was especially common in the zones occupied by Austrian, Prussian, and other

German-speaking forces. Gradually, however, through the efforts of select Allied commanders, including the Duke of Wellington, as well as French administrators themselves, such arbitrary martial law gave way to a new approach to law and order, one that was based on a clear division of labor—but also a sense of cooperation—between French and Allied officials.

Surveillance and Discipline

French and Allied authorities worked hard to keep the peace by monitoring and regulating relations between occupied and occupiers. In the early years of the Second Restoration, French officials exercised tight surveillance over the occupied zone in particular. Following the chaotic summer of 1815, when they were often too preoccupied with the pressing demands of invading armies to compose reports, local officials began by early 1816 to report regularly to the central administration. According to a circular of February 1817, except for military intelligence, officials were required to inform the minister of police in particular of all incidents related to the Allied troops in their locality: "[F]rom the moment that it is a question of order, security, difficulties in relations, brawls, complaints, recriminations, investigations, etc., it is indispensable that I know what has happened, who is responsible, what there is to fear, what it is necessary to explain, stop, or prevent. . . . The Police is the sentinel of the Government."[17] To fulfill this mission, the police minister relied heavily on officials lower down the administrative chain, especially subprefects and mayors, but also gendarmes and policemen.

To reduce the number of incidents on which they had to report, local officials made efforts to manage relations between locals and occupying troops. The delicacy of this task was suggested by the prefect of the Haut-Rhin—whose inhabitants spoke the same language as the Austrian troops stationed there—who notified the ministers of interior and police that there were two traps to avoid: "that of letting the allied generals acquire an impolitic popularity and of engendering a dangerous affection between the two peoples whose similar customs and habits are brought even closer together by the same language; and the other, a more immediate danger: discord and division."[18] To prevent both threats, local authorities instituted a number of disciplinary measures. In September 1816, for instance, the mayor of Charleville ordered that, in the interest of "good intelligence" between the town and the Prussian garrison, inhabitants were forbidden from smoking tobacco in front of guard-boxes and, in case the corps sounded an alarm, they were not to leave their workplace or home, unless there was a fire.[19]

Allied officers also insisted on strict discipline. This was especially important to the Russians, particularly the commander in chief, Vorontsov. Raised in England before entering Russian military service in 1801, Vorontsov was, in the words of one contemporary, "more an English lord than a Russian dignitary." Selected by the tsar for his Westernization and reliability, the commander earned a reputation for his insistence on humanity and justice. From the beginning of the occupation, Vorontsov issued strict orders against arbitrary requisitioning, smuggling of contraband, and hunting or fishing outside of the conventional seasons, reminding his troops that "no individual belonging to the army corps including entrepreneurs, roadmenders, etc., may take advantage of the Russian name for the least gain." In a memorandum to local authorities in the arrondissement of Rocroi in January 1816, Vorontsov insisted, given that he had no power to change overall troop numbers and locations, the only way he could help the inhabitants was through "police measures" to prevent "the inconveniences that at present troubled their peace." In addition to encouraging local authorities to ensure that alcoholic drinks were distributed only by official suppliers, that troops were lodged separately from inhabitants, and that officers were given rations in money rather than in kind whenever possible, he urged that all "excesses" by his troops be reported to him so he could investigate and punish them in conformity with military law. Hoping that these measures, along with a bit more "exactness" in provisioning to alleviate grievances among occupying troops, would put a stop to such excesses, he concluded, "After that, with patience and good will on both sides, I have reason to believe that everything will arrange itself so that the troops and the inhabitants are content with their fate and in good intelligence. I assure you that that is my primary desire, and that on my part there are no efforts I am not ready to make to contribute to it."[20]

Similar disciplinary measures were taken by other Allied authorities. The Duke of Wellington required British troops traveling through French villages to register with local authorities and ordered officers to be present on Sundays and festivals when troubles were most likely to occur. To maintain order, Wellington insisted that his officers perform unannounced inspections, submit daily reports, and cooperate with French civil authorities, including limiting the hours of taverns where British troops might congregate. Like General Sir Richard Hussay Vivian, who asked his soldiers to consider how they would feel if their hometown were occupied by foreign troops, British leaders imposed strict limits on drinking, dancing, and curfew.[21]

Although reputed for their violence, even the Prussian and Austrian soldiers were restrained by their officers during the occupation of guarantee. In March 1816, following a brawl between his soldiers and the inhabitants of a town in which a local cobbler was injured, a Prussian officer forced the troops to camp in the countryside all night.[22] According to a report on the Austrian troops encamped in the east of France, which were compared favorably to the Württembergers in the same region, "The perfect discipline of the Austrians, and the regular movement imprinted on the spirit of these troops by their worthy General [Baron de Frimont], greatly helps the inhabitants of this beautiful part of France to forget the pains of an Invasion, and the burdens inseparable from the presence of Foreign troops."[23]

French and Allied authorities occasionally cooperated in law enforcement. In the department of the Nord, an adjunct to the mayor of Lille was attached as a commissioner to the Russian general staff to collect information on offenses committed by local inhabitants. Danish troops from the battalion called "The Queen" in the town of Carvin assisted French customs officers in combating a smuggling ring along the border with the Netherlands; as a reward, the customs director offered 400 francs to the troops, who in turn gave the money to the mayor to distribute to the poor. More commonly, French and Allied officials organized joint patrols of national guardsmen and occupying soldiers. Such patrols were especially common in the Russian sector, where, according to the subprefect of the arrondissement of Avesnes in March 1817, "The Russian Army comports itself according to the principles of its general [Vorontsov]. The officer and the soldier live in peace with the inhabitant, and the army joins with the national guard to conduct the night patrols and prevent the disorders that might be occasioned, either by the military occupation, or by the horrible misery that reigns in this country." Elsewhere, local authorities seem to have been more reluctant to allow such mixing between French and foreign militaries. In the Bas-Rhin, despite orders from the prefect and subprefect, as late as February 1818, the mayor of Oberbronn, among other towns, had failed to organize a *garde bourgeoise*, or civil militia, to perform night rounds with the foreign troops stationed there.[24]

Effective as they were, these efforts at surveillance and discipline did not alleviate complaints. To handle such complaints, the two sides worked out a formal procedure whereby authorities on the ground would pass them up the chain of command to the Duc de Richelieu on the French side, or the Duke of Wellington on the Allied side. Together they would find a resolution. But this procedure was not without problems. In addition to leaving unanswered the question of how to determine and remedy guilt, it was open to abuse by both sides, especially French inhabitants, who were bound to find fault with foreign occupiers. On several occasions, after Allied officers complained of exaggeration or inaccuracy in charges against their troops, the Duc de Richelieu had to remind local authorities to conduct their own thorough investigation before forwarding the accusations to him.[25]

Justice under Occupation

Despite the efforts of authorities on both sides to address incidents, countless offenses inevitably occurred, raising one of the thorniest issues of the occupation of guarantee: how to render justice for the victims, whether Allied or French. Initially, the justice was haphazard, with both Allied officers and French administrators deciding ad hoc whether and how to investigate and punish offenders. In some cases, Allied soldiers were arrested by French officials, or French civilians were tried by foreign military courts, provoking complaints about overextension of power. French and Allied leaders then negotiated a policy whereby offenders could only be tried by officials of their own nation. Beginning in the spring of 1816, this procedure constituted a new approach to justice under occupation.

When foreign soldiers committed offenses against local inhabitants, they were often punished by their superior officers. During the British army's evacuation from Paris to home via Calais at the end of 1815, two

Irish soldiers charged with attacking and robbing a farmer were sentenced by court-martial—with the approval of Wellington—to be hanged. According to grenadier William Lawrence, the entire brigade was assembled to watch the execution, which "was supposed to serve as a lesson." In October 1815, in response to a complaint, the Russian chief of staff ordered a joint investigation, by a civil commissioner and a Russian officer, of a Russian soldier garrisoned in the commune of Lenoncourt who was accused of injuring the mayor's adjunct with a sword. Following the investigation, the soldier was "very severely" punished. Later in the occupation, in August 1817, several English soldiers in Valenciennes who had been condemned to hang for theft were saved only by the people of the town crying, "Grace! Grace!"[26]

Russian officers were reputed for their intolerance of misbehavior, often forcing guilty soldiers to run a gauntlet of lashes, which equated to a death sentence. In early 1816, a Russian court-martial made an example of a soldier in Nachembourg, who in a drunken state had "mistreated" his host, by sentencing him to five hundred lashes. In Landrecies, a Russian sergeant entered a house whose mistress was doing laundry, locked the door, threw her on the ground, kicked her hard all over her body, and scratched her mouth and face before stealing objects. He was sentenced, after investigation by the French justice of the peace, by court-martial in January 1818 to degradation of rank and a thousand lashes.[27] Similar—or even worse—punishments were meted out for crimes committed by troops of other Allied contingents. For instance, an Austrian chasseur of the Eighth Battalion, quartered in the countryside around Belfort, having been found guilty of assassinating a local civilian, was executed at dawn by a firing squad, after which his body was exposed in the town square until sunset.[28]

Although they lacked the authority to punish perpetrators without trial, French civilian authorities responded to Allied accusations against their subjects by launching investigations and pressing charges. In June 1817, the Prussian chef-de-brigade at Bar-le-Duc informed the prefect of the Meuse that the robber of a watch belonging to a fusilier of the battalion quartered at Ligny had been arrested by French gendarmes, proving "the good harmony that exists between the authorities and the inhabitants of Ligny and the garrison of this town."[29] Around the same time, a peasant in Blangy who mistreated an English officer crossing his fields was condemned to a month in prison by the tribunal of Saint-Pol.[30]

In addition to punishing perpetrators, Allied commanders and, less frequently, French authorities indemnified their victims. Following a fire in the village of Fontaine-Notre-Dame caused by a British artillery forge, Wellington ordered not only a court-martial of the officers responsible—who were ultimately acquitted of endangering the village—but also a report on the damage inflicted. With the exception of those who had actively refused to assist in extinguishing the fire, the inhabitants were eventually indemnified by the British cavalry staff corps to the tune of over 19,000 francs. In 1817, the duke also insisted on indemnifying two villages in the Nord that had suffered from the passage of his troops following the Battle of Waterloo, with 2,247 francs, which had been promised but not yet delivered by the British war department.[31] In the absence of a tradition of military justice, such indemnities were employed especially by the Russian officer corps, particularly Vorontsov. In April 1818, the prefect of the Nord reported that Vorontsov had paid 400 francs to a cotton spinner in Villers-Outreaux who had been attacked by two Russian soldiers. While he was not sure whether the soldiers had been punished, the prefect concluded, "I cannot insist upon more ample information on this point, now that the mistreated individual is reestablished and has been suitably indemnified." In another case, Moinot de Contrisson, a Frenchman who had thrown a rock at the head of a Russian noncommissioned officer, consented to give him 100 francs; meanwhile, the Russian officer, who had mistreated the Frenchman with a whip, was subjected to corporal punishment.[32]

Such disciplinary actions and compensatory damages did not eliminate all grievances, and as they transitioned to the occupation of guarantee, Allied and French authorities had to figure out how to adjudicate offenses by each side. The biggest difficulty was the question of jurisdiction: Whose law prevailed, and, in case of violation of the law, who had the authority to judge the offender? According to Article VI of the military convention attached to the Second Treaty of Paris, the French administration was not to be hindered by the foreign occupation. However, given the exceptional circumstances, at least some Allied officers insisted on military justice, even in cases involving civilians. In early 1816, after disputes between Prussian officers and French courts over the right to judge various cases, the issue was taken up by the French ministry, in consultation with the Duke of Wellington. Rejecting previous legal practice in the case of military conquest, the minister of justice, François Barbé-Marbois, a moderate royalist, developed a novel approach for this new sort of temporary peacekeeping occupation. Rejecting Richelieu's assumption that the occupying army always retained jurisdiction over criminal matters whenever either accused or victim belonged to it, Barbé-Marbois maintained that because the Allies occupied France as "auxiliaries," not as enemies, they did not have the right to try French civilians, who remained under the jurisdiction of their own sovereign. Renouncing the sort of extraordinary justice imposed by the Napoleonic Empire on the peoples it conquered, the justice minister insisted, in a separate note to the king, that according to the treaty of 1815, as well as national law, the "natural judges" of French civilians were their own courts.

As a compromise, some French and Allied leaders, particularly Prussian commander Count von Zieten, proposed the establishment of "mixed commissions" of French and foreign judges to investigate and try offenses. Consistently rejecting such a proposal for suggesting the occupation was semipermanent, the justice minister instead instituted clear guidelines for determining whether offenses were subject to military or civilian jurisdiction. In formal "rules" issued to the general and royal prosecutors of the departments of the East on February 25, 1816, Barbé-Marbois ordered that while Allied troops accused of misdemeanors or crimes should be delivered to the relevant military authority, subjects of the king arrested by Allied troops must be relinquished to French authorities, who were responsible for following the procedures of the Criminal Code. In addition, he instructed, Allied and French authorities were to cooperate in obtaining testimonies from witnesses. Following a complaint by Wellington that some Allied forces would allow their troops to appear before only military courts, Barbé-Marbois's successor, the ultraroyalist Charles Dambray, had to issue in August 1816 "supplementary instructions" regarding military witnesses for civilian trials. These instructions permitted the collection of testimony from troops at their regimental headquarters, but only by a member of the French, not military, justice system. Accepted by the French foreign minister as well as by the Allied command, this new division of justice was implemented throughout the zone of occupation.[33]

This split system for judging crimes generated some complaints by Allied and French authorities. While Allied leaders found French courts too partial to their own subjects, French commentators deemed courts-martial too lenient with Allied soldiers. Russian officers repeatedly complained that the punishments imposed by French courts against civilians charged with offenses against their troops were too soft. For instance, when a royal court in Amiens sentenced two gendarmes convicted of brawling with a Russian officer to only fifteen days in prison, Vorontsov appealed the decision, seeking a harsher punishment. To ensure that justice was rendered in such cases, Vorontsov even hired his own French-speaking lawyer to monitor court proceedings.[34]

Such dissatisfaction with the French judicial administration was shared by other Allied leaders, including the Duke of Wellington. Six months into the occupation of guarantee, he became so disgusted with the laxity of justice in the British sector around Cambrai that he petitioned not only the French foreign minister but also the Council of Allied Ambassadors to intervene with the local administration. After four British soldiers were assaulted by seven French officers in June 1816, Wellington bemoaned the discrepancy between Allied discipline and French impunity toward such violence, in a letter to Richelieu that was forwarded to the Council. "The general officers who command the different army corps," he argued,

> have given the example of the most severe discipline among the troops, and I defy the authorities of the Country to name one case where an offense has been observed, where the offender was not punished with severity. Just recently I submitted to the Royal Prosecutor at Cambray [*sic*], to be treated according to the laws, two English attached to the Commissariat against whom there were complaints, and all the decrees of the courts martial, whether against officer or soldier, even those of death, are executed right away—I regret to be obliged to say that the same Justice is not rendered to us by the authorities of the Country, and the consequence is the brawls, of which it is question in this letter, which will have even more grave results if the French authorities do not do their duty.

In response, Richelieu assured Wellington that he had ordered French officials to pursue the guilty in this case and that he would initiate measures to prevent such problems in the future.[35]

Nonetheless, Wellington continued to complain that French offenders were getting off easier than Allied soldiers. Despite numerous entreaties to the French ministers of foreign affairs and police, as well as the king, he continued to receive almost daily complaints from the different contingents of the occupation army about the partiality of the French courts. "This state of affairs cannot last," reportedly said Wellington, who threatened to "leave unpunished the troops, who would make their own justice, until it was rendered to them by the competent authorities." In an 1817 letter to the prefect of Pas-de-Calais demanding punishment of the inhabitants of Landrethun-lès-Ardres, who had attacked the billeting sergeants of a regiment they refused to lodge, the duke insisted that his troops be given the same treatment he had consistently ensured for French civilians:

> I have given countless examples of my desire to conserve the best discipline among the Troops, and good Harmony with the inhabitants of the Country; and I have never received a complaint, against an officer, or a soldier, whose Trial was not made, and who was not punished according to the rigor of military laws. I demand nothing but justice, but I hope that the authorities of the Country will see the bad that may result from this conduct of the Inhabitants of L . . . les A . . . , and that they will make a real effort so that on this occasion the guilty are punished according to the laws.[36]

As Jean Breuillard concluded about the Russian sector in the Ardennes, there remained a large gap between the conciliatory policy of the diplomatic authorities and the recalcitrant practice of the local civilian authorities regarding offenses by French inhabitants against Allied troops.[37]

On the other hand, French authorities complained that Allied justice was too lax or arbitrary. During the transition to the occupation of guarantee in late 1815, a report from the gendarmerie on the political situation in the departments of the Moselle, Meuse, Marne, and Ardennes protested that some Prussian soldiers who had injured a deputy public prosecutor and his wife in Charleville with saber blows had not been fairly punished: for their offenses, which "for our Troops and in time of War on a conquered country would have been punished with death," these soldiers had received only one month in prison with bread and water. Later, from Mézières, a French official groused to the police ministry that when a Russian officer was assassinated by a Frenchman whose wife he had seduced, and a French customs officer was assassinated by a Russian soldier who wanted to rob him, the Frenchman was brought before the courts, while the Russian was set free by order of his general. Another report from Arras on two cases of rape—one by a Frenchman, who was punished by the civil courts to seven years in prison, and one by a British soldier, who was set free—complained that Allied courts-martial often failed to convict troops charged with this particular crime.[38]

While some offenders slipped through the cracks in this system, however, the division of labor between French civilian tribunals and Allied courts-martial proved remarkably effective at rendering justice in the occupied zone. Contrary to the complaints of Wellington and other Allied leaders, French courts did try inhabitants for crimes against Allied soldiers. While some of these defendants escaped punishment, many did not. Given the scattershot nature of judicial archives from this period, it is impossible to provide exact numbers of cases of French soldiers and civilians prosecuted for offenses against occupying troops. But on both the national and local level, there are numerous records of such cases, which suggests that most police and judicial authorities took such offenses seriously. In September 1817, the royal prosecutor in the department of the Nord reported to the police ministry that relations with the English and Russians there had improved because of a series of decisions in which locals had been punished for offenses against Allied troops. For instance, the tribunal of Cambrai had, without even receiving a formal complaint, sentenced to five years in prison an inhabitant charged with stealing the clothes of a bathing British soldier. The same tribunal condemned an inhabitant who had fired on a Cossack in the act of stealing at Le Cateau-Cambrésis to 60 francs in amends, to the satisfaction of the Russians, who had threatened to disarm the population near their encampments. In February 1818, two young people of Clermont found guilty of insulting and attacking two Prussian soldiers were condemned to one month in prison, 16 francs amends, and court fees. In October of the same year, one of two customs officers charged with killing a Russian Cossack suspected of smuggling from the Netherlands was sentenced to forced labor in perpetuity. Occasionally, such convictions were overturned after the Allies departed, as in the case of two customs officers charged with assault against Allied soldiers, who were sentenced to five years of prison in September 1816 but pardoned by the king in late 1819. On the whole, however, crimes against occupying troops were prosecuted by the French judiciary.[39]

Most Allied authorities were at least as diligent in prosecuting offenses by their troops against the occupied population. For the British, there are extensive records of courts-martial in this period. From 1815 to 1818, there were between 125 and 220 courts-martial per year. Of these, most related to troops stationed outside of France—for instance, in Jamaica, India, Australia, Gibraltar, or Ireland—or charged with "routine" offenses such as profiteering, neglect of duty, disobedience, or desertion. But a significant handful—roughly, one-tenth—concerned officers and soldiers in the occupation zone accused of crimes against the French. Already in 1815, a Private Fenton McEvoy of the Seventy-First Regiment was court-martialed for "Scandalous and Infamous Conduct in Stopping Francois Rossignol an Inhabitant of Barraills on or about the 8th November 1815, at night in conjunction with three other men unknown, on the Highway from Paris to Barraills, near Virasfoi, and forcably [*sic*] robbing the said Francois Rossignol of a Silver Watch, of 3 five franc's pieces and of 20 sous in copper money" and some apparel, as well as for attempting to assault a volunteer in the Ninety-Fifth Regiment with intent to rob him. Although he was acquitted of the second charge, for the first he was sentenced to be hung to death. In December of that year, in Montmartre in Paris, Private Richard Malony and Private Richard Dinan of the First Battalion, Twenty-Seventh Regiment, were court-martialed for stealing fabric from a shopkeeper: while Malony was acquitted, Dinan was sentenced to life service in the British army abroad. In October 1816, a Private Kelly of the Eighty-Eighth Regiment in Valenciennes was sentenced to six weeks of solitary confinement for assaulting an inhabitant. As late as 1817, the British adjutant general reminded the assistant quartermaster general stationed in Calais, Major Shaw, that he had the power to convene a general court-martial for any offense committed by a soldier against an inhabitant. According to Thomas Dwight Veve, over the course of the three-year occupation, the British returned home over two hundred soldiers after sentence by court-martial or commutation of punishment.[40]

Although such court-martial records seem not to have survived for the other Allied powers, anecdotal evidence suggests that such procedures were used by all forces, including German and Russian. In the summer of 1818, according to the archives of the French ministry of police, the Bavarian judicial authority condemned some of its soldiers to ten days in prison, plus expenses, for drunken "excesses," including a knife blow to the head against a young man from Teuteling and "violences" against a woman from Obergaille. According to scholars of the Russian army in this period, it had its own court-martial system, complete with specially organized campaign prisons, for crimes of alcoholism, brigandage, theft, and rape.[41]

If found guilty, Allied troops were sentenced to a variety of punishments, depending on the occupying contingent as well as the crime. According to the British register of courts-martial between 1815 and 1818, typical punishments included: 500–900 lashes for theft; 700–1,000 lashes, or even death, for robbery; 600–800 lashes, or 6 weeks' solitary confinement, for assault; 28 days' imprisonment for manslaughter; from 1 month imprisonment to hanging, for murder; 500 lashes or 4 months' solitary imprisonment, for rape; and 6 months' solitary imprisonment or hanging, for counterfeiting money. Such comprehensive data on punishments is lacking for the other Allied contingents. However, the relative severity of punishment for robbery and counterfeiting—as opposed to, say, assault, manslaughter, or rape—suggests that crimes against property were penalized more harshly than those against persons. Sometimes, such punishments were commuted to indemnities, as in the case of a former soldier of the British First Regiment, who, for injuring an inhabitant of Valenciennes, was sentenced by court-martial to receive three hundred lashes but was instead allowed to pay his victim 25 francs.[42]

In sum, justice was rendered to a remarkable extent under the occupation of guarantee. To ensure that the French, as well as the Allies, obtained satisfaction, Wellington himself often intervened in cases of crimes committed by Allied troops, approving or increasing penalties. As Veve concluded about the commander's approach to justice: "Wellington refused to tolerate exploitation of the French, violation of French law, or abuse of French subjects. . . . Everything considered, the incidents between occupied and occupier may be classified as normal for the situation, perhaps even minimal, as no stress arose between the government and the occupational command." Distinguishing the occupation of guarantee from traditional military conquest, Wellington's insistence on punishment of occupiers, as well as occupied, facilitated peacekeeping.[43]

For the occupied French, perhaps the most symbolic example of Allied justice was the court-martial of British officer Lieutenant Colonel C. F. Smith, Royal Engineers, at Cambrai, in December 1816. Charged with "unofficerlike and disorderly conduct" for insulting and assaulting French tradesman Louis Clide Joseph Marlière, who had come to his residence in Valenciennes the previous month to collect payment of a bill for about 400 francs for household goods, Smith pled not guilty. According to the plaintiff, when presented with the bill, the officer not only refused to pay but exclaimed "Vaten!" ("Go away!") three or four times before kicking Marlière with "considerable force." When Marlière swore "Jean Foutre" (*j'en foutre*, in the original French, meaning "I don't give a f***"), the officer reportedly gave him a "beating of the severest description." According to the testimony of a public health officer, the shopkeeper suffered contusions on his head, including both eyes, and was confined to bed for two or three days. In the court-martial, Marlière's testimony was countered by Lieutenant Colonel Smith, who presented his own defense. Asserting that the bill presented by Marlière was under adjudication by a police commissioner, he denied having insulted or kicked the shopkeeper. While Smith acknowledged that he had beaten Marlière, he justified this action under British law by insisting that the shopkeeper had first insulted his honor, arguing, "If I am to endure such language, who is there among you, Gentlemen, whose rank will protect him?" Noting that under French law one witness, however honorable, was insufficient to prove a charge, Smith called several in his own defense. For Smith, the issue at stake was "not whether a British officer can with impunity commit an assault upon a French subject, but whether British officers are tamely and patiently to endure every indignity[,] insult and outrage which language can command, from those without the pale of our Laws, and under the sanction of their own." Following this defense, the court-martial declared Smith "most honorably acquitted" of the first charge of insulting and kicking Marlière. Although it could not deny that he was guilty of the second charge, of assault, the court sentenced him only to a fine of one shilling.[44]

This mere slap on the wrist did not go unnoticed by the commander in chief of the army of occupation, who ordered a review of the sentence. In a letter dated December 11, 1816, Wellington objected to the verdict of an honorable acquittal. Insisting that a legitimate decision was important for the discipline and the reputation of the occupying army, he wrote, "I directed that Lt. Col. Sir C. Smith should be brought to trial on this occasion, because I wished to show to the Government and People of this country, that no officer, whatever his rank or merits, should be permitted to commit an act of this description with impunity; and I wished to mark my disapprobation of the mode, but too common among the officers of the Army lately, of making use of their fists upon every occasion, on which their anger might be excited." Noting that British troops were having trouble receiving justice from French courts, Wellington emphasized, "[I]t is important that I should be able to show, not only that I have done my duty in maintaining the discipline of the Army, but that Courts Martial have done theirs, in the trials, which have come before them, without partiality to any body, and above all without adverting to the Conduct of the French Courts of Justice, to which their Brother Officers and Soldiers have been obliged to appeal." Calling the original sentence rendered by the court-martial a "joke and mockery," as well as "an encouragement rather than a preventative of the offence," the commander in chief demanded that it revisit the case. The second time around, the court again acquitted Smith of "unofficerlike and disorderly conduct," but without the distinction of "honorably," and, still noting the extenuating circumstance of the offensive and provocative language used by the shopkeeper, increased the sentence for the second charge of assault to 20 shillings.[45]

Although the new verdict was not much more punitive than the first, the intervention of the Duke of Wellington in this case provoked a "noticeable change" in the attitude of the occupied toward the occupiers, which prior to December 1816 had been one of sadness and anger, according to a report from the prefecture of the Nord early the next year. While this thaw in relations could be attributed to the discipline of Allied leaders and the firmness of French authorities, the report concluded, the court-martial of Lieutenant Colonel Smith provided a "severe example for the troops, and inspired confidence in the inhabitants."[46]

Through 1817 and 1818, as the French grew increasingly impatient for liberation from the occupation of guarantee, this new attitude of confidence was often tested. Nonetheless, the new approach to peacekeeping enacted by the treaty of 1815 and enforced by the Allied leadership, particularly the Duke of Wellington, provided a context for more or less smooth relations between occupiers and occupied in most locations, and at most moments, between early 1816 and late 1818. By establishing a clear division of labor over policing and justice, French and Allied authorities were able not just to keep the peace between former enemies but also, in some cases at least, to make it.

Chapter Five

Accommodation

ALMOST THREE YEARS into the occupation of guarantee, in response to reports that inhabitants of the Nord were becoming recalcitrant toward British forces, the minister of interior wrote to the prefect, urging him "to direct the spirit of his subjects for the general interest of France." Concerned that the "sudden impatience" of the inhabitants not threaten upcoming negotiations over the departure of the occupying army, he insisted, "The security and even more the dignity of the French nation requires that the last moments of the sojourn of the foreign troops be marked by reciprocal regards and good will which they cannot resist . . . it is necessary that they may depart *as guests who separate themselves from us, and not as enemies that one pushes away.*"[1]

Hospitality toward the occupiers was a major preoccupation of authorities throughout the occupation of guarantee. The prefect of the Pas-de-Calais urged the mayors of his department to impress upon their subjects the importance of avoiding conflicts with occupying troops, "That they should see us *as friends and as true allies.*" Similar language was employed by a subprefect in Sedan describing his efforts to preserve "harmony" in the area around the Prussian headquarters: "I have too often made the leaders of my Communes understand the extent of the obligations we have to the allied armies, since without them we would never have had the happiness of enjoying the Presence of our good King; *that they regard them as our true friends,* and suffer quietly the inconveniences that are inseparable from their Presence."[2] These efforts by French officials were reciprocated by Allied authorities, who also had an interest in smoothing relations between the two sides. Throughout the occupation, leaders on each side worked hard to ensure the other was treated not as an enemy but as a friend.

Such a goal proved more attainable at some moments and in some communities than in others. To a remarkable extent, however, the occupation of guarantee did promote amity between the French and their former enemies. French estate-owner François-Simon Cazin, who lived in the Russian sector in the Nord, may have been exaggerating when he later recalled that, as soon as the cannons ceased in 1815, dancing and singing recommenced, with "noblewomen and market women, warriors of the banks of the Don and those of the banks of the Seine mixing their steps and extending their hands to each other."[3] But numerous other memoirs and letters from both sides attest to at least superficial cordiality, if not genuine friendship. In addition, there was considerable fraternization between occupiers and occupied between 1815 and 1818.

This by-product of military occupation has been well documented for the twentieth century, when it often assumed a negative connotation of "collaboration." The rich literature on the First and Second World Wars has analyzed the cooperation and fraternization between occupiers and occupied, including "horizontal" collaboration, in a number of different contexts, particularly the post-World War II Allied occupations of Germany, Austria, and Japan. Moving beyond the simple dichotomy of collaboration versus resistance, it has revealed a wide spectrum of experience of occupation, from hostility and ambivalence, through patience and acquiescence, to curiosity and even amity.[4]

The more positive end of occupation has been overlooked in the cursory summary of the occupation of guarantee provided in most histories of the Restorations, which—aside from occasional references to the "gentility" of some officers, especially from Russia—tend to emphasize the violence and humiliation of the foreign presence.[5] However, perhaps even more than in other contexts of occupation, when the social stigma of collusion was greater, there was considerable cooperation and even camaraderie in the aftermath of the Napoleonic Wars in France. While it is anachronistic to speak of "collaboration" in this period, there was at least accommodation between French inhabitants and foreign troops. At the time this was characterized as "good intelligence," "tranquillity," or "harmony." Often encouraged from above by national officials, this positive interaction was most common among the upper classes, who had the monetary resources, shared manners, and language skills to socialize together. However, in many localities, amicable relationships developed farther down the social scale.

Alexander, the "Liberator"

During the invasion of 1814 and, to a lesser extent, 1815, occupying troops were characterized by at least some commentators—whether out of genuine conviction or in an effort to appease the Allies—as "liberators." Both times around, these liberators were personified by the Russian tsar, Alexander I, celebrated as a hero for freeing the French from the yoke of Napoleon. There were a slew of poems, songs, and images in honor of this "friend" of France.

For orchestrating a relatively generous occupation and restoration in 1814, Alexander was given a warm welcome. As the tsar entered Paris on March 30, crowds lined the streets to cheer the victor over Napoleon. During his two-month stay, he was invited everywhere, including to the Louvre, the royal palace at Versailles, the home of Joséphine Bonaparte at Malmaison, and the Académie Française, where he was awarded a prize as a new "Marcus Aurelius," philosopher-king. In his honor, writers composed numerous pieces, including one "epistle" dedicated to "His Majesty the Emperor of Russia, Liberator," by a veteran of the Napoleonic Wars now devoted to Alexander for returning peace and monarchy to France, and another dedicated to "M. de Saint-Victor," which concluded "He is a vanquishing hero! He is a king, he is a father! / Benefactor of the French and avenger of the earth."[6] Alongside these texts circulated portraits of Alexander with captions such as "Be Happy Now" and "Returned Happiness to France." Such glorification became so widespread that it constituted a genre called "Alexander-mania."

This Alexander-mania shaped the reception of the tsar following the second defeat of Napoleon. Early in 1815, the publisher Lemercier issued a collection of *Alexandrana,* or "bons mots" uttered by Alexander during his stay in Paris, along with a description of Allied operations to restore Louis XVIII to the throne of France. Including a portrait of the tsar, this collection contrasted the "magnanimity" of Alexander with the "scourge of the human species," Napoleon. Among the "remarkable words" quoted, it noted that "upon his entry to Paris, the tsar said to the immense crowd that was pressing around his august person: I come not at all as an enemy; I bring peace and commerce to you."[7] Even after the second, more brutal invasion of France, the Russian emperor was welcomed as a friend of France. According to the *Journal de Paris,* on a walk through the streets of the capital Alexander was encircled by several national guardsmen as well as a large number of citizens, "drunk with the pleasure of seeing a good and great monarch," exclaiming "Vive l'Empereur!"[8] The Russian emperor was also lauded outside the capital. During a religious service for the festival of Saint Louis in Maubeuge, the local priest expressed gratitude for the role of the "magnanimous and generous sovereign" who had facilitated the return of Louis XVIII.[9] The Russian tsar symbolized the occupier as a "friend" of France.

Courting the Other

Alexander was not the only foreigner to receive such a welcome. Most French military and civilian officials were at least superficially hospitable to their Allied counterparts, especially once the initial military invasion gave way to the more systematized occupation of guarantee. Such hospitality was easier for upper-level administrators, like ministers and prefects, than for lower-level ones, especially mayors, who had to deal daily with the demands of hundreds of soldiers. But by treating the occupiers as "allies," not enemies, these officials set the tone for a more positive reception of the foreign army. By reciprocating with various courtesies, foreign officials in turn cultivated this more positive relationship with their "hosts."

At the highest levels, hostility between former enemies was dissipated in official meetings, ceremonies, and reviews. Within days of the second capitulation of Paris, the French monarch was joined by Allied dignitaries for official events, religious services, and military parades, to shouts not just of "Vive le Roi!" but also of "Vivent les Alliés!" As soon as they arrived in Paris, the tsar of Russia, the emperor of Austria, and the king of Prussia together paid court to Louis XVIII, leading the government newspaper to editorialize, "The capital delivers itself without reserve to the hope that the reunion of these monarchs with him who is returned to us, will soon establish the foundation of a peace henceforth inalterable, and will tighten for ever the ties that must unite France, returned to a stable and legitimate government, with Europe."[10] Two days later, the *Journal de Paris* reported, the tsar, with two of his brothers, and the king of Prussia, with two of his sons, dined at the Tuileries Palace with Louis XVIII. When they appeared together at a palace window, cries of "Vive Louis XVIII!" "Vive the Emperor Alexander!" and "Vive the King of Prussia!" filled the air.[11] When the Austrian emperor was "indisposed" in mid-July, the French king paid him a visit. He also awarded decorations to foreign princes, such as the Order of Saint-Esprit to Michael and Nicholas of Russia.[12]

Similar courtesies were exchanged between the French royal family and Allied officers and statesmen. In mid-July 1815, the general staff of the Allied army, composed of about three hundred generals and superior officers under the command of Wellington, appeared at the Tuileries to pay its respects to the king. After having all the staff presented to him by name, the king addressed Wellington in English, expressing his personal gratitude for the "humanity and good behavior of the Allied army toward his subjects," according to one news report.[13] In recognition of Wellington's role in restoring him to the throne of France, Louis XVIII regularly addressed him as "My cousin, the duke of Wellington."[14]

Following the institution of the occupation of guarantee in the northeast, foreign officers and local authorities participated in each other's ceremonies. In May 1816, for instance, British troops stationed in Valenciennes joined in a thanksgiving service for the second anniversary of the initial return of Louis XVIII. In July, the new mayor of Tourcoing invited the Saxon contingent there to attend his installation ceremony, after which he promised to distribute drinks to the troops. Foreign officers and local authorities also cooperated to welcome Allied dignitaries for visits or reviews, such as when the Prussian king Frederick-William III and Prussian commander Count von Zieten accompanied Wellington to Mézières in September 1817.[15]

French and Allied leaders joined in celebrating each other's holidays. In Colmar, festivities were held on the birthday of the Austrian commander, Baron de Frimont, and emperor Francis I. As local schoolmaster Georges Ozaneaux reported to his mother, on the emperor's birthday in February 1818, forty thousand Austrian troops were encamped around the town in preparation for an open-air mass and a grand ball, complete with illuminations and "transparents," at the prefecture, to which he and other local elites were invited. Of this party, the *Moniteur universel* wrote, "It is thus that in mutually offering each other testimonies of esteem and affection, in uniting their voices for the prosperity of their respective sovereigns, these nations show themselves to be deserving of the benefit of the peace owed to them, and coooperate to assure its maintenance and endurance." For the Prussian king's birthday in 1818, the *Moniteur universel* reported, "[The Prussian] commander gave a grand dinner, to which the principal functionaries [of the town] were invited . . . The greatest cordiality reigned in this gathering, during which the soldiers on their side rejoiced with order and decency." Even the commander of the small Danish contingent, Prince Frederick, was fêted by the French court on a visit to Paris in February 1817 and by the villages in the Danish zone around Bouchain on his birthday, with banquets, balls, illuminations, and fireworks in which local inhabitants partook "with great joy."[16]

Foreign troops reciprocated by participating in festivities on French holidays, especially the feast day of Saint Louis (Louis IX), on August 25. At Berlaimont in the Russian sector, soldiers marked this holiday by shooting fireworks while exclaiming "Vive le Roi, vivent les Bourbons, vive l'Empereur Alexandre." At Maubeuge, on July 1, 1816, Russian troops joined in festivities for the marriage of the Duc de Berri. Following a parade, church service, and banquet, a ball was hosted by the municipality at which "was never seen more union," according to a local official. "The French and the Russians battled for the attentions, the actions and the regards [of the crowd]. In one word, it was a family party."[17] Similarly, on the feast day of Henri IV and the anniversary of the second return of Louis XVIII in July 1816, Russian officers in Lille shared in the "communal joy, and one noticed with pleasure that their soldiers had hung, in the middle of their barracks, a white flag, with the inscription Vive le Roi!"[18]

To promote more amicable relations, the French and the Allies paid reciprocal courtesies to each other, especially in times of grief. In the Haut-Rhin, according to the ultraroyalist newspaper *L'ami de bon sens,* local officials attended funeral services for the empress of Austria and in memory of troops killed in the Battle of Leipzig. In turn, in Landrecies in January 1818, a funeral for a French general named Catelain was attended by Russian troops garrisoned in the region, along with a Muscovite "pope" and a large number of officers. Allied troops participated regularly in memorial services for Louis XVI each January 21. On the occasion in 1816 in Charleville, the Prussian commander assured the mayor, "We all respect too much a dynasty for the reestablishment of which we have shed our blood, not to want to express a sincere regret on the anniversary of the death of a monarch, who was once so loved by his subjects and whose unfortunate end placed France in mourning for more than twenty years."[19]

French and Allied authorities cultivated their relations by bestowing thank-you letters, gifts, and decorations on each other. When they left their post to assume another or return home, Allied commanders often received written declarations of thanks from local authorities. Some of these took the form of official certificates of "good conduct," demanded by the departing officers themselves for their superiors. Others, however, were more spontaneous expressions of gratitude. In September 1815, a civil official in the Haut-Rhin wrote an effusive letter to the Austrian commissioner for Alsace thanking him for his "humanity," "moderation," and "justice" in the difficult initial invasion. French and Allied authorities also exchanged a variety of gifts. In Colmar, Austrian commander Baron de Frimont was so appreciated for his "moderation and wisdom" by the local elite that in 1816 he was given a copy of the lavishly illustrated book *Grand ouvrage sur l'Egypte*. In July 1816, the Prussian king conferred the Third Class of the Order of the Red Eagle on the mayor and commander of the national guard of Versailles, in recognition of their cooperation with the Prussian army during the occupation of 1815. Such mutual recognition was especially widespread as the occupation drew to a close in late 1818.[20]

"Good Intelligence"

Even if they did not always feel true "friendship" for each other, French and Allied authorities went to considerable effort to ensure at least tolerance and peace. Both sides aimed to promote what they called "good intelligence" between local inhabitants and foreign troops. On the

French side, under pressure from the central government, local authorities endeavored to ease tensions. To minimize opportunity for conflict, they introduced or reinforced regulation of threats to public order, such as drinking, smoking, public assembly, and even bell ringing. To smooth relations, local administrators cultivated contacts with—and channeled complaints from—Allied officers. The subprefect of Verdun, for example, took it upon himself to get to know the Prussian commanders—all the way up to General von Zieten—via regular correspondence and visits. "We do not like the Prussians," he reported to the minister of police in February 1816. "We would see them leave with pleasure, but we tolerate them with wisdom."[21]

To appease the troops stationed in their sector, local administrators focused above all on ensuring their comfort. Beyond the required provisions, they arranged small favors. With Saxons as well as Russians in the Nord, the subprefect of Avesnes reported in early 1817, "Experience has taught us that, by ceding in good time and with good grace a host of small objects whose supply is not at all rigourously demanded by the treaties, one obtains from the military leaders some concessions for the maintenance of police, the security of the country, etc., which at least equal these sacrifices." In the Russian sector around Givet, where the commanding officer Loewenstern tried to lighten the burden of occupation, the municipal administration rushed to satisfy the demands of the Russian troops for baths, workshops, sheds, barracks, an exercise field, an interpreter, and even a chapel for practicing their Orthodox religion.[22] In their own effort to facilitate "good intelligence," Allied officers reciprocated by enforcing good behavior among their troops. For instance, the Russian officer General Count Barclay de Tolly required his soldiers to obtain for their commander each week a certificate of good conduct from the mayor of the place where they were stationed.[23]

Mutual Aid

In their efforts to maintain "intelligence" in occupied communities, the Allies offered *secours,* or aid. In return, French men and women provided assistance to the occupying troops beyond the lodgings and provisions required by the treaty of November 20, 1815. The mutual aid between occupiers and occupied took a variety of forms, including physical labor, donations in money or kind, rescue from disaster, and care of sick and dying.

When not training, Allied troops sometimes did work for the local communities. In Bouchain, two companies of Danish troops fixed a number of fortifications, bridges, tunnels, and other structures.[24] One of the most common ways in which the occupiers assisted the occupied was in gathering crops at the end of each summer. Realizing that such assistance was in their own interest, to ensure a regular supply of food and forage, Allied officers often permitted, or even ordered, their troops to help with the local harvest. During the occupation of the Paris region in summer 1815, the *Moniteur universel* reported, both Field Marshal Blücher and the Duke of Wellington offered troops and wagons to local landowners to harvest grain. As British general Cavalié Mercier remembered: "What strange things we live to see and hear! . . . English soldiers and French peasants are seen everywhere side by side, sickle in hand, or binding sheaves, &c—the invader and the invaded alike peaceably occupied, and reciprocating kind offices one with the other. 'Tis a goodly sight, truly."[25]

While the British were particularly quick to assist local peasants in this way, other contingents also helped to harvest the crops in a number of localities, especially in the bad growing seasons of 1816–1817. In August 1816, in the Ardennes, Prussian general-in-chief von Zieten agreed to permit his troops to assist (without payment) in the harvest, in response to a formal invitation from the prefect, solicited by the subprefect of Verdun, who desired "by all possible means, to establish some ties of affection between the inhabitants of this arrondissement and the Prussian troops whom they must keep for several years; thinking . . . that the services rendered by the latter would make more tolerable to the former all of the sacrifices that they must make for their subsistence and lodging."[26]

In addition to providing labor, Allied contingents offered material assistance. When local communities had trouble supplying the food or forage demanded of them, Allied officers arranged loans or shipments to make up the deficits. In February 1817, Prussian general von Zieten loaned the arrondissement of Sedan 50,000 francs to pay for three thousand hectolitres of oats to remedy a lack of forage. During the same winter, Russian general Loewenstern obtained authorization from

Wellington to order regular shipments of grain from the Netherlands (payment of which was guaranteed by the department) to the region of Givet, where some seven thousand troops of his nation were stationed. For his generosity, he was later awarded a sword by the commune of Givet, as well as a cross of the Legion of Honor.[27]

During the grain crisis of 1816–1817, but also in response to particular disasters, Allied officers and their soldiers took up collections and handed out grants to struggling individuals and communities. Already in September 1815, the mayor of Soultz asked the prefect of the Haut-Rhin to publicize in the departmental newspaper a donation of 300 francs for the poor given by a departing Austrian colonel. In January 1817, in the midst of the grain crisis, officers of the Alexiopolski Regiment offered a party to the inhabitants of Landrecies, at which a gift of 1,000 francs was given by the colonel and 3,000 francs raised by the regiment to help the town's poor. The same year, the Prussian brigade in the arrondissements of Bar-le-Duc and Commercy collected 800 francs for the victims of a fire in the commune of Brillon. Informed of the gift, the subprefect at Verdun praised the Prussian officers for doing "everything they can to relieve the pain they witness, and . . . alleviat[ing] as much as possible the burden of the occupation. I can only praise them, in all the relations that it has been necessary for me to have with some of them, and I have to admit that we owe to them in particular perhaps the calm which we have enjoyed in the middle of the misery that has afflicted us in the last ten months." In 1816, Prussians in the Meuse likewise contributed to a subscription for victims of fires in several Alsatian villages during the invasion of 1815.[28]

There are numerous accounts of occupying soldiers helping to put out fires or to rescue local inhabitants from various catastrophes. In the Pas-de-Calais, Danish troops helped to extinguish several fires, including one in the commune of Angres, where Mathies Mathiessen, a cannoneer, became a hero for saving a young man who was battling a fire on a roof when it crumbled—and then donating the reward given to him by the commander of the Danish brigade to the victims of the fire. Another 100 francs were donated to these victims by the Danish general de Gerstenberg. In response to such generosity, which "could not be too honored," the prefect wrote to the general to convey the appreciation of the town's inhabitants. On the eve of the liberation in 1818, when a "violent" fire broke out in Rocroi, the Russian commander, Major Brawkow, whose troops were away for a review at Maubeuge, enlisted sick soldiers in the military hospital to aid the inhabitants. In August 1817, two lieutenants attached to the Russian Twenty-Third Company of Artillery in the arrondissement of Avesnes, who "had the generosity to throw themselves into a pond to retrieve a child of ten years who was drowning," were recommended by the subprefect for a commendation. In Tourcoing, Saxon troops rescued a child half-dead from cold in January 1818. The same year, when six Saxon soldiers responded heroically to the collapse of a wall, their general, von Gablenz, refused an indemnity offered by local authorities, insisting they "only did their duty."[29]

Such humanitarian acts were not one-sided. Throughout the occupation, French men and women offered kindnesses, big and small, to Allied officers and soldiers. They were particularly compassionate toward wounded and sick foreign troops. Perhaps inspired by the legend of "Sister Martha," a nun in Besançon who was widely celebrated for her work during the invasion of 1814 to nurse foreign as well as French troops, inhabitants of communities throughout France succored injured or ill troops. Following a decree by the war ministry in February 1816, designated towns in the occupation zone were required to supply ambulances and hospitals for occupying troops. In enacting this order, however, local authorities emphasized the duty of humanitarianism. As the prefect of the Haut-Rhin instructed the mayors of his department in early 1816, "In executing this measure, commanded by the humanity and the interest inspired by each suffering soldier, I recommend, Monsieur the Mayor, that you dispose right away of the civil hospice, if there exists one in your commune, or another space to receive sick troops who are not at all transportable, as well as those suffering from mild illnesses. The duties of hospitality and the sentiments that distinguish you assure me of the care that you will give to them."[30]

French inhabitants exhibited remarkable concern for the foreign dead, especially given the administrative and religious constraints on mortuary care. As Jacques Hantraye has eloquently shown, the solicitude shown demonstrates the extent to which the "Other" was accepted in France. On a few occasions, French churches held funeral services for foreign officers, if not usually soldiers. While religious officials often refused to allow foreign troops, especially of a different faith, to share the same space as their parishioners in cemeteries as well as churches, they were frequently inhumed in French burial grounds, often in communal graves (sometimes alongside unidentified French soldiers), in a Protestant section or with unbaptized children. Of 476 death certificates of foreign troops examined by Hantraye for the department of the Seine-et-Oise in 1814 and 1815, there are burial acts for 152. Of these, only 34 percent were buried in the cemetery of the Catholic church. In the Russian sector, some seventy-six soldiers who died during the occupation were buried in a military cemetery at Bayot. Near Nancy, another burial ground remained known as the "Russian cemetery" for the next several decades. The French went to considerable effort to record and communicate the deaths of Allied troops. Sometimes noting their last words, they wrote letters to the deceased's kin. Following a law of 1814, local administrators forwarded all death certificates of foreign troops to Allied authorities. As Hantraye argues, such treatment of foreign dead suggests "the conception of a sort of community of families in mourning, outside of national differences."[31]

Brothers in Christ

In mutual aid, religion often played a role. Although not all Allied troops shared the Catholic religion practiced by most French, they—or at least their officers—attended services, or at least social events, with local religious authorities. In many communities, religious officials insisted on spatial separation between Catholic and other sects, including Russian Orthodox and German Protestants. Nonetheless, there was considerable fraternization between foreign troops and local inhabitants in the name of Christ.

The example for cooperation in the name of religion was set by Tsar Alexander who, soon after his arrival in Paris in 1814, orchestrated a public mass on the Place de la Concorde on Easter Sunday. In pursuit of his dream of universal peace, the tsar proclaimed to his troops, "Our revered faith teaches us, by the very mouth of God, to love our enemies, to do good to those who hate us." Echoing such language, French religious authorities urged local inhabitants to welcome the Allies. In a circular letter to local priests on April 30, 1814, the vicars of the Catholic Church praised these "liberators" for returning the French "to [their] Religion, to [their] liberty, to [their] laws, to [their] sovereigns." Following the second invasion, in a thanksgiving service for the return of the king, the bishop of Clermont paid homage to the "brave and respectable" officers of the Austrian army in the region, who by the "moderation and honesty of their behavior had come to conquer our hearts." While ecclesiastical authorities such as archbishops and vicars tended to be more hospitable to Allied troops than parish priests, clergy at all levels provided them with a variety of religious services.[32]

Between 1815 and 1818, there are numerous examples of French clergy succoring foreign soldiers. While some foreign troops, especially British, were accompanied by their own clergy, they often lacked adequate numbers, especially outside Paris, where Anglicans, among others, had their own church. Hence French priests, chaplains, and nuns played a significant role in providing material and spiritual assistance to the occupiers, especially in hospitals and prisons. In June 1817, the vicar general of Metz asked his subordinate in Ville-au-Montois to accompany an "unfortunate" Russian soldier who had been condemned to death in his "painful voyage" without sacraments.[33]

In general, the French insisted on physical separation between sects. In numerous towns, Catholic priests denied requests from Allied contingents to use the local church for their own religious services. When they did permit Allied forces in their establishments, they insisted that foreign troops hold their services at a different time or, preferably, on a different altar, separated by a curtain. However, whether out of generosity, politics, or fear, French religious authorities made a number of concessions to occupying troops. Local priests dispensed communion to Catholic officers. In January 1816, at the request of Bavarian officers, the vicar general of Metz authorized celebration of a mass and singing of a *Te Deum* for their contingent. That May, in the Russian sector, Orthodox "popes" were permitted to celebrate services in five churches, including those of Vouziers and Rethel. In Colmar, based on the letters of local schoolmaster Georges Ozaneaux, the wife of the general-in-chief of the Austrian army, Baron de Frimont, regularly attended mass in the local church, escorted by the general staff. The local priest, Louis Maimbourg, fulfilled ecclesiastical functions at all military festivals of the Austrian army, which decorated him for his services.[34]

For their part, Allied authorities practiced Christian faith and charity. Where they could not obtain a space of their own, foreign troops often worshipped outside. In Bouchain, Danish troops attended services "in the fresh air" led by their own pastor, K. Nyholm, who would remind them that France and Denmark were "the most loyal friends and allies." At these services, money was collected for the families of Danish troops, but also for local French in need. In Rethel, Russian general Loewenstern donated money for the repair of the organ, iron grill, and bell of the parish church. In Colmar, the Austrian commander paid for the restoration of the Chapel of the Virgin in the college of Saint-Martin—in exchange for which he later took with him some stained-glass windows from the former church of the Dominicans.[35]

Even when they did not worship together, there was considerable socialization between French clergy and Allied authorities, at least at the higher end of the social spectrum, which reinforced a sense of "brotherhood" among occupiers and occupied. As Jacques Hantraye has shown, on parish tours vicars cultivated relations with foreign officers. In the diocese of Metz, the vicar general, Monseigneur Jauffret, paid a visit to Russian troops ten times; Prussians, four; Bavarians, twice; and Dutch, once. At Rethel in July 1816, at a traditional Russian dinner hosted by the general staff, the French prelate gave a toast to Alexander I, "moderator and pacifier of all of Europe," while the Russian generals drank to the health of Louis XVIII. Five days later, the same vicar celebrated a mass attended by Russian officers; at a dinner afterward, when the Russian colonel Count von Konski learned that the parish church's organ had burned, he launched a subscription for it, to which he himself contributed 250 francs. While this sort of socialization between religious and military authorities was more frequent with Russians than, say, Germans, it did contribute to a certain rapprochement across national lines, at least among elites.[36]

Socializing with Allied "Guests"

In addition to worshipping together on occasion, Allied troops and French inhabitants mixed in a variety of other social arenas, including at festivals, banquets, balls, theater performances, hunts, salons, reading rooms, Masonic lodges, taverns, peasant festivals, and evening *veillées.*

Such mixing is attested to in numerous letters and diaries by foreign as well as French witnesses, especially among elites. The socializing was more frequent among some classes and nationalities than others, particularly those that shared French as a lingua franca. While Russian and, to a lesser extent, Austrian officers were perhaps the most sociable with French aristocrats and bourgeois, the English, let alone the Prussians, were perceived by locals as more reserved. Nonetheless, even among the German contingents, and even among the common people, there was considerable fraternization—including sexual—across national lines. In fact, such sociability was encouraged by local officials, who recognized its role in ensuring "tranquillity" and promoting understanding between former enemies.

Allied and French elites frequently dined together. Across the occupation zone, as well as in Paris, Allied officers and French authorities hosted lavish meals to which they invited their counterparts. In September 1815, on the festival day of Emperor Alexander, the Russian intendant and commandant in the department of the Meuse organized a banquet to which were invited eight hundred guests, including the prefect and town authorities. After the meal, the Russian officials, followed by the guests, carried a bust of Alexander to the people in the street, to whom they distributed wine and money. This gesture was followed by a "general illumination," at which local families mixed with Russian troops. According to a report in the *Journal de Paris,* "The celebrants of the two nations erupted in the most pure and frank joy." In July 1818, at his field headquarters in Cambrai, the Duke of Wellington hosted an outdoor banquet for 108 people, including the Prince of Hesse, several French functionaries, Allied officers, and a large number of "charming ladies." The meal was followed by dancing in the garden, illuminated for the occasion. Other times, Allied officers and local administrators shared less formal, more impromptu meals. In the British sector, officers received numerous invitations from local authorities for family dinners, as well as banquets, balls, and spectacles. At these dinners, each side often toasted the other's sovereign.[37]

Eating and drinking were often accompanied by dancing, and Allied and French elites attended numerous balls together during the occupation. In the Russian sector, Loewenstern, Vorontsov, and other officers regularly organized balls for local elites at which Russian and French dances alternated, sometimes by local ordinance. In Rocroi, the "brilliant parties" organized by the French-speaking Russian officers, to which local functionaries were invited, helped to heal the wounded pride of the occupied. Russian officers were such good dancers that, whenever a ball was organized for visiting sovereigns, they were asked to attend. But other Allied contingents also danced with local elites. The Saxon contingent in Tourcoing was reported to give "very pretty parties." In June 1818, the officers of the British garrison in Valenciennes gave a party in the local theater to celebrate the birthday of the king of England. Attended by Russian as well as English dignitaries and all the "beautiful and elegant women" the region could supply, this party featured a mix of French and English symbols. Such parties were most frequent at holidays, especially Carnival, when they involved masking and cross-dressing, and increased toward the end of the occupation.[38]

In addition to dancing, Allied officers, including the Duke of Wellington, enjoyed hunting with French notables. In the area around Givet, Russian officers joined in hunting parties with local lords. For his exploits in these parties, the Russian general Loewenstern was proclaimed *Roi de la Chasse,* or "Hunting King." According to his memoirs, this general also enjoyed trout fishing with young ladies from Givet.[39]

In their leisure time, Allied leaders attended the theater, where they mixed with local elites. In Paris, the theaters were full of foreign, especially English, statesmen, officers, soldiers, tourists, and their female companions. Soon after their arrival in Paris, Allied sovereigns and officers, including Wellington, attended a performance at the Academy of Music, where they joined in applauding exclamations of "Vive le Roi!" in the presence of Louis XVIII. Around the same time, a rumor circulated that the Russian emperor and Prussian king had rented boxes at the capital's main theaters for the next three months. Theater was a popular pastime among Allies in the provinces, too. In September 1815, after arriving in Caen, Blücher attended the local theater, which performed *The Prussian Major* and an intermède in his honor; afterward, the actors presented him with flowers and a crown of laurels. In Strasbourg in January of the next year, two Austrian generals (one stationed at Molsheim; the other, Hagenau) attended the theater with the department's prefect and commander, demonstrating (in the words of the *Journal*

La Russe, ou les Alliés à Tivoli. Print, ca. 1815. Musée Marmottan, Paris/Bridgeman Images.

de Paris) that "[T]he good accord that reigns between the royal authorities and the chiefs of the allied troops is a certain guarantee of tranquility between these two countries." To entertain their troops, Allied officers organized theater performances, which provided occasions for mixing with French inhabitants. At Valenciennes, the British commanders organized a society of amateur actors; their performances were attended by local French, as well as Wellington himself in May 1816. In the Russian sector, to amuse his garrison of two hundred officers, "young, lively, ardent, and avid for pleasures," General Loewenstern procured a French theater troop from Reims, who not only entertained them but also taught them some French.[40]

Allied and French elites also mixed in reading rooms, philosophical societies, and salons. In 1816, a popular English guidebook to Paris marveled, "The liberality of the French in admitting foreigners into the greater parts of their literary societies and public edifices, in many of which they will not suffer the attendants to accept a donation, is the theme of universal praise among our countrymen." In Colmar, Georges Ozaneaux recounted, the weekly soirées hosted by the prefect Comte de Castéja were attended by a "crowd" of local notables and Austrian officers, including the general-in-chief Baron de Frimont, whom he called a "very brave man." French aristocrat François-Simon de Cazin remembered, during a voyage to the Loire to retrieve his convalescent brother, spending soirées in the salon of a local bourgeoise with two Prussian officers "belonging to families of the high aristocracy of Berlin," whose behavior was "always dignified and irreproachable." Back home in Rocroi, Cazin socialized regularly with Russian officers, for whom he developed a real affection.[41]

One of the most common and consequential arenas for socializing with French elites was Masonic lodges. During their stay, numerous Allied officers—some of whom were already Masons—joined lodges in France. According to a local historian, in Cambrai several British officers became members of the Thémis lodge, which hosted a banquet for their British brothers. Prussian officers were also eager to participate in Masonry; however, whether because they were not welcomed by French elites or because they were prohibited by Prussian authorities, who viewed any such secret society with suspicion, Germans did not become as active in these associations as other Allies, especially the Russians. In the area around their headquarters in Maubeuge, Russian officers and local bourgeois often socialized in Masonic lodges. According to historian André Boyer, based on the archives of the Russian general staff, there were some 471 Masons among the Russian occupation force in 1814–1815, including 62 generals and 150 colonels. In Avesnes, the single lodge Aménité counted as many as twenty-five Russian officers, who had demanded admission as affiliates or initiates. In these lodges, Russian and French Masons developed cordial, even close, relations. In Maubeuge, for instance, a Russian military lodge was invited by the Avesnes lodge to a banquet celebrating the feast day of Saint Louis, at which the Russians assured their French brothers of "their esteem and their love." During another gathering of the two lodges at Maubeuge, the French "Vénérable" of the lodge in Avesnes declared in his toast, "Alexander and Louis love each other, esteem each other. Following the example of their sovereigns, the Russians and the French feel, toward each other, the same sentiments." Participation in Masonry cultivated more than amity between Russians and French. It also engendered liberal ideas among at least some Russian officers, as evidenced by the concern expressed by French and Russian authorities surveying them. In fact, their experiences in these lodges is acknowledged by historians to have influenced the Decembrist movement, in which many of these officers played a part, a decade later.[42]

Some Allies were more sociable than others. In contrast to the Russians, the British were often viewed by the local population as reclusive. According to one local historian, based on sources from the garrison town of Valenciennes, "the English did not seek out contact with the population and did not try to participate in local life, beyond official obligations. They kept rather to themselves, if only for linguistic reasons. The officers lived among their family; sending their servants out to the market—where one reproached them for making prices increase due to their ignorance of local practices." Another local historian, quoting a contemporary report, concurs that "no rapport existed between the English troops and the inhabitants. The opposition of their customs is the most apparent, if not real, cause."[43]

If the British sometimes had difficulty making friends with the French, the various German contingents—especially the Prussians, who had developed a reputation as brutal barbarians—had even more trouble. In some places, Austrian, Saxon, Württemberger, and even Prussian officers managed to conciliate themselves with local elites. But they were generally perceived by the French as less friendly than the British and, certainly, the Russians, who—overcoming the widespread fear of the "Cossack"—soon established themselves as the most "gentle" occupier. According to a local historian of Landrecies in the Russian sector, "Everywhere it was agreed that one would prefer to lodge ten times the number of Russians or even Prussians than a single Saxon," reputed to be the most demanding occupier. With Russian officers, local inhabitants developed a "great intimacy": "The city-dwellers were in real sympathy with the Russian officers, who were very affable and a few of whom spoke fluent French. In balls, redoubts, banquets, private soirées, the two nations fraternized openly like two friends."[44]

Of course, the "friendliness" between occupiers and occupied also varied with class. The "gentleness" of even the Russian contingent, described by French elites, is called into doubt by numerous sources from farther down the social scale. The picture painted by a notable such as Cazin did not match the reality of much of the population in his hometown of Rocroi, which was subject to heavy requisitions.[45] Historian

Marc Blancpain likewise emphasized the differences in experiences between bourgeois "collaborators" and suffering people: "Even if it eventually had, for the Russians and the French, some consequences that one might interpret as happy, and even if the discipline, the good will and the charm of many of the tsar's officers often left rather agreeable memories to some, the occupation of guarantee was experienced, by the population as a whole and as are all occupations, as an insupportable and ruinous humiliation."[46]

Painful as the occupation was, however, even among the lower classes there is significant evidence of sociability between occupiers and occupied. Already in 1815, describing how British troops were helping French peasants harvest the fields around Paris, General Cavalié Mercier recounted:

> Further good consequences are very perceptible in our village. All mistrust and dislike of each other are at an end; and our people are now quite on an intimate and friendly footing with the peasantry. Many an amicable little knot may be seen of an evening sitting at their doors enjoying at once the cool air, their pipes, and the pleasures of conversation, or rather of trying to understand each other. Some of the villagers have already picked up a little English, and our men a little French. The gayest of the latter occasionally mix in the rustic dance; and although rather rough and bearish in their manner of swinging the girls about, yet are they sought after as partners, the pretty *paysanne* who has for her partner *un canonier* evincing in her look and manner a degree of satisfaction not to be mistaken. Already symptoms of jealousy have made their appearance among the young *paysans,* and I have consulted M. Bonnemain on the subject, expressing my fears lest it might disturb the harmony already subsisting. "A bah ! n'y a pas de danger !—n'importe, n'importe," is always his answer; and accordingly neither I nor my officers have observed anything like a diminution of friendship among the males.[47]

During the occupation of guarantee in the northeast, there is considerable evidence that foreign troops mixed with local inhabitants in homes, churches, fields, squares, dance halls, and taverns. Based on the number of administrative regulations and police reports concerning cabarets—for example, in Tourcoing, which in April 1816 and again in October 1817 ordered all establishments selling alcohol to close by nine in the evening in winter and ten in summer—these were sites of regular fraternization between French inhabitants and Allied soldiers. In the Danish zone around Bouchain, where on the anniversary of the return of Louis XVIII in July 1816 three Danish military bands participated in a music competition alongside French national guards, relations became so amicable that a local inhabitant reportedly said to a Danish officer, "Your soldiers are such good boys, one could even entrust them with the key to one's house." In the Russian sector, in 1818, soldiers joined villagers in celebrating the first good harvest in several years. Russian general Loewenstern recalled in a (perhaps overly) rosy light: "Our soldiers mixed with the villagers, waltzed, danced the Cossack to the great joy of the women, courted everyone, and did not seem the least bit astonished to find themselves engaged in the French contredanse."[48]

Sleeping with the (Former) Enemy

Such social contacts sometimes led to more intimate relations. The close proximity between occupiers and occupied provided plenty of opportunity for sex—both paid and unpaid.[49] Based on the number of illegitimate births, which rose in the occupied zone between early 1816 and early 1819, its seems that many foreign troops coupled with local women. In some cases, such couples stayed together, even marrying. Some of these couples settled in France, while others moved to the foreigner's homeland. While both French and Allied authorities sometimes frowned on the "moral corruption" of local women by foreign troops, they did not usually interpret this coupling as a "collaboration" with the enemy. To the contrary, it was often seen as a natural, mostly positive outcome of the "good intelligence" between occupiers and occupied.

In occupied communities, women tended to be more "friendly" than men toward foreign troops, whether out of curiosity, romantic sentiment, or self-interest. During the occupation of Dijon in 1815, local officials denounced the "overly hospitable welcome given to Austrian officers by certain women of high society." In the village of Kientzheim, in the Haut-Rhin, on the feast day of the Visitation in 1816, the wife and daughter of a landlord were refused communion because the girl was suspected of intimacy with the Austrian officer billeted on them. According to a special police commissioner in August 1817, resentment against the Württemberger troops stationed around Wissembourg was limited to the men: "the women are far from sharing it, to the contrary they see these foreigners as friends, toward whom the most complete hospitality, and even the sharing of their purse, becomes for them a gentle duty to fulfill." Similarly, in the Nord, local bourgeoises tended to dote on Russian officers.[50]

Sometimes, French women seduced Allied soldiers for political sabotage or material gain. In March 1816, in the Haut-Rhin, the Austrian military leadership protested that "a quantity of vagabonds and girls of *mauvaise vie,* coming from Belfort, hide in the different garrisons occupied by the troops and debauch the young soldiers, either to pass them on to Swiss recruiters, or solely with the bad intention of distracting them from their duty." To prevent such desertion, which was prohibited by the Second Treaty of Paris, the Austrian general requested the assistance of local subprefects and mayors.[51]

Of course, some Frenchwomen sought to profit by prostituting themselves. Allied armies already had experience with French prostitutes when they invaded the second time. In fact, despite efforts by the Parisian police to limit solicitation, fraternization between Allied—especially Russian—officers and the prostitutes of the Palais-Royal became a source not just of satire but even of legend. As many as three decades later, when the young writer Ivan Turgenev returned to St. Petersburg after his first visit to Paris, the now elderly officers of Russia asked him, with a gleam in their eyes, "Well, and how is our grand old Palais-Royal."[52]

Prostitution was not limited to Paris. In the northeast, countless *filles publiques* plied their trade in the vicinity of Allied garrisons. While it is impossible to provide exact statistics, the frequency of this sort of "fraternization" is attested by the number of complaints lodged by Allied commanders with French authorities. In Tourcoing in December 1816, for instance, Saxon officer Bucher protested, "The captains commanding the two companies in garrison in this town, have just let me know that, once again, several public women keep establishments in different cabarets, one of which is called, I think, *la pomme d'or* [the golden apple]. Already, they have shared with several soldiers of the garrison a bad illness, and it is in consequence that I beg you, to give your orders to put an end to this problem." As this complaint suggests, Allied officers were concerned that prostitutes were infecting their soldiers with venereal disease. In 1817 and 1818, authorities received similar complaints from British, Russian, Prussian, and Austrian as well as Saxon

L'Autrichien sentimental. Colored print by David Noël Dieudonné Finart (artist), Blanchard (engraver), and Basset (publisher), ca. 1815. Anne S. K. Brown Military Collection, Brown University Library.

officers. Although some local officials in turn complained that the foreign officers needed to keep their troops from frequenting such *femmes publiques,* authorities at all levels stepped up their efforts to subject these women to regular medical visits, as required by law, and to deport those not native to their department.[53]

In addition to paying for sex with prostitutes, Allied officers and soldiers seduced local women. In many communities, authorities complained of the "degeneration" of their women and girls by Allied soldiers. In May 1816, the mayor of Niederbronn reported that the occupation of his town by troops from Württemberg had caused an "almost complete moral corruption." Attributing the fraternization between these troops and local girls to the idleness of the soldiers and the commonality of language (German), he wrote, "I have noticed that, since the presence of these troops the depravation of morals has increased to such a point that it surpasses the imagination. Fathers of families suffer, due to the difficulty of containing their daughters, and masters, their servants. . . . News has reached me . . . that . . . several young women have secretly sold, on behalf of their soldier-lovers under arrest, some sugar and coffee belonging to them, in order to bring to them the product of these sales in prison."[54] Among the Russians, the agents of such "moral corruption" were mainly officers, who as soon as they arrived in France rushed to find a mistress. According to Cazin, in Rocroi the commander took as his mistress a young girl of only sixteen years, whose mother "had sold her to pull themselves out of misery." In the same town, an artillery colonel appropriated a young woman of twenty-three, a "virtuous seamstress until then," who initially resisted his advances but ultimately ceded to his "brilliant offers" to aid her mother, a widow with three small children. The colonel gave the mother 5,000 or 6,000 francs, with which she paid her debts and reestablished "her little grocery trade."[55] However, if official complaints are any indication, seduction seems to have been most widespread in the British sector, where troops often promised to take women home with them.[56]

At least some of the liaisons between Allied troops and French women resulted in offspring, often illegitimate. In the diocese of Metz, there are at least two records of single women presenting children for baptism with godfathers in the Bavarian army. In Tourcoing, at least two Saxon troops presented daughters for baptism. In Sedan, on July 12, 1817, a boy named Jules-Nicolas was born to Jean-François-Gérard Junghans, a native of the Ruhr and secretary of the artillery train of the Prussian army, and a local seamstress. Nine months later, on April 11, 1818, this same Junghans married a different resident of Sedan, an eighteen-year-old girl. Also in Sedan, on November 28, 1817, a Prussian quartermaster and member of the "mixed commission" for requisitions, Frédéric Auguste Schober, registered himself as father of a boy, Charles, born to a twenty-year-old Frenchwoman, Caroline Alexandrine Dupuys Some, native of Versailles. Even more revealing than this anecdotal evidence is the rate of illegitimate births in the occupied departments. In the Moselle, the departmental council allotted some 60,000 francs for public assistance to such illegitimate children in the years after 1815. In Sedan, the rate of foundling, illegitimate, and "natural" births topped 15 percent over the course of the occupation, double the usual rate. In at least some of these cases, the couple may have been prevented from marrying by religious differences or administrative hurdles.[57]

Indeed, such mixed marriages were officially frowned upon. According to the papers of the Reverend G. G. Stonestreet, who accompanied the Duke of Wellington from Waterloo to Cambrai, before a British soldier could marry a Frenchwoman, he was supposed to obtain approval from the commander in chief of the occupying army. One reason British soldiers tried to lure their romantic conquests across the Channel was that their requests for permission to marry local women were rarely approved by Wellington: in 1816, he granted such permission to only one soldier; in 1817, to seven; in 1818, to thirty-three. In mid-1816, the commander in chief of the Horse Guards, Adjutant General Harry Calvert, issued a general order specifying that every regiment and battalion must keep a registry of marriages and births, certified by the adjutant. Other Allied commanders were also reluctant to approve such marriages, and French authorities—both religious and civil—demanded extra documentation from foreign soldiers seeking to marry local women. In Tourcoing, before a Saxon minister would marry an army musician to a local girl, he insisted that the mayor certify that the mother of the bride did not object and that, following a public announcement of the wedding in accordance with French law, no one was opposed. In the Bavarian sector, even demobilized soldiers could not obtain a French marriage contract until they had provided not only a birth certificate but also proof that they were unmarried and discharged from the army. In Alsace, although civil authorities were more lenient, at least one priest, in the town of Thann, admonished his female parishioners to frequent the "grand mass" rather than the military camp of the Allies, to avoid marrying foreigners.[58]

In spite of these obstacles, numerous Allied officers and soldiers did in fact marry Frenchwomen during or shortly after the occupation. Although exact statistics of such mixed marriages are impossible to compile, there were at least a handful in most towns where Allied forces were stationed. Soon after the capitulation of Paris, near his camp at Saint-Germain, English grenadier William Lawrence married a local shopkeeper's daughter, with permission of his colonel. In 1817, when he was ordered back to Britain, he took his wife with him, and the couple ultimately settled in Plymouth, where they established a small cabaret. During their stay in Cambrai, other British soldiers took French wives, most of whom came from outside the town to service the foreign troops. For instance, on September 25, 1816, a bootmaker, Thomas King, married Joséphine Lebel, a washerwoman from Clary; on March 4, 1818, a corporal in the English royal artillery, William Livingston, married Adélaïde Céléstine Haquet of Béhéricourt, with four British soldiers as witnesses. In Tourcoing, on June 11, 1818, army musician Karl Wugk, a Saxon native, married Mademoiselle Sophie Vercambre. "Monsieur Charles," as he came to be known, would soon found the municipal symphony of nearby Roubaix. In Colmar, on November 2, 1816, the pharmacist of the Austrian army, Gustave Eisenlohr, married the daughter of a local pastor, and on October 22, just days before the end of the occupation, the Austrian commander's cook married the daughter of a schoolteacher. In the Danish sector, at least twenty soldiers married local women. All but one took their new wives back to Denmark. One of these women was later immortalized for assuming her husband's job—and uniform—as a night watchman to support their family after he fell ill.[59]

Farther up the social scale, numerous marriages were contracted between British officers—as well as statesmen, businessmen, writers, and tourists—and French women. In Givet, three Russian officers contracted alliances with local women. In nearby Landrecies, the frequent social contacts between Russian officers and local inhabitants resulted in at least one union, contracted on October 7, 1820, between Christophe-Simonin Nikszyez of Odessa and Amélie-Constance-Josephe-Bernardine Fanyau, born to a local landowner; their witnesses included a Russian colonel. In Sedan on November 6, 1817, was celebrated a "grand marriage" between Ernest Auguste Maurice de Froelich (native of Silesia, major in the Hussard Regiment of the Royal Guard of Prussia, and aide-de-camp to commander Count von Zieten) and demoiselle Adélaide Perret (native of Neufchâtel, Switzerland, then domiciled in Sedan). Even after the end of the occupation, Allied troops returned—or remained—to marry local girls, as in Sedan, where one Charles Guillaume Hny, treasurer of the Prussian army, married Marie-Anne Garet, daughter of a pensioner. From such marriages issued two of the most well-known families in Sedan.[60]

Making France Home

Whether they married local girls or not, Allied soldiers demonstrated their affinity for France—or at least their ambivalence toward their own country—by staying beyond the end of the occupation. Numerous Allied troops deserted their armies. Whether they were rejecting a military life, feared political repression at home, or were searching for economic opportunity, these foreigners left their families and friends behind to settle in France more or less permanently—sometimes in violation of French law, which restricted immigration. In order to obtain civil rights, including military pensions, some of these foreigners attempted (often by marrying Frenchwomen) to obtain domestication or naturalization—a complicated, lengthy, and rarely successful process.

Following the invasions of 1814 and 1815, there was a wave of desertion among the Allied armies, especially the Russians. In May 1814, dozens of Russian soldiers deserted in the Marne, and the Russian government appointed a lieutenant to hunt for them. Following the invasion of 1815, desertions multiplied among the Russians, including the commandant of the Forty-Ninth Regiment of Infantry, Nahum Gerasimof. In Champagne, Russian troops fled into the woods, where they were often protected by local peasants, who felt no antipathy toward them and needed extra laborers. But desertion was not limited to the Russian contingent. In October 1815, three Austrian cuirassiers deserted on the eve of the departure of their unit from Verrière, where they had been quartered since the end of July. In the northeast, desertions continued, for example among British forces in the Cambrésis.[61]

According to the official military convention regulating the occupation of guarantee, such deserters were supposed to be turned over to Allied officials. There were numerous incidents of foreign deserters being transferred, by French or Allied police, back to their units. In July 1815, a Russian deserter, guilty of theft and suspected of murder, was arrested by a national guard patrol in Brieulles-sur-Meuse and returned under Prussian escort to his commanders. In November, according to the study of the Seine-et-Oise by Jacques Hantraye, three inhabitants of Sèvres were arrested for having "excited" some Allied soldiers to desert as well as to support Napoleon. In December 1816, six deserters from Russia, arrested by French gendarmes after stealing cabbages and potatoes, were detained in the prison of La Force before being turned over to the commandant of the Russian army.[62]

In late 1818, at the moment of the evacuation, there was another rise in desertion. Many men were not eager to return home, especially if—as in Russia—they faced additional years of military service. Already in September, in anticipation of the end of the occupation, there was a wave of desertion among Prussian troops around Sedan. In Alsace, based on the reward of 20 francs per arrested deserter offered by Austrian commander Baron de Frimont, many soldiers stayed beyond the end of the occupation. As one contemporary noted, "Upper Alsace has become a sort of promised land, a land of Cockaigne for a mass of foreigners, heteroclite residues of the armies of invasion." While some of these deserters lived on the margins of society in their new homeland, suspected of "delinquency" by the authorities, most assimilated into their adopted communities, practicing agricultural or artisanal trades, socializing with fellow ex-soldiers and tradesmen, and even marrying local women. Although statistical data is lacking, anecdotal evidence of such deserters suggests that at least some Allied troops developed relatively close relations with the communities in which they were stationed.[63]

With the occupation of guarantee over, French authorities were more reluctant to turn deserters over to their respective governments. In November 1818, the prefect of the Meuse refused to extradite to the Prussian army commander, now in Luxembourg, some deserters, unless instructed by his superiors. Early the next year, the prefect of the Nord reported to the interior minister:

> Several troops of the regiment of the [British] Prince Regent garrisoned in the Department during the occupation of part of France by the foreign army, most carrying leave papers, have just returned to the communes where they were garrisoned and propose to stay there by forming alliances with some Demoiselles of these communes who, with the permission of their parents, consent to marry them. I think, Monseigneur, that for these holders of leaves who have a means of subsistence, that there is no disadvantage to permitting them to establish themselves in France, but I would like to know your intentions on the procedure to follow with regard to deserters from the foreign corps who take refuge in France and desire to settle here.

In response to queries regarding desertions, the minister of police issued a memorandum, in May 1819, stating that Allied troops found in France after the evacuation should be considered as any other foreigners seeking asylum, according to the law. Some of these immigrants applied for official status as "domiciled" (requiring five years of residence) or "naturalized" (requiring ten) in France. However, only a handful managed to become French citizens.[64]

Although it is next to impossible to quantify the Allied troops who stayed in France beyond the occupation, some of them left traces well into the nineteenth century, across multiple generations. Decades later, their descendants may be identified, living in the same communities. One such case was a Pole, Jean Bartholomovy, who on May 15, 1816, married, in the church of Auvers-sur-Oise, a Frenchwoman, Marie Dubac, with whom he had several children. In 1851, listed as a day worker, he resided in the same commune with his wife and children. In 1866, his wife, now widowed and aged seventy-four, still lived in the same place with their thirty-two-year-old son, a building painter. In their genealogical research on British families who settled around Cambrai in this period, Arnaud Gabet and Christianne Lepie noted a similar rootedness. As Hantraye concludes of the occupation, it "modified, if only temporarily, the landscape of communes. Even if the contingents succeeded each other rapidly, they were present even in the heart of the domicile of civilians."[65]

"The Greatest Harmony Reigns"

Even if they did not integrate over the long term, during the occupation of guarantee Allied troops and French inhabitants cohabited in relative peace. While the French did not always embrace their former enemies as true "friends," many of them adopted a range of relatively benign attitudes toward the foreigners, from bare tolerance, through bemusement and respect, to camaraderie and even romance. Despite the challenges of agricultural crisis as well as foreign occupation, between 1815 and 1818 daily life went on more or less as normal in most communities in France, even along the northeastern frontier. This sense of normalcy enabled at least some reconciliation between occupiers and occupied.

"Harmony" was the word used most commonly by observers on both sides to characterize relations between French inhabitants and foreign troops. Along with "good intelligence," reports from local informants employed synonyms such as "tranquillity," "calm," and "order" to describe the situation in the occupied zone. Following the disruption of the initial military invasion, by mid-1816 relations between occupiers and occupied had improved: according to reports, Calais, for example, seemed to "enjoy a rather satisfying tranquillity," and around Lille, "the Foreign soldiers forming the garrisons and encampments in the department of the Nord continue to comport themselves with discipline and to live with much intelligence with the inhabitants of the country." Similar reports of "harmony" between occupiers and occupied continued into the next year. In July 1817, the subprefect of Avesnes reported to the minister of police, "My Arrondissement is quiet. The greatest harmony reigns between the inhabitants and the Russian Troops of which the majority are encamped in the neighborhood of Maubeuge: in this camp has occurred no disorder." Of course, local authorities often sugarcoated the situation, to reassure the central administration that they had firm control over their jurisdictions.[66]

But Allied officers concurred that, for the most part, "harmony" reigned. When he was removed as commander at Valenciennes due to the troop reduction in spring 1817, British general Sir Charles Colville wrote to the mayor to thank the town notables for the welcome they had given him. Assuring them he would "never forget the good will and spirit of conciliation with which they aided in all the measures it had been his duty to propose during his command," he wrote, "The good result of such conduct on their part was demonstrated by the harmony that existed between the inhabitants and the Garrison, which was so satisfying for us." Concluding that the reorganization of his division was a consequence of the "state of current tranquillity of France," he congratulated the authorities of Valenciennes "that the entry of a British Army in France had so happily succeeded in its object."[67]

Even if such official reports overstated the "harmony" between occupiers and occupied, other evidence, such as the correspondence of mayors and the minutes of municipal council meetings, suggests that in most communities daily life remained largely unchanged by occupation. Throughout this period, these municipal records are remarkably banal in their concerns. Following the initial invasions of 1814 and 1815, when they struggled to react to waves of soldiers moving back and forth, community leaders in the northeast barely noted the foreigners in their midst, at least in their official records. Instead, they focused on such routine matters as excise taxes on drinks and tobacco; maintenance of infrastructure; night patrols; regulation of bakers and butchers; recruitment for the national guard; poor relief; hospitals and schools; wild dogs; the official start of the wine harvest; and royal and religious festivals. While they sometimes skipped traditional illuminations or fireworks for lack of funds, most communities continued to celebrate their usual calendar of festivities, often in conjunction with the occupying troops. In Alsace, each year of the occupation, the town of Strasbourg held its annual Christmas market, though without strolling musicians.[68]

In this context of relative normalcy, French inhabitants and foreign troops were able, in at least some instances, not just to accommodate but even to appreciate each other. Over the course of thirty-six months, the occupation of guarantee promoted international understanding and reconciliation. As one local authority, the subprefect of Thionville in the Prussian sector, concluded in November 1817, "Finally, a two-year stay among us has taught these foreigners to better appreciate a nation that they knew only by its armies, and a deeper knowledge of our national character has necessarily revived their esteem and confidence, dissipated their unfavorable prejudices and moderated, if not entirely destroyed, the profound hatred with which they were animated in the initial period following the peace of 1815."[69] This dissipation of hatred, which worked both ways, facilitated one of the most surprising but significant outcomes of the occupation of guarantee: a spike in cross-cultural exchange and cosmopolitanism.

Chapter Six

Cosmopolitanism

IN MID-1817, as the northeast remained under military occupation, in Paris a less serious "battle" was being waged in gardens and on stages, one that suggested a more symbiotic relationship between the French and their former enemies. The "Combat of the Mountains" involved entrepreneurs who, in their struggle for a share of the leisure market, built dueling *montagnes russes,* or "Russian mountains," in parks including Belleville, Tivoli, and Beaujon. Early versions of roller coasters constructed of wood, these "mountains" were inspired by the Russian tradition of sledding on hills made of ice, which was imported to France following the invasion of 1815. Beginning in late 1816, when the foreign minister's sister, the Marquise de Montcalm, remarked in her journal that they were "a pleasure very much in fashion," these *montagnes russes* were so popular that they became the subject of numerous lithographs and plays. The piece that garnered the most attention was *Le combat des montagnes,* which depicted the battle between various entrepreneurs of amusements—as well as their sidekicks, including a vaguely Russian-looking shop clerk named Calicot—at the Théâtre des Variétés in mid-1817.[1] Integrally connected to the occupation of guarantee, the "Combat of the Mountains" illustrates the tension between cosmopolitanism and nationalism. Frequented by foreign dignitaries, officers, and tourists as well as French elites, on the one hand the *montagnes russes* exemplified a gentler side of the postwar occupation: a cosmopolitan culture, centered on Paris. On the other hand, the cultural "combat" provoked by them reflected a growing concern about foreign influence.

Cosmopolitanism, in the sense of tolerance of and curiosity about peoples of different nations, religions, and races, predated the revolutionary period. Since at least the reign of Louis XIV, the French capital had been a center of exchange between elites from around Europe. Even in the United Kingdom, Francophilia prevailed among at least the aristocratic class, for whom the Grand Tour, with a requisite stay in Paris, became a rite of passage. Peaking during the Enlightenment, when elites traveled far and wide and *philosophes* forged an international Republic of Letters, cosmopolitanism was threatened by the outbreak of the French Revolution and the ensuing wars, which divided the educated classes and separated the French from other nations. For over two decades, cross-cultural contact had been limited to officers and soldiers on campaign and émigrés in exile from revolutionary regimes.[2]

With the return of peace, there was a revival of international travel and cosmopolitan sentiment, not just among the hundreds of thousands of troops who invaded France but also among tens of thousands of civilians who could now move freely across the Continent. Officers, royals, diplomats, and their entourages renewed contact with each other, first in Paris, then in London, where they were welcomed by the British prince regent, and finally in Vienna, where the congress to reconfigure the map of Europe met (with a brief interruption to remobilize against Napoleon) from September 1814 until June 1815. As Brian Vick has shown, this period saw a resurgence of cross-cultural elite sociability, in festivals, salons, newspapers and prints, religious services, balls, theaters, and other amusements, which served to cement a cosmopolitan "European" identity.[3]

Once the Congress of Vienna concluded, this cosmopolitan culture centered in France, particularly Paris. Beginning in the summer of 1815, as Allied troops covered two-thirds of the country, foreign statesmen journeyed to Paris. Over the next few months, they were joined by tens of thousands of foreign civilians, who traveled to France to assist the Allied diplomats, service the occupying troops, or merely amuse themselves. Alongside a number of former imperial officials and demobilized troops from the Grand Empire who were now refugees from their homelands, this massive foreign presence created an unprecedented opportunity for cross-cultural contact.[4] Noted in contemporary travelogues, themselves a product of resurgent cosmopolitanism, this large diversity of peoples in a relatively small space promoted considerable exchange of different customs, including linguistic idioms, foods, fashions, dances, and literary styles, as well as political ideas. This (sometimes forced) contact encouraged a new, or renewed, familiarity with other cultures at virtually all levels of society, generating a practical sort of cosmopolitanism among popular classes as well as an aesthetic and intellectual one among more elite groups. At the same time, however, this contact provoked anxiety on all sides, fueling the rise of nationalism.

While the literature on nationalism has raised awareness of the role of the Revolutionary and Napoleonic Wars in forging national identity in Britain, Germany, and other countries fighting against France, it has tended to overstate the breadth and intensity of anti-French sentiment, while overlooking the role of the postwar occupation in reshaping this identity, sometimes in a less exclusively nationalist way. Important intellectual movements such as romanticism, historicism, and liberalism blossomed during the transition from war to peace, when Paris was reopened to the writers and artists of Europe. The period also saw the rise of modern consumer culture and public spectacle, often identified with the Belle Époque but already ubiquitous in Paris in the late 1810s. All these developments were intimately linked to the aftermath of war, particularly the multinational occupation. In this context, the French endeavored to reappropriate foreign fashions—and Fashion more generally—to reassume a position of cultural dominance in Europe. The occupation of guarantee was thus key to remaking Paris as the capital of the world in the nineteenth century.[5]

A Factory of Nations

The invasions of France in 1814 and 1815 introduced its inhabitants to foreign peoples, as unprecedented numbers of troops from all over Europe blanketed most of the country. Riding on horseback or marching on foot, these men and accompanying women made quite an impression. In northern Alsace, a Lutheran pastor, Heinrich Hermann Weissmann, recounted the 1815 invasion in the parish register: "As incredible as it may seem, yet it is proven that, during three months over the summer, eighty thousand soldiers of all the nations, supplied with billets for lodging, were sheltered and nourished in the houses of the inhabitants . . . No one at Soutz [*sic*] remembers having experienced such passings of men." In Marseille, inundated by Sicilian as well as English troops, the royalist Julie de Pellizzone employed similar language in her diary: "Never have so many extraordinary figures been gathered here, I believe there are some come from the four parts of the world. One hears only foreign languages, one sees only forbidding faces." Viewing this sudden flood of peoples out of their "ancient beds" through the lens of the history of the barbarian invasions by Gregory of Tours, the republican writer Edgar Quinet later recalled, in perhaps the most evocative characterization of the invasions, "I too had seen the *fabrique des nations* [factory of nations] engender peoples upon peoples to engulf us."[6]

Over the succeeding months, this *fabrique des nations* remained on display in France, not only in their daily routines in the towns where they were garrisoned, but especially in periodic reviews, exercises, and celebrations, which attracted crowds of spectators. Following the arrival of the Allies in Paris in July, there were several reviews of troops, including a joint inspection of two hundred thousand soldiers on the fields of Saint-Denis. Overseen by the sovereigns of Russia, Austria, Prussia, Holland, Bavaria, and Württemberg, as well as the Duke of Wellington, and attended by a crowd of sullen Parisians, this two-hour maneuver involved, according to British observer Captain Gronow, "one of the most illustrious and numerous staffs ever brought together." In mid-September, on the Plain des Vertus, in Champagne, there was a review of 150,000 Russian troops, hosted by Alexander I, who brought the chef Marie-Antoine Carême from Paris to supply elaborate dinners over three days. Intended to impress, this show of force served to introduce the Russians to other foreign armies as well as French civilians, as noted by Harriet Leveson-Gower, Countess Granville: "Here also, for the first time, the people of Europe watched the mass of the turbulent ranks of the Cossacks, the wild cavalry of the steppes, whose exploits during Napoleon's retreat had given them a worldwide reputation." Even after the departure of the Allied sovereigns in October, such spectacles continued on a semiregular basis, particularly during the annual reviews of Allied troops by Wellington on the plains of Denain and the joint exercises and ceremonies on the eve of their departure from France in late 1818.[7]

Menacing as they could be, the foreigners aroused considerable curiosity among the French, who profited (sometimes literally) from their presence. In the Russian sector, General Loewenstern recalled how one contingent's summer camp on an island in the Meuse River attracted spectators: "A crowd gathered on the island, especially on Sunday, to watch our divine service, which took place under a beautiful and spacious tent, in a portable church." The locals were no less intrigued by the steam rooms set up by the Russians along the river: "There is nothing more curious," he recalled, "than the stupefaction of the inhabitants at this spectacle [of Russian soldiers jumping from steam room to icy river and back]! The women especially were fond of watching our soldiers exiting the Meuse as intrepid gladiators. I made some excuses to some of them, but there was no way to find screens for so many grenadiers, and they continued to focus their eyeglasses on them, which reassured me about my scruples."[8]

Such curiosity is vividly attested by contemporary illustrations, produced in great number in the second half of the 1810s. Sketches, paintings, and prints of foreign troops and civilians were ubiquitous in galleries, periodicals, and shop windows. Rendered by some of the best artists of the day—including Eugène Delacroix, who captured the invading troops in drawings and prints such as *Campaign Baggage*, an etching depicting a British soldier accompanied by a pregnant wife, two children, and household belongings—these illustrations satirized the "national" traits of foreign troops.[9] Often appearing in the popular "Bon Ton" series published by Martinet, they typologized the various foreign contingents. This stereotyping is best seen in a series called *Types et costumes de soldats étrangers* by Carle Vernet, which captured the physiognomies of the Allies.[10]

French observers were particularly struck by the uniforms of the foreign troops. As the troops arrived in the capital, Parisians came to gawk at the foreign mode of dress. Of his arrival on the Champs-Elysées in Paris, the British captain Gronow remembered, "Being in uniform, I created an immense amount of curiosity amongst the Parisians; who, by the way, I fancied regarded me with no loving looks." In Marseille, Julie

Pellizzone admired the blue uniforms and classical helmets of the Sicilian cavalry, whose officers looked "rather like theatrical heroes."[11]

The foreign invaders also impressed French observers with their sounds, especially their music. During the initial invasion in 1815, crowds gathered in the Jardin du Luxembourg in Paris every evening between six and seven o'clock to hear a concert given by musicians of the Second Regiment of the Prussian guard. In Marseille, Julie Pellizzone praised a concert given by English and Sicilian troops to a large crowd: "Neither English nor Sicilian music is superior to ours, but their trumpets are worth infinitely more than ours[;] they have a grave and majestic sound that pleases me a lot, and every time I hear them, I believe I am hearing the overture of a grand opera." In Tourcoing, locals gathered each day on the Grand Place to hear the music of the Saxon contingent, while in Valenciennes, according to an English soldier, the British military band was a "great object of attraction. It played every morning, and all the beauty and fashion of Valenciennes assembled to hear it." In Colmar, Georges Ozaneaux noted in his diary that crowds gathered in the town square to hear concerts by the Austrians each Sunday and holiday. Finding the music "brilliant," if somewhat repetitive, Ozaneaux regretted it would end with the occupation. In August 1818, he wrote, "It is true that we will no longer have their delicious music, but one will sacrifice this loss for the happiness of being liberated from the musicians."[12]

Of all the Allied contingents, most intriguing to the French were the Cossacks and the so-called "English Cossacks," the Scottish Highlanders. In Napoleonic propaganda, the Cossack had been stereotyped as a barbarian with a large bonnet, thick beard, long lance, and strong odor, who subsisted on raw or grilled animal flesh, was known to steal (especially watches), and took pleasure in setting fire to houses, harvests, and whole villages.[13] This caricature of the Cossack was modified, however, by actual experience with soldiers from the Russian Empire. In part as a result of a concerted campaign of "seduction" by the Russian leadership, fear of these eastern troops dissipated. While "Cossack" remained synonymous with "thief" in popular culture, Russians were increasingly characterized by French observers as gentle and humane, if still exotic.

Equally exotic—but, given French animosity toward the English, more sympathetic—to the French were the Scottish. During the military occupation of Paris in summer 1815, Highland troops attracted crowds of spectators. As Countess Granville reported to her sister of a visit to the Louvre, where a contingent of such troops was guarding the painting gallery: "The whole length of it was filled with soldiers of every nation, some Highlanders, who attracted great attention and took it as a great compliment. One of them said, 'They look more at us than at the d——d pictures.'" Similarly, a collection of amusing anecdotes about the British remarked:

> Among the Allied troops who entered and stayed in Paris in 1815, those who attracted the attention and fixed the curiosity of the women of the capital, were some Scottish regiments, whose singularity of dress was a totally new subject for them. These Highlanders, instead of pants, wear little kilts which do not even cover their knees. The slightest movements exposed their large posteriors which caused to flee the *spectatrices* who, nonetheless, while running away glanced back with a furtive eye. . . . At the Palais-Royal, one followed them like beings who had fallen suddenly from the sky.

Publishers capitalized on the curiosity about these foreigners by producing numerous prints, satires, and plays about the Scottish Highlanders, as well as translations of some of their native tales. Depicted with muscular legs emerging from tartan kilts, the Scottish Highlanders symbolized, in a more benign way than the often menacing Cossacks, the exoticism of the occupying forces.[14]

"The Most Wonderful Show-Box"

The exotic troops were accompanied by numerous foreign dignitaries. In 1814, one English observer in the capital wrote to a friend, "Paris is certainly at this moment the most wonderful show-box in the world. It has within its walls as many live emperors, kings, generals, and eminent persons of all kinds, as the ingenious Mrs. Salmon ever exhibited in wax."[15]

This show-box returned the following year after the Battle of Waterloo. As they moved toward Paris, Allied sovereigns were sighted, often together, at several points in eastern France. On the evening of July 9, for instance, the three sovereigns arrived at Châlons-sur-Marne to acclamation from the local people—the same people, one commentator noted, who only eight days before had cried "Vive the Emperor

Napoleon!"[16] Once in Paris, the sovereigns and their entourages were on display for the capital and, via the press, much of the rest of the country. Ensconced in the Elysée Palace, Tsar Alexander attracted crowds of admirers everywhere he went. By early August, the *Journal de Paris* reported, the sovereigns were joined by their wives—provoking "emulation" among local novelty merchants who hoped to profit from their stay—and their families, including the Russian grand dukes Nicholas and Constantine, the Prussian royal prince Wilhelm, and the Austrian archduchess Léopoldine, who was pledged to marry a French prince.[17]

At the same time, foreign ministers and diplomats rushed from their home bases to the French capital, which by late July received Russian ministers Pozzo di Borgo and Count Karl von Nesselrode, the Prussian foreign minister Karl August von Hardenberg and ambassador Wilhelm von Humboldt, Austrian foreign minister Klemens von Metternich, and British ambassador Sir Charles Stuart and foreign minister Viscount Castlereagh. Lady Castlereagh, accompanied by a lady-in-waiting, courier, and entourage, settled into a new embassy on the fashionable rue du Faubourg Saint-Honoré, in a house previously owned by Napoleon's younger sister, Pauline. Here she hosted many a soirée, for French and foreign elites. Among her frequent guests were Madame de Staël, Sir Walter Scott, Prince Schwarzenberg, General Blücher, Tsar Alexander, and the Duke of Wellington.[18] The dignitaries remained in Paris for at least three months, until the signature of the Second Treaty of Paris.

During their stay, the foreign sovereigns and statesmen appeared often in public. In late July, the king of Prussia, his son, and Grand Duke Nicholas of Russia viewed a Panorama of Calais.[19] The Austrian emperor and his son toured a number of educational institutions, including the royal boarding school in Saint-Denis for the daughters of Legion of Honor members; a nursery for foreign plants; and the royal library.[20] Meanwhile, as they had in 1814, the Prussian king and his son visited a number of palaces around Paris. Such visits influenced the worldview of a generation of sovereigns. In 1814, the future Wilhelm I of Prussia accompanied his father on a visit to Versailles; fifty-five years later, after his victory in the Franco-Prussian War, he chose the palace as the site for his proclamation of the German Reich.[21]

In the fall of 1815, the foreign sovereigns headed for home. En route, they stopped in various towns in eastern France, where they again made an impression on the local population. Many foreign statesmen, including Metternich and Castlereagh, departed from the French capital, and the Duke of Wellington moved his headquarters to Cambrai. However, throughout the occupation of guarantee, a number of foreign diplomats and generals remained in—or returned to—Paris, to consult with counterparts and seek out amusements. On several occasions, the Allied sovereigns also returned to France. After a review of his troops on the frontier in August 1817, the king of Prussia paid another visit to Paris, provoking the Marquise de Montcalm to remark in her diary, "One would have found it more appropriate that he postpone his trip to France to the era when the foreign troops would have departed; but there are some matters of tact that are too fine to penetrate the German skin." Criticizing his "common" behavior, she continued, "the king of Prussia is continually alone on foot in the streets, goes every day to the Variétés [Theater], and seems to have developed such a taste for Paris that he would, I believe, voluntarily trade his realm for a pretty hôtel in the Chaussée d'Antin."[22]

"All the World's in Paris"

This "show-box" contained ordinary civilians, too. In the winter of 1814, a song popular in London demanded, "London now is out of town/Who in England tarries?/Who can bear to linger there?/When all the world's in Paris?"[23] By the next summer, it seemed indeed that all the world was rushing to the French capital. Tens of thousands of tourists invaded France, touring monuments and museums, patronizing restaurants and theaters, frequenting salons and pleasure gardens, and mixing with local inhabitants. Coming from all across Europe, especially Great Britain, these foreigners sometimes settled in the capital for months or even years, contributing to the revival of Paris as a cosmopolitan metropolis.

After two decades with little access to France, European travelers of all classes were eager to partake of its sights, sounds, smells, and tastes. As British artillery officer Cavalié Mercier recalled, "Be it remembered that, at that period, the continent of Europe was almost a *terra incognita* to Englishmen, to whom everything, therefore, even trifles, bore a degree of interest, which our present intimate acquaintance may cause to appear puerile at the present day." No sooner did the Allied armies enter French territory than the country was flooded with thousands of foreign aristocrats, businessmen, artisans, writers, artists, and tourists, including many women and children. In the words of historian Margery Elkington, "It was a true invasion, a peaceful army marching in the steps of the soldiers."[24]

Many of the visitors in this "peaceful army" came from Great Britain. Already in 1814, according to visitor J. W. Ward, "There are a great many English here [in Paris]; however, I think the stock don't increase; as many go as come. They proceed in the old way—grumbling and enhancing the price of everything."[25] Beginning the next year, however, the stock of English across the Channel increased dramatically. According to the *Moniteur universel,* in 1815, 13,832 British travelers arrived in France; in 1818, the number rose to 19,038. By 1816, 68 percent of the foreigners in temporary lodgings in the capital were British. In July of that year, the *Times* of London quoted the *Gazette de France* as boasting, "[M]any English of distinction arrive in Paris. A great number take apartments in Paris, or country houses, for the whole of the fine season . . . They now come to study our manners, our customs, our language, our urbanity, and our arts, and do so like good neighbours, sincerely reconciled." That year, more British than French subjects were presented at the court of Louis XVIII. By 1817, according to an English publication, 1,500 British families had established themselves in Paris, where the cost of living was cheaper than at home. While some stayed at the newly established Hôtel Meurice on the rue de Rivoli, many of these visitors rented *hôtels garnis,* or furnished apartments, usually in the western sector of the Right Bank.[26] During the Restoration, the British formed a veritable "colony" in the French capital.

Under the occupation of guarantee, the British established similar, if smaller, outposts in other localities, too, especially the port of Calais and the occupied towns of Cambrai and Valenciennes. Of this latter town, one English visitor in 1816 recounted, "The streets were crowded with English, French, Germans, Prussians, Russians, Flemings, and Dutch, in every possible variety of costume. Some were reading the journals on the Grande Place, some canvassing the affairs of Europe, and others listlessly watching the passing scene. English equipages, English grooms leading English horses, English dogs, and English shops, met the eyes at

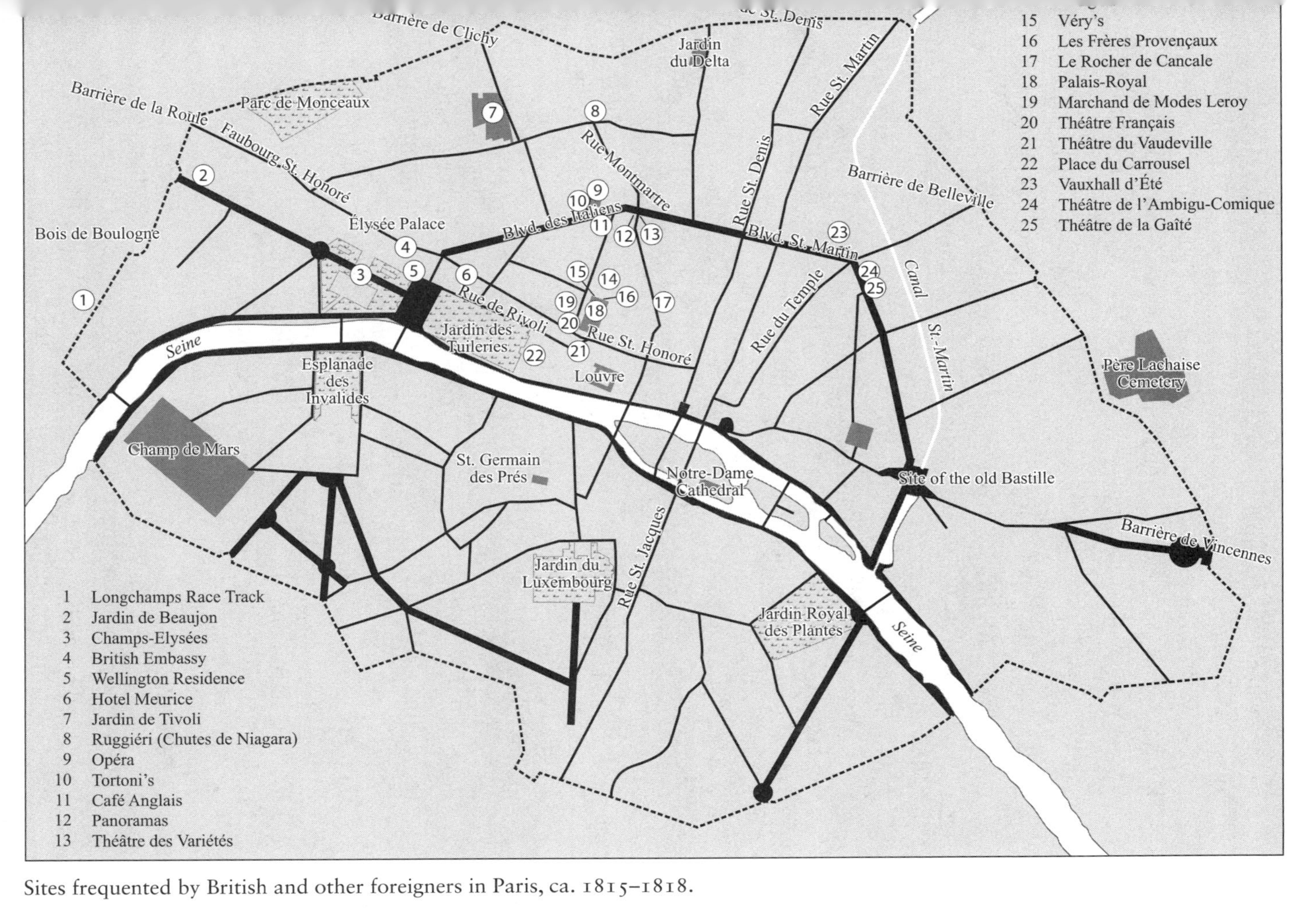

Sites frequented by British and other foreigners in Paris, ca. 1815–1818.

every turn; indeed, the number of English trades-people was surprising; almost every other shop exhibited an English name."[27] Among these visitors were a number of English women, who came to accompany British soldiers or seek new opportunities—or men—abroad. This influx of women and their families became so great that it attracted the attention of both French and British officials. Despite efforts to restrict their entry, by February 1816, some 1,700 Englishwomen and a similar number of children had arrived in the department of Pas-de-Calais, burdening local authorities with demands for lodging and food.[28]

The British were not the only foreigners to visit France in these years. Following a long tradition of Russian pilgrimage to Paris, Russian aristocrats established a small colony in the French capital. Suggesting that there was also a sizable contingent of German travelers, in summer 1815 the French diplomatic representative in Prussia wrote to Talleyrand, "Berlin is now more on the Seine than on the Spree."[29]

The foreign colonies became so substantial that they generated concern among commentators back home, who launched campaigns against "emigration" to France. In Britain, already in September 1815, a published *Letter Addressed to an English Lady of Fashion at Paris* discouraged the exodus abroad: "Let us then, my dear friend, exert all the persuasion in our power to prevail on our countrymen, after having gratified curiosity, to leave the shores of France, and return to the post allotted them." Despite such pleas, in July 1816 the *Times* of London reported, "The emigration from England to France continues to be indeed alarming . . . They [the tourists] take the bread from the mouth of the slaving workman in England and lavish it on French luxuries and French amusements . . . The words *national bankruptcy* begin to be familiar to our ears." The same year a poem, "Emigration; or England and Paris," complained that the exodus was draining labor and corrupting morality in Britain.[30] In 1817, a satirist, William Jerdan, tried to counter emigration to France with a three-volume mock travelogue, *Six Weeks in Paris, or a Cure for the Gallomania, by a Late Visitant.*[31]

Ignoring such pleas, foreigners swarmed the cities of France. For civilian as well as military visitors, the most popular sites included the Louvre Museum (even after much of its art was removed by the Allies), theaters and restaurants, the pleasure gardens—including the *montagnes russes*—on the city outskirts, and especially the Palais-Royal, where for-

Palais-Royal: La sortie du n° 113. Drawing in pen, washed in Chinese ink, by Georg-Emmanuel Opiz, 1815. BNF.

eigners indulged in food, drink, gambling, and prostitutes while mingling with French elites. The scene was depicted by British captain Gronow in memoirs published half a century later:

> France has often been called the centre of European fashion and gaiety; and the Palais Royal, at the period to which I refer, might be called the very heart of French dissipation. . . . Mingled together, and moving about the area of this oblong-square block of buildings, might be seen, about seven o'clock P.M., a crowd of English, Russian, Prussia, Austrian, and other officers of the Allied armies, together with countless foreigners from all parts of the world. Here, too, might have been seen the present King of Prussia, with his father and brother, the late king, the Dukes of Nassau, Baden and a host of continental princes, who entered familiarly into the amusements of ordinary mortals, dining *incog.* at the most renowned restaurants, and flirting with painted female frailty.[32]

Following the departure of most Allied troops and statesmen at the end of 1815, the numbers of foreigners decreased, but Russian and

German as well as British visitors remained a common sight in Paris. The British remained ubiquitous at the capital's main attractions, including the Jardin des Tuileries, the Longchamp racetrack, and the Opéra, and the streets of Paris resounded with English shouts and songs. From their headquarters in the border town of Maubeuge, Russian officers made frequent trips to the capital. General Loewenstern sojourned regularly in Paris, in his view "the only city in the world in which one may live as one intends," where he frequented salons hosted by the likes of Madame de Staël, before whom he trembled not to make a mistake in French. Parisian salon society was infiltrated by foreigners to such an extent that, in 1817, the former director of the Louvre, Vivant Denon, warned his lover, about to arrive from Italy, "you will not find this Paris that you have heard described, this brilliant urbanity that characterized its society. One no longer knows where to find this society which is divided [politically] and meets anymore only without confidence in a few households which are most often foreign." Similarly, in April 1817, the American George Ticknor, on a Grand Tour of Europe, wrote of the salon of Madame de Staël, which included Wilhelm von Humboldt and Augustus Schlegel, "[I]t is curious that on this occasion more than half the company were foreigners, and . . . the two who entertained the rest more than any others were Germans." Even the English were heard to complain that they were "sorry to see London transferred to Paris and to rediscover there their England, in which, during so many years, they had found themselves prisoners."[33]

In addition to visiting French attractions, the various foreign "colonies" established their own institutions. In Paris, special schools, churches, groceries, and pharmacies were created for the British. The British Embassy served as a center for receptions, dinners, balls, and even Anglican church services. British visitors also frequented a Café Anglais on the Boulevard des Italiens, as well as the more exclusive Cercle Anglais, patronized by Wellington, among others, before it was banned by the French government in 1825. (A similar project for a German *casino littéraire* was blocked in 1816 by the French administration as a political threat.)[34]

One of the most popular institutions was the international bookshop Galignani's, then located on the rue Vivienne near the royal library and still in existence today on the rue de Rivoli. Founded around 1800 by an Italian as an "English, French, Italian, German and Spanish library," focused on publishing a collection of British classics for foreign readers, its business exploded with the influx of foreigners. In addition to creating a circulating library with over two hundred English and continental periodicals, the bookdealer founded a daily newspaper, *Galignani's Messenger.* Alongside news of Paris and London and reviews of French plays, the paper featured correspondence from English men and women residing in Paris to their compatriots back home, and advertisements for goods and services of relevance to British expatriates. In the aftermath of the Napoleonic Wars, Galignani also published a number of other periodicals and guidebooks for foreigners in the French capital.[35]

The flood of foreigners to France was a boon to publishers. In the mid-1810s appeared a number of publications devoted to promoting—and satirizing—cross-cultural exchange, including a "political tableau" of the German lands, aimed at improving Franco-German understanding following a decade of reciprocal invasion and occupation; the periodical *Panorama d'Angleterre,* published briefly in 1816 to report in French on English affairs; and the *Éphémérides anglaises,* which replaced it. For English-speaking audiences, there arose a veritable subgenre of literature about British living in Paris, including the best-selling *Fudge Family in Paris* by Thomas Moore, framed as a series of letters from a penny-pinching British civil servant on mission in France and his young adult children, who revel in the food, fashions, and amusements of Paris, including the *montagnes russes.*[36]

Beginning in the mid-1810s, there was also a surge in guidebooks for foreign visitors to France. Describing a similar itinerary of monuments and attractions, most of these guides commented on the sad condition of the Louvre in the wake of the reappropriation of art by the Allies. For British travelers, some guidebooks were published in English, such as Peter Hervé's *How to Enjoy Paris: Being a Guide to the Visitor of the French Metropolis in Two Volumes,* which included the history of France since the Second Restoration. Written as a series of letters from a Briton in Paris to a friend back home, it began, "Go hasten to Paris, my dear friend, with all your susceptibility of grand impressions."[37]

First Impressions

Many foreign visitors shared their "grand impressions" in letters, journals, memoirs, and travelogues. Following the tradition of military memoirs by participants in the campaigns of the Revolutionary and Napoleonic Wars, they recorded their observations of the country and its inhabitants. Part and parcel of this cosmopolitan moment, their writings share some common themes about the characteristics of the French versus other nationalities while also highlighting the way in which the occupation promoted a mixing of peoples and customs.

Of the foreign descriptions of France under occupation that have survived, most are British. However, the few extant diaries and memoirs from other nations suggest that German and Russian troops shared many of the same impressions. Like the British, these other foreign observers tended to express incredulity, and even melancholy, at the whirlwind of events during the previous few years. Exhibiting nostalgia even for their archenemy Bonaparte, they lingered over the ruins of his regime. Praising the improvements made to Paris by the revolutionary and especially the imperial regimes, they often bemoaned the damages wrought by the Allies during the invasions. Regarding French mores, foreign commentators criticized their moral degradation, their political inconstancy, and especially their frivolity in the face of defeat and poverty. On the other hand, they lauded the French sense of pride, love of liberty, and joie de vivre. Mary and Percy Shelley concluded after a tour of the country in 1817:

> The manners of the French are interesting, although less attractive, at least to Englishmen, than before the last invasion of the Allies: the discontent and sullenness of their minds perpetually betrays itself. Nor is it wonderful that they should regard the subjects of a government which fills their country with hostile garrisons, and sustains a detested dynasty on the throne, with an acrimony and indignation of which that government alone is the proper object. This feeling is honourable to the French, and encouraging to all those of every nation in Europe who have a fellow feeling with the oppressed, and who cherish an unconquerable hope that the cause of liberty must at length prevail.[38]

In general, foreign travelers emphasized the ease of life in France. Although Allied visitors occasionally complained about a particular lodging, they mostly relished the good life available to them. Of his quarters in an Alsatian village in 1815, for instance, a Bavarian soldier,

Johann Michael Antlsperger, noted, "After the Conclusion of the Peace we had it a lot easier. We stayed put for the whole of August in Buschweiler and all were happy here."[39] In fact, soldiers such as Antlsperger often expressed regret when ordered to leave France.

Foreign travelers often viewed the French as more "civilized" than other peoples. Travelogues from this period hierarchized various nationalities, with Cossacks, Austrians, and especially Prussians ranked the lowest. These nationalities were often disparaged for their "barbarism," not just by the French but also by other foreigners, especially the English. On their tour of France, Mary and Percy Shelley blamed every desolate village and stolen cow on the "Cossacs" [*sic*] who had passed through two or three years earlier. The Prussians were denounced even by other German speakers, such as the Bavarian Antlsperger.

Babel on the Seine

As noted by many travelogues and memoirs, the influx of foreign tourists and troops made France, especially Paris, a veritable Babel. In public spaces throughout the capital and occupied region one heard—and read—English, German, Russian, Hungarian, Polish, Danish, Italian, Gaelic, and even Latin, among other languages. Visiting a deserted *maison de plaisance* in Montmartre, Seth William Stevenson noted, "Its interior stucco, covered with innumerable scribblings in French, German and English, told us who had been the last successive occupiers of this forlorn and ruined habitation." During the invasion, an inhabitant of Lunéville, in Lorraine, remembered, "It was very remarkable to hear the merchants of the town established at the camp [of the Allies], negotiate prices and dispute each other in French, German and Russian words; because, more or less, everyone knew a few words of each." In Paris, as well as around Cambrai, English began to challenge French as the lingua franca. In the country around Étreillers, General Cavalié Mercier observed a group of French farmers chatting with English soldiers, trying on their helmets and belts, and laughing: "[T]heir chief source of amusement appeared to be reciprocally teaching each other English and French words—the attempt at pronouncing which causes infinite fun."[40]

This Babel constituted a source not just of amusement but also of challenge, for both occupier and occupied. Among elites, this challenge could often be overcome by relying on the old lingua franca, French. Still written, if not always fluently spoken, by many aristocratic officers and tourists, French enabled them to communicate with local elites. In British, German, and Russian as well as French archives, many of the letters and decrees by Allied officers to local inhabitants (and each other) are written in French. The use of French by Allied officers is attested by numerous contemporaries, who expressed admiration for their language skills. Often, they remarked on the "beautiful," "unaccented," and "almost native" French of officers from Russia especially.

But for many French as well as foreigners, especially farther down the social scale, the events of 1814 to 1818 were experienced as a literal lack of comprehension. In a vivid anecdote about the invasion of 1814, Edgar Quinet recalled that, with four cavaliers lodged with his family, he could communicate only in the dead language of Latin: "These men, who were Hungarian, spoke Latin to me. I was very astonished to understand them. I did not imagine that one could understand Latin, let alone speak it. Hardly was I convinced that the ancients had been capable of it. However, out of curiosity, maybe out of necessity, I mustered my courage to pronounce several words; from this moment my tongue was loosened. What I would never have dared before my friends, or before my master, I did boldly and fluently with these barbarians." Quinet served as interpreter, until one of these cavaliers insulted him with the Latin phrase, "Te verberabo," meaning "We will whip you." Even when they tried to speak the language of the occupier, the French struggled to make themselves understood. In the summer of 1815, the Englishwoman Helen Maria Williams observed several Parisian ladies parading on the Champs-Elysées who "spoke to the sentinels in their lisping English, and were sometimes answered by the smiling soldier with 'Eh, Ma'am?' for not one word did he comprehend of his own language pronounced with a foreign accent."[41] Although Allied authorities tried to bridge the language gap by issuing bilingual decrees in, say, German and French, such miscomprehension caused frustration and tension.

To meet the challenge of communication, entrepreneurial linguists, translators, interpreters, publishers, and language teachers rushed to offer their services to both French and foreigners. The Allies relied heavily on interpreters, either from their own forces or from local populations, to mediate between their troops and French inhabitants. In August 1816, a Saxon officer at military headquarters in Tourcoing asked the mayor to consider hiring their interpreter, "because we have need of such an interpreter at every moment, as much for lodging as for every other service, because no supply officer knows how to speak French." Although such interpreters were often mistrusted by both sides as spies, they served a crucial role in the occupation of guarantee.[42] To supplement the services of interpreters, professors of English and German among other languages taught courses, as attested by numerous advertisements in French periodicals, and instruction in French was offered to foreigners by Galignani's and other institutions in Paris and elsewhere. To obtain training in French, officers from Denmark, among other countries, even traveled from their headquarters in the northeast to Paris.[43]

But the clearest indicator of the demand for language instruction is probably the number of bilingual and multilingual dictionaries produced in the mid-1810s. Following the model of German-Russian dictionaries published during the campaign of 1813, French and foreign publishers quickly released vocabulary, grammar, and conversation guides for English, German, Russian, and a number of other languages. Beginning in 1814, French booksellers such as Barrois requested official permission to import bilingual dictionaries from British and German publishers. By fall 1815 publishers were advertising a compact *Vocabulaire français, allemand et russe, précédé d'un dialogue à l'usage des militaires français,* with German and Russian words spelled phonetically for French speakers. Over the next few years followed a wave of other manuals to foreign languages, particularly English. Probably the most useful for the occupying forces was Denys de Montfort's sixteen-page vocabulary, published by Plancher in 1815, containing translations for everyday words such as *bread, chicken, salt, pillow, tobacco, soap,* and *hello.*[44]

Aided by such dictionaries, French and foreigners adopted a number of expressions from each other. This linguistic cross-fertilization left its mark. In the region around Landrecies, for instance, popular language retained a number of German and Russian locutions, including *Schnapps* (eau-de-vie), *capout* (kill), *schafen/schlof* (sleep), and *broute/brod* (bread). Contrary to legend, the French *bistrot* did not originate from the Russian word meaning "quick." Not recorded until the 1880s, it seems instead to have emerged from regional dialect for either "lesser servant" or a drink of brandy and coffee. But the occupation did engender other idioms, such as the English expression "mounting Cossack" for riding horseback.[45]

By mixing peoples on French soil, the occupation relied on but also undermined the dominance of French as the lingua franca of Europe. It promoted what Jacques Hantraye has termed an "apprenticeship" of other linguistic and cultural frameworks. This unintended consequence of occupation was recognized at the time. Within a decade of the conclusion of the Napoleonic Wars, a newspaper article concluded, "We have come back a little bit to less exclusive ideas; the hazards of war have made us see close up other nations, other customs; their language has become less foreign to us." Although the author doubted most French would undertake intensive study of another language anytime soon, he highlighted one of the most significant, if also neglected, consequences of the occupation of guarantee. In this Babel, French and foreigner had indeed gotten to know—if not always understand—each other.[46]

Inter-National Taste

French and foreigners also shared culinary traditions. In the context of occupation, food was a source of significant tension. While the French struggled to supply the Allies with the requisitions required by treaty, the Allies often complained that these provisions were inferior to their normal diet. If food solidified differences between nations, however, it also constituted a site of international exchange. Between 1815 and 1818, occupier and occupied had a chance to sample each other's cuisine. While they did not always like what they tasted, this experience helped to spread a cosmopolitan culinary culture down the social scale as well as across the Continent.

The occupation reinforced stereotypes of "national" cuisines. For French observers, each invading force was identified with particular foodstuffs. German-speaking and Russian-speaking forces were associated with potatoes and schnapps or vodka. The British were reputed to consume vast quantities of beef and mutton, washed down with punch or gin. The most barbaric cuisine, however, was identified with the Cossacks, who in one caricature were shown roasting over an open fire whatever they could find. Culinary difference became a tool for the French to reassert their own sense of national superiority in the wake of defeat. This is seen in numerous caricatures of the British as corpulent, gluttonous, ill-mannered, and indifferent to pleasure and taste, such as *Punch in the English Manner,* in which a group imbibes "punch" (urine) from a garden urn; *L'Anglais et le Français, ou Chacun son goût* ("The Englishman and the Frenchman, or To Each His Own"), in which an Englishman lays into a lavish spread of meat and liquor while a Frenchman cuddles a woman; and a duo of images, *Arrival* and *Departure,* showing a Briton before (all skin and bones) and after (supporting his enormous belly on a wheelbarrow) visiting a Paris restaurant, while in the background the cook chases cats for the pot.[47]

The occupation also strengthened the "national" taste of foreigners. In French restaurants, which in this era specialized in restorative soups, British visitors missed hearty meat dishes. Russian troops longed for more familiar foodstuffs, in their case vegetables. Emphasizing that his troops were relatively well provisioned, General Loewenstern nonetheless noted, "The French soup with a tranch of white bread did not at all agree with the stomach of the Russian soldiers. They required cabbages and onions! We rented fields, and the soldiers cultivated them with success." With a supplement of grain provided by Commander Vorontsov, these troops were able to fabricate their preferred beverage, a drink of fermented barley called kvass, which Loewenstern termed "the Bordeaux of the Russian soldier."[48] For occupier and occupied, food was a vector of national identity.

But food also operated as a mechanism for cross-cultural exchange. As a result of the foreign presence, new products and dishes were imported into France. To the French, the Russians bequeathed a taste for the potato, particularly along the route of their invasion in 1815, on the Marne River. From the gardens established by General Loewenstern in Landrecies, the Russians grew enough salted cucumber salad to sell to local inhabitants, "who ended up developing a taste for it." In this period, the French grew so enamored of a number of English products—including punch, beefsteak, pudding, and tea—that popular literature soon urged them to remain true to their own taste. Defending the culinary tradition of France, a poem entitled "Anglomania, or the Anti-French," insisted, "In the art of cuisine and lifestyle,/No people, one knows, can yet surpass us."[49]

Even as the French were sampling foreign dishes, their own cuisine, which had already constituted the international standard, became even more popular among not just elites but ordinary soldiers and tourists, too. Already in 1814, Allied officers and diplomats had indulged in French cuisine to such an extent that during the subsequent invasion of 1815 at least one pamphlet framed a call for resistance as a campaign to keep foreigners from frequenting the restaurants of Paris. "It is not surprising," it exclaimed, "that their Generals and Officers burn to enter France; they would like to try again the restaurants of the Palais Royal." Informed by a proliferating number of guidebooks to restaurants, such as *Le guide des dîneurs, ou Statistique des principaux restaurans de Paris,* which declared itself "indispensable to Foreigners as well as Persons who do not keep house," visitors indulged in lavish meals at the capital's finest establishments. Such meals often featured in letters, travelogues, and memoirs by Allied troops and tourists. One English soldier stationed in the Bois de Boulogne in the summer of 1815 described his delight at experiencing such a "place of refreshment" for the first time:

> Our old comrade in arms soon hushed us into a "Caffe" or, what we would call in England an eating house or cook shop. We were at first struck with the splendor of the place, and thought there was some mistake. The room is boxed off, each box contains cushioned seats, a marble slab table at the end of which is a large looking glass. In one of these we seated ourselves, when a bill of fare was handed to us out of which we ordered such dishes as suited our inclinations. We soon had a dinner set before us fit for noblemen. This done, we retired to another room, where we regaled ourselves with wine etc. Smoking our cigars, reading the news and chatting to our old friend for an hour. When calling for the bill we were astonished to find that each of us had to pay only the trifling sum of two francs and a half, or two shillings and one penny English money.

Symbolizing the English everyman in Paris, the fictional Bob Fudge wrote to his friend: "There's nothing like feeding;/And this is the place for it." Fattening like Louis XVIII and "Boney" until he eventually breaks his stays, the Fudge son exclaims, "How can one not love a country with 685 ways to cook an egg?"[50]

Outside Paris, Allied generals sampled local delicacies while also ordering deliveries of foodstuffs and even hiring chefs from the capital. During his stay in Dijon in the summer of 1815, one Austrian commandant became a "fervent admirer of *produits bourguignons,*" expressing a desire to prolong his stay "in order to refine his taste and encourage local commerce." To satisfy his taste for the finest French cuisine, Russian general Loewenstern ordered from a Mme. Chevet in Paris regular provisions, as well as a professional chef to prepare them. When the Allies returned home, they exported many French dishes with them, helping to forge a French-based cosmopolitan cuisine that dominated cookbooks and restaurants across Europe for much of the nineteenth century.[51]

Mutual Borrowing

Early in the Restoration, a print in the popular "Bon Ton" series depicted two English women dressed in French fashion and two French women dressed in English fashion. Entitled *L'emprunt mutuel,* or "Mutual Borrowing," this print included a caption reassuring viewers: "Since the borrowing is limited to clothing and the form otherwise remains the same, no one needs to worry about mistaking an Englishwoman for a Frenchwoman, and a Frenchwoman for an Englishwoman." With its stereotyping of British versus French women, this print reified national difference while also accentuating cross-cultural mixing, suggesting that, in spite of small differences in styles of dresses, bonnets, and accessories, a more international style was developing in the aftermath of the Napoleonic Wars. As people traveled across the Continent, especially to France, they borrowed from each other not just fashions but also a wide variety of customs and ideas, from dance steps to measurement systems, from pedagogical methods to political ideals. While the occupation itself was not always a direct cause of exchange, it provided the context for hundreds of thousands of men and women to encounter—whether in person or through print—foreign ways of doing things.

This cross-cultural exchange is exemplified by the practice of dancing. At the end of the war, each nation had its own preferred dance style. Within a short time, French and foreigners were learning each other's steps. According to the memoirs of Captain Gronow, the French quadrille was not introduced to Britain until Lady Jersey brought it back from Paris in 1815. Similarly, according to the daughter of the French ambassador to London, Adèle d'Osmond, Comtesse de Boigne, before

L'emprunt mutuel: Anglaises habillées à la Française, Françaises avec des tailles à l'Anglaise. Le Bon Genre, No. 112, from *Observations sur les modes et les usages de Paris pour servir d'explication aux 115 caricatures publiées sous le titre de Bon Genre depuis le commencement du dix-neuvième siècle* (Paris: Vassal et Essling, 1827). Bibliothèque Historique de la Ville de Paris/Roger Viollet.

1816, no English damsel waltzed, until that dance was imported from Germany by the Duke of Devonshire. During the occupation, the Duke of Wellington developed a passion for the Russian mazurka. At a ball in Maubeuge, General Loewenstern later recalled, "The duke clapped his hands, stamped his feet; there was even something burlesque about contemplating the hero of the Peninsula and of Waterloo, writhing in place, and making his feet move with the beat, striking his spurs one against the other, his eye on fire, and following each movement, so to speak, with a smile of sensuality." In the Russian sector around Maubeuge, the French bourgeois François-Simon Cazin remembered that the balls funded by officers from their savings began with a Polonaise before proceeding to German and English steps, waltzes, quadrilles, mazurkas, and military dances, and that the local French ladies "had easily learned these figures and steps." By 1818, these foreign steps had become so popular that in Austrian-occupied Colmar the schoolteacher Georges Ozaneaux told his mother he was taking waltzing lessons, because "one does nothing but waltz here."[52] The role of war in promoting the spread of the waltz was satirized in a poem by a Russian colonel published in the *Journal de la Marne* in the summer of 1815: "Animated by the desire to please/We have seen from our country/Imported the light waltz/Which one still likes in Paris./If you have taken our dance/We owe to you some other successes/And we have learned in France,/Friends, to fight like Frenchmen."[53]

Alongside dance steps, international elites borrowed a number of other ideas and practices, contributing to the creation of a more cosmopolitan culture in Europe. A pedagogical method of mutual education developed by the Englishman Joseph Lancaster was exported to Russia via France. Taken with the method during his visit to England in 1814, Tsar Alexander I sent four young scholars there, at state expense, to investigate schools employing it. During the occupation of guarantee, Vorontsov ordered Loewenstern to establish a school based on this method for his soldiers in Givet. Within three months, according to Loewenstern's memoirs, these soldiers had developed rudimentary reading and writing skills. This experiment was so successful that, when one of the Russian scholars sent by Alexander to England, who had written a long study of the method, came to visit, he was "very surprised to observe the progress that we had accomplished before even having read his book." This sort of exchange had long-lasting consequences not just for educational theory but also for political consciousness in Russia—and elsewhere where the Lancaster method was adopted—well into the next decade.[54]

But the revival of cross-cultural exchange in the context of occupation is perhaps best seen in the realm of fashion. Although France had been the center of fashion since at least the seventeenth century, two decades of revolution and war had limited exposure to the French mode elsewhere in Europe. As Englishman J. W. Ward wrote from Paris in May 1814, "The last twenty years have, I suspect, very much altered the relation betwixt the two countries on things in which the French used to be our acknowledged superiors. We have been advancing, and they have receded, so that in taste and elegance we are much nearer a match for them than we were. The Paris fashions in dress used to be regularly and servilely copied, and perhaps they will be so still, but I confess I see nothing in them worth following."[55]

This discrepancy in fashion was viewed differently by French commentators, who criticized the English as outmoded. Looking back on the period 1814–1815, the French noblewoman Victorine de Chastenay remembered, "Our fabrics of all kinds, our bronzes, even our steels, down to our lamps fashioned in so many different ways, everything was new for the English. Their styles had become grotesque, and in just a few days it was necessary for the women of this nation, recently disembarked, to reform their outfits entirely. The men, whose simple and correct dress had once served as a model, were obliged to follow in their turn the models offered by our young people of all classes." Other French observers were equally critical of English modes. In late 1815, the *Journal de Paris* ran a number of articles describing the "bizarre" dress of English of both sexes. Englishmen were critiqued for their "not very gallant" and "seasonally inappropriate" dress, especially their large neckties and long vests; Englishwomen, for their flat hats, high-buttoned coats, and jarring mix of colors. The next year, the same paper ridiculed an Englishman for riding horseback on the boulevards in cloth gaiters, spurs, a yellow straw hat, and an open umbrella: "We warn him that he is six months in advance of Carnival." On another occasion, the newspaper concluded, "In spite of the quantity of foreigners for which Paris has become the rendez-vous, we have remarked that Parisian fashions have made almost no borrowing from those of other countries. . . . [T]hus the two peoples [French and British] conserve their particular fashions, and it is easy to recognize them in the streets and public meeting places."[56]

In the context of the occupation, however, French ladies—and gentlemen—did adopt foreign fashions. After gawking at the Scottish troops encamped on the Champs-Élysées, Frenchwomen acquired a "sudden taste" for their costume. Already in July 1815, the *marchand de modes* Louis Hippolyte Leroy marketed a "*habit complet à l'écossaise*" that included a rose "spencer" (short jacket), a knee-length skirt of Scottish taffeta, Scottish booties, and a black hat decorated with pink feathers and tied under the chin with a Scottish ribbon. By 1818, according to the *Journal des dames et des modes,* there was a widespread fashion for "Scottish hats," in bright colors, most recently in a plaid of yellow and green. Over the next few years, according to the same fashion review, the British "spencer" jacket became the mode among French women. The mania for British styles was shared by French men. In 1818, in occupied Colmar, the schoolteacher Georges Ozaneaux was delighted to receive as a new year's present from the local prefect a "pretty English cane," complete with scissors and blades. Meanwhile, from Russia French women adopted "witz-chouras," or fur-lined (usually wolf) coats.[57]

Even as French women—and men—began to imitate foreign styles, foreigners were quick to appropriate French fashions. Already by 1815, Victorine de Chastenay remembered, "The ridiculousness of the outfit of the [English] women gave way to French styles, from the very first ball which they attended; after just a few weeks in Paris, the name and the insipid pretentions of the [English] dandys had disappeared." On the road from Calais to Paris in the summer of 1815, Countess Granville quickly had her bonnet redesigned according to the French mode. As she reported to her sister back in England, "We saw varieties of French bonnets, sat with two agreeable old milliners, who trimmed mine up half a mile high, and called one another Rosalie and something else, and bore it all like saints." Once they arrived in the capital, foreign visitors revamped their wardrobes. Like the fictional English Miss Biddy in *The Fudge Family in Paris,* they found the French capital to be a shopper's paradise, an "Eden of milliners, monkies and sights," whose gowns and dresses were "*superbe*" and "*magnifique.*" Between 1815 and 1820, foreigners were the prime clients of French *modistes,* particularly the milliner Louis Hippolyte LeRoy, whose customers included Russian and British aristocrats such as the Duchess of Wellington and Lady Stuart. Even the king of Prussia, not known for his fashion sense, frequented the boutiques in the French capital to procure a new wardrobe for his daughter.[58]

As a result of this shopping frenzy, within a year or two of the end of war, French fashion had taken hold among elites throughout much of Europe, to the extent that it became impossible to distinguish between a "British," a "German," or a "French" style. By May 1817, on another trip to Paris, Countess Harriet Granville informed her sister that there was "scarcely any difference of dress between French and English women."[59]

Literary Cosmopolitanism

Mutual borrowing also shaped the development of postrevolutionary literature, particularly romanticism. Compared to the role of empire, the context of the Napoleonic Wars and their aftermath has not received much attention among scholars of this literary movement.[60] However, this context—and, especially, the circulation of hundreds of thousands of foreigners in France during the late 1810s—was central to the re-emergence of, but also resistance to, a more cosmopolitan literary culture in the early nineteenth century. As new scholarship has begun to show, in France the battle of the romantics against the classics was largely a reaction to foreign influence in the context of occupation.[61]

During precisely the same years that France was under occupation, some of the most important works of the "romantic revolution" were produced. From this period date many of the iconic poems and novels by authors such as William Wordsworth, Sir Walter Scott, Jane Austen, and Mary Shelley, whose *Frankenstein: The Modern Prometheus* was drafted in the summer of 1816 during a stay in Switzerland following a trip through post-invasion France. These years were also fecund for romantic music and painting, including Caspar David Friedrich's *Wanderer above a Sea of Fog* (1818), which is often taken to encapsulate the movement. This romantic revolution had already been brewing since the late eighteenth century in Great Britain and Germany, whence writers such as Germaine de Staël had imported its ideas into France, in her multivolume work *De l'Allemagne,* first published toward the end of the Empire but reprinted multiple times at the beginning of the Restoration. But after 1815, romanticism exploded across the Continent—and, again, with renewed force, in Britain.

There are a number of reasons for this resurgence of romanticism, including a reaction against Enlightenment rationalism and early industrialization, the aftershocks of the French Revolution, and a fascination with national myths and historical ruins.[62] But one of the most important is the postwar settlement, which promoted unprecedented circulation of books as well as peoples across national frontiers. In this period of relative peace and scant protection of literary property, the literary market became international to an extent not seen even in the "Republic of Letters" of the seventeenth and eighteenth centuries.

The postwar era saw in France a profusion of foreign-language, especially English, publishers, bookstores, periodicals, and reading rooms, as well as producers of French publications abroad, especially Belgium. Because they did not have to pay rights to authors, which were guaranteed—if at all—only in their country of origin, these producers, most famously Galignani's, were able to offer compact editions of foreign works at cutthroat prices. Although they thus became a thorn in the side of authors and publishers, these literary pirates served to spread new (and old) works across Europe—and beyond. They were single-handedly responsible for introducing French audiences to British romantics such as the Shelleys, Byron, and especially Scott, who by the late 1810s was among the best-selling authors in France. Referring to Scott in particular, one British soldier stationed in France remembered, "Few things will more strongly prove the approximation of the two nations, than the attention that has been paid of late years to the literature of England, and the number of people who now speak our language. Almost all our modern works of note are immediately translated into French, and a greater number still reprinted in Paris by the literary pirate of Rue Vivienne." During these years, listings of publications in the trade journal *Bibliographie de la France* contain countless titles by and about the Scottish as well as the English, including catalogues of works imported from London by publishers such as Théophile Barrois. Read and discussed widely by the French, for example in the English-language study group formed by Étienne-Jean Délécluze, these works influenced a generation of authors, including Lamartine, Hugo, Balzac, Stendhal, and De Vigny. French romantics were also influenced by German and Russian ideas, including the spiritualism of Alexander I, to whom Stendhal dedicated his 1817 history of painting in Italy. As Jean-Yves Mollier has concluded of this period in French literary history,

> The openness to the rest of the world and, particularly, to England beginning in 1815, played an important role in the renewal of intellectual horizons. With the arrival in force of Walter Scott, but also of Byron, even the American Fenimore Cooper and the great German romantic authors, France was confronted by other writings, other systems of thought and other methods of analysis.

> Even if the commercial balance, in book production, remained weighted in the direction of exports, the arrival of British newspapers and reviews liberated space for criticism and unleashed the winds of liberalism in the France of the Restoration.[63]

The multinational occupation fueled intellectual exchange.

The Reaction against Xenomania

Within a few years of the Battle of Waterloo, cosmopolitanism had resurged to such an extent that it provoked a nationalist reaction in France, especially against Great Britain, whose cultural and economic influence it had long feared. This reaction against what the French termed *étrangomanie,* or "mania for the foreign," is encapsulated in an engraving from early 1818, *L'étrangomanie blamée, ou d'être Français il n'y a pas d'affront* ("Xenomania Impugned, or There Is No Shame in Being French"). One Frenchman, pointing to a list of French accomplishments in the realms of "Valor," "Genius," and "Fine Arts," says to another, "Let's take the Russian, the English, for what he is, there is nothing like being French." The other man, seated with a list of the best products of French industry on his lap, replies, "When the English will have done as much, chickens will have teeth." Under his foot lies a paper reading "Products of Foreign Manufacturies." In the back, an English civilian and a French soldier fight for dominance. At the top, a female angel blows a trumpet from which flies a banner reading "To Immortality."

This message was echoed widely in popular culture in France. In an 1814 song entitled "The Good Frenchman," Pierre-Jean de Béranger warned: "Beware Anglomania,/It has already spoiled everything./Let us not at all go to Germany/To seek the rules of taste./Let's borrow from our neighbors/Only their women and their wines./My friends, my friends,/Let us be true to our own country,/Yes, let us be true to our own country." The next year, the satirical newspaper *Le nain vert* also cautioned against Anglomania, in a piece written in the voice of an Englishman, who claimed to be less surprised to find himself in Paris than to see and hear constant references to the example of England. Noting that Parisians were imitating English fashion and literature, he admitted that the French and English could learn from each other's industry, but insisted that they would be wrong to adopt each other's

L'étrangomanie blâmée, ou d'être Français il n'y a pas d'affront. Engraving by Charon; published by Martinet, 1818. BNF.

political institutions, concluding, "The Anglo-French of 1815 will never be worth the French of 1600 to 1750."[64]

Satire proved the best weapon against xenomania. Beginning in the second half of the 1810s and continuing through the July Monarchy, when Anglomania peaked, French authors, journalists, artists, printmakers, and playwrights generated a wave of caricatures of foreigners, particularly the British. Although they varied in form and style, caricatures of the British tended to poke fun at a common list of "national" traits: impolite manners, bad food, lack of style, materialism, corpulence, humorlessness, penchant for suicide, wife-selling, boxing, foxhunting, and, especially, imperfect French. To take just one of many examples, the collection of amusing anecdotes about the British published in 1815 characterized them as eating "fatty meats" and drinking "detestable" coffee to excess, without napkins. Beginning with a frontispiece illustration, depicting a Scotsman in a bar calling "Célibataire, apportez un miroir!" ("Bachelor, bring me a mirror!") to ask the waiter (*garçon)* for an ice cream (*glace),* this collection satirized the British inability to speak the French language. In another anecdote, it contrasted the French quest for fun to the British penchant for drama, concluding, "One gains no more by boring a Frenchman than by amusing an Englishman." Another satire, performed in theaters during the occupation, revealed its purpose in the very title: *Les Anglais pour rire* ("The English, for Laughing"). (When a French lady expressed surprise that British theatergoers could laugh at this piece, one English officer reportedly retorted, "Yes, madam, those who win may laugh!")[65] Comparable to the reaction against "Americanization" following World War II, the campaign against "xenomania" aimed to reassert cultural superiority after military defeat.

The Battle of the Mountains

Both the revival of cosmopolitanism and the reaction against it are exemplified in the "combat" over the *montagnes russes* in 1817. First noted in Paris toward the end of 1816, these amusements were modeled after ice-covered sledding hills, 40–50 feet high and 800–900 feet long, built on the frozen Neva River in St. Petersburg. In Paris, they were constructed of wood and descended on rails, in wheeled carriages, which were lifted to the top by horse power.[66] The "extreme rapidity" of the descent was described by the Marquise de Montcalm in her journal on October 22, 1816:

> This pleasure, which is not without danger, may be compared, according to the opinion of several people, to the impression that one would feel if one fell from a fourth-floor window, which does not seem very seductive. These mountains are made of ice in Russia, and one hopes, in spite of the difference in climate, to imitate them in winter; a man said, in speaking of them, that he was surprised that this fashion does not elicit complaint against the influence of Russia, which it is very common today to render responsible for everything.[67]

In spite—or because—of their foreign origin, within a year the *montagnes russes* were a ubiquitous form of amusement in the French capital. Quick to profit from the fad, a number of entrepreneurs invested in the new entertainment. By early 1817, they were inundating the ministry of commerce with requests for patents for technical improvements to the roller coasters. Evoking their exotic origin, the new coasters were named after a wide range of foreign attractions, including "Swiss" mountains, "Egyptian" mountains, "Illyrian" mountains, "Aeolian" mountains, and (in perhaps the first water ride) "Niagara Falls."[68]

The most extravagant was the *promenade aérienne* in the Jardin Beaujon at the Barrière de l'Étoile, on the site of a hospice built in 1784 by a financier named Beaujon. The terrain was transformed into a pleasure garden at great expense, roughly a million francs, earning it the moniker of "Folie Beaujon." After inspection by a police commission, the *montagnes* at Beaujon were inaugurated on July 8, 1817, the second anniversary of the return of the king. Surmounted by a belvedere, from where riders had "the best" view of Paris, and surrounded by a lush garden with numerous other amenities, including dance halls, lemonade stands, and fireworks, Beaujon quickly surpassed Tivoli, a popular pleasure garden under the First Empire, as the premier entertainment in the capital, despite growing competition from other roller coasters, including Tivoli's own "Montagnes Aeoliennes."[69]

To fuel the popularity of these mountains, the entrepreneurs orchestrated a publicity blitz. In July 1817, according to the *Journal des débats,* they hosted a "magnificent banquet," to which they issued a mass invitation to all journalists and playwrights in the capital. Knowing that "people of all opinions and of all colors may rise and descend equally," they allowed these writers to try the mountains before dining at their expense.

At the banquet (and in the press that followed), "The *bons mots* flew as rapidly as the aerial carts."[70] The roller coasters were also promoted by a doctor, F.-F. Cotterel. Positioning himself as their Hippocrates, probably for a fee, he published a book, first in 1817 and again in 1821, enumerating the health benefits of these "gymnastic" amusements, including outdoor "exercise," cleansing of the lungs, movement of the digestive organs, and cure of nervous maladies. According to him, the *montagnes russes* constituted an antidote to the inactivity of the "opulent class."[71]

Despite almost continual rainfall during the spring and summer of 1817, the new roller coasters drew thousands of visitors, including foreign as well as French dignitaries. On his second trip to Paris, the Prussian king, who had asked his army's chief doctor to procure him a copy of Cotterel's medical defense of the *montagnes russes,* visited the Folie Beaujon. On August 2, 1817, the king of France paid a visit to the same pleasure garden, whose proprietors he praised for their entrepreneurship. As Cotterel noted, comparing the leisure gardens of the Restoration to the émigré capitals of the revolutionary and imperial era, "Thanks to the lighting that gives it all desired security, the *contre-allée* that extends from the place Louis XV to the Jardin Beaujon, and which one now calls the *Path of the French Mountains,* has become for elite society the Coblenz or the Ghent in fashion, and for the merchants, on festival days at Beaujon, a fair day."[72] Appealing to people of every age, sex, and nationality, if not—depending on the fees at each garden—class, these attractions were soon imitated in other cities, including Bordeaux, Lyon, Marseille (where Julie Pellizzone sketched them in her diary), and, farther afield, Berlin.[73]

This new fashion was attested by popular culture. Reporting on the opening of the *montagnes russes* at Beaujon, the *Journal de Paris* commented, "An immense crowd came, and the Champs-Elysées looked like a day at [the horsetrack at] Longchamp. Men, women, children, everyone wanted to be among the number of aerial promenaders, and all the runs succeeded perfectly. . . . If this continues, each neighborhood in Paris will have its *Montagnes.*" Within a short time, this amusement became so popular that a pastry shop in the rue Croix des Petits-Champs was reported to have taken as its ensign "Aux Montagnes."[74] In addition to newspapers, the *montagnes russes* figured in countless images,

Promenades aériennes, Jardin Beaujon, Honoré de Sa Majesté, le 2 août 1817. Designed by Garneray; engraved by Lerouge, 1817. BNF.

many in the popular "Bon Ton" series, including a commemorative print of the visit by Louis XVIII to the Folie Beaujon in August 1817.

The popularity of the *montagnes russes* is evident in the number of theater productions featuring them between 1816 and 1818. Playwrights penned countless couplets, pantomimes, vaudevilles, and *pièces de circonstances* featuring the entrepreneurs of and the visitors to the mountains, playing on words such as *monter* ("to rise"), *descendre* ("to fall"), *dégringoler* ("to tumble"), and *ramasser* ("to pick up"). Already in late 1816, at least two plays entitled *Les montagnes russes* were produced in Paris. The first, subtitled *Le Temple de la Mode* ("The Temple of Fashion"), featured a Russian inspector named Poussikoff; the second included a British gentleman named Milord Plum-Pudding.[75] By mid-1817 there were more plays about the *montagnes russes*.[76] Although they did not rise to the level of high literature, these plays generated laughter—and sales—among Parisian audiences. As the *Journal général de France* concluded in a review in July 1817,

> One might fear that, after having turned in twenty different ways the pretty little puns on *ramasser, dégringoler,* and many other similar whimsies, the genius of the vaudevillists would be exhausted; but, habituated to constructing

> their frail edifices on the point of a needle, the singing architects of the Rue de Chartres and the Panorama find themselves suddenly inspired by the new *montagnes*, which differ from the earlier ones only by their elevation and their extent. . . . [I]f, with such a production, one does not much enrich either the repertoire or the cash register, one does not neglect to round off the sum of the author's rights received at the end of the month.[77]

The plays about the different *montagnes russes* featured some common characters, including a comic antihero variously named Arlequin, Philibert, or Fanfan; one or more doctors, to attest to the beneficent effects of these rides; a British or Russian inspector; male or female novelty merchants, either profiting from or competing against the new pleasure gardens; and, typically, a personification of "Fashion," known either as "La Folie" or "La Mode," on whose caprice depended the success of the mountains. In addition to the message about the fickleness of fashion, the plays shared a number of other themes, including the return of pleasure to France after war, the mixing of different peoples and classes at the pleasure gardens, the promotion of romance (often pre- or extramarital) by the roller coasters, and the celebration of freedom, including sexual license. In these dramatizations, the *montagnes russes* also constituted a metaphor for the ups and downs of life. As *Les montagnes russes, ou Le Temple de la Mode* moralized, in the voice of the Russian inspector Poussikoff, "Because in this world,/It is a constant fact,/Each one in his turn/Sooner or later descends./Come everyone to learn,/To learn/How to descend./Come everyone to learn/How to descend/Gaily." Although they did not refer explicitly to Napoleon, such pieces evoked his sudden fall from fame and fortune.[78]

Another central theme in the plays was the foreign inspiration for, and presence at, the pleasure gardens of Paris. The vaudeville *Les montagnes russes, ou le Temple de la Mode* included an air about how these amusements brought Russia to Paris: "Renouncing even the countryside/Of Saint-Cloud and of Passy,/Many a good bourgeois comes here;/And, thanks to our Mountains!/In leaving his suburb,/Believes himself to be in Saint-Petersburg." In another fictionalized travelogue, a "Champenois," underwhelmed by the Folie Beaujon, counters a criticism by an Englishman of the amusement's "excess" by emphasizing its international character: "And anyway, where is the crowd of French:/I see only foreigners in this immense garden;/Don't we owe to them these foolish novelties/Which are far from unpleasing to your young beauties!"[79] Depicting battles between exotic-named mountains, whose fictionalized promoters and riders came from the different nations of Europe, these plays showcased the cosmopolitan culture of the postwar capital.

At the same time, however, the caricatures of the *montagnes russes* revealed intense anxiety about foreign influence on French culture. These seemingly innocuous imported amusements constituted a foil for grappling with the serious issue of postwar trauma, especially foreign occupation. For instance, a slight *à propos épisodique* about the *montagnes russes* in 1816 questioned why it was necessary to import these amusements from Russia, as if there were no mountains in France, asking facetiously: "What a nice effect it would have been if someone were to transport the butte Montmartre to St. Petersburg?" The vaudeville subtitled *Le Temple de la Mode* pilloried the mania for English as well as Russian fashions with a chorus exclaiming, "What will become of the women of Paris?/If this continues, one is going/To take them for some miladies. . . . Because one does not recognize genius,/I see that soon it will be necessary for us/All to leave for Russia,/After the Opera." Countering this anxiety, a character called "La Mode" insisted that French women should feel free to borrow coats and shawls from the Russians, to brave the icy "mountains" that were now the "bon ton," concluding: "What difference does one cashmere make/It's milord who will pay for it." With such dialogue, the plays about "Russian" mountains crystallized nationalist resistance against "foreign-mania."[80]

The use of the *montagnes russes* as a foil for anxiety about cosmopolitanism is best exemplified in the most acclaimed but controversial of the plays, *Le combat des montagnes, ou La Folie Beaujon,* a one-act vaudeville penned by the popular playwrights Eugène Scribe and Henri Dupin and performed at the Théâtre des Variétés in July 1817, at the height of these amusements.[81] Like many of the other plays about the roller coasters, it satirized the foreign origin of the new vogue for "rising" high above ground. In the first scene, a character named La Folie appears at the Beaujon garden before the Hermit of the Chaussée d'Antin, a well-known but reclusive Parisian journalist, who does not recognize her. Explaining that she has been touring the world and is arriving from England, where she received the warmest of welcomes, La Folie remarks:

> There, it is true, I was forced to assume a physiognomy so grave, so serious, that many people were tricked, taking me for Reason. . . . But the name is not important; it was always me! I attended cockfights, races at Newmarket, boxing matches! And I did not miss a single one of the political meetings that take place in the taverns of London. . . . But in the matter of follies, the gayest are the best; and I am returning to Paris to rediscover my loyal subjects; I am going to find them much changed.

To revive amusement in Paris, La Folie undertakes construction of a new Mount "Olympus" at the barrier of L'Étoile, with help from a cast of characters on whom she bestows names of ancient gods and goddesses. In this endeavor, she is opposed by another entrepreneur, dubbed Titan, whose "Russian mountains" she abandoned the year before. Carrying a model of his mountains, Titan initiates a lawsuit against her for counterfeiting, proclaiming, "Yes, in spite of your tricks, we are going to see a lawsuit regarding my mountains, which are made by Russians." To this challenge, La Folie replies, "And ours are made by French!" Their legal battle is soon joined by the entrepreneurs of a number of other mountains, including Swiss, Illyrian, Egyptian, Niagara Falls, and even the natural mountain of Montmartre.

In the end, the battle between the mountains of Paris is won by the new "Olympus" constructed by La Folie, who overthrows the "Titans" of the other *montagnes russes,* proclaiming "Those protected by La Folie/always triumph." While she allows the other roller coasters to continue to operate at least on Sundays, she concludes that by public judgment the Folie Beaujon will remain the busiest as well as the tallest amusement in the capital. Claiming that her mountain is the only true French one, she insists that, in the realm of art and honor, no nation builds more enduring monuments. Naturalizing the "Russian" mountains and foreign fashions more generally, she concludes, "We want to achieve peace,/But let us forbid anyone ever,/From rising above us." In this play, as in a number of others, the figure of Folly or Mode serves to combat xenomania by repatriating the center of fashion in France.

Alongside La Folie, this dramatization included a new character, Calicot, who also satirized the foreign origin of much of postwar culture in France. Named after the cotton fabric imported or imitated from

India, a "calicot" was a sales clerk for a fashion merchant. Too young to have fought in the Napoleonic Wars, this type nonetheless often assumed the air of a veteran. As played by the popular actor Mira Brunet in *Le combat des montagnes,* Calicot was caricatured as vaguely eastern in appearance, sporting a stuffed jacket, Cossack-style pants, spurs, and a mustache, and wielding a yardstick as a weapon. Embodying the foreign origin of much of postwar French culture, this character—on whom La Folie bestows the name of Mercury, god of commerce—was satirized as the very antithesis of the heroic French soldier whose manners he imitated.

To this satirical representation of them, the real merchant clerks of Paris took great offense. In late July, between two hundred and three hundred clerks invaded the parterre of the theater each evening, armed with leaded canes, interrupting performances and threatening brawls; the actor Brunet had to be escorted by gendarmes; and the police arrested some fifteen to twenty real-life "calicots." According to the *Chronique parisienne,* "One half of the human species laughs at the other half. . . . There is talk only of the *combat des montagnes,* which would have become a combat to the death if the sage prevention of the police had not restored order." Over the course of the next few months, this combat was widely covered in the press, inspiring a number of commentaries, including a poetic "pot-pourri" entitled *Grand combat du combat des montagnes, ou La campagne des calicots,* by "Jérôme, the Peaceful," who criticized the fashion clerks for taking so much offense at a "bagatelle," or trifle. One of the first "news" items exploited by the new technology of lithography, the "battle" of the calicots was also depicted in a series of prints. In one, modeled after David's famous painting *The Oath of the Horatii,* the calicots take an oath to fight against their "enemies" in the pit at the Théâtre des Variétés. Another, the *Charge de M. Calicot et Cie. au Théâtre des Variétés*, featured a clerk leading the attack in the parterre of the theater, armed with a yardstick. Yet another represented his return home, exhausted and demoralized. Such images in turn provoked more fighting in the streets, endangering the shop window of at least one printseller.[82]

The combat of the calicots was resolved only when the writers of *Le combat des montagnes* composed a new epilogue to the play, *Le Café des Variétés*, which constituted a peace treaty written in couplets "as

Charge de M. Calicot et Cie. au Théâtre des Variétés: La Guerre en temps de Paix. Hand-colored lithograph published by Martinet, 1817. BNF.

spiritual and clever as those that had occasioned the war," according to one critic. To appease the sales clerks who had taken offense at the characterization of Calicot, it included a couplet praising commerce as equivalent to war as a means of obtaining glory. Complaining that no profession was safe for comedy, the epilogue ended with a merchant singing to the audience: "We propose to you/A treaty of alliance: It is not enough/Alas, that the war is over;/By a more gentle noise, Messieurs, prove to us/That the peace is signed." This "peace" did not fully resolve the combat of the calicots, who continued to be satirized for their role in commerce long after the fashion for the Russian mountains waned. But it did work to legitimize new—often foreign—commercial practices in postwar France.[83]

The "combat" of the mountains served to empower the French—at least in Paris, at a safe remove from the occupation zone—against foreign influence. By reclaiming the *montagnes russes* and their sidekicks, the calicots, as "French," the promoters of the roller coasters reasserted the cultural and commercial, if not military, superiority of their nation. The identification of the Folie Beaujon as the genuinely "French" mountain was widely adopted by the French public. An illustrated guidebook to the monuments of Paris in this period said of the Folie Beaujon, "The richness and elegance that shines in all of its details gives it first place among the numerous establishments of this genre, and the public suffrage has sanctioned the title it has taken of *Montagnes françaises.*" Within a short period, the *montagnes russes* were refigured—by foreign as well as French commentators—as distinctively "French."[84]

By the time that guidebook was published, the *montagnes russes* had begun to disappear from Paris, most closing by the end of 1818. They would not appear in France again until reimported, this time from England and the United States, during the Belle Époque. Why did the "Russian" mountains rise and fall so quickly in public favor? As the character of La Folie suggests, they may simply have fallen victim to the fickleness of fashion. In addition, they suffered from the general trend toward a separation of classes and reprivatization of leisure by 1820.[85] The demise of the roller coasters was also certainly caused by concern over safety. In the fall of 1817, at the *montagne française* at Beaujon, a

Madame Sauveur and accompanying "monsieur" were thrown from a car when it hit an obstacle on the track; she suffered the fracture of her clavicle and tibia, and he endured a wound to the face. Less than a year later, at the same garden, a former quartermaster, Dufrère, along with his daughter of sixteen years and nephew of eight, were ejected from a carriage when it stopped too brusquely; Dufrère and his daughter both died.[86]

However, the downfall of the "Russian" mountains may also be attributed to the complications of cosmopolitanism in postwar France. Given their connection to the foreign presence in France, it is not coincidental that the *montagnes russes* disappeared at exactly the same moment that this presence declined, with the evacuation of the army of occupation in the fall of 1818. Following the often vitriolic satire of these foreign imports in the theater, the amusements had already begun to lose popularity when they also lost a large contingent of their public, many of whom now left France for home.

Part Three

Regeneration

Chapter Seven

Reconstruction

EIGHTEEN MONTHS after he parodied the "demoiselles" of the Palais-Royal anticipating a boom in business, in November 1816 the songwriter Béranger penned a "Complaint by One of These Demoiselles, Regarding the Affairs of the Times," bemoaning a precipitous decline in business since the previous year: "Thi' commerce brings nothing anymore./But if th' public bankrupts us,/It is because business is no' going well." Listing the types of men who could no longer afford her services, the song repeated the refrain: "It seems tha' lord Villain-ton [Wellington] has taken everything,/There's no more money in thi' beggarly Paris."[1]

Whether or not Wellington himself was to blame, by late 1816 France was indeed beset by economic crisis. The foreign presence may not in fact have harmed the affairs of prostitutes, but it certainly imposed financial burdens, which squeezed consumption as well as investment in other industries.[2] The Napoleonic Wars left French commerce and industry in shambles. Already a generation behind Great Britain in industrial development, the country fell even further behind under the naval blockade by Great Britain beginning in 1806. As a result of the Revolutionary and Napoleonic Wars, it also lost much of its colonial trade. The collapse of the Grand Empire in 1814 further disrupted trade patterns. Following the second defeat of Napoleon, France was burdened with heavy requisitions and reparations, as well as war debts, both foreign and domestic. As it struggled to handle this financial crisis, the country was hit with an agricultural one, due to a freak climatic occurrence that made 1816 and 1817 unprecedentedly cold and wet. Lacking money for investment, French merchants and manufacturers faced renewed competition from foreign suppliers, including occupying troops themselves, who encouraged and even practiced smuggling along the reimposed frontier in the northeast. In this context, French business often languished.

Even as the "Affairs of the Times" suffered under the Allies, however, the occupation of guarantee prompted new enterprises, institutions, and policies, which over the long run promoted the nation's financial health and industrial development. As illustrated by the *montagnes russes,* the occupiers provided new products as well as markets for French entrepreneurs. Although many French suffered from the heavy damages, requisitions, and reparations, others profited from the new opportunities provided by the peace settlement. In occupied communities, including Paris, foreign troops generated business for local farmers, artisans, and shopkeepers. Even their horses provided an economic benefit in the manure coveted by local peasants for their fields. Like the burdens, the benefits of occupation were centered in the Paris region and the northeast. Though they still endured extra taxes, other regions, such as the southwest, suffered less. But they profited less, too, especially given the simultaneous shift from colonial to continental trade, which favored the northeast.

The occupation also encouraged a rethinking of political economy in France. To fulfill its financial obligations while relaunching commerce and industry, the French government adopted a number of policies to rebuild not just the public treasury but the overall economy, too. Understanding the link between fiscal and political legitimacy, the restored monarchy worked hard to reestablish public credit. Under foreign pressure, the new regime managed to prioritize fiscal health over partisan ideology, most notably in its first major finance law, of April 28, 1816. Along with many governments in the postrevolutionary period, this regime rebalanced commercial policy between liberalism and protectionism, restoring a number of defenses and incentives for domestic agriculture and industry, including strict customs controls. Together, these measures put France on a stable, if somewhat "separate," path toward industrial development in the nineteenth century. Despite the setbacks of war and occupation, growth rates averaged a relatively high

3.7 percent between 1815 and 1820, while the balance of trade in manufactures improved.[3] Contrary to the complaint of Béranger's "demoiselle," the occupation did generate business, contributing to a remarkably quick economic recovery in France.

The Most Expensive Hundred Days in French History

For France, the Battle of Waterloo constituted not just a military but also a financial disaster. As Pierre Branda concludes in his masterful study of the role of money in the reign of Napoleon, the Hundred Days after the emperor's escape from Elba were the most expensive in French history.[4] Already drained by fifteen years of imperial largesse (following decades of monarchical and revolutionary insolvency), the French treasury was ruined by this defeat. Even more than the first, the second Allied invasion exacted a heavy financial toll on the French, well into the nineteenth century.

The military glory of the Napoleonic Empire exacted a steep price. For over a decade, Napoleon met the challenge of financing his campaigns, without bankrupting the state, through a strategy of making war pay for itself, by exacting "contributions" from occupied territories such as Italy and Prussia. Supplemented by "indirect" taxes on goods like alcohol and tobacco, this strategy eventually undermined itself, by provoking opposition to the Grand Empire, especially in Spain. Meanwhile, the British were more successful in financing their war effort, mobilizing vast sums through a mix of exchequer bills, fiscal reforms, tax increases, and massive debts. These policies, combined with the failure of the Continental System instituted in reaction to the naval blockade, enabled the British government not only to increase the budgets of the army and, especially, the navy, but also to offer military subsidies to other members of the Allied coalition.

By the time Napoleon abdicated on April 11, 1814, the French treasury was nearly bankrupt. According to the restored king's minister of finance, Baron Joseph-Dominique Louis, the emperor had left some 1.3 billion francs in arrears, of which 759 million were due at once. According to Branda, the real gap was closer to 670 million, or one year's worth of revenue. Rather than renouncing the debt, the finance minister assumed it, arguing, "A State must pay everything, even its mistakes."

To pay its war debts, the new government collected *centimes additionnels* from all taxpayers (to the tune of 86 million francs) and reinstituted the *droits réunis,* or excise taxes, which it had initially promised to abolish. It also slashed the budget for the military, sending some two hundred thousand men—including over ten thousand officers—home without pay, and proposed to sell three hundred thousand hectares of national lands and forests. Provoking substantial opposition to the restored monarchy, especially among beverage distributors, soldiers, and former proprietors of the *biens nationaux,* these measures paradoxically promoted the return of the emperor whose spending had necessitated them in the first place.[5]

The brief return of the emperor had devastating consequences for the French treasury. During the Hundred Days, the remobilization of the military did not in itself aggravate the public deficit too much. In fact, the budget for 1815 had a surplus of 29 million francs. However, the defeat at Waterloo entailed unprecedented financial costs. In addition to the war debts of 1814 and 1815, which at the time of Napoleon's last battle still amounted to some 500 million francs, the new regime was now faced with paying a slew of contributions and requisitions to the 1.2 million troops who poured into France. Excluding appropriations from localities that were never recovered, for the summer of 1815 alone these costs totaled almost 500 million francs in documented claims, plus 186.2 million francs in state payments for maintenance and equipment. These expenses were daunting for the finance minister Baron Louis, who continued to insist that his primary duty was to "respect and repay scrupulously all engagements contracted in the name of the state."[6]

Systematizing the maintenance of the occupying army, the Second Treaty of Paris went well beyond the first in the financial burden it placed on the French. In addition to all expenses for the remaining troops, including not just rations for two hundred thousand men and fifty thousand horses but also 50 million francs per year for salary and equipment, the treaty required the French to pay substantial reparations to the Allied powers as well as war claims to foreign nationals. In 1814, the French government was required only to assume the Empire's debts to foreigners. In 1815, that requirement was redefined and extended "to cover all loss or damage of any nature suffered by public or private property as well as compensation for services rendered," which opened the door to all kinds of exaggerated claims. Along with reparations, these claims—the amount of which remained to be negotiated—had to be paid before the Allies would agree to end the occupation. As a result of Napoleon's return to power, France would owe over 1.8 billion francs in occupation costs and indemnities.[7]

To meet these obligations, the French government employed a mix of tax increases and bond issues. Following the elections of August 19, 1815, Baron Louis was replaced as finance minister by Comte Corvetto, who was already serving as president of the Commission on Requisitions. By early the following year, the new minister had acknowledged the semi-bankruptcy of the French treasury. With the aid of a financier named Gabriel-Julien Ouvrard, who had helped Napoleon pay for the 1815 campaign, Corvetto began to arrange loans, mostly from Protestant financiers abroad, in exchange for government securities. At the end of 1815, to begin to address the budgetary arrears inherited from Napoleon, the government issued a first round of *rentes,* or annuities. Sold at an average price of 51.23 francs on a face value of 100, these annuities raised 35.8 million francs, with a nominal interest rate of 9.8 percent. This approach was also used to repay the invasion expenses, as well as to fund the war reparations, occupation costs, and Allied claims. As a result, between 1814 and 1825, public debt in France increased threefold. The policy restored the credit of the French government, but at a steep cost: with interest rates close to 10 percent, the cost of financing this debt consumed 20 to 25 percent of public revenues over the next decade. As Branda concludes, Napoleon's method of paying for war by war constituted only an advance, to be reimbursed over several generations. The return of the emperor in March 1815 left a long legacy for public finance in France.[8]

Indemnifying the Victims of Invasion

One of the first tasks of the returning monarchy was to indemnify the victims of invasion not only from 1814—undertaken by the First Restoration but interrupted by the return of Napoleon—but now also from 1815. For the new regime, this task was crucial for restoring not just its financial credit but also its political credit at home and abroad. This sort of indemnification was not entirely new. Since the Old Regime, the state had a tradition of reimbursing victims of fires and other natural disasters. However, as Thomas Gauchet notes, "[T]his desire to reimburse the expenses of war reveals all the same a change in perception. . . . To repair a damage supposes a principle of equality between victims, as between citizens."[9] In assuming responsibility for these costs, the restored monarchy aimed to legitimize itself in the eyes of its subjects, especially in the region most affected by occupation—the northeast—where a large number of demobilized troops and military suppliers increased discontent. In particular, the new government was concerned to repay the extraordinary taxes, the *centimes additionnels,* imposed on property owners to finance the expenses of war, which had caused considerable resentment in local communities, where they were sometimes used as tools to punish political opponents.[10]

The Second Restoration made indemnification of such expenses a centerpiece of its first budget proposal for 1816. First presented to the Chamber of Deputies by the finance ministry in December 1815 and then revised in March 1816, the proposal contained over 120 articles related not just to ordinary revenues and expenditures but also to the additional burdens of occupation costs and reparations. In addition to imposing a long list of income taxes, consumption taxes, and customs duties, this bill proposed to guarantee the extra contributions levied on both the local and national level during the crisis of 1815 as well as 1813–1814. It also promised to indemnify inhabitants of occupied departments for the costs they had incurred from the two invasions. Proposing to revive the *Caisse d'Amortissement,* or sinking fund used to back public debt, the bill aimed to stabilize public finances.

The finance bill of 1816 provoked considerable debate. In committee, there was significant opposition to the provisions regarding indirect taxes and customs duties, as well as to the financing of occupation costs through government bonds. But one of the most divisive issues was whether and how to reimburse the damages caused by the invasion of 1815, especially in those departments occupied by the Allies. Against the objections of ultraroyalists who repudiated the debts of the Napoleonic Empire and demanded instead indemnities for returning émigrés, supporters of the bill insisted that it was vital to reassure creditors of the state and to compensate those departments that had borne the burden of invasion.[11]

Finally, under pressure from the Duc de Richelieu, the bill passed on April 28, 1816. Prioritizing the interests of the state's creditors, the law guaranteed repayment not only of all previous arrears but also of all additional taxes, including the "extraordinary contribution" of August 1815 and the requisitions incurred as a result of the invasions of 1814 and 1815. To manage this process, the law instituted two types of commissions in every affected department: a "settlement commission," to standardize the additional taxes levied during the invasion of 1815; and a "verification commission," to reimburse the requisitions provided by local inhabitants. Each of these commissions was composed of six notables named by the *conseil général* of the department. Each department also created a "settlement bureau" to receive and investigate claims, with one section for the costs of the invasion of 1813–1814 and another for those of the invasion of 1815. To discourage any favoritism, the interior minister insisted, in an explanatory instruction in June 1816, on an "equitable division" of indemnities, to be funded by new property taxes and government annuities.[12]

Under occupation, the French state thus began the complex process of indemnifying its subjects for the costs borne during the transition from empire to monarchy. In each department, the settlement commission began to review the extraordinary contributions levied on the richest taxpayers in 1815. Once the amount paid by each taxpayer was verified, it was either deducted from the current tax bill or reimbursed by the state. Under pressure from local authorities, however, individual taxpayers often donated these indemnities to the community. According to the *Journal de Paris* in early 1816, many property owners relinquished their right to this money, which was then used to rebuild public infrastructure damaged during the invasions, such as bell towers, hospitals, and town halls.[13]

Even more complicated was the work of the verification commissions, charged with assessing and reimbursing the costs in money and in kind of the invasions of 1813–1814 and 1815. These commissions, established only in those departments that had suffered invasion, faced the formidable task of sifting through thousands of claims from local inhabitants—many of them Jewish entrepreneurs—for requisitions, supplies, contracts, and outright pillages by the invaders. Some of the claims were based on straightforward receipts for provisions. Others demanded compensation for broader losses, such as one from an "unfortunate" stocking merchant, F. Webber of Valenciennes, who in May 1816 petitioned for reimbursement of a long list of expenses incurred during the siege of that town in summer 1815, including moving the effects of his shop and household, as well as his wife and five children, and closing his business for several weeks, which he estimated to total at least 374 francs. Based on a note in the margin, he seems to have been reimbursed only 200 francs.[14]

Such claims, which now fill hundreds of boxes in municipal and departmental archives, took months, even years, to be settled. In the designated departments, the verification commission reviewed the contracts and receipts submitted by claimants—ordering additional investigations and enlisting outside experts where necessary—before deciding on the sum (usually only a portion of the total claim) to award, or, in cases where the claim was denied, providing justification for the decision. Once a reimbursement had been approved by the local commission, it was reviewed by the prefect, who then submitted it to the finance ministry, which in turn arranged payment through a credit order issued against the account of the ministry of war, redeemable in Paris. According to reports from prefects compiled by Roger André, for 1815 alone these claims totaled a minimum of 495,664,833 francs.[15] Given the complexity of the settlement process, a veritable industry of public writers and intermediary agents emerged to help creditors to negotiate with administrators and financiers in Paris. Politicized from the beginning, this process often magnified resentment among claimants whose demands were not fully satisfied.

Moreover, this process continued long after the occupation of guarantee. In its budget for 1817, the government approved a new issue of annuities, to be reimbursed by lottery beginning in 1821. In 1818, the government limited claims for arrears up to 1810 to 61.8 million francs, and up to 1816 to 297.6 million francs. The reimbursement of these debts culminated in a budget law of August 22, 1822, that accorded to the finance ministry a credit of over 13 million francs in bonds to be distributed to creditors who filed claims for expenses from the invasions of 1814 and 1815 by April 1, 1823. Following the revolution of 1830, Adolphe Thiers, then undersecretary of finance, decreed a definitive end to the liquidation of such claims. But individual claimants continued to petition the government for reimbursement as late as the 1850s. Many never received anything. In the Moselle, out of 9,747 claims for requisitions, 3,680 were rejected; out of 2,602 claims for losses, 1,740 were deemed unjustified. As Henri Contamine concluded, this settlement was organized in the interest not of individual creditors or even departments, but of the central state, concerned above all with maintaining a strict economy.[16]

To supplement these indemnities, in September 1816 the monarchy granted 11 million francs in *secours,* or aid, to those departments that had suffered most from the invasion of 1815. This aid was used by local communities to reconstruct damaged buildings, replace lost livestock and crops, purchase new furnishings and equipment, indemnify the damages of the smallest taxpayers, and finance poor relief. But it was often too little, too late. For example, the department of the Moselle, which claimed some 2 million francs in damages from occupation, received only 246,450 in aid, most of which went to Longwy in the Prussian sector.[17]

Nonetheless, the unprecedented effort at indemnification helped place the restored monarchy on a more stable financial footing. Along with the finance bill of the next year, which required ministers to provide a public accounting of their budgets, the finance bill of April 28, 1816, began to restore public credit. In the view of many historians, these finance bills were among the most successful measures of the Restoration, ending a century of financial crisis and placing the state budget on firmer ground.[18] As one early history of the Restoration argued, the occupation engendered a financial system "which will remain one of the great benefits of the parliamentary regime that established them."[19]

The Biggest War Reparations Ever Paid

Among the many financial burdens faced by the French, the war indemnity was the most significant. Set at 700 million francs, this indemnity constituted something new in the history of war termination. In contrast to previous "contributions" imposed by victors on losers to recoup particular costs, it was intended as a general punitive "reparation" for past suffering and a guarantee against further aggression. As economic historian Eugene White concluded, "Reparations now became part of a tougher peace package, assessing a penalty for threatening the new European order and a deterrent against future ventures. Payment of reparations was also an incentive, whose fulfillment would allow France to resume its role as a Great Power in the management of European affairs."[20] To ensure payment, the Allies provided the French with two main inducements: the military occupation of their territory, which would be reduced only in proportion to payment; and a security deposit of 7 million francs in 5 percent bonds, representing a nominal capital of 140 million francs, to be held by the Allies as a guarantee of payment.

According to the convention annexed to the treaty of November 20, 1815, after delivering its security deposit to the Allied powers by the end of the year, the French government was to pay the indemnity of 700 million francs over five years, in fifteen quarterly installments of 46,666,666 francs in negotiable bonds ranging from 1,000 to 20,000 francs. The bonds were to be redeemed daily by the treasury in equal amounts. These payments were verified regularly by Allied commissioners posted at the royal treasury. Once the first 600 million francs had been paid, the Allies would accept the bonds held in security in settlement of the balance. Upon receipt, these reparations would be divided among the Allies according to a separate protocol. Of the total of 700 million francs, the four Great Powers were each allotted 100 million francs. The remaining German states, along with the Netherlands and Sardinia, received 100 million francs between them, shared at the rate of just over 425 francs for each man furnished to the original war effort, with the largest sum (a little over 25.5 million francs) going to Bavaria. (Württemberg, Baden, and Saxony received much smaller amounts—8 million francs or less.) Spain, Portugal, Denmark, and Switzerland received 12.5 million francs between them. For their efforts at Waterloo and in Paris in the summer of 1815, the armies of Wellington and Blücher each received 25 million francs. Finally, 137.5 million francs were allotted for the construction of fortresses along the French frontier, mainly in the Netherlands.[21]

In order to pay the reparations, the French government had to overcome political intransigence at home to obtain financial credit, mostly abroad. In early 1816, with the political and economic situation still unstable, the French government could not meet its financial obligations through either taxation or credit at home. With the legislature dominated by the ultraroyalist party, still threatening to default on the debts left by Napoleon, the government also had trouble obtaining loans from foreign bankers, forcing it to rely on short-term borrowing in the form of treasury bonds at the expensive rate of 12 percent. To restore the trust of foreign lenders required much effort on the part of the finance minister, Comte Corvetto, and the foreign minister, the Duc de Richelieu. At their suggestion, the government reestablished the *Caisse d'Amortissement,* or sinking fund, with 20 million francs for the amortization of the public debt. Later that year, under foreign pressure, the Duc de Richelieu finally convinced the king to dissolve the legislature, which then agreed to increase the endowment of this *Caisse* to 40 million francs. At the same time, the French government lobbied for a reduction in the number of troops occupying France, in order to decrease the amount it owed for requisitions, but the request was initially rebuffed by the Allies. In the meantime, the French government found it increasingly difficult to meet the financial obligations of the treaty of 1815. Despite the dissolution of the Chamber, the government missed the deadline for paying the third installment of the reparations. In December, short of money, it temporarily suspended payment of the indemnity for January and February, causing the Allies to threaten to raise the number of troops in France.[22]

Recognizing that the current strategy, based on tax revenues and short-term debts, was not working, the finance minister began to search for a substantial loan from foreign bankers, whose funds needed a new market now that the British government was no longer indebting itself to subsidize the war effort. To facilitate such a loan, in January 1817 the Duke of Wellington finally agreed to reduce the number of troops in France by thirty thousand, effective April 1. Following negotiations mediated by Ouvrard, on February 10 the government signed a contract with the bankers Baring Brothers, of London, and Hope & Co., of Amsterdam, according to which they agreed to purchase 100 million francs' worth of bonds at 55 percent of par (versus the price on the Bourse of 60), in exchange for a commission of 2.5 percent on the nominal value of those bonds, or 4,545,454 francs. On March 11, a second loan of

100 million francs was arranged with the same bankers, with bonds at 58 percent of par; on 22 July, a third was arranged, this time with French as well as foreign bankers, for a capital of 115 million francs, at the rate of 64. After subtracting the commission charges, the rate of interest on these loans averaged close to 9 percent. Nonetheless, the strategy proved effective at restoring the credit of the French treasury and hence the confidence of the Allied powers. As André Nicolle concluded over half a century ago, "Burdensome as these conditions were, the government could hardly be blamed for subscribing to them, in view of the reluctance of French bankers to take any initiative and of the necessity of dealing with houses of international repute without whose participation neither the allied governments nor Wellington would have consented to the reduction. That the operation was, after all, a success was shown by the improvement of the government's credit and the steady upward trend of the *rente* since the first loan."[23] Combined with higher revenues from tax receipts and land sales, as well as sharp reductions in expenses, the loans enabled the treasury to cover the significant costs of reparations, occupation expenses, and war claims. By the spring of 1818, the government was confident enough in its creditworthiness to borrow directly from its own people. On May 9, it opened a domestic subscription for 292 million francs' worth of bonds. In less than three weeks, this loan was oversubscribed. Having demonstrated its ability to raise money on its own, the government was then able to arrange a final deal with Baring Brothers and Hope & Co. to settle its remaining reparations debt of 280 million francs.[24]

Given the constraints, Corvetto and Richelieu were remarkably successful at fulfilling France's financial obligations to the Allies and obtaining an early end to the occupation. As Eugene White has argued, by most measures the reparations paid by the French after the Napoleonic Wars were the largest ever paid in full. Referring to a second round of reparations paid (within two years) by France following its defeat to Germany in 1871, White notes that the French had some reason to insist on the post-World War I reparations: "Not once, but twice the French paid in full and ahead of time. . . . From a French viewpoint, France had not shirked from meeting its reparations obligations. The Germans might protest that they could not pay because their country was exhausted after a prolonged war, a great portion of territory had been lost, and their new government was not firmly established. But the French could point to very similar conditions in both 1815 and 1871."[25]

Other historians concur that the post-Waterloo settlement, especially the war indemnity, was a "godsend" for French public finances. Only three years after that historic defeat, public credit had been restored. Not only was the new government able to place a large amount of sovereign debt on the international market, but the spread between French *rentes* and British consols decreased dramatically. Close to 5 percent in the wake of Waterloo, it dipped to only 1 percent within a decade, indicating that investors once again trusted the French state to repay its debts. Making France an intermediary for the transfer of capital from English bankers to continental governments, the war indemnity also promoted the financial recovery of Europe.[26]

In the short term, however, this relative success at "repairing" the damages of war through creative financing came at a high—and enduring—cost for the French economy. At the end of the First Empire, government debt totaled 1.266 billion francs, costing 63.6 million francs annually; by the time the French finished paying reparations in 1821, it had reached 4.174 billion francs, costing 238.8 million francs annually. Much of this debt—maybe half the total value—remained in the hands of foreign investors, such as David Ricardo, who held approximately 11 million francs' worth of French bonds at his death in 1823. Moreover, the reparations alone constituted approximately 18–21 percent of one year's GDP, estimated at 9.2 billion francs, meaning a transfer of 6–7 percent of national income per year over three years. In other terms, they represented 195–231 percent of annual tax revenues at the time, or 65–77 percent spread over three years. By comparison, the German reparations burden after 1918 was some 83 percent of one year's national income, or 350 percent of tax revenues, but it was left largely unpaid.[27]

While the precise consequences of reparations for the French economy are difficult to evaluate, especially given the absence of macroeconomic data for the period before 1820, the mix of borrowing and taxation used to meet the obligation certainly contributed (to a lesser extent than would have taxation alone) to the economic distress experienced by the French from the late 1810s through the 1820s. Although this distress has often been blamed on the agricultural crisis of 1816–1817, it was undoubtedly exacerbated by the burden of reparations. This is supported by recent research on the volume of loans intermediated by notaries, which declined sharply in this period. As White concludes, "[The] evidence suggests that government borrowing crowded out private investment. Gross capital formation to GDP remains low in the 1820s and the growth of GDP only appears to pick up in the 1830s. The effects of reparations may have been cloaked by the bad harvests, but there is good reason to believe that they were a significant drag on the economy."[28] To the extent that the French economy lagged behind the British in the nineteenth century, it was largely because of the debts inherited from the Empire, particularly the war reparations.

The Year without a Summer

The difficult economic situation was exacerbated by a freak climatic occurrence that made the years 1816–1817 two of the most difficult on record in terms of subsistence. The resulting agricultural crisis provoked hunger, poverty, and unrest in many parts of France. Already suffering from two waves of invasion, as well as the loss of territory now incorporated into the Netherlands and German Confederation, the northeast was especially hard hit by the weather in 1816–1817.[29]

The agricultural crisis of 1816–1817 was caused by an event halfway around the world. On April 10, 1815, a volcano in Indonesia, Tambora, erupted. Blasting at least 150 cubic kilometers of ash some 40 kilometers into the air, this was one of the biggest volcanic eruptions in recorded human history, dwarfing even Vesuvius or Krakatoa. For many months afterward, the ash remaining in the stratosphere created a reverse greenhouse effect, causing a decrease in seasonal temperature of as much as five or six degrees Fahrenheit in some places, including northern Europe. Affecting Asia and North America as well as Europe, the eruption is now acknowledged to have caused what contemporaries called the "Year without a Summer" in 1816, when much of the northern hemisphere experienced cold, wind, rain, hail, and even snow, with precipitation levels some 80 percent higher than normal. In France, many inhabitants reportedly huddled around fires in their cottages while fields and vineyards were decimated by rain and hail. Some of the worst weather hit the already devastated region of the northeast, which experienced heavy hail in August, just as the crops were beginning to ripen. That year harvests were roughly two months behind schedule, around October 29 on average in France and Switzerland, the latest recorded since 1601. Moreover, the grain harvest was sparse and mediocre.[30] Unfortunately for the French, this coincided with the presence of foreign troops and their horses, which stressed the locals' capacity to feed themselves.

The result of this unlucky confluence was what the French called a *disette,* or "dearth," verging in places on outright famine. Exacerbated by bottlenecks in distribution, as well as by extra demands for grain and forage for the occupying armies, the shortage occurred in two main phases: the fall and winter of 1816–1817, following the disastrous growing season of 1816; and the spring and summer of 1817, before that year's crop was harvested, as a result of speculation on grain. During these periods, the price of grain increased dramatically. Between 1815 and 1817, wholesale cereal prices almost doubled, before declining to less than the average for 1815 by the end of the decade; the prices for other agricultural products, especially potatoes, beef, and wine, followed similar patterns.[31]

As prices rose, people began to go hungry. Unable to obtain wheat bread, a staple that claimed about half of a working family's income even in normal times, peasants were forced to consume substitutes, including bran, bean pods, berries, wild herbs, roots, acorns, and (previously unpopular) potatoes. In the mountains of the Vosges, numerous families reportedly lived for months on "herbs boiled in water, without fat, with no bread and with no other seasoning than a little salt." Some were sickened or killed after ingesting poisonous plants.[32] Despite these desperate measures, many suffered from famine. According to an account of the years 1816–1817 by a pastor in northern Alsace, the excessive precipitation of 1816 brought to the normally prosperous region "a painful shortage and price increase such as one had never known. Our streets were covered with famished people of a cadaverous appearance, everywhere one heard cries of hunger, orphaned children left for faraway regions and many an infant perished at the dried-up breast of its mother." As historian Nicolas Bourguinat notes, "Malnutrition was often such that observers described a population in a state of languor and stupefaction, and that deaths from hunger were not rare."[33]

In the face of such hunger, criminality and unrest increased. Begging became a significant problem. So did emigration. In Alsace and Lorraine, there were twenty thousand requests for passports from agricultural laborers, headed for the Russian Empire or the United States in search of land and food. During the first half of 1817 alone, five thousand families from rural communes in the Bas- and Haut-Rhin applied for passports.[34] As the crisis worsened, throughout the winter of 1816–1817 and especially in the spring of 1817, there were widespread reports of theft of food and obstruction of grain markets. In May 1816, inhabitants of the port of Caen tried (unsuccessfully) to prevent the departure of a ship suspected of carrying grain. The growing discontent was manifest in police reports in and outside Paris, which by 1816 began to note numerous "clamors" about the dearness of wheat.[35]

To defuse such discontent, national and local authorities adopted a mix of old and new measures, mitigating the official "pedagogy of liberalism" toward the grain trade with ad hoc intervention. Already in September 1815, the king revived the so-called Commission des Subsistances, employed during the Revolution and Empire, to monitor the quantity and price of basic foodstuffs throughout the country, especially in those provinces occupied by Allied troops, and ensure the free circulation of such goods by commercial enterprises at just prices. Maintaining relations with the ministries of finance, war, and police, as well as the Reserve of Paris and departmental authorities and military commissaries, this commission continued the Old Regime practice of compiling *mercuriales,* or bulletins, on harvests, reserves, and prices; debated policies to recommend to the government; and contracted with merchants in France and abroad to supply strategic regions. Especially concerned with maintaining the reserve for the capital, the subsistence commission deviated from the official policy of liberalism to assist particular localities on a case-by-case basis.[36]

To alleviate the subsistence crisis, the administration took a variety of other, often haphazard, measures. Before the weather turned bad, in April 1816 the state had prohibited imports of grain in an effort to protect French landowners. In August, as it became clear the harvest would not happen in time to prevent a shortage, it lifted this restriction, instead prohibiting exports. However, this measure was only partially successful at bringing more grain to market, because in the meantime the surrounding German and Italian states had themselves prohibited exports. To encourage more imports, the government then revived an old practice of offering *primes,* or bonuses, for shipments from abroad. Exploiting his connections in the Black Sea region, the Duc de Richelieu himself even helped to arrange contracts with grain merchants in Odessa. However, in comparison to the British, who instituted the Corn Laws in response to this agricultural crisis, the French maintained a relatively liberal market for grain.[37]

When these policies failed to alleviate hunger, the state accorded emergency *secours,* or grants, to particular communities. This aid was often administered by the Commission des Subsistances, which redistributed grain from one region to another. In April 1817, it ordered the shipment of wheat from Orléans to Chalon-sur-Saône to mitigate a rise in price there.[38] Elsewhere, the government distributed some grants for damages caused by the bad weather. Following a decree of September 4, 1816, indemnifying the Moselle for a hailstorm, for instance, 3,000 francs were granted to the arrondissement of Metz and 7,000 francs to the other three arrondissements of the department.[39] Such aid was not terribly effective. As Bourguinat concludes, "The exceptional grants were not negligible, but seem to have been only drops of water in an ocean of misery, always reserved for local situations and never systematized."[40]

To supplement national measures, local authorities took action to regulate bakers, to police markets, and even to restrict manufacturing of other grain-based products, especially eau-de-vie and beer. In the Haut-Rhin, authorities attempted to "tax" bakers by setting their prices. In Valenciennes, in March 1817 the mayor imposed such a "tax" even on meat, declaring that, if butchers refused to sell their product at the regulated price, they would be punished as an illegal coalition. In the Haut-Rhin, the prefect ordered the suspension of all distillation of grains and potatoes. In Strasbourg, the municipal government also forbade the distillation of potatoes, to preserve more for subsistence. While some communities, such as Boulogne, deemed their stock of grain sufficient to avoid such prohibitions, many others, including Dijon, suspended brewing.[41]

In addition, local authorities took charitable measures to alleviate hunger. In both the Haut- and Bas-Rhin, civic leaders organized traditional *greniers d'abondance,* or public warehouses, of grain, as well as British-inspired *soupes économiques,* or soup kitchens. In Strasbourg, which distributed potatoes and rice to families in need, charitable workshops struggled to nourish 2,145 indigents in January 1817. The official local newspaper, the *Courrier du Bas-Rhin,* published instructions on how to reduce bones to gelatin for soups.[42] In the Meurthe, Pont-à-Mousson adopted a mix of measures: in addition to imposing a "tax" on bread, it organized a special subsistence commission; distributed bread to the poor in lieu of funding illuminations on the festival day of Saint Louis; and instituted new taxes on wealthy inhabitants to create a charity fund for the town's poor.[43] In the canton of Charleville in the Ardennes, some two thousand households, out of a population of little more than fifteen thousand, qualified to receive bread from the local subsistence commission.[44]

These more paternalist measures were supplemented by heavy policing and extraordinary justice. Following the lead of the tough police minister Élie Decazes, authorities at all levels took a "no tolerance" approach to vagrancy, theft, and protest, even when clearly motivated by famine. Relatively unsympathetic to the real hunger, they insisted that gendarmes, national guardsmen, and police commissioners stop any threat to the free market for grain. Moreover, anyone arrested for such crimes was liable to be prosecuted by special *cours prévôtales,* or semi-military courts. Dating from the Old Regime and used by Napoleon against smuggling, these courts were revived in the early years of the Second Restoration to try crimes committed by returning soldiers or involving highway violence, customs violations, vagabondage, or rebellion. Of the cases tried by these special courts before they were discontinued in 1818, many involved theft or smuggling of food or disturbance of "public order" as a result of hunger. In 1816 and 1817, the number of defendants before French criminal courts also jumped to 9,890 and 14,084 respectively, before in August 1817 the king pardoned all persons convicted of crimes arising from dearth.[45]

As the court records show, the subsistence crisis provoked political instability, often fueled by religious millenarism. At first, during the winter of 1816–1817, the unrest was scattered and disorganized. However, in the first half of 1817, as speculation and rumormongering increased, it became more violent. (Paradoxically, the unrest was greatest in regions threatened least by grain shortages, such as Paris and Lyon; by contrast, the northeast, where prices were highest, remained relatively calm, due to the foreign military presence.) Ringing the tocsin to rally their fellow villagers, bands of peasants, often armed, blocked transports of grain, appropriated provisions from merchants, and forced entrepreneurs to sell foodstuffs at lower prices. Blaming the subsistence crisis on the restored monarchy, as well as on the foreign occupation, they circulated images of Louis XVIII as a grain-eating pig and shouted cries of "Vive le roi, mais du pain!" In the southwest, according to one prefect, a widow named Martinet in Lussac "excited the people by saying that the King (using offensive expressions) sold all the wheat 'to pay for the potatoes that he had eaten [while in exile] in England': I repeat these odious words . . . because I have found the same ones from the Pyrenees to the Poitou." Recalling the Maximum (price controls on grain and bread) of 1812, some peasants began to demand the return of Napoleon. Engendered during the Hundred Days, Bonapartism was exacerbated by the subsistence crisis of 1816–1817, often around grain markets.[46] To nip such sentiments in the bud was one of the main reasons the Duke of Wellington finally agreed to a reduction of the occupation force in early 1817.

The Costs and Benefits of Occupation

The foreign occupation certainly exacerbated the economic distress. Beyond imposing heavy requisitions and reparations, the postwar settlement disturbed commerce, especially in industrial regions tied to the Continent. With the end of the Continental System, France was now open to imports from Great Britain. At the same time, with the collapse of the Grand Empire, it lost tariff-free supplies of raw materials, including grain, and ready-made markets for manufactured goods in neighboring territories such as Belgium, the Rhineland, and northern Italy. With the new regime struggling to enforce revised customs barriers, French producers faced considerable competition from foreign troops and entrepreneurs, in the form of smuggling, counterfeiting, speculation, theft, and fraud.

At the same time, however, the foreign presence did provide some unanticipated economic benefits. Along with the civilians who accompanied them, the occupying troops required all kinds of goods and services, which were often supplied by French artisans and merchants. During the three years of the occupation, the troops spent much of their pay in the towns where they were stationed. While the benefits of occupation varied with the nationality of troops and the class of inhabitants, they did not go unnoticed by contemporaries, including state officials, for whom they constituted an argument against more equal distribution of the costs of occupation. Although it is impossible to quantify the total costs versus benefits for occupied communities, both must be considered in accounting for the economic effects of the occupation of guarantee.

By reconfiguring the boundaries of France, the Second Treaty of Paris disrupted the trading patterns of the last two decades. By August 1815, according to a report from a stagecoach driver in the Nord, Holland and Belgium had ceased commercial relations with the department: "One no longer sees any foreigner from the Netherlands in the city of Lille. The Lillois themselves engage in no commercial speculations. They have even interrupted their relations with Paris. The Diligences that are ordinarily full of merchants and loaded with their merchandise, have anymore only English and other foreigners."[47] Similar reports came from other regions. In November 1815, the municipal council of Mézières, in the Ardennes, complained that the end of war had brought economic disaster: now that the formerly prosperous royal manufactory of firearms was "without activity," its more than 1,200 workers were "without bread and . . . forced by hard necessity, abandoning their wives and children to public charity, to take their industry to foreign manufactories."[48]

The collapse of the Empire exacerbated the problem of contraband from abroad. During the occupation, much of this contraband was imported by occupying troops themselves, in cahoots with locals. This problem was perhaps greatest in the Nord and Pas-de-Calais, where smugglers, with the participation or the backing of British soldiers, introduced alcohol, tobacco, and merchandise from abroad without paying taxes. The smuggling of alcohol in particular became so egregious that it provoked formal complaints from the Chamber of Commerce in Paris.[49] Smuggling was also a problem in the Russian zone, where an old chapel near Rocroi was transformed into a warehouse for the sale of contraband coffee, tobacco, salt, and cloth.[50] Contraband became prevalent along the Rhine in Alsace, where economic activity declined significantly as a result of the fall of the Empire, which cut the region off from the German and Swiss lands with which it had been trading extensively. In the area around Wissembourg, local authorities complained relentlessly that Württemberger troops were importing tobacco and other goods from their homeland across the border. While this contraband was welcomed by local peasants, who opposed the excise taxes, it became a source of serious friction with French customs officials.[51]

In addition to smuggling, Allied nationals engaged in fraud and theft. In December 1815, in Abbeville, several English soldiers were arrested for fabricating one-franc coins.[52] In September 1817, in Paris, a police commissioner reported that a foreigner, probably English, asked to change some foreign money for 35,000 francs of French gold coins, upon receipt of which he disappeared, leaving the moneychangers with a bag containing only copper.[53] Domestic industry also continued to be threatened by foreign espionage, which had long been a problem in France. In April 1817, a designer and a mechanic, both of Russian origin, were arrested by French authorities for planning to export processes for manufacturing silk. Although the court in Lyon judged this to be an "abuse of hospitality," the Russian ambassador, Pozzo di Borgo, insisted on a retrial, arguing that "[O]ne might not, without extreme injustice, arrest a Russian under pretext that he had the plan to return to his Patrie; and to put to use there knowledge that he had acquired on his voyages."[54]

Dishonesty aside, foreign visitors hurt French suppliers and consumers just by affecting supply and demand. After causing a rush on lodging in Paris during the summer of 1815, Allied statesmen, officers, and accompanying civilians provoked a crisis among hoteliers at the end of that year when they either found cheaper sublets or departed Paris altogether. According to a report from the police commissioner in Montmartre at the end of December 1815, "The *maisons garnies* have become deserted. The lodgings still occupied rent for a cheap price. The hoteliers and lodgers, whose expenses have become very high, renew their complaints and demands, because of the infinite number of individuals who with or without permission sublet rooms without being subject to any public expenses or obligations, which allow them to rent at a discount, to the prejudice of those whose profession it is."[55] During the subsistence crisis of 1816–1817, foreigners were criticized for exacerbating price increases by buying up items of primary necessity. According to a report from a stagecoach driver in Caen in December 1817, the English had excited considerable discontent by purchasing an immense quantity of eggs in the Calvados, raising the price by almost 100 percent.[56] At other times, the foreign visitors depressed prices by reselling provisions. In June 1816, following a reduction in administrative personnel among the English and Danish armies, their mounts were sold, thereby diminishing the price of horses from Flanders.[57] The economic distress was aggravated by certain Allied policies. In February 1818, for instance, the mayor of Valenciennes in the Nord protested a proposal by the Duke of Wellington to forbid masked balls during Carnival, for removing "from several individuals the means of earning some money to help them live, which is all the more bothersome in these circumstances, when one has been deprived of commerce."[58]

When they did business with French shopkeepers, foreign visitors did not always pay what they owed. Allied officers, statesmen, soldiers, and tourists racked up numerous debts for food, drink, entertainment, and gambling. This was especially true during the summer of 1815 in and around Paris, as the Allies celebrated their second victory over Napoleon. But they also left such debts in the provinces. In the spring of 1817, the mayor of Valenciennes struggled to obtain payment for rental of the town hall and for labor provided by local workers for an English "Dramatical Society" brought to entertain the soldiers; failing to obtain a response from the director of the society, he closed the hall, confiscating the troupe's belongings.[59] The same mayor compiled a list of debts owed by an Irish officer to about twenty locals, totaling 19,876 francs.[60] Meanwhile, in the Russian zone around Avesnes, inhabitants complained that officers were leaving unpaid debts. Although the Russian command kept a third of the salaries of officers, to acquit debts that they acknowledged, the subprefect of the arrondissement nevertheless urged mayors to warn local merchants not to offer them credit.[61] In Tourcoing, the Saxon contingent racked up debts totaling 17,429 francs, for workshops, candles, wine, labor, furniture, and fuel. By the end of the occupation, only 3,847 francs were paid; the rest were settled out of receipts from sales of the furnishings left behind.[62] Foreign civilians also accumulated considerable debts, many of which remained unpaid when they departed at the end of 1818.

However, the occupation was not all bad for business. By the end of 1815, factories and shipments had begun to resume "ordinary activity." Although the agricultural crisis, along with the war indemnity, squeezed growth in 1816–1817, continental and colonial trade began to revive.[63] This recovery was stimulated by demand from the occupying troops and foreign civilians. Together they contributed in no small measure to the reconstruction of the economy in France. In addition to purchasing goods from French manufacturers and shopkeepers, they imported technology, capital, and labor. Some of them established businesses in France that continued to operate after the liberation.

Between late 1815 and 1818, economic activity in France was encouraged by the occupation itself. The occupiers required not only food, drink, and forage, but also large quantities of other supplies, including clothing, furniture, bedding, kitchen equipment, office supplies, horseshoes, saddles and bridles, and tools. Much of this material was ordered from local suppliers. As one study of the Moselle has suggested, in an otherwise difficult economic context, the foreign occupation permitted artisans and merchants to find a market for their products: "In a general fashion, one may ask whether all these deliveries of supplies, and, especially, the fulfillment of services (outside of the summer season) were not, often, a godsend for these villagers, who thereby found a supplementary revenue or, in any case, a compensation, however limited, for their suffering."[64] This "compensation" was fueled by a building boom, as local communities, especially in the northeast, constructed or renovated buildings to use as barracks for foreign troops and repaired damages to structures caused by invasion. Such projects put numerous architects, engineers, entrepreneurs, and laborers to work.[65]

In some places, French businesses also profited from the foreign demand for French goods and services, including the *montagnes russes*. This was especially true in Paris, where Allied officers, statesmen, and tourists spent large sums at hotels, restaurants, cabarets, tailors, bookstores, theaters, gambling dens, amusement parks, and brothels. In the capital, *marchands de nouveautés* marketed the latest fashions to foreign visitors. To cater to the British colony there, shopkeepers erected English signs—of which some two thousand were counted circa

1816—and restaurateurs printed English menus.[66] Shopkeepers and restaurateurs were also kept busy at Cambrai, where the Duke of Wellington had his headquarters. At Wellington's residence in Mont-Saint-Martin, the Duke and his wife spent some 10,000 francs per day, to the profit of nearby communities.[67]

In the northeast, foreign soldiers infused cash into the local economy. According to the terms of the treaty of November 20, 1815, the annual payment of 50 million francs toward salary and equipment for occupying troops was to be distributed monthly, in cash, by Allied commissioners. Some Allied commands, such as the Russian and the Saxon, seem to have retained any money in excess of the normal salaries of their soldiers for their general military budget. However, others distributed it to their troops, who (if they did not send it to family back home) spent it where they were stationed. This opportunity for profit-making did not go unnoticed by local leaders. With a Russian army corps camped in the area in September 1816, the mayor of Charleville informed local merchants: "Those of you who would transport abundant provisions of food and liquid there will find a great advantage, because the officers and servants will receive nothing from the warehouses."[68]

Beyond such spending, the occupation yielded other, often unexpected benefits. One of the most important—and sometimes controversial—of these was the manure produced by the fifty thousand horses of the occupying troops. According to an instruction from the French war ministry publicized by Allied commanders, the manure was Allied property only if the horses were stabled in their garrisons and provisioned with straw from their warehouses. If they were stabled with local homeowners, the manure became the property of the inhabitants, who sought it for their fields. This by-product, which literally fertilized the French economy, became a source of dispute. In March 1816, the Prussian commander in Charleville ordered the mayor to instruct a local inhabitant named Pierlot, who had been appropriating the manure of the horses stabled on his property even though he was not feeding them, either to turn the manure over to the Prussians or to reimburse the Prussians for each wheelbarrow of it applied to his fields. Later that year, the prefect of the Bas-Rhin asked the commander of the Württemberger contingent to remind his cavalry to relinquish their manure to the local inhabitants on whom they were lodged.[69]

The biggest economic boon from occupation seems to have occurred in the British sector. Although some merchants were surprised by the "excessive economy" of British officers, compared to Hanoverian or Saxon ones, most commentators found British troops to be liberal spenders.[70] According to a report on the British embarkation from Calais on December 1, 1818, "The entire pay of the English soldier was spent by him, during the three years of the occupation."[71] After the British left Valenciennes, business declined to such an extent that an English traveler returning five years later bemoaned, "[G]ood Heavens, what a change! It was like a body from which the soul had departed. The buildings were the same, and the beautiful spires still glittered in the sun, but the vivifying principle was gone. Grass was growing in the streets; half the shops were shut up, and mine host of the *Grand Canard* [a hotel], instead of asking three guineas for a bed, thanked me most humbly for three francs. *Vive la Guerre!*"[72] The British were reputed to be far more prodigal than, say, the Prussians, who, according to the report on the Pas-de-Calais in December 1818, "lived with Economy and have always sent their funds home."[73] However, even in the Prussian sector around Sedan, it was reported after the evacuation in 1818 that "those persons who protested with the most vehemence against the occupation of this town by foreign troops are those who regret their departure, for the reason that the money they spent fueled commerce, and they complain today of the insufficiency of the [returning French] garrison."[74]

Varying with the nationality, the benefits of occupation were mitigated by the fact that Allied troops often brought their own suppliers from abroad. In Valenciennes, inhabitants complained that they "had hoped to make great profits with a significant garrison and proportional general staff; but they find themselves, for the most part, disappointed in their hopes: many merchants and artisans of different types have arrived here from England, and thus take from us the benefits of the sojourn of the troops of their nation."[75] The Russian contingent was often accompanied by its own suppliers, such as the merchant Sieur Hickmann, who in 1815 assumed responsibility for provisioning Russian troops in the Ardennes with a third of the materials they required, including sheets, fabrics, canvasses, and leathers, at the expense of the department.[76] In both the Russian and Prussian sectors, inhabitants complained that, out of economy or hostility, troops opened their own cafés and cabarets, thereby depriving French shopkeepers of business. According to one report in June 1816, "The establishments, such as restaurants, cafés and cantines, formed by the Prussians at Sedan, cause considerable damage to the inhabitants and paralyze Commerce entirely. All the soldiers gather there and those of the inhabitants are deserted. For this behavior, the principal motive seems to be the animosity that reigns between the French and the Prussians."[77]

In fact, during the occupation a new generation of foreign artisans and traders poured into France. Many came to do business with the Allied troops. In the Moselle, in the spring of 1816 arrived approximately twenty suppliers per week from such places as Bohemia, Rotterdam, and Mayence, to furnish provisions to the contingents in the region.[78] Foreign occupiers may have helped launch the brewing industry in France, around Valenciennes and elsewhere.[79] In the Auvergne, which was occupied by the Austrian army between August and October 1815, some Slavic troops seem to have demonstrated the art of brewing—and, in some cases, stayed to practice it—in local towns, which experienced an "explosion" of brasseries, with eastern names like Fusch or Wertz, in the late 1810s.[80] Around Cambrai, a number of British landowners, merchants, and "mechanics" came to seek their livelihood in the late 1810s.[81] English artisans brought a number of new technologies to France, including three important inventions: gas lighting, introduced to Paris by the British firm Winsor; the Leavers lace-making machine, smuggled into Calais by three artisans from Nottingham; and the steamboat, first exhibited on the Seine in March 1816 and then reproduced in a factory at Charenton by the British firm Manby & Wilson. Such foreigners were instrumental in jump-starting factory production in places like Lille, Le Creusot, and Saint-Étienne.[82] Often surveyed by the police, who suspected them of importing materials without paying proper customs duties, many of these foreign entrepreneurs and workers stayed beyond the liberation. According to business historian Jean Lambert-Dansette, by 1825 there were thousands of technicians and workers from England, among other countries, in French industry. These "adopted French" reinvigorated the capitalist elite of nineteenth-century France.[83]

While the economic benefits of the occupying forces are difficult to calculate with any precision, they were notable enough to garner the attention of the French administration. On at least one occasion, the ministry of interior cited such benefits as an argument against collective responsibility for the financial burden of the occupation. Rejecting a request by the prefect of the Meuse for an extraordinary tax to be levied on the department as a whole, the ministry concluded that, while the presence of Allied troops gave rise to some expenses, "it also gives birth to some profits; by pouring their pay into the occupied country, they increase the value of the productions of the soil, sustain commerce and industry, generate growth of capital, and give it a greater activity; what is considered by the prefect and the council as a troublesome situation, is reduced to a simple momentary bother, from which will result some very real advantages." In lieu of authorization for such an exceptional tax, the ministry offered a royal donation of 30,000 francs, for the prefect to distribute as he saw fit. Explaining this decision, the ministry elaborated in a letter dated July 31, 1816: "The Department of the Meuse has been more than any other subject to the disasters of the last invasions; but the troops that occupy it are today friends, who observe an exact discipline; they consume, but they pay . . . It would thus be unjust that, the advantages being local, the expenses be considered as departmental. Each locality must face that which concerns it, either by means of habitual resources or from extraordinary communal taxes, or even by loans that it will pay by means of such taxes."[84] Even if local authorities did not always see it that way, the occupation did bring some economic benefits to the communities affected.

Revising Economic Policy

In addition to encouraging the revival of business activity, the occupation of guarantee forced a revision of economic policy in France. As the French government struggled to pay its debts, requisitions, and reparations, it grappled with the question of how best to promote economic reconstruction, especially how to rebuild agriculture, industry, and trade. This question, which provoked an outpouring of pamphlets, petitions, and treatises, constituted one of the main preoccupations of ministers and legislators between 1815 and 1820. Concerned about foreign competition, especially from the British, who had emerged as the economic and military victors of the wars, the French government pursued a middle path between Old Regime mercantilism and revolutionary liberalism. Following the lead of Jean-Antoine Chaptal, who had served Napoleon as minister of interior until the advent of the Continental System, the new administration moved to encourage industry via investments in education, infrastructure, and credit. Inheriting a number of men from the previous regime, it adopted much the same approach of balancing state protections and individual rights. Initially less restrictive than British economic policy, this French path proved no less effective. Despite the difficult conjuncture of the foreign occupation and grain shortage, it set the French economy on the road not just to recovery but to actual growth by the end of the 1810s.

The collapse of the Empire unleashed a flood of discussion on the subject of political economy among theorists, statesmen, landowners, manufacturers, and merchants. Beginning in 1814 and 1815, this subject was revived—and vulgarized—by a slew of administrators, intellectuals, and industrialists, some of whom traveled to Britain in search of new ideas about how to promote commerce and manufacture in France. From this period date some of the most important and enduring works of political economy published by French before the mid-nineteenth century, including Jean-Baptiste Say's treatise on industry in Great Britain, *De l'Angleterre et des Anglais* (1815) and Jean-Antoine Chaptal's extensive survey of the state of industry, *De l'industrie française* (1819).[85] Alongside such philosophical treatises and investigative reports appeared a slew of manuals, dictionaries, and periodicals related to commerce and industry. Political economy was also discussed in editorials in newspapers and, especially, in petitions to the chambers, by merchants, manufacturers, and commercial associations. Between 1814 and 1820, dozens of such petitions—often printed—were submitted to the legislature on issues ranging from government loans to consumption taxes, from the state monopoly on tobacco to the revival of guilds, from transit and warehousing rights to customs duties.[86]

Many of these publications were aimed at helping the government solve its financial problems, especially its debts from the end of the Napoleonic Wars. With titles such as *Very Equitable Method for Repairing a Large Part of the Disasters of France* and *Method of Paying All the Debts of the State without Recourse to Either the Loans or the Taxes Rejected by the Last Session of the Chambers*, these petitions debated various options for restoring the public credit of France.[87] Other such publications, however, were focused on determining what sort of policy would best help rebuild French agriculture and industry after two decades of revolution and war. Many of these were motivated by anxiety about competition from the neighboring economic powerhouse, Great Britain. During the occupation of guarantee, much of the debate over political economy concerned questions of international trade—for instance, which cities held privileges for the transit and warehousing of goods from abroad; the extent to which imports should be discouraged through tariffs; and how exactly to encourage the development of domestic industry.[88] These issues, which tended to divide the maritime regions of the Atlantic and Mediterranean from the landlocked east, which had benefited from the Continental System, ultimately united the bulk of property owners, whether of land or industry. With few exceptions, agricultural, manufacturing, and merchant interests all favored some state protection of commerce in the interest of national industry.[89]

Pushed by manufacturers, merchants, and landowners, the Restoration government maintained a compromise between liberalism and protectionism. Following the approach charted by Chaptal in the early years of the Empire, the new regime sought to encourage trade in the domestic market, especially in niche industries, while also protecting this market from international competition. Rejecting the revival of Old Regime corporations, it instead focused on promoting industry through government incentives, educational institutions, and, especially, customs duties. As Jeff Horn has argued, "During the Restoration (1815–1830), a period of diminished political expectations, state industrial policy focused on expanding the profitability and range of what France did well and reserving the home market for domestic manufactures. . . . If this led to slower growth than across the Channel, it did allow France to recover from its ordeals and to profit from its own competitive advantages."[90]

This path between liberalism and protectionism is exemplified by the finance law of April 28, 1816. In addition to resolving the public debt from the invasions of 1814 and 1815 and revisiting the thorny issue of excise taxes, this law imposed a host of tariffs on foreign imports, including colonial goods such as sugar. Legislators argued that such protections were the only way to revive French manufacturing in the face of foreign competition. As deputy Cornet-d'Incourt asserted during discussion of the bill on April 16, "If ever grave and extraordinary circumstances had been able to determine the legislator to deploy a great severity in repressing contraband, it was in the circumstances where events without example had placed our unfortunate country."[91] To enforce these tariffs against smugglers, the law also strengthened the power of the customs administration, especially in the east. In an effort to restore the commercial "morality" of the French after the fall of the Continental System, the law prohibited imports of colonial goods via land, instituted domestic searches for foreign textiles, and increased penalties for smugglers. Under the leadership of its director, Pierre de Saint-Cricq, the Administration of Customs, which grew to some twenty-five thousand employees, or 20 percent of all state agents, during the Restoration, symbolized the new regime's commitment to "purification" of French commerce. Reconfiguring the old prohibitionist system, this customs regime would be reinforced by additional regulation of foreign commerce in succeeding years.[92]

At the same time that it strengthened the customs regime, the Restoration government provided a number of encouragements to industry within France. In line with Chaptal's mantra that "Today when it is generally recognized that commerce, agriculture and manufacturing industry constitute the force and the richness of a nation, governments can have only one goal, that of protecting and encouraging them," the new regime established institutions to facilitate investment and enterprise in France. In addition to a better-funded Caisse d'Amortissement, it instituted a Caisse des Dépôts to ease credit. To encourage contributions to this institution, in 1818 the government created the so-called Livret A, which remains one of the main types of savings accounts to this day. To promote investment, it also approved the incorporation of the first insurance companies in France, starting in the late 1810s. To oversee commercial policy, in 1816 the government established a Conseil Général du Commerce, to supplement the Conseil Général des Manufactures created by Napoleon in 1810; in 1820, it would add a Conseil Général de l'Agriculture. In 1816, it also established the public École des

Mines, or mining school, to encourage the field of metallurgy, crucial for industrialization. Recognizing the importance of communication and transportation for industry, the Restoration government invested heavily in roads, canals, and ports, including for the new steamship, which made its first transatlantic crossing in 1819. In an effort to catch up to the British, the new regime focused above all on preferences for certain manufacturers, especially in the textile and steel industries. Already during the First Restoration, the administration imported from England an entrepreneur, James Jackson, to establish a coke-burning blast furnace at Saint-Étienne, which would continue to receive numerous subsidies and contracts from the French government. A similar strategy was used by the administration to revive the steel industry at Le Creusot in 1816.[93]

Continuing into the 1820s, this Chaptalian approach would put France on its own effective path to industrialization in the nineteenth century. The policy enabled the nation to recover quickly from the military and economic disasters of 1814 and 1815–1818. Already by 1819, the French economy was growing at a healthy rate of over 3 percent per year, a rate of growth that would continue for much of the rest of the century. As Horn concludes, "Despite the constraints imposed by English political, technological, and industrial dominance, France's economic performance under Bourbon stewardship was impressive. Sustained by the industrial revival after 1815, the Bourbon regime postponed revolution until 1830."[94] Out of the crux of dire financial and agricultural crisis was forged a revived political economy in France.

The National Industrial Exposition of 1819

Symbolic of the new regime's support for industry, as Horn has noted, was its revival of the national industrial exposition, beginning in 1819.[95] First organized by the Directory in 1798 to showcase the work of artisans and manufacturers in France, the industrial exposition was continued by Napoleon during the early years of his reign. But one had not been held since the advent of the Continental System in 1806. In January 1819, within a few weeks of the liberation of the country from occupation, Élie Decazes, now minister of interior, proposed to organize a new industrial exposition. Asking prefects to solicit samples of the best executed or most economical works of manufacturers in their departments, the ministry of interior offered to pay the cost of shipping them to Paris for display. To judge these products, the ministry appointed a jury of nineteen notables, presided by the Duc de Rochefoucauld, a reformist noble who was, among other things, inspector of the École Nationale Supérieure d'Arts et Métiers in Châlons-en-Champagne. The vice president of this jury was Jean-Antoine Chaptal, who as interior minister under Napoleon had organized the expositions of 1801 and 1802.

Opening on the king's festival day, August 25, the exposition of 1819 was held at the Louvre, which only four years earlier had been emptied of many of its treasures by the Allies, but now was transformed into a "national sanctuary of industry." Over the next month, well over a hundred thousand visitors, including approximately twenty thousand English, toured this "sanctuary" to view the manufactures on display. Among the wide variety of products displayed were fabrics, including the latest cashmeres and silks; dyes; metallurgical arts, including tools and arms; jewelry; pottery and porcelain; glass and crystal; paper, typography, lithography, and bookbinding; clocks; chemical arts; alimentary products; scientific instruments; heating and lighting appliances; and machines for agriculture and manufacturing. The exposition also featured the work of trade schools, royal manufactories, poorhouses, and prisons. Overall, some 1,662 manufacturers competed for five different distinctions. In the end, 886 medals were awarded, among them a Legion of Honor presented to Joseph-Marie Jacquard for the process of silk weaving. More famously, in the salon attached to the exposition, Théodore Géricault exhibited his painting of the shipwreck of the *Raft of the Medusa* off the coast of Mauritania in July 1816, whose anticlassical style and anti-imperialist message provoked a public outcry.[96]

For observers inside and outside of France, the industrial exposition of 1819 signified the economic recovery of France after three years of foreign occupation, financial difficulty, and agricultural crisis. In the introduction to the catalog of the products, the reporter for the jury, Louis Costaz, enumerated the causes of progress in the industrial arts since the last such exposition in 1806, including scientific research, the École Polytechnique, the Society for the Encouragement of Industry, local expositions, and especially new legislation regarding commerce and industry. "Such are the principal causes that have produced the

Flourishing state at which the industrial arts have arrived," he wrote, "and as these causes still persist, since they act with a growing energy, one can predict for French industry a brilliant and stable destiny."[97] The economic recovery was detailed by Chaptal in his comprehensive survey, *L'industrie française,* published the same year. The speedy recovery of industry in France was noted even by foreign observers, such as William Somerville, who remarked of the industrial exposition of 1819: "[N]o scene could be more brilliant than that which Paris exhibited during the months of September and October. A crowd of foreigners flocked in from every country of Europe to enjoy the exposition. . . . The disheartened vanity of the French was re-vivified by this admiration of their productions, and the press consequently teemed with extravagant encomiums on the perfection of the arts in France, and on the charms of Paris, as the metropolis of civilization, and the centre of all earthly elegance."[98] Little more than four years after the Battle of Waterloo, France had not only paid its war debts and reparations, but also reconstructed its economy. Despite the setback of military defeat, it was now ready to compete with its former enemies on the new battlefield of industry.

Chapter Eight

Recuperation

In the salon at the Exposition of 1819, alongside the controversial tableau of the *Raft of the Medusa* was exhibited a porcelain tray with a painting of *The Apotheosis of Henri IV* by Louis-Bertin Parant, part of an eight-piece service by the royal Sèvres manufacture. Commissioned by Louis XVIII himself, the service was presented as a gift to his nephew, the Duc d'Angoulême, in December 1818 before being exhibited to the public. Featuring the first Bourbon king, who had reunited France after almost a century of religious warfare by converting from Protestantism to Catholicism in 1593, it was intended to honor the newly restored king as a similar hero of national reconciliation following civil war. In the painting, a seminude, laurel-crowned Henry is greeted by Jupiter, surrounded by classical heroes including Alexander the Great and Julius Caesar; below them, an allegory of France mourns the Bourbon king, while a group of putti raises a sword left by him to the country. Under the descendant of this Bourbon monarch, the painting suggests, France may rise again.[1]

While it has long been overshadowed by Géricault's masterpiece, Parant's *The Apotheosis of Henri IV* is more representative not just of official but also of popular culture during both Restorations. In the wake of foreign invasion and civil war, the French took refuge in history. To face the national trauma of regime change under foreign occupation, they resurrected two figures from the distant past: Henry IV, who had died over two hundred years before; and Joan of Arc, the "Virgin of

Orléans" who fought the English during the Hundred Years' War. While both historical figures had been common subjects of art and literature since long before the Revolution, they spiked in popularity in the years after the collapse of the Napoleonic Empire. In 1814 and again between 1815 and 1818, both Joan of Arc and Henry IV featured in countless histories, poems, panegyrics, plays, paintings, monuments, prints, decorative arts, and even fabrics.[2]

Joan of Arc and Henry IV served as malleable, sometimes contradictory icons for the French nation. Initially, the "Virgin of Orléans" was revived as a symbol of resistance against foreign invasion. During the Hundred Days, she was invoked in a two-page call to the "courageous women" of the capital to avenge themselves against the "savage" enemies who had invaded the year before: "Before these dirty barbarians force cries from your modesty; before the air polluted by their breath is mixed with the gentle odor of your virginal breath, learn at least to strike your executioner; . . . Avenge your *patrie;* avenge your family; avenge yourself; avenge your honor: it is sacred to Frenchwomen!"[3] Once these foreign enemies conquered Napoleon, however, Joan of Arc came to represent the triumph of monarchy over empire. This shift is exemplified by a print depicting a group of French "Amazons" raising their swords to a statue of Joan of Arc. Originally intended to rally the French against foreign invasion, this print was recycled as royalist propaganda by changing the flag from tricolor to white and adding the figure of the king's niece, the Duchesse d'Angoulême.[4] Following the Second Restoration, Joan of Arc remained a popular symbol of monarchy and faith as well as patriotism, in histories, odes, household furnishings, sermons (particularly in her hometown of Orléans), and especially plays.[5] In fact, this heroine became such a common subject of theater that she was satirized in a burlesque farce at the Théâtre de la Porte Saint-Martin in 1819, *The Sword of Joan of Arc, or the Five Demoiselles,* which depicted a contest between five different "Joans" from five different Parisian theaters.[6] Following the collapse of the Empire, Joan of Arc came to symbolize the regeneration of France out of defeat, through royalism and Catholicism.

Where Joan of Arc was employed to inspire support for monarchy in general, Henry IV was resuscitated to encourage attachment to Louis XVIII in particular. The link between these two monarchs was made explicit from the beginning of the First Restoration, when the returning king was greeted by crowds singing couplets to the tune of "Henry IV" and by a plaster copy of the equestrian statue of the earlier king that had been erected on the Pont Neuf in 1614 but destroyed during the Revolution. Commissioned by interior minister Jacques-Claude Beugot from sculptor François-Frédéric Lemot, the reproduction included an inscription in Latin: "With the return of Louis, Henry lives again."[7] The analogy between the two monarchs was also drawn in songs, histories, paintings, prints, and plays, many of which were performed in the provinces (often in conjunction with a visit by a member of the royal family), as well as in Paris.[8] Often referencing Henry's promise to put "a chicken in every pot," these representations accentuated the humanity of the first Bourbon monarch and, by extension, the newly restored one.[9] To legitimize the restored king, they often depicted Henry IV surrounded by admiring subjects. The effort to popularize Louis XVIII is exemplified by the new regime's project to erect a permanent statue of Henry IV on the Pont Neuf, funded by public subscription. Cast by Lemot from metal melted down from the imperial Vendôme column, the new statue was inaugurated with much pomp on August 28, 1818, only weeks before the opening of the Congress of Aix-la-Chapelle to end the occupation of guarantee. Numerous prints depicted the statue being pulled by a crowd of enthusiastic people to the bridge.[10] Emphasizing the king's role in restoring peace and prosperity, the various representations of Henry IV aimed to reconcile the French to each other as well as to their restored monarch.

Together, in the context of yet another national trauma, Joan of Arc and Henry IV were weapons in a battle of symbols between two Frances: one for the Emperor Napoleon, symbolized by the violet, and one for King Louis XVIII, associated with the lily. The use of such symbolism to reconcile the two Frances has long been noted by historians of the Restoration, who emphasize the regime's dual—and hence unsuccessful—strategy of forgetting and expiation of the past.[11] Less well known is the way in which the conflict between the two Frances was shaped by foreign occupation. As the revival of Joan of Arc in particular highlights, the restoration of monarchy occurred in the context of foreign invasion. Although it compromised the legitimacy of the restored king, the foreign occupation spurred political reform, which stabilized the new regime. Constraining civil conflict, the foreign presence was critical to the development of a more liberal political culture in France.

Revisiting the political history of this period through the lens of the occupation of guarantee revises our understanding of the Restoration. Long a no-man's-land in the historiography on modern France, this regime has recently attracted attention from scholars on both sides of the Atlantic interested in political culture. Focusing on the role of the regime in inventing the institutions, symbols, and practices of partisan politics, this new work has tended to conclude that it was by no means reactionary but actually quite innovative. In fact, following a contemporary commentator named "William, the Straight Talker" who said "It is not a Restoration we need, it's a Regeneration," some recent historians have reinterpreted the regime less as a "restoration," than as a regeneration or even revolution, which in the name of reversing the Revolution of 1789 nonetheless created a modern political culture.[12] In rehabilitating this regime, however, the new work has not addressed the international context in which it was incubated. Meanwhile, even as diplomatic historians have also begun to revise their understanding of this period as "revolutionary" rather than conservative, they have remained focused on the Congress of Vienna and the Concert of Europe, at the expense of the institutions and practices through which the goals of the Great Powers were put into effect.[13] By failing to bring these two strands of research together, historians have missed the extent to which political reconstruction within France was shaped by foreign occupation.

Between 1815 and 1818, as the new regime was determining its main institutions and laws, it was under surveillance by Allied leaders, especially the occupation's commander in chief, the Duke of Wellington. Although the Allied leadership did not orchestrate a comprehensive propaganda campaign of the type seen in later peacetime occupations, it still exerted considerable influence over policy in France, mainly through the Council of Allied Ambassadors. This council's goal was not just to contain civil war but also to remake the political culture. Concerned less with legitimacy than with moderation, it sought to forge a middle path between Jacobin revolutionaries on the one hand and extreme conservatives on the other. Encouraging the ministry of Louis XVIII to resist the demands of ultraroyalists such as his brother the Comte d'Artois, Allied leaders like Wellington, Castlereagh, and

Nesselrode played a key role in the political "recuperation" of France after twenty-five years of revolution.[14] Promoting the establishment of a parliamentary system, the repoliticization of the public, and the rise of a relatively free press, the foreign guardianship of the French government created a window for liberalism. As this fanned the flames of Bonapartism, however, the window was soon slammed shut by the Concert of Europe, whose main concern shifted from conservative reaction to revolutionary activity. Enabled by the occupation, the shift toward liberalism ended—not just in France, but across Europe—soon after the troops returned home.

Violets versus Lilies

When they arrived in France in 1815, the Allies found a divided nation. The brief episode of the Hundred Days had split the country between supporters of Napoleon and of Louis XVIII. In the wake of the emperor's defeat at Waterloo, the country endured not just foreign invasion but also civil war, the so-called White Terror of royalists against *fédérés*. In an era when news still took over a week to travel from one end of France to the other, this power struggle generated widespread uncertainty and anxiety. By mid-1815, the French were suffering from what Pierre Serna has termed political "nausea." To survive the multiple shifts in political winds, many had become *girouettes*, or "weather vanes," as satirized in a slew of guides to these political shape-shifters.[15]

The nausea was only exacerbated by the return of Louis XVIII, an unpopular leader imposed by the Allies for pragmatic rather than legitimist reasons. Under pressure from the occupying powers to pacify the French nation, the restored monarchy adopted a strategy of *oubli*, or "forgetting." However, by highlighting certain symbols at the expense of others, this policy of forgetting only exacerbated political divisions. As the monarchy returned with the Allied armies, it launched an attack on the symbolism of revolution and empire. The royal administration ordered local authorities to remove all revolutionary and imperial symbols from public spaces and destroy them in public ceremonies, called *mises-en-place*. Within a short time, Bourbon symbolism, especially the *fleur-de-lis*, or lily, was substituted for imperial iconography, including not just the initials NB but the golden bee, the eagle, and the violet, favorite flower of Hortense, wife of Napoleon's brother Louis and Queen of the Netherlands.[16]

This iconoclasm was sometimes initiated spontaneously by local populations. As Allied armies approached first in 1814 and again in 1815, French communities changed their flags and cockades from revolutionary red or tricolor to white, and official iconography rotated rapidly between eagles or violets and fleur-de-lys. Even shop signs were replaced, multiple times.[17] As soon as the siege was lifted in Valenciennes in July 1815, the municipal administration raised a white flag and sent an address to the restored king.[18] Farther south, in Nancy, in addition to flying the white flag on public buildings, local authorities reprinted their official stationery and forms with the old royal filigree, burning all paper with the imperial one, as they had a year earlier in 1814.[19] In Strasbourg, the mayor prohibited the wearing of buttons with eagles in the royal secondary school.[20] This revolving symbolism was noted in the letters and diaries of ordinary citizens. For instance, an artisan in Chinon, Claude Bailly, observed that on July 18, 1815, a portrait of Bonaparte was removed from the local fountain and a tricolor flag was replaced by a white one.[21]

Once the monarchy was firmly reestablished, this "forgetting" became far more systematic. In November 1815, the minister of police ordered prefects to destroy all reminders of revolution. Given how many private, as well as public, objects carried these symbols, this was a daunting task. Often, this happened in mass burnings on public squares, accompanied by sermons, processions, speeches, and cries of "Vive le Roi!"[22] In Strasbourg, following an order that any individual found to possess Bonapartist symbols would be delivered to the courts, a bonfire of "outdated emblems" was held on the Place d'Armes, in front of the local national guard and departmental legion.[23] Meanwhile, outside city hall in Dunkirk, in front of a crowd crying "Vive le Roi! Vive le père des Français!" authorities destroyed a number of revolutionary flags, tricolor cockades and scarves, red bonnets, buttons with eagles, two paintings commissioned by the emperor in 1814, and even a clock decorated with an eagle, which despite the fact that it referred to Jupiter was deemed unacceptable.[24] Around Lunéville, in the Meurthe, the subprefect certified that all liberty trees—symbol of freedom since the Revolution—had been cut and sold, with most of the proceeds donated to the public treasury.[25] Similar renewals of symbols occurred in cities throughout France, including Paris, where at the cathedral of Notre-Dame such revolutionary emblems as Phrygian caps were replaced with royalist ones such as lilies in stained-glass windows, medallions, and wood paneling.[26]

Despite the efforts at removing all signs of the previous regime, some signs remained in circulation, often in secret. In "private intelligence" forwarded by the Duke of Wellington to British authorities in August 1815, it was noted that while green and white cockades were pervasive in the west of France, the popular actress Mademoiselle Mars, who had previously caused offense by wearing violets, had in her latest role found a new way to indicate her political sensibilities by changing her dress three times, from red to white to blue, provoking much amusement.[27] In October 1815, an artillery company in Strasbourg glued a tricolor cockade and eagle on a door inside their barracks.[28] For years after the second defeat of Napoleon, symbols of the imperial regime continued to circulate, often hidden under royalist ones, for instance in fans and snuffboxes, in which a portrait of the emperor was embedded under a representation of Louis XVIII. Such revolutionary symbolism became a rallying point for opposition to the new regime. As Sheryl Kroen has emphasized, the project of "compulsory forgetting" reinforced rather than erased ideological differences, creating new sites and symbols for memory of the Revolution and Napoleon. The violet came to symbolize the hope that Bonaparte would return again, like the flower, in the spring.[29] Ultimately, the restored monarchy's project of "forgetting" the past proved impossible.

The goal of forgetting the past was further undermined by the regime's strategy of "expiation" for the sins of the revolutionary regimes, especially regicide. This approach was encouraged by the Allies, who often participated in funerary services and anniversary celebrations for the royal family. However, like forgetting, expiation failed to reconcile the French. As Emmanuel Fureix has shown, because this approach to expiation centered on royal as opposed to ordinary victims of the Revolution, it ultimately exacerbated divisions between royalists and liberals.[30]

Although it began under the First Restoration with multiple funeral services for victims of the Revolution, the monarchy's insistence on collective penance was fueled by the Hundred Days. On September 1, 1815, the new regime declared a day of "solemn and expiatory prayers" to be said all over France, for the excesses of the Revolution against the Catholic religion. It sent members of the royal family, including the Duc d'Angoulême and the Duc de Berri, on a tour of France, to ensure atonement and allegiance among local populations. The re-restored regime also reinstated a calendar of funerary anniversaries, especially January 21, which was decreed a day of public mourning to be celebrated with expiatory masses throughout France. The anniversary of the death of Louis XVI became a sort of national holiday, but of a negative kind. Carefully scripted by police orders and episcopal mandates, the anniversary was marked in virtually every town in the country—and as far away as Russia—with black streamers, processions, and funerary services in local churches, in which the former king was represented as a Christ-like figure, soaked in blood. To avoid controversy, the monarchy forbade local clergy and administrators from giving eulogies or orations on this day. Instead, local authorities were to read the last will and testament of Louis XVI. Alongside the annual service for Marie Antoinette in October, the anniversary of the king's death was intended to redress French culpability for the sin of regicide.[31]

To encourage devotion to the restored monarchy, the regime celebrated a new holiday on the king's feast day, August 25. As one mayoral decree in Strasbourg characterized it, "This day is linked to the most touching memories: it reminds the French what they owe to the best of Kings, it promises them, in the future, more happy destinies, fruit of devotion, union and recognition; it penetrates all hearts with the most pure sentiments, the most sacred duties." In Strasbourg, Saint Louis was celebrated with a solemn mass in the cathedral, as well as Protestant and Jewish services, followed by a fair in the Orangerie garden, complete with games, drinking, dancing, entertainment, gifts to the *patrie,* and prizes to schoolboys.[32] The regime also continued to mark the anniversary of the return of the king to Paris on July 8, 1815. Through at least the end of the decade, it was commemorated with masses, festivals, charitable gifts, and illuminations. In these celebrations, foreign officers and diplomats often participated, noting that such an event interested "all of Europe," in the words of Russian diplomat Alexey Orlov.[33] During the difficult years of 1816 and 1817, local authorities sometimes refrained from ordering the customary illumination of private houses, but they continued—despite strained budgets—to organize public celebrations for these royal occasions.

In expiation for the sins of the revolutionaries, the new regime also orchestrated a number of commemorative monuments. In addition to restoring the Basilica of Saint-Denis as a site of royal power, it commissioned the Chapelle Expiatoire, dedicated to Louis XVI and Marie Antoinette, which was funded by Louis XVIII and the Duchesse d'Angoulême and inaugurated in 1824, shortly before the king's death.[34] Although meant to reconcile the French, these projects—like the other monuments, ceremonies, holidays, and symbols intended to erase or absolve past transgressions—only served to remind them of historical trauma. They exacerbated the division between lilies and violets.

Foreign Trusteeship

To keep division in check was the main goal of the occupation of guarantee. In addition to constraining political violence on the ground in the particularly recalcitrant region of the northeast, the occupation enabled Allied leaders to oversee and, when necessary, intervene in political debate in the French capital. In particular, the Council of Allied Ambassadors played a major role in moderating French politics during the formative years of the Second Restoration. At the beginning of the occupation, the Allies were concerned primarily about counterrevolutionary reaction in France; toward the end of the occupation, however, they became more worried about a revival of revolutionary sentiment, in France and across Europe. Their multinational "foreign trusteeship," as it was termed by at least one historian of the period, represented a new development in international politics, a development that was at least as important as the Congress of Vienna and the Concert of Europe.[35]

Between 1815 and 1818, the French government was monitored especially by the British and the Russians, including Alexander I. Given the tsar's role in restoring the monarchy, he continued to be suspected of holding too much power over Louis XVIII, especially once his former governor of Odessa, the Duc de Richelieu, was appointed minister of foreign affairs in September 1815. As the constitutional royalist statesman Comte de Corbière remembered, "The emperor Alexander was only too habituated to meddling in our affairs, which he understood very badly." The "Russian tinge" of the French ministry was decried even by British secretary of foreign affairs Castlereagh. But the British, too, intervened in the affairs of the new government, even going so far as to send the Speaker of the House of Commons, Charles Abbott, to Paris to teach the French government about parliamentary procedure. As Pierre de la Gorce remarked almost a century ago, referring to the demand by the Allies in October 1815 to obtain a draft of the king's annual speech to the legislature, "France was treated like a convalescent barely escaped from a long fever."[36]

The most significant player in the foreign trusteeship of France was the Council of Allied Ambassadors. Organized during the invasion of 1815, this council comprised the ambassadors of the major powers involved in the occupation, including Sir Charles Stuart (Great Britain), Pozzo di Borgo (Russia), Baron de Vincent (Austria), and Count von der Goltz (Prussia), as well as the occupation's commander in chief, when he was in Paris. Brainchild of the Duke of Wellington, the council was designed to ensure execution of the treaties of Paris and Vienna and to protect Europe not only against direct attack from France but also from revolutionary convulsion more generally. Assuming that the newly restored government of France required tutelage, the council was supposed to survey the government, aid the king, monitor public opinion, and mobilize the occupying army, if necessary. Meeting twice a week throughout the three years of the occupation of guarantee, the council examined a wide range of issues, from refugees "proscribed" from France to problems with requisitions for the occupying army, from jurisdiction over offenses committed by Allied troops to financing the reconstruction of fortresses outside the frontier of France, from war claims by foreign individuals and enterprises to relations between Spain and Portugal, especially regarding their colonies in South America.[37]

But the council's main role was to monitor the new government in France. In the words of Charles H. Pouthas, it was an "organ of surveillance and of pressure on the French government."[38] Under the leadership of Russian ambassador Pozzo di Borgo in particular, it worked to ensure that the government upheld the principles of its founding Charter. With the acquiescence and even encouragement of the French foreign minister, the Duc de Richelieu, the council gathered information, issued opinions, and even sought modifications regarding the French government, including the decisions of cabinet ministers and royal family members. The ambassadors kept close watch over debates in the legislature, especially regarding the budget, which was of vital interest to the Allies, who depended on it for payment of requisitions and reparations.

When the Chamber of Deputies elected in the fall of 1815 proved to be a little too "introuvable," especially in resisting payment of financial obligations, the Council of Allied Ambassadors began to pressure the king to limit the influence of the ultraroyalists. Concerned that the Chamber's opposition to the budget was "contrary and offensive to the constitutional rights of the King" and might provoke a change in ministry, "which would threaten the direct interests of the Allies and the tranquility of the country," the council asked Wellington to intervene with Louis XVIII. In February, the duke sent a letter to the king urging him to rein in the members of his own family, especially his brother the Comte d'Artois, who were pushing the Chamber to obstruct his budget proposal: "I owe to truth and to my attachment to Your Majesty and the tranquility of Europe to warn Your Majesty," Wellington wrote. "The moment has come where it is absolutely necessary for Your Majesty to declare himself with firmness and to support his ministry with all of the influence of the Court, which is at present most harmful to him." Early the next month, the commander in chief met with the Comte d'Artois to insist on the danger of destabilizing the ministry and hence the peace settlement. Such intervention had an effect on the king: fearing that the extreme politics of the ultraroyalists would prolong the occupation, as soon as the budget was passed in April he pronounced the legislature adjourned until October.[39]

This adjournment did not satisfy the Allies, who remained concerned that the Chamber's counterrevolutionary tendencies would destabilize France and, by extension, Europe. In instructions to Nesselrode, Pozzo di Borgo insisted on the need for a "less passionate" legislature, going so far as to support the outright dissolution of the Chamber, and, in an interview with the French ambassador to St. Petersburg, the tsar himself reportedly deplored the reactionary tendency of the Chamber of Deputies, which he saw as an obstacle to the liberation of France from occupation.[40] Over the next few months, the Council of Allied Ambassadors continued to pressure the ministry to persuade the king to dissolve the Chambre Introuvable, as a condition of considering a reduction in the size of the army of occupation and thereby of the annual financial obligation. Although the ministry was initially reluctant to act, by late summer 1816, under the influence of Pozzo di Borgo, Wellington, and Castlereagh, the Duc de Richelieu became convinced of the necessity of dissolving the Chamber of Deputies, which he now called a "head of Medusa frightening French and foreigners alike."[41] He argued that the monarch needed to reassert the royal prerogative over the Chamber, whose opposition to the ministry regarding the budget and other matters was exacerbating the concern of the Allies and thereby prolonging the occupation of French territory. Finally, invoking the Charter, Louis XVIII moved to dissolve the Chamber of Deputies in a meeting of the council of ministers on August 20, 1816. In a decree dated September 5 and published in the *Moniteur universel* two days later, the king ordered new elections to occur within the next month. This news was welcomed by the stock market and the public; following the king's decree, Richelieu was cheered at the theater. Despite strong reaction by ultraroyalists such as François-René de Chateaubriand, who published a vitriolic pamphlet against the ministry, the elections were organized by the minister of police Decazes via instructions to prefects.[42]

The dissolution of the Chamber was heartily approved by Allied leaders. In its first meeting after the decree of September 5, the minutes of which it forwarded to the Duke of Wellington, the Council of Allied Ambassadors concluded that this measure "may be envisaged as a proper means of reconciling the different parties, improving public credit and strengthening the Government, and thereby of fulfilling a goal equally useful and necessary and in conformity with the true interests of France and of all the other Governments." In the occupied zone, Allied commanders urged French administrators to promote candidates supportive of the king's agenda. In the Bas-Rhin, where he was reviewing German troops in September 1816, Wellington was heard to say to French functionaries that the dissolution of the Chamber was a "useful and salutary measure" they needed to support, to ensure the tranquillity of France and hence the interest of Europe. At a dinner following an inspection of Bavarian troops at Sarreguemines in mid-September, when told that "all of France" supported this measure, the duke remarked,

"I am charmed to see the French satisfied with a measure that the allied powers themselves have delivered." The decree was endorsed by the Baron de Frimont, commander of the Austrian contingent at Colmar, and the king of Bavaria, who is reported to have said, "The king of France did very well to repress the ultraroyalists; they are not his friends."[43]

Wellington's comment in Sarreguemines to the contrary, not all French were satisfied with the foreign trusteeship of their government, particularly the Allied role in the dissolution of the Chamber. According to the report on the duke's visit to Sarreguemines by a regional police commissioner, his comment was met with "invectives" by a local coterie, which loudly demanded, "Why do foreigners want to meddle in our affairs?" The same sentiment was expressed in a number of pamphlets, such as *The Coalition and France,* attributed to liberal politician Narcisse-Achille de Salvandy, which asserted that, rather than protecting France, its "allies" were oppressing it.[44]

But the "foreign trusteeship" was critical to the development of a parliamentary government in France. In the elections of October 1816, the ultraroyalists lost seats to moderates. Out of 232 total seats, 160 were won by constitutional monarchists and liberal independents. The new legislature undertook a number of important reforms that eventually enabled the liberation of France. Within a few months, the shift in government encouraged the Allies to consider a reduction in the size of the occupying army. By pushing the monarchy to counteract ultraroyalism, the Council of Allied Ambassadors promoted political reconstruction in France. As historian Pierre Rain observed, writing during another occupation in World War II, "By surveying the public peace, by guaranteeing it by its arms, by fortifying it by its advice, Europe saved France from anarchy. This trusteeship, which was for the defeated power the supreme humiliation, was yet to be the greatest aid to its regeneration."[45]

A Political Laboratory

By provoking the dissolution of the ultraroyalist Chamber, the foreign trusteeship paved the way for political experimentation in France. The new legislature initiated a number of seminal liberal reforms, including new laws on electoral procedures, military recruitment and advancement, and press crimes and regulations. As many recent histories have concluded, this period was formative for the nation's political development.[46]

The Chamber's first important reform was a new electoral law, passed on February 5, 1817. It was, in the words of Emmanuel Waresquiel and Benoît Yvert, "one of the most important political developments in the history of the Restoration." Revising the terms of the Charter and even of past revolutionary legislation, the law gave a direct vote, via a single electoral college in each department capital, to all men over thirty who paid at least 300 francs in taxes, proportional to the amount of income deemed necessary by doctrinaire liberals for political "capacity." Requiring renewal of one-fifth of the Chamber of Deputies each year, the law also deemed eligible for office any man over forty who paid at least 1,000 francs in taxes. Although the tax qualifications limited the electorate to less than a hundred thousand men, this still represented a significant expansion of the franchise into the urban middle class. Despite some last-minute opposition from Allied authorities concerned that annual elections would introduce too much instability, the law passed by a narrow margin. Although it would be partially overturned by the law of the double vote (for voters paying more than 1,000 francs in annual taxes), proposed in February 1820 right before the assassination of the Duc de Berri, the electoral law of 1817 enabled a loyal opposition, committed to both king and Charter. In the words of the Comte de Rémusat, it was "the act of investiture of the middle class as the governing class."[47]

The second major reform passed by the more moderate legislature was a law to reorganize the military, which had dwindled to little more than a hundred thousand royal guards and volunteers, into a national—versus imperial or royal—force. A condition for the end of occupation, the establishment of an army loyal to the new regime was a major step in the recovery of France. To raise the size of the army to 240,000, the new minister of war, Gouvion Saint-Cyr, proposed, in November 1817, to levy each year a contingent of forty thousand new recruits to serve terms of six years. They would be chosen by lottery from all twenty-year-old men certified fit for service. Those who drew a "bad" number could hire a substitute. A revision of Napoleonic conscription, this system also allowed veterans (many of whom had served the emperor) to remain in a reserve army. Promotion to officer could occur only after two years of active service or military school; after that, two-thirds of all promotions would be based on seniority. Although this provision in particular generated substantial opposition from ultraroyalists, who wanted to preserve noble prerogative, Gouvion Saint-Cyr's proposal was ultimately passed on March 10, 1818. Proven effective during the war in Spain in 1823, it was maintained by subsequent regimes.[48]

Although the last of the three main liberal reforms of the late 1810s was not officially passed until after the occupying army had left France, it was initiated under the foreign trusteeship. Allied leaders pushed the government of France to draft a new press bill that would forge a moderate path between the extremes of license and censorship. The press law of May 1819 was comprised of three provisions: holding authors, printers, and publishers responsible for attacks on public morality or the monarchy; placing such offenses under the jurisdiction of juries rather than judges; and requiring publishers and printers of periodicals to make declarations and pay security deposits to the official Administration of the Book Trade. For the prepublication censorship regime of the old absolutist monarchy revived by Napoleon, this law substituted post-publication liability. While it placed some limits on publishing, it represented a major step toward freedom of the press and helped link the new regime to public opinion. Like the laws on electoral procedure and military recruitment, it would remain a legislative landmark until the Third Republic.[49]

With these reforms, the new regime instituted parliamentary politics in France. Under the "trusteeship" of the Council of Allied Ambassadors, it steered a moderate path between the Scylla of counterrevolution and the Charybdis of Jacobinism. Out of the occupation emerged a more liberal compromise between Old Regime and Revolution.

Resurgence of "Public Spirit"

Under foreign occupation, the new regime permitted considerable political activity. According to one of its first historians, Baptiste Capefigue, the Second Restoration imprinted a "powerful action on the public spirit." Compared to the Napoleonic Empire, when this spirit had been restrained by strict censorship, the new regime generated a political "effervescence." Although censorship was not fully lifted until 1818, popular as well as elite classes were quickly repoliticized, yielding real partisanship, if not formal parties. This surge in partisanship was noted at the time by the government, which devoted new attention to observing public opinion with the help of prefects, gendarmes, and commissions of various kinds.[50]

Politicization commonly took the form of "noises," "news," and "rumors," very diffuse and often false, which both reflected and shaped the political imagination, especially of the popular classes. Engendered by the political vacuum between 1813 and 1815, these "noises" persisted under the Second Restoration, especially during the subsistence crisis of 1816–1817. Related to what François Ploux has called a "psychosis of conspiracy" inherited from the revolutionary era but revived by the fall of the Empire, these rumors usually involved threats to the regime of Louis XVIII, including the renewal of war and especially the return of Napoleon.[51] Another prevalent rumor held that the son of the late Louis XVI, Louis-Charles, who had in fact died in the Temple prison in 1795, was still alive. To counter such "noises," British troops in particular worked to rebuff false rumors and destroy Bonapartist propaganda.[52] But the rumors continued to fuel popular opposition to the new regime.

Some opponents of the new regime engaged in more overt forms of political activity, in town squares and marketplaces, underground clubs, universities, and, especially, theaters. In Paris, students at the École de Médecine were surveyed by the police for various liberal activities, such as posting seditious inscriptions, usually in praise of the "Usurper," on the walls of classrooms in 1815–1816; organizing a subscription in favor of the Bonapartist refugees of the Champ d'Asile in December 1818; and circulating petitions against revision of the electoral law in November 1819. In Aix-en-Provence in February 1818 there were "disorders" in the theater after law students applauded "on several occasions and with a sort of affectation" some verses against the English. The *habitués* of the parterre, particularly artisans who were profiting from the presence of the English and tended to be more royalist than the liberal students, countered their applause by throwing potatoes at them. Exiting after the first play, the students returned with their pockets full of stones, which they proceeded to launch at the artisans. According to a police report, "Several people who were in the parterre received bad contusions and if Mr. the Mayor, who just arrived at the spectacle, had not instantly taken severe measures, this brawl would have inevitably had disastrous consequences." Following this incident, the students tried to form an association, but were prohibited from engaging in any further political activity by local authorities.[53]

The repoliticization of public opinion is best seen in the explosion of the press. Despite continued restrictions, particularly on publications of less than twenty pages, authors, editors, and printers took advantage of the overthrow of imperial censorship to unleash a flood of publications on the issues of the day.[54] This period saw a slew of petitions and brochures with proposals for solving the "misfortunes" of France. Some of these—such as Chateaubriand's *De la monarchie selon la Charte,* which initiated ultraroyalists in parliamentary procedure—provoked extensive and vitriolic pamphlet wars.[55] There also appeared a long list of new political periodicals, including the *Mercure, Minerve,* and *Conservateur.* The role of the press in politicizing even the most popular classes was recognized by a German visitor to Paris in 1817, who marveled, "If one wanted to extirpate the interest that everyone takes in public affairs here, it would be necessary to turn over the soil of France. Everyone reads: the coachman on his seat while awaiting his master, the fruit-woman at the market, the porter in in his box. In the Palais-Royal, in the morning, a thousand people have newspapers in hand and show them to each other in the most diverse positions."[56] In comparison to the Napoleonic Empire, this was a golden age for the political press in France.

Dwarves versus Giants

The resurgence of public debate may be seen in the slew of semi-regular partisan periodicals that appeared during the regime changes of 1814 and 1815. The most famous were the *Nains,* or "Dwarves." Often produced by radical exiles across the border in the Netherlands, reportedly with financing from Russian officers, they were usually identified by a politically tinged color, such as the *Nain jaune,* the *Nain blanc,* the *Nain couleur de rose,* and, most subversively, the *Nain tricolore.* They tended to the left of the political spectrum, though the *Nain vert,* or "Green Dwarf," was affiliated with the royalist camp in France. These "Dwarves" were countered by another series of politically tinged periodicals, called "Giants," such as the *Géant noir* ("Black Giant") produced in 1816. These periodicals became a concern not just for the government of France but also for the Council of Allied Ambassadors, which spent many a meeting deliberating how to address the "license" of the press coming from the Netherlands.[57]

Born during the tumultuous months between the fall of Napoleon in April 1814 and the return of Louis XVIII in July 1815, all of the *Nains* participated actively in ideological struggles. Produced by radical writers and publishers, often outside of France, most defended the ideals of the Revolution against despotism, whether imperial or monarchical. A prime example is the *Nain jaune*, which became a voice for revolutionary ideals in the turmoil of the first half of 1815. Across the Hundred Days, this "yellow" Dwarf denounced the emperor Napoleon, whom it likened to the "foreigner" William III of England, while exonerating the French people of any responsibility for his return to power. Persecuted by the revived imperial regime, it went underground, metamorphosing into a number of other publications, including a brochure called *Bluettes*, appearing on an irregular basis in the summer of 1815.[58] In the wake of the second return of Louis XVIII, however, the *Nain jaune* was challenged by several new Dwarves, including a *Nain rose*, a *Nain blanc*, and a *Nain vert*. The struggle between these partisan publications was even depicted in a print produced by Martinet, *The Three Literary Dwarves, or the Bastards of the Yellow Dwarf, Fighting Each Other over Its Remains*, in which three devilish simian creatures raid the coffin of their predecessor and fight over his quill.[59]

The pro-revolutionary message of the first Dwarves was countered by the reactionary *Nain vert*, which, taking the color of the royalist *Verdets*, constituted a weapon in the White Terror of 1815. This publication in turn inspired a *Géant vert*, as well as a *Géant noir*, after the color of mourning, which explicitly distinguished itself from the *Nains* by rejecting the Revolution and Empire. In its most direct assault on the legacy of 1789, the *Géant noir* sarcastically listed the "advantages and benefits" of a revolution:

> The demoralization of all classes of society; an artificial food shortage; famine; roads infested with brigands; the most beautiful provinces devastated by civil war; public instruction destroyed; emigration; the torture of all men of talents; millions of French drowned, guillotined, speared, shot, bombarded; no

> more navy; the colonies invaded; no more commerce; freedom of the press destroyed; property pillaged; lands left uncultivated for lack of manpower; requisitions of all kinds; state creditors ruined; honest people despoiled; the public fortune in the hands of scoundrels; crime unpunished; a Robespierre, a Directory, a Fructidor, a conscription, and to finish you off, a Bonaparte . . . So, go ahead, make revolutions!

Over the next year or so, the legacy of the Revolution remained a subject of vitriolic debate between the Dwarves and the Giants.[60]

By mid-1816, this debate became so intense that the Administration of the Book Trade prohibited the import of *Nains* published in the Netherlands. Nonetheless, police informants continued to report that Belgian smugglers were spreading the "abominable pamphlet" of the *Nain jaune,* thereby keeping spirits in a "dangerous fermentation." That same year, the authors, publishers, and distributors of the *Nain tricolore* were put on trial. As a result of such censorship, as well as the high cost of publication, neither the Dwarves nor the Giants lasted long. But for a brief time beginning in late 1815, they fueled political activity in France and elsewhere. Russian officers, who frequently crossed the border into the southern Netherlands, carried these publications back to their encampments in France and, presumably, all the way back to Russia. Across the Channel, British journalists founded a *Black Dwarf* to defend the cause of liberty against government oppression in the wake of the Battle of Waterloo.[61]

Attack on the Iron Duke

In early 1818, the political activity took a violent turn that threatened to derail the progress the French government had made in convincing the Allied leadership that the country was ready for the removal of the occupying army. On February 11, the Duc de Richelieu wrote to the French ambassador in London, "There has just occurred a deplorable event." Early that morning, a shot had been fired at the carriage of the Duke of Wellington as he returned to his residence in Paris. Blaming this attack on a "horrible machination of our enemies," the foreign minister feared the scandal it was going to cause would be "disastrous." "One understands nothing of such an extravagant attempt. . . . The effect will be no less fatal, and, in truth, it seems that a bad demon has attached itself to our affairs, and dogs us to create difficulties, as if we did not already have enough in the natural state of things."[62]

This was not the first time the life of the Iron Duke had been threatened. From the beginning of the occupation, he had been subjected to insults and attacks. In summer 1816, the police ministry investigated a suspicious fire at the duke's residence in Paris. A few months before the assassination attempt, a rumor had circulated in London that Wellington, on a visit to Lille, had wanted to go to the theater but had instead been detained at an "eternal" dinner by the prefect, who had learned that several "turbulent" spectators were preparing to boo him. In the days before the attack, rumors were already circulating that Wellington was going to be or had already been assassinated and that the British army was planning to move on Paris.[63]

But this incident was more serious. As Wellington himself described the attack, in a letter to the British minister of war, the Earl of Bathurst, the following day:

> My Dear Lord, I have to inform you that a pistol was fired at my carriage, close to my own door, at about half-past twelve on the night before last, by a well-dressed person, who immediately ran away and made his escape. The sentries at the door were, at the time, within the *porte cochère,* as they usually are in the night; and it appears that the man had accompanied the carriage, at an accelerated pace, about sixty or seventy yards along the street (Rue des Champs Elysées); he then took post behind the sentry-box while the carriage was turning to enter the *porte cochère,* and fired at the moment it was entering . . . The government, the police, and indeed every individual here, are doing everything in their power to discover the criminal; and, besides the ordinary means, we have another channel [an anonymous tip] not unlikely to be successful.

Suspecting a veteran, Wellington reassured the war minister that he did not fear for his safety, but would nevertheless arm his carriage and take an escort of gendarmes when out in public.[64]

The incident provoked quite a commotion. Domestically, news of the attack generated anxiety and unrest. At the stock market, where it was already known by the opening, contradictory reports unsettled the majority of traders, causing a fall in prices and a fear of "disastrous" consequences. In the capital, police agents reported that the attempted assassination had spread "consternation in all spirits." Many supposed it was a plot by the English or perhaps the ultraroyalists to justify continuation of the occupation, but "reasonable people" thought it was a personal vengeance or small conspiracy to spread anxiety. Some brazen satirists even suggested the attack was a joke. In the provinces, where it was even more difficult to obtain accurate information about the incident, similar rumors circulated, with many supposing that it was only a "simulacra" of an assassination, a "coup" organized by the enemies of France, perhaps even the English themselves, as a pretext for moving or extending the army of occupation. Over the next few weeks, as inhabitants of the countryside accosted drivers for information from Paris—rumored to be in insurrection—this suspicion became so widespread that, in Nantes for instance, theater audiences were excessively applauding epigrammatic lines against the English.[65]

Outside of France, the incident caused not only concern for the safety of the occupation's commander in chief but also tension between French and Allied—particularly British—leaders. Within three days, the prince regent wrote to Wellington to express his relief but also horror at this "foul attempt." "I have only," wrote Prince George, "in common with the rest of the nation, to return my most grateful acknowledgments of the superintending goodness of Divine Providence in having protected a life so important to the best interests of your own country, as well as to the preservation of the tranquility of Europe." The Earl of Bathurst prevailed upon Wellington to leave Paris for Cambrai. Saying he would rather die respected, the duke insisted that such a move would threaten the stability of the financial settlement and exacerbate the animosity toward the occupation.[66]

Nonetheless, Wellington was irritated by the French reaction—or lack thereof—to the attack. Complaining that the notables of France, including the Duc de Richelieu, had not expressed adequate indignation over or even belief in the plot, Wellington wrote the Earl of Bathurst: "I don't think such a declaration [of public outrage] would make the smallest difference in regard to my safety; but it must be considered that I am not a common person here, and the honour of France would have stood upon better ground if there had been a general public manifestation of indignation at this attempt." Richelieu worried that the incident would undermine negotiations between France and Britain, along with the rest of the Allies, to end the occupation of guarantee: "Between us,"

Caricature faite contre le Lord Wellington, lors qu'on lui tira rue des champs-élisées [sic] *un coup de pistolet à poudre*, by Charlet, 1818. BNF.

he wrote to Osmond, "I fear very much that we are not as happy here, and that the Duke of Wellington has received from this event, and from the manner in which it has been interpreted by a certain segment of the public, an impression that will be most unfortunate for our affairs." For several weeks, Richelieu continued to fear that his relationship with Wellington had degenerated.[67]

Immediately after the attack, an investigation was launched, under the direction of police minister Decazes. In Paris, police visited boarding houses to identify residents who had returned after one o'clock that night; among the names they collected was that of the liberal writer and politician Benjamin Constant. To try to identify the purchaser of the weapon used against Wellington, they questioned arms dealers. They also interrogated women, including prostitutes, who were said to know the suspects. Given that rumors of an assassination had been circulating even before the attack occurred, the police also surveyed postal and passenger carriages in the northeast. As various leads began to point to radical circles across the border in Brussels, they enlisted the assistance of police and judicial officials in the Netherlands.[68]

The investigation soon centered around a British lord, Charles Kinnaird. A Scotsman born in 1780, he had violently opposed the war with France as an MP and then Peer; by the early 1800s he was spending most of his time on the Continent, where he mixed with radical political refugees, especially in Brussels. In these circles, he got wind of a plot to assassinate Wellington, which he then reported to the duke's chief of staff, Sir George Murray. In a letter dated ten days before the attack, Kinnaird informed Murray that a French refugee in Brussels had heard that a man had been hired by a group of conspirators to kill Wellington; the assassin had been following the duke for four months and was now in Paris. Kinnaird requested that British and French authorities grant safe passage to Paris to the informant, plus two of his friends, writers who had been proscribed from France.[69] Neither Murray nor Wellington would agree to deal with these refugees. After Wellington was attacked, however, they pressed Kinnaird to reveal the name of his informant, to no avail. On February 19, Kinnaird and his informant departed on their own for Paris, where they were taken into police custody but soon released.[70]

The police in Paris developed a long list of suspects, including a former officer named Kellermann, who had been condemned a year or two before for seditious writing and had been seen on several occasions in the proximity of the duke's residence, and a former colonel of the imperial chasseurs called "Brice," who had been heard saying he would assassinate the duke himself but also had in his service a soldier willing to do it. Also implicated were several "proscribed" radical Frenchmen, many of whom were called as witnesses in the case. In their effort to pin the assassination attempt on a foreign conspiracy, the police ministry even extended their web of suspicion to the Prince of Orange and the tsar of Russia, who were thought to want to take over command of the occupation of guarantee. After about a month, however, the police singled out a Bonapartist lawyer exiled in Belgium, Louis-Joseph-Stanislas Marinet, otherwise known as Nicolle, who had been employed as a tax collector by the government of France in 1815. According to the French ambassador to the Netherlands, after Napoleon's return to power, Marinet "ran away from France with the Caisse, but not for the King's use, and has thus become rich. A pretty confidant and *compagnon de voyage* for a peer of the United Kingdom [Kinnaird]!" Following the Second Restoration, Marinet had been condemned to death in absentia. To commit the assassination, Marinet had hired another "proscribed" former sergeant of the imperial guard, Marie-André-Nicolas Cantillon. By mid-March, Marinet and Cantillon had been arrested in Paris.[71]

There the investigation stalled. Decazes could obtain no definitive evidence or denunciation against Marinet or Cantillon, who continued to protest their innocence. As Wellington complained in mid-July, "Although . . . the government have plenty of proof of the plot, of those who formed it, and of those who carried it into execution, and they have Marinet, who was one of the conspirators, and Cantillon, who was one of the assassins (for there were two employed), in Paris, all those who have given them the information having stipulated that they should not be brought forward as *dénonciateurs,* they have no positive proof to produce in a court of justice."[72]

Without sufficient evidence, the suspects could not be tried. They remained in jail, provoking protests from their defenders. Already in mid-April, Lord Kinnaird petitioned the Chamber of Peers against the detention of Marinet, who had offered to divulge the plot against Wellington in exchange for safe passage to Paris over a week before the assassination attempt.[73] Over six months later, when Cantillon still had not been brought to trial, his lawyer published a brief protesting the "preliminary defamations" and "perpetual interrogations" to which his client had been subjected, as well as the length of his detention, which for the first four and a half months had been secret. The lawyer blamed Cantillon's bad treatment on the victim of the attack: "Does the generosity of the duke of Wellington match the level of his rank?" he wrote. "The general of all of the armies of Europe, one of the arbiters of the world, has descended to searching for the slightest clues to a pistol shot that did not even attain his carriage, and for eight months, he leaves forgotten an unfortunate who is only suspected. Ah! That a more noble role remained to him!"[74]

Not until after the liberation of France from occupation, on May 12, 1819, were Marinet and Cantillon tried before a jury in Paris. According to the statement by the prosecutor, both Marinet and Cantillon were known to hate foreigners as well as royalists, and both had come into money in the months before the attempted assassination. In the end, both Marinet and Cantillon were acquitted, ostensibly due to a lack of proof, but also presumably because of the departure of the victim of the attack.[75]

Although he avoided conviction, Cantillon was later rewarded for the attempted assassination of Wellington by none other than Napoleon. In a codicil to his will, Napoleon promised 10,000 francs to Cantillon, arguing he

> had as much right to assassinate this oligarch, as had he to send me to perish on the rock of Saint-Helena. . . . Cantillon, if truly he had assassinated Wellington, would have been covered and justified by the same motives [as Wellington in protecting his country]: the interest of France to rid herself of a general, who besides had violated the capitulation of Paris, and by that had rendered himself responsible for the blood of the martyrs of Ney, Labédoyère, and of the crime of despoiling the museums, against the text of the treaties.

The 10,000 francs were paid to Cantillon by Napoleon's executor in 1823. To this reward, Wellington responded, "I sincerely regret that, in the testament of Saint-Helena, Napoleon lowered himself to this point to accord a reward to him who had thus struck an adversary of the battlefield. Those are the kind of stains that cannot be erased, even on the greatest historical physiognomies."[76] Cantillon died in 1869, on the eve of the collapse of the Second Empire.

Despite its inconclusive outcome, the trial of Marinet and Cantillon revealed the extent of opposition to the restored Bourbon monarchy and the Allied coalition buttressing it. In investigating the attack, French and Allied authorities uncovered a vast underground, transnational network of radical writers, activists, paymasters, and even would-be assassins. Centered in Brussels, many of these were Jacobins or Bonapartists who had been "proscribed" from their homeland of France.

The Invention of Bonapartism

One of the paradoxes of the definitive defeat and exile of Napoleon Bonaparte in 1815 is that it spurred the development of Bonapartism as a political movement. The Hundred Days initially divided, but ultimately unified, the liberal opposition to monarchy in France and much of the rest of Europe. This opposition was made all the more intransigent by the foreign invasion and White Terror. Whereas in 1814 Bonaparte had been supported mostly by demobilized soldiers, in 1815 his cause became more inclusive. As Robert Alexander has argued, the twin threats of invasion and restoration demanded compromise between Jacobins and Bonapartists: "It was indeed an unnatural alliance in many ways, but it held—perhaps because Napoleon's government fell long before its own actions could have compromised revolutionary Bonapartism." In the context of the Second Restoration and foreign occupation, liberalism and nationalism were "Napoleonized."[77]

The cult of Napoleon was born at the moment of his defeat in 1815, in the context of popular mobilization against foreign invasion. Originally, the cult was promoted by the paramilitary *fédérés* who supported him in his return to power that spring. Motivated by their experience of invasion the year before, these *fédérés* were located mainly in the eastern part of France, with as many as four thousand in the region of Lyon. Consisting of a mix of old revolutionaries, devotees of Napoleon, and future liberals from the lower and middle classes, they continued to brandish the name of Bonaparte in opposition to the monarchy—especially against the reestablishment of excise taxes, the reversal of electoral reform, or the reconsideration of sales of national properties. But the cult of Napoleon quickly spread beyond these circles. Already in the second half of 1815, seditious words and popular demonstrations in favor of Bonaparte were widespread throughout both urban and rural areas of France. In addition to cries of "Vive l'Empereur!" and displays of eagles and violets, popular classes engaged in spontaneous celebrations of the emperor's birthday, the Saint Napoleon, on August 15.

Over the next few years, the cult of Napoleon continued to grow, often underground, through the circulation of *mauvais discours, fausses nouvelles,* songs, posters, and publications regarding the former emperor, especially around dates significant in his life, including not only his birthday but also the anniversary of his return to power in 1815. Throughout the occupation, police and judicial authorities collected countless reports of Bonapartist comments and activities. Beginning in 1816, in Chalon-sur-Saône, the police were monitoring an establishment known as the Café de l'Île d'Elbe, a "meeting place of all the enemies of the government among which were counted a lot of retired officers" and where was produced "all the alarming news that is then spread throughout the town." Another center of Bonapartist sentiment was Colmar, where former soldiers nostalgically remembered the "splendors" of the Empire. In Paris in 1818, following an order from a local judge, a police agent visited the shop of the printer Michaud, where he seized a "rather large number" of copies of a history of Bonaparte in which was inserted most of a work called "The 18th Brumaire." Endless rumors circulated about Napoleon: he had escaped again; his wife, Marie Louise, was plotting to place his son on the throne of France. Such rumors, many of which were propagated by agents provocateurs or occupying troops, were especially prevalent on the anniversary of Napoleon's escape from Elba, in March 1816 and again in 1817. As François Ploux has emphasized, in the context of messianic expectation produced not only by the foreign occupation but also by the grain crisis, such rumors were an integral part of the political imaginary.[78]

The growing cult around Napoleon can also be seen in the proliferation of images and objects featuring the former emperor that circulated, often under the cloak. In addition to portraits and miniatures, consumers could purchase a wide array of objects, including prints, medals, busts, pins, clocks, knives, dishes, toys, fans, snuffboxes, and even candies and elixirs bearing his likeness or another symbol of the Napoleonic Empire, including the eagle, the violet, the tricolor, or the initials *NB*. In January 1818, on the road between Strasbourg and Nancy, a police agent found a small engraving folded in different directions circulating among the peasantry. On first sight, it offered a fleur-de-lys, but opening the first fold, it represented an imperial eagle, and after being entirely unfolded, it revealed a seditious allegory, as well as an inscription so injurious to the king that the report of it was not inserted in the official briefing given to him. That fall, around Toulouse, peddlers were reported to have sold a large quantity of wooden snuffboxes topped with an engraving of a French grenadier whose flag some English soldiers were trying to take and a quotation from an imperial guardsman at Waterloo, "A Frenchman dies, but does not surrender." Inside, underneath a false bottom, was a portrait of Bonaparte. Much of this anti-monarchist propaganda was smuggled into France from Belgium, often sewn into the dresses of travelers.[79]

Bonapartists did not limit themselves to spouting seditious phrases, spreading false news, and collecting imperial memorabilia. They also participated in meetings, demonstrations, riots, and even conspiracies, the most famous of which were the (failed) insurrectionary coups at Grenoble in 1816 and Lyon in 1817. While these revolts cannot be linked with any certainty to revolutionary organizations, at least some of the participants may be identified as *fédérés*, according to Robert Alexander.[80] This Bonapartist activity peaked in 1816–1817, in the context of the food shortage and the foreign occupation. In 1818, as the supply of grain increased and the end of occupation neared, it declined, at least in France. As the new regime began to implement liberal reforms, the Bonapartist opposition began to focus its energy on electoral politics. It would regain steam the next decade, first with Napoleon's death in 1821 and then with the posthumous publication of his *Memoirs of Saint-Helena* in 1823.[81]

As suggested by the attack on the Iron Duke, Bonapartism was by no means isolated to France but spread—again, even before the definitive fall of the Empire—throughout much of Europe and even farther afield, including to the Americas. French Bonapartists were linked to international networks of revolutionaries, with centers in Brussels, London, Wartburg, Milan, and, eventually, St. Petersburg. Across Europe and beyond, young people, especially soldiers and veterans, but also students and artisans, developed a fascination, sometimes bordering on obsession, with Napoleon. As in France, there was a veritable craze for objects associated with the former emperor across Europe, including in Great Britain, where an exhibition of memorabilia—including the emperor's carriage—toured London, Bristol, Dublin, and Edinburgh in 1816 and 1817, and where a Napoleon museum was opened at Piccadilly a few years later, each attracting over a hundred thousand visitors. Among the generation that came of age circa 1820, the cult of Napoleon was so widespread that it became a literary trope, for instance in Stendhal's *The Charterhouse of Parma* and *The Red and the Black,* and in Pushkin's novel in verse *Eugene Onegin.* Some of these Bonapartists participated in the many secret societies formed in this period, whether Masonic lodges, *Burschenschaften,* Carbonari, or Decembrist societies in Russia. According to some estimates, by the 1820s and 1830s there were as many as 400,000–600,000 Carbonari promoting revolutionary ideas, threatening the peace settlement of 1815. Helping to keep the legend of Bonaparte alive until the revolutions of 1848 (following which the nephew of Napoleon was elected to the presidency of France), these young radicals struck fear in the hearts of the conservative elder statesmen of Europe, including the architect of the Congress of Vienna, Metternich.[82]

Closing the Window of Liberalism

Not for a few years, however, would Metternich succeed in reining in these young radicals, whose activities were not significantly limited by French or Allied authorities, even after the assassination attempt on Wellington. For a brief moment between 1815 and 1818, France and much of Europe enjoyed a real resurgence of liberal political activity. Central to this window for liberalism was the occupation of guarantee, which constituted a new mechanism not just for ensuring peace but also for promoting political reform and debate. The role of the Allies in opening this window was recognized even by diehard Bonapartists such as General Maximilien Lamarque, who from exile in the Netherlands wrote, "Let us console ourselves for the outrages against our national glory. The liberty of the world will emerge from the very triumph of our enemies. What a singular chain of causes and effects! It's to the Baskirs, it's to the Cossacks that Europe owes a constitutional regime."[83]

In time, however, France's political recuperation was cut short by a reactionary backlash, outside as well as inside the country. While in

France it is usually associated with the assassination of the Duc de Berri by Louis-Pierre Louvel in February 1820, this backlash actually began toward the end of the occupation. Already by late 1817, the Council of Allied Ambassadors expressed concern about the "spirit of vertigo and rebellion" coming from opposition papers and student organizations in the German lands.[84] Following the attack on Wellington, Allied leaders became increasingly anxious about the resurgence of liberalism, including Bonapartism. As Wellington himself commented in a letter to the British minister of war that otherwise downplayed the threat of insurrection in France:

> [T]he [French] Ministers are running as hard as they can in pursuit of a low, vulgar popularity, which they think the best support of the King's authority and their own. This is the real motive of all their measures, of their encouraging the cry against the Allies, of their Jacobin laws of election and recruiting, of their persecution of the Royalists and encouragement of the opposite party, and of their silence and apathy respecting the attempt upon me. But it must not be supposed that in this race they can run as fast as the liberal Jacobins, or as any of those factions whose object it is to overturn the existing order of things. Every step they take tends to weaken the Royal authority, and I think it is much to be apprehended that as soon as the Allies withdraw from France the whole fabric will crumble to pieces.[85]

Admitting that the Allied occupation was now so onerous to the French that it could not be extended, the Iron Duke suggested that he now regretted the push toward liberalism he himself had initiated. As the Allies began to negotiate the end of the occupation of guarantee, they became increasingly anxious about revolutionary activity spreading around Europe. As Francis Démier has noted: "Henceforth, foreign ambassadors addressed to their governments memoranda expressing more and more concern about the progress of the liberal left, which they associated with a rise in the revolutionary current in Europe."[86] The occupation of guarantee had provided the security and direction necessary for relatively open political debate, internationally as well as domestically. Paradoxically, this window of liberalism was closed by the "liberation" of France.

Chapter Nine

Liberation

In September 1818, the foremost British portrait painter, Sir Thomas Lawrence, traveled to Aix-la-Chapelle, or Aachen (then in Prussian territory), where representatives of the four major powers, plus France, were soon to meet to consider ending the occupation of guarantee. Lawrence had spent the Revolutionary and Napoleonic Wars making a name for himself painting the British elite. Now he was commissioned by the prince regent to paint commemorative portraits of the Allies who had defeated Napoleon. Including Alexander of Russia, Francis I of Austria, and Frederick-William III of Prussia, as well as Nesselrode, Metternich, Castlereagh, and (on a subsequent visit to Vienna) the young Napoleon II, this series has since 1830 been displayed—along with his famous portrait of the Iron Duke—in the Waterloo Chamber at Windsor Castle. Among them is a striking Romantic portrait of the Duc de Richelieu, the foreign minister charged by Louis XVIII with ensuring the liberation of France from foreign troops. Seated in front of a stormy background, the minister is depicted holding a rolled-up paper, presumably some sort of official communiqué. Staring off into the distance, he wears an expression of determination and weariness, but also of hope, at the moment when he was about to realize his prime goal of liberation.

In comparison to its precursor at Vienna, the conference at Aix-la-Chapelle in the fall of 1818 has been all but ignored by historians. But it was attended by many of the same dignitaries, who enjoyed many of

Portrait of the Duc de Richelieu by Thomas Lawrence, 1818. Royal Collection Trust/© Her Majesty Queen Elizabeth II 2016.

the same amusements in the spa town as they had in the capital of the Habsburg Empire. And its consequences were just as significant for the future not just of France but of all Europe. From the perspective of the occupying troops, as well as the French, the Congress of Aix-la-Chapelle marked the definitive end of the Napoleonic Wars. It also effected the rehabilitation of France as a European power.[1]

To obtain the liberation settled at Aix-la-Chapelle, Richelieu worked long and hard for three years. From the beginning of the occupation of guarantee, he labored, along with finance minister Corvetto, to uphold the terms of the treaty of November 20, 1815, so the Allies would evacuate as early as possible. In little more than a year, he managed to persuade the Allies to reduce the troops by thirty thousand. Between the fall of 1817 and the spring of 1818, with the help of Wellington, he addressed the last obstacles to liberation: settlement of the claims by Allied nationals for war damages; and payment in full of the indemnity required by treaty. By orchestrating a series of bond issues, he channeled money from British and Dutch financiers via the French government to the peoples who had suffered the greatest losses during the wars. By May 1818, when the Allies announced the plan to meet at Aix-la-Chapelle, the French were hopeful that the occupation would conclude by the end of the year, two years ahead of schedule.

Once the end of occupation was approved on October 9, 1818, the Allies had little time to evacuate their remaining 120,000 troops and 50,000 horses from France. The massive demobilization required extensive organization on the part of French and Allied officials. As soldiers departed and French troops returned to the northeastern frontier, the French celebrated with illuminations, banquets, balls, speeches, prints, poems, and plays. Among the Allies, however, the end of the occupation elicited more ambivalent feelings. Many were not happy to see their stay in France come to an end. Moreover, the glow of liberation was short-lived. Over the next few months, France, like much of the rest of Europe, was beset by economic and political crisis. Like the "end" of war itself, the "liberation" from occupation was a long and complex process, with repercussions extending across Europe through the nineteenth century.

The Troop Reduction of Spring 1817

In arranging the evacuation of 1818, the Allies had a blueprint in the troop reduction of 1817. Following a half-year of negotiation with the government of France, in February 1817 they agreed to send home one-fifth of their forces—thirty thousand men—by April, decreasing the burden on the occupied country.

Since agreeing to the treaty of November 20, 1815, Richelieu had made it a personal mission to liberate his country as quickly as possible. Only six months into the occupation of guarantee, he was already seeking a reduction. Arguing that a reduction was critical to strengthening the new government of France, he first raised the issue with Wellington in June 1816. Wellington, with Castlereagh, insisted that such a move would require the support of the British government as well as the Allied leadership. They wanted to wait for the next session of the Chamber of Deputies, to ensure that the French achieved political and financial stability. In the meantime, Richelieu began to seek Russian and Austrian approval for a reduction, emphasizing that, without a decrease in the cost of occupation, France might fail to make its reparation payments on time. He did not yet approach Prussia, which was most opposed to softening the treaty terms. Although they gave qualified support, both Russia and Austria indicated they would follow the lead of the commander in chief on this matter. Fearing that a reduced force could not guarantee against either political disturbances or reparation defaults, Wellington postponed his decision until the end of the year.

Within just a few months, however, the Allies acceded to the reduction. In early September, a major concern was eliminated when the ultraroyalist Chambre Introuvable was dissolved by Louis XVIII. While Wellington insisted on waiting to see the results of elections to the new Chamber, this move toward political stability—combined with the new government's increase in reserves of the Caisse d'Amortissement and sale of 150,000 hectares of royal forest—encouraged the Allies to uphold their end of the agreement. They were also pushed by French public opinion, which was becoming more vocal against the occupation. Among others, Narcisse-Achille de Salvandy argued in *The Coalition and France* that there was less to fear from the "interior dangers" within France than from the "peril" located outside it. Insisting that the members of the coalition were allies of Louis XVIII, not "liberators" of the French, he suggested that by crushing them with expenses and debts the Allied sovereigns were provoking war again.[2] Meanwhile, British public opinion, which had always feared a standing army, began to shift in favor of a reduction, in the interest of stationing more troops at home to repress popular unrest. At the same time, the Austrians became concerned that the huge cost of the occupation was making it impossible for the French to make reparation payments.

In fact, by fall 1816, faced with the worst harvest on record, the French government was forced to suspend its payments to the Allies while it sought a foreign loan. Fearing grave supply problems, Wellington ordered all Allied contingents to adjust their troop rolls, often inflated by several hundred men to account for illnesses and transfers, back to the levels stipulated in the treaty of 1815, thereby saving the French about 10 million francs per year. Concerned to prevent even more political unrest, he then agreed to pursue a more substantial reduction, once the French government had developed a plan to pay its reparations. Beginning in January 1817, with the help of financier Gabriel-Julien Ouvrard, the government negotiated (with mostly foreign bankers) three payments totaling some 300 million francs, in exchange for about 30 million francs in government 5 percent bonds. In exchange for this financial guarantee, the Allies agreed to reduce each of their contingents by one-fifth. Wellington insisted this solution would maintain both the multinational character and the adequate strength of the occupation army. For the reduced force, rations would be decreased from 200,000 to 160,000, and the cost of maintenance and equipment from 50 to 40 million francs per year. However, forage was maintained at fifty thousand rations per day. Approved by the Council of Allied Ambassadors and the French legislature, this plan was signed by the ambassadors of Austria, Great Britain, Prussia, and Russia in a "Note" of February 10, 1817. Emphasizing that France had met the conditions of "good faith" and credit stipulated by the treaty of 1815, the note scheduled the troop reduction for April 1.[3]

Before that date, all troops in excess of the new maximum of 120,000 needed to leave France. Beginning in mid-February, Allied commanders organized the evacuation of their extra troops. In Alsace, the Württemberger command plotted the march of a contingent back across the Rhine. Meanwhile, the Saxon leadership negotiated with the Russian diplomatic corps to avoid having Russian troops traverse their country on the way home. From the region around Givet, a Russian regiment embarked at Calais on a ship sent from Kronstadt; the Thirty-Eighth Regiment of Chasseurs, the infantry regiment of Apsheron, and the dragoons of Courlande marched across Germany and Poland. Before leaving, the officers of the Thirty-Eighth thanked their commander, General Loewenstern, for the welcome he had given them and the "little annoyances" he had saved them.[4]

The troop reduction of 1817 did not go off without a hitch. Following publication of the note of February 10, Allied commanders complained that local inhabitants were harassing the troops. French national officials instructed local authorities to "calm spirits and console hearts" and to submit regular reports on conditions. On their march out of the country, some foreign troops committed excesses. As they crossed the Meurthe, a Saxon corps of 400 men and 250 horses inflicted "*mauvais traitements*" on a number of inhabitants, including a woman who "fled precipitously from her house to remove herself from the violence of these soldiers, who demanded wine, liqueurs, coffee." These soldiers rendered the region around Bourg de Foug a "theater of disorders that were hardly seen in the most difficult moments of the first invasion." And the consequent reduction in payments created some problems, for instance among the minor powers, whose officers complained that the monetary allowances provided them in lieu of rations were now too low, especially proportional to those given to the officers of the major powers. Nonetheless, the troop reduction of 1817 marked a turning point in relations between the Bourbon regime and the occupying powers, preparing the groundwork for the eventual liberation of France.[5]

Impatience for Liberation

Rather than calming public opinion in France, however, the troop reduction aggravated it. Authorities noticed that the French, particularly in the occupied zone, were ever more impatient for definitive liberation. Over the next year, as Richelieu continued to press for liberation ahead of schedule, French inhabitants increasingly needled Allied troops, including Wellington, who during the spring and summer of 1818 was insulted by locals near his headquarters in Cambrai.[6]

By early 1818, as Allied and French authorities began to discuss the end of the occupation, the impatience for liberation reached a boiling point. In the first half of the year, reports from officials on both sides are full of references to French "lassitude," "mis-intelligence," "bad harmony," and even "hatred" against the occupiers. In the wake of the attempted assassination of Wellington in Paris on February 11, the British liaison to the Prussian army in Sedan, Lieutenant Colonel Sir Henry Hardinge, reported: "With regard to the public feeling generally in this quarter, it may be said that the people betray more impatience against the occupation than last year; and, as to the public opinion, as far as it can be collected, towards the Bourbon government, it is supposed by no means to have ameliorated. . . . General Zieten's view of the state of things is an unfavourable one. Without any particular facts to go upon, he has strong suspicions of a convulsion in France being a very likely event." French authorities tended to concur in this assessment of public opinion. The same month, the subprefect of Verdun, worrying that it would be dangerous to assemble the youth of his arrondissement for military recruitment, noted: "[A] rather extraordinary nuance to observe, is that those people who at one time invoked the allies as liberators, today desire their removal with as much ardor as the men who, at their arrival, lost the status they had under the preceding government." Their hopes were fed by rumors—fueled by supply agents—announcing "as soon" the departure of the allies.[7]

Countering such hopes, Allied troops spread other rumors suggesting they had no intention of leaving anytime soon, which only inflamed French hostility. In April 1818, the Verdun subprefect remained concerned that the Prussian "spirit" toward the French and their king was not what it had been a year ago:

> It is easy to see that the Prussians would be delighted if we became agitated about a certain matter, to have a motive for advancing, repressing, dominating especially, because they suffer impatiently not to be entirely the masters, and I do not think I am mistaken in believing that the Prussians are perhaps not foreign to all the talk, all the opinions that might have or could still circulate among us, that can have no other goal than that of dividing us, and provoking

> us to some act, that might offer the allies a plausible pretext for staying longer among us.

If they did stay in the department of the Meuse beyond the first of 1819, however, he said "it would require much precaution, much wisdom, much force, to quiet the murmurs, stop the indiscretions, and prevent the misfortunes, whose consequences would be incalculable."[8] By spring 1818, tension between occupiers and occupied had mounted to such an extent that central authorities became concerned it would endanger the possibility of an early liberation.

Fortress-Building and Debt-Paying

Before the Allies would agree to end the occupation, there were a few sticking points to resolve. According to the treaty of 1815, before France could be liberated, it had to demonstrate that its government and military were stable enough not to endanger the general security of Europe. In addition, with the help of reparations from France and funds from Great Britain, the string of fortresses outside the frontier in the Netherlands needed to be reconstructed, to serve as a defensive bulwark against France. Finally, in addition to paying off the indemnity owed to the coalition, the French government had to settle its debts with private individuals and collectivities in Allied nations from the wars of the last twenty years. After the new Chamber of Deputies passed several reforms, including the reorganization of the military, the French government was able to persuade the Allied leadership of its stability and proceed with negotiation of the remaining points.

The first of these points was really out of French hands. According to the 1815 treaty, before the Allies would leave, they required a fully operational string of fortresses outside the northeastern frontier. Such a string existed—in twenty-three towns now belonging to the Kingdom of the Netherlands, including Charleroi, Tournai, Ypres, and Ostend—but they were in disrepair. They were to be reconstructed by the British Royal Engineers, with financing provided from French reparations as well as the British and Dutch governments. Wellington was charged with inspecting the fortresses on a regular basis. While delays in the reconstruction threatened to postpone the end of the occupation, by early 1818 the commander in chief had determined that they were close enough to completion to consider a complete evacuation. (Following the Revolution of 1830, in which Belgium obtained independence from the Netherlands, many of these fortresses would be destroyed, due to the inability of the new nation to garrison them, in exchange for French recognition of Belgian neutrality.)[9]

The other major issue, war claims by Allied subjects, proved harder to settle. Dating from the First Treaty of Paris, which did not force France to pay reparations to Allied governments but did require it to repay debts to their subjects, this stipulation was reiterated in the Second Treaty of Paris. The amount of these claims was to be determined jointly by French and Allied commissioners. Predicted to total no more than 200 million francs, the claims soon began to accumulate, including, according to historian Bertier de Sauvigny, "the oldest and most absurd sort of debts: for example, the Duke of Anhalt-Bernburg claimed the settlement of a contract for furnishing mercenary troops by one of his ancestors to Henry IV!" By the filing deadline of February 1817, there were some 135,000 claims, totaling 1.6 billion francs. Anxious about the effect on public credit, Richelieu complained to his ambassador in London, "What a situation to be struggling thus in this cage of vultures!" Through the summer and fall, these "vultures" repudiated any compromise with the French. Although they were pursued by the French ambassador to Vienna all the way to Carlsbad, where they were taking the waters at a spa, the representatives of Prussia, Austria, and Russia—Hardenberg, Metternich, and Johannis Capodistrias—refused to moderate their claims.[10]

To mediate between these "vultures," the Allies finally turned to the Duke of Wellington. Beginning in November 1817, he worked tirelessly to get the various creditors to abandon some claims in the interest of a realistic financial settlement. Despite encountering fierce resistance, especially from smaller powers such as Denmark, Hamburg, Switzerland, and Bavaria, Wellington succeeded, with help from the Rothschild family of bankers, in persuading these creditors, including the Prussian, Austrian, and British governments, to accept much less than the full amount due them. Although his goodwill toward France was dampened by the attack on him in February 1818, by that spring the duke had reduced the remaining claims to an amount acceptable to Richelieu: 240 million francs (excluding some 80 million francs already paid). In a convention dated April 25, 1818, the French government agreed to meet this debt by raising another payment from Baring Brothers, in exchange for another bond issue of 12 million francs, to be distributed by the Allied powers to individual claimants. Of this, 6 million francs were awarded to the British, 3 million to the Austrians, and 2.6 million to the Prussians. In two separate conventions, the British obtained another 3 million francs; the Spanish, 1 million. (Although the Austrians and Prussians had certainly suffered most from the wars, the British had the longest-enduring claims, dating back twenty years.) In interest, limited to the period since March 1816, the French agreed to pay 32 million francs in liquid money. This settlement was criticized by most Allied leaders, including Wellington himself, who expressed his disgust in a letter to the British ambassador to the Netherlands on April 23, 1818: "The French government have behaved most shamefully in this question, and have taken advantage of the general eagerness to come to a settlement to make a better bargain. I always thought that the prosperous state of the French funds afforded means of accommodation on this question of back interest, but not for sacrificing the interests of the Allies entirely. However, I believe the sacrifice was necessary, and that we should have got nothing if we had not made it." The settlement paved the way for an early end to the occupation.[11]

All that was left to arrange was the final indemnity payment due the Allies for the last two years of the projected five years of occupation. As of summer 1818, the French still owed 280 million francs in reparations, which the Allies agreed to reduce to 265 million, of which 100 million were budgeted as interest on bonds as allowed by the treaty of 1815. To pay the remaining indemnity due in 1819 and 1820, Richelieu proposed to issue 24 million francs in bonds in exchange for another payment of 165 million francs from foreign financiers. To meet the remaining bill for 1818, he proposed another bond issue of 16 million francs, to be used to raise money from the French themselves, at the rate of 66.5 francs, 2.5 francs below the market price. Richelieu's proposal for fulfilling the reparations was approved by the Chamber of Deputies in a somber session on May 6.

Domestic response to the bond issue was overwhelming. Despite their recent economic woes, within a month French investors subscribed some 144 million francs, ten times more than the government requested, causing the *Minerve française* to opine that there were "more people flocking to the treasury to offer money than ever did to receive some." Following this vote of confidence in the French government, the bond rate rose quickly to 80 francs by August. For the remaining indemnity, finance minister Corvetto contracted again with Baring Brothers and Hope & Co., at the rate of 67 francs, for bills of exchange to be delivered to the Allies in installments over nine months, beginning in January 1819.[12]

With these financial details settled, the Allies agreed to consider ending the occupation of guarantee. However, they disagreed over the form of the conference to settle the liberation. In particular, they debated whether it should include all the powers involved in the occupation or only the four major ones, with Metternich pushing the latter. Finally, on May 25, Allied leaders announced that a conference of the four major powers, plus France, would occur that fall. For symbolic and strategic reasons, they chose to hold the conference at Aix-la-Chapelle, site not only of the imperial capital and burial place of Charlemagne over a thousand years earlier but also, more recently, of French peace treaties with Spain (1678) and Austria (1748).[13]

Rumors and Conspiracies

Even as the negotiations toward liberation were proceeding, however, a number of rumors and conspiracies threatened to derail them. Endless gossip circulated about the nefariousness of the Allies and even of some French themselves. In early 1818, police reports and newspapers in France were full of references to various rumors, including that the occupation would be extended for another two or more years, that the foreign armies would remain stationed along the frontier, or that the foreign powers themselves were on the verge of war. While Richelieu's announcement of the financial settlements in late April gave the French reason to hope, similar rumors persisted through the summer.

Some of the anxiety in France was due to machinations outside its borders. In late January, in response to the annual address by the British prince regent to the opening session of Parliament, the Earl of Stanhope gave a speech questioning whether the French government was really stable enough to permit evacuation of the occupying army. Calling the

French "a people the most unprincipled on the face of the globe—a people who had pursued the career of slaves and robbers, and were now the most abject of the human race," Stanhope insisted that "nothing but the most perfect security" against revolution and aggression by France could, in his view, "justify the removal of the army of occupation." In conjunction with the attack on Wellington just a couple of weeks later, this speech provoked widespread reaction against the foreign presence in France.[14]

Soon publicized across the Channel, Stanhope's speech was denounced by many French. As early as February 8, the police commissioner at Cambrai reported that the lord's discourse "has had a bad effect and agitated several heads." As Wellington himself admitted in a letter to the British prime minister, the Earl of Liverpool, on February 4, "Lord Stanhope's speech has made a good deal of impression here. The Duc de Richelieu, who is rather irritable upon all subjects, mentioned it to me with a good deal of anger last night."[15] Warning Stanhope not to come to Paris, the *Chronique parisienne* noted that some twenty writers had taken up pens against him. Numerous authors wrote pamphlets and editorials refuting the right of a foreign power to intervene in the government of France. Representative of these was an anonymous response to the speech, first published in London and then reprinted in Paris, which asserted that the "liberation" of France from Napoleon had come at great cost to its people: "We are horrified to see this deliverance ensured by 120,000 jailers, nourished by the sweat of the inhabitant, keeping him under their yoke, in the name of friendship and the holy alliance." Insisting that the British needed the French as allies, this pamphlet urged them not to extend the occupation.[16] Such "license" against the coalition was criticized by more moderate supporters of liberation, including Richelieu. Nonetheless, the foreign minister maintained that the dangers of evacuation were much less than those of ignoring the treaty article that provided for the end of occupation after three years.[17]

Rumors that the Allies did not intend to evacuate soon seem to have been encouraged by French ultraroyalists themselves in an effort to undermine the authority of the moderate constitutional ministry of Louis XVIII. As the Comtesse de Boigne later remembered, in its efforts to obtain liberation, the ministry was "thwarted by the Ultra party which felt, or feigned, a great alarm to see the foreign army leave France," with the king's brother the Comte d'Artois reportedly warning Wellington, 'If you go away, I want to go, too.'" Already in 1816 and again in 1817, ultraroyalists opposed to the Charter had drafted a "Secret Note" denouncing the French ministry as too sympathetic to revolutionary ideology. In early 1818, playing on Allied anxiety of unrest across Europe, they commissioned the Baron de Vitrolles to circulate another such "Secret Note" on the political situation in France to foreign courts, to get them to press for a change in ministry in France. Directed at the Prussians, thought to be most opposed to ending the occupation, this ploy backfired when the note fell into the hands of the minister of police, Decazes, who published it, provoking a backlash against the ultraroyalists. In France, this note pushed the liberals to launch a defense of the Charter against the reactionary opposition and its cynical use of the threat of Allied force. Abroad, the secret note failed to stop the movement toward liberation. British foreign minister Castlereagh, who had received a true appraisal of the French situation from Wellington, is reported to have remarked: "If this description is exact, we should be obliged to recall our troops forthwith, form a cordon around France and leave the inhabitants to devour one another. Fortunately, my lord, we have less terrifying information to oppose to yours."[18]

In June, the French police revealed yet another last-ditch attempt by the ultraroyalists to discredit the monarchy and postpone the evacuation, the so-called Conspiracy at the Water's Edge. Uncovered—or constructed—by some police agents, this "conspiracy" involved a plot by a group of ultraroyalists, including Vitrolles and Chateaubriand, to use a segment of the royal guard to force Louis XVIII to replace his moderate ministry with a reactionary one or, if he refused, receive the Paul I (of Russia) treatment—in other words, assassination. Publicized by Decazes via an anonymous article in the *Times* of London, which connected it to the king's brother, this "conspiracy" served as a pretext for a government crackdown. Over the next few weeks, the leaders of the supposed plot were arrested and the Comte d'Artois dismissed from his post as head of the national guard.[19]

Amidst such intrigues, the rumor mill suggested that for one reason or another the congress to settle the end of occupation would be delayed. Through the summer of 1818, inside and outside France circulated endless "noises," many of which were blamed on the ultraroyalists: the entire occupation would be extended for at least two more years; the Austrian army planned to establish an "army of observation" across the border; inhabitants of western France were plotting an insurrection. In the wake of the Conspiracy at the Water's Edge, Alsace was beset by rumors that Austria and Prussia were making "great preparations" for war and that the Austrian army had renewed its contracts with local suppliers for another year. Even once the congress at Aix-la-Chapelle was underway, rumors circulated that it was not going well for France. Around Besançon it was said that Richelieu had been so badly received at Aix-la-Chapelle that he left.[20]

At the same time, though, other "noises" hinted that liberation was at hand. From Sedan in early July a police informant reported, "One reports that the Prussian General-Staff has sold lots of objects found in the military warehouses in Sedan and begins to pack its bags; which reanimates the hope, which the inhabitants had conceived but which had been weakened, to see the foreign Troops depart soon." Around the same time, from Châlons-sur-Marne a maréchal de camp reported that the Prussians were melting lead into portable cylinders, distributing wood to make trunks, and selling 1,876 pounds of biscuit, all in preparation for departure. From Metz the police commissioner noted that orders had been given in Trier, across the border, to prepare lodging for thirteen thousand troops. He concluded, "This noise, which seems positive, is the happy foreshadowing of the evacuation of the French territory."[21]

"A Prettier Little Conference I Have Never Seen"

Despite efforts to sabotage the liberation, by August 1818 preparations were under way for the Congress of Aix-la-Chapelle. Great Britain was to be represented by Castlereagh and Wellington; France, by Richelieu, assisted by the French ambassador to Vienna, the Marquis de Caraman; Prussia, by Prince Hardenberg and Count Bernstorff; Russia, by Capodistrias, Nesselrode, and Pozzo di Borgo; and Austria, by Metternich and his aide, Friedrich Gentz, who would serve as conference secretary, as he had at Vienna. These diplomats were to be joined by the sovereigns of Prussia, Russia, and Austria.

Their staffs—as well as hundreds of accompanying tradesmen and spectators—had arrived early to prepare. According to a letter from an inhabitant of Aix in early August printed in the *Moniteur universel,* "One is occupied at this moment in renting a mansion for Lord Castlereagh. A crowd of foreign negociants, merchants and speculators is already arriving inside our walls. Vast warehouses are established, and our town begins to take on the air of a big city. . . . One cannot imagine the activity that reigns in this moment in our city. The plasterers, painters, carpet-makers, and carpenters are overwhelmed with customers, and charge what they want: it is the foreigners who will pay in the end." The only people having trouble finding houses, according to this informant, were the English, who had developed a bad reputation for parsimony.[22] Within a month, the town was full of socialites, bankers, journalists, suppliers, mercers, tailors, servants, preachers, tutors, restaurateurs, actors, and artists—including Sir Thomas Lawrence—from England, Germany, Russia, and France. The influx of visitors was strictly monitored by police on both sides of the border. In France, they required passports of inhabitants crossing the frontier; in Aix-la-Chapelle, they ejected foreigners whose documents did not provide a sufficient reason for their stay. Nonetheless, by mid-September, there were some 2,117 foreigners in Aix-la-Chapelle.[23]

There they awaited the sovereigns and diplomats of the major powers. According to information provided to Sir George Murray in Cambrai, the emperor of Russia would pass through Berlin and proceed with the Prussian king to Mainz. There they would be joined by the emperor of Austria and proceed to Aix-la-Chapelle, where they were expected to arrive in late September. Awaiting the Russian tsar upon his arrival were three "superb" carriages imported from London—for which customs fees alone reportedly cost 1,600 francs—a gift from the prince regent, who did not attend the congress.[24] Also absent was Louis XVIII, too ill to make the trip. In mid-September, the king had met with Richelieu to convey his two main goals for the conference: the end of occupation, in exchange for the final reparations payment of 265 million francs, and the readmission of France into the international community. The king insisted on the first goal in particular: "Make every kind of sacrifice in order to obtain the evacuation of the territory," he told Richelieu. "It is the first condition of our independence. . . . Explain to my allies how difficult the position of my government will be as long as one attributes to it the misfortunes of the country and the military occupation. . . .

Obtain the best conditions possible, but at any price let us not have any more foreigners on our soil." On September 27, Richelieu arrived in Aix-la-Chapelle, and three days later the negotiations began.[25]

Once in Aix-la-Chapelle, diplomats and spectators alike amused themselves splendidly. Because the conference lasted little more than a month, there may have been less dancing than in Vienna. However, there were plenty of concerts, parties, banquets, and balls. Lady Castlereagh hosted many a card party, and Goethe was on hand to attend a stage version of his *The Sorrows of Young Werther.* The Austrian emperor visited incognito a dye manufactory producing the famous Prussian "blue." Although a boxing match sponsored by the British was not to the taste of the foreign spectators, a performance by a Prussian aeronaut, Mademoiselle Mina Reinhard, in which she floated for a long time above the town, covering spectators in flowers and prints, was applauded by a large audience, including the king of Prussia. As the self-appointed "Observer" of the Congress reported in late September, "Since the sovereigns have reunited at Aix-la-Chapelle, one notices an incredible movement and activity; but one speaks more of balls, of parties and of dinners than of political conferences."[26]

Once Richelieu arrived, it did not take long for the congress to get down to business. According to protocols exchanged ahead of time, the congress was to consider four main issues that had not been effectively resolved at Vienna, in addition to the question of the liberation of France: the political reorganization of the German Confederation, particularly a territorial dispute between Baden and Bavaria; the problem of the Barbary pirates; the conflict between the revolutionaries of South America and the Spanish government; and differences between Spain and Portugal over their colonies. There was also some discussion of whether Napoleon should remain in captivity. Ultimately, the conference boiled down to a "political stock-exchange," as one reporter labeled it. Attended by a number of financiers, including the Rothschild brothers as well as representatives of Baring Brothers and Hope & Co., it focused on negotiating the end of the occupation of guarantee in exchange for payment in full of the indemnity. Or, as another commentator put it, referring to the author of a popular accounting manual from the early eighteenth century, "All the science of diplomacy resides today in Barrême." After some last-minute maneuvering over the financing of the remaining 265 million francs in reparations, the Allies agreed to evacuate their armies.[27] The treaty signed on October 9 required the occupying armies to evacuate the territory of France by November 30, after which the French were no longer responsible for financing their supplies or salaries. On this point, Richelieu found the Allied leadership very amenable, particularly Wellington, whom he characterized as "perfect for us, it seems that he has in some way adopted us."[28]

Although they came to a quick agreement on ending the occupation of guarantee, the Allies had a harder time settling the other issue of concern to Louis XVIII: the place of France in the community of Europe. Here, the main question was whether the Pact of Chaumont of 1814 would continue as a Quadruple Alliance or expand to include the newly liberated France. While Richelieu insisted that the stability of Europe necessitated France's rehabilitation as an equal power, most of the Allies, with the exception of Russia, were nervous about including it in the coalition. Anxious about a Franco-Russian alliance, Metternich was vehemently opposed to its inclusion. While not averse to allowing France to participate in the alliance, Castlereagh was concerned about the reaction of the British Parliament, some of whose members were quite anti-French.[29]

Interrupted by the five-year anniversary of the Battle of Leipzig on October 18—which was celebrated "pompously" by Wellington and the sovereigns of Prussia, Russia, Austria, and the Netherlands, to the chagrin of the French—the congress continued to weigh this issue for another month. Finally, in early November, the Allies adopted a two-pronged approach to the question. Publicly, they invited France to participate in the international meetings that were supposed to occur on a regular basis. In a note to Richelieu, they wrote:

> The August Sovereigns have seen with satisfaction that the order of things so happily established in France by the restoration of the legitimate and constitutional monarchy and the success which has crowned up to now the paternal efforts of His Most Christian Majesty fully justify the hope of a progressive strengthening of that order of things so essential for the repose and prosperity of France . . . [Therefore they invite the king] to unite his efforts and counsels with theirs and take part in their present and future deliberations, devoted to the maintenance of peace, of the treaties upon which it depends, and of the rights and mutual relations established or confirmed by their treaties.

As representative of France, Richelieu was invited to join the ministers of the Quadruple Alliance in signing the official protocols at the end of the Congress of Aix-la-Chapelle, on November 15, 1818. But the same day, unbeknownst to Richelieu, the ministers of these four powers renewed the Pact of Chaumont by secret treaty. Requiring each of them to maintain a force of sixty thousand in case of revolution in France, this contingency was never executed before the Congress System dissolved in the 1820s.[30]

The Congress of Aix-la-Chapelle was widely celebrated as a success. Klemens von Metternich himself remarked, "A prettier little conference I have never seen." As a history of the liberation of 1818 written in the aftermath of the Franco-Prussian War concluded, from this conference the Quadruple Alliance "emerged strengthened in its action, less uncertain in its attributes; it had grown from the adhesion of France but survived no less against her in case of some attack, on her part, against the regime that governed her."[31]

As news of the treaty circulated, the French rejoiced. On October 11, a stagecoach driver reported, "This news has produced a great sensation, and one impatiently awaits official confirmation." As word traveled south to Bordeaux, it produced "an excellent effect," especially as French troops in the region departed to reoccupy garrisons in the Nord; when official word arrived in the city, it was received "with enthusiasm and to cries of: Vive le Roi!"[32] In London, the Comtesse de Boigne recalled, the day the news arrived the diplomatic corps and the British cabinet rushed to visit her father, the French ambassador, to "share our satisfaction." Among foreigners in Paris, however, news of the evacuation was less welcome, causing some who had rented rooms in the neighborhood of the Palais-Royal, for instance, to depart for home.[33]

Meanwhile, the spa town of Aix-la-Chapelle emptied of visitors as the aides-de-camp of the various armies returned to their corps to organize the evacuation and the clerks, journalists, tradespeople, and entertainers lost their customers. Following the departure of the Allied sovereigns in November, the magistrate of the town renamed the streets where they had stayed rue d'Alexandre, rue de Frédéric-Guillaume, and rue de François.[34]

Evacuation

Given the short period between the convention on October 9 and the deadline for evacuation by November 30, the Allies began to prepare for their return home even before the congress had ended. Within a week of the convention, the English Reverend Stonestreet wrote from Cambrai, "The decision of Congress sets us all on the move. The heavy baggage of the Army is already on its way to Calais; and as the next week will be a scene of confusion difficult for any body to conceive who has not seen a large army on the march, I am stealing off a day or two in advance." Even as they began to plan detailed schedules and routes for the evacuation of each national contingent, Allied officers proceeded with one last annual joint exercise on the fields of Denain, to the southwest of Valenciennes. Concerned that the evacuation not look like a hasty retreat, they organized a march of massive numbers of troops, first from their garrisons for review and, then, mere days later, from the garrisons across the border to their home countries. For this grand review, the Allied dignitaries took a break from the negotiations at Aix-la-Chapelle to visit Valenciennes, which scrambled to procure extra lodging, transport, and food as well as to fund the illumination and decoration of public edifices. After several delays in the arrival of various Allied contingents, the grand review finally occurred on October 23. Before the Russian emperor and the Prussian king, Wellington reviewed the army of occupation for the last time before "an immense crowd of curious" inhabitants. This review was followed by a parade near Mont Houy and, in the evening, a grand ball hosted by the Iron Duke.[35]

From Valenciennes, the two sovereigns visited the headquarters of their national contingents at Maubeuge and Sedan. In Sedan, where they were expected from October 18 to 20, the municipality repaired the theater, where a troop from Reims came to perform a comedy, and constructed large barracks. They also built three floating bridges on the Meuse, to facilitate the movement of the Allied leaders to and from a review of troops that had not made the trip to Valenciennes. At this review, in which 24,000 soldiers and 7,500 horses paraded before the two sovereigns, local authorities earned praise from the Prussian intendant general for provisioning his troops on short notice.[36] Before returning to Aix-la-Chapelle, at the request of Richelieu, the Allied sovereigns made a brief visit to Paris to pay their respects to Louis XVIII.[37]

Even as their troops were being reviewed by Wellington for the last time, the Allied contingents began to pack their bags for their definitive departure. Already in May, Wellington had solicited from his quartermaster and commissary general information on the time and expense needed to transport artillery and ordnance via cart and boat. Over the succeeding months, he arranged for duty-free transport of equipment via the Netherlands, as well as for payment of remaining salaries and rations. Within a week of the settlement, a police informant reported, "The English Troops are making all the arrangements necessary for their departure. One sees in Valenciennes only packing of loads for wagons, sales of horses, of equipment, &c. The inhabitants are ready to make great celebrations the day that they will reassume the guard of their own city."[38]

As they packed, the Allied armies took stock of their possessions, selling unnecessary supplies, including weapons and horses, and purchasing extra provisions for the trip home. On October 8 in Sedan, the Prussian commander in charge of artillery, Colonel de Roehl, announced on a printed poster a public auction of used equipment, provoking the staff of the French war ministry to investigate whether this matériel was actually Prussian in origin. From Mulhouse, an informant noted that, having received the evacuation order, Allied troops were "selling all the effects, utensils, and baggages, which had become useless to them" but were also buying all sorts of merchandise to import to their own countries. Over the succeeding months, municipal authorities from Tourcoing, in the north, to Ribeauvillé, in the south, reappropriated furnishings, tools, office supplies, excess provisions, and even buildings that had been procured for the Allies. Returning those that had been loaned to their owners, they sold those that had been purchased by the municipality or department at public auction to the highest bidder. In Tourcoing in late November a collection of armoires, clocks, tables, mirrors, curtains, chamber pots, and spoons—valued at some 4,400 francs—was auctioned off. Along with another cache of tools, the town also sold off a blacksmithing hangar and some stables, which had been used to house the Saxon cavalry. In Ribeauvillé, a similar building used by the Austrians was sold to a local property owner. Meanwhile, in Wissembourg, the commander of the contingent from Württemberg ordered extra wagons and horses for the transport of baggage and staff.[39]

As the Allies prepared to depart, there were some last-minute incidents. Tension between occupiers and occupied was especially palpable in the British sector around the time of the last grand review. Already in August 1818 in Cambrai, according to the police commissioner, a song circulating among the townspeople threatened to spark conflict with the English. Set to the tune of "Peuple Français, Peuple de Frères," this song demanded the departure of the English who had inflicted such a reversal on the French: "Depart, hero of one day;/One day victors, one hundred times defeated;/France however unfortunate/Conserves its thousand virtues;/Tremble before the noble audacity/Of a people that you irritate;/It accuses you, it menaces you,/Depart, retreat, depart." In the following two months, there were several reports of "disorders" in Cambrai and Valenciennes. As the British began to worry that the French would mistreat them during the evacuation, they in turn became more aggressive with the locals. From Valenciennes, a stagecoach driver reported that a number of English officers had committed "excesses" during the night of October 16–17, removing a number of street lamps, which they threw in wells, and replacing them with straw bundles. In turn, local inhabitants demonstrated that they were tired of their British guests. During the evacuation of Cambrai, according to local legend, a toiletry merchant who had been forced to lodge two "drunk and debauched" English infantrymen, when asked to refill their gourds one last time, replied drily, "You will have no more, go away." When one of the soldiers, furious, threatened to pierce him with a sword, the merchant grabbed a bar of iron and hit the soldier in the chest, killing him on the spot. The body of the Englishman was thrown, along with his gun, sack, and shako cap, in a hole under the courtyard of the merchant's house. According to the legend, there remained no witness to this incident except the iron bar, which "served now to break ice and clear sewers."[40]

Such last-minute violence was not limited to the British sector. In early November, Russian troops were reported to be firing shells in the area around Maubeuge. Some of this tension was provoked by the French themselves. In Sedan, for example, in the "happy tumult" surrounding the evacuation, local inhabitants lodged insults at Prussian troops until the very last moment. In response to such disorders, French authorities and Allied commanders issued a number of decrees, demanding strict discipline of inhabitants and soldiers, and urging quick resolution of any remaining business between the two.[41]

To minimize opportunity for conflict, Allied and French officials took great care in organizing the evacuation. Four times bigger than the troop departure of the previous year, the evacuation of November 1818 was a monumental undertaking, straining the capacity of roadways and communities in France and neighboring territories. In little more than a month, the Allies had to move 120,000 soldiers and most, if not all, of their horses and equipment, via wagons, barges, and ships, lodging and feeding them at each stop along the way. As Allied wagon trains moved through, local French authorities were directed by the war ministry to house and feed them. According to the plans approved by British quartermaster general Sir George Murray, who was in charge of the operation, the Russians were to evacuate first, followed by the Saxons, Prussians, Austrians, and others, with the British artillery departing from Anvers and the rest of the British army embarking from the single port of Calais. By the end of October, many of these troops were on the march, their every move tracked by the French war ministry and the Allied military staff. To alleviate tension, Allied leaders even negotiated indemnity rates for German states through which Prussian, Austrian, and Russian troops would pass on their march home.[42]

Immediately after the review at Valenciennes, the British began their evacuation via Anvers and Calais. Between October 27 and November 13, the Russians, split into two columns, departed the region around Maubeuge for their long march home via the Netherlands on the one hand, and the Rhine at Mannheim on the other, reaching the German town of Kaiserslautern at the end of November. Before they left, their commander, Vorontsov, distributed to each soldier one ruble, a pound of meat, and a glass of wine. The Russians were followed closely by the Saxons, who did not want to be left alone in the hostile territory of the Nord, and the Hanoverians and Danish, who had already contracted with a shipowner in Dunkirk to transport their weapons and baggage by sea. Departing the area around Bouchain between November 8 and 18, the Danes marched in six columns of eight hundred each to the town of Mons, in what is now Belgium, provoking some complaints from local inhabitants. Beginning on November 4, the Prussians moved in columns of three to five units each along five different routes, with stops in Koblenz, Triers, Cologne, and Luxembourg. With an average travel time of ten days, the final Prussian unit arrived in Cologne on December 9. With the help of bridges constructed by the French war ministry, by early November troops from Württemberg and

Austria had begun to cross the Rhine out of Alsace. Likewise, the Bavarians crossed from the area around Bitche and Sarreguemines into Baden, whose inhabitants were enraged by their presence given the territorial dispute between the two nations. The British, who began to leave for Calais in late October, evacuated Cambrai on November 18 and Valenciennes a day later. From Calais, the first troops, a regiment of Scots, embarked around October 27. Over the succeeding weeks, hordes of British soldiers, as well as officers and accompanying civilian men, women, and horses, gathered in the port city. Following official restrictions against the export of Frenchwomen and more than one horse per infantry officer, some embarking military men took desperate measures: many officers shot their excess horses rather than sell them cheaply, and one police informant reported, "One assures that there was discovered at embarcation in a trunk to which an English officer was giving a lot of care, a young girl that this officer had taken from St. Omer, or rather who had consented to follow him." On December 1, according to a report from Calais, 22,481 men, 6,475 horses, 2,200 women, 2,700 children, and an enormous quantity of baggage were shipped to England. As the last British troops departed, the French lieutenant overseeing the embarkation at Calais wrote to the war minister, "The reign of England died yesterday at one past noon." By the beginning of December, all but a handful of Allied troops had been evacuated from France. On December 5, the Council of Allied Ambassadors, which had surveyed the French government, also discontinued their meetings in Paris.[43]

As the Allied troops departed, they were bid adieu in numerous ceremonies, banquets, and parties organized by French authorities, as well as with official letters, discourses, and decorations. In Sedan, the prefect of the Ardennes hosted a party, followed by a ball, for foreign military leaders. In Rocroi, despite their joy at liberation, the inhabitants "did not forget to address their farewells to the Russian officers, with calm and dignity," by offering them a meal "in which reigned the most sincere cordiality."[44]

As they bid farewell to Allied commanders, French authorities recognized "good conduct" with certificates and awards. In Valenciennes, the mayor and his adjuncts wrote to the British commandant and his majors to attest "their satisfaction with the honest procedures and regards they had taken toward us and all French public functionaries during their three years" there. In language typical of these testimonials, the letter continued, "Receive as a proof of the honorable memories that you leave to us, the expression of the sentiments of esteem that you have inspired in us, it is shared by our inhabitants who are pleased to render justice to your moderation toward them and your firmness in maintaining Discipline among your troops, it is these two qualities that distinguish you as military Chiefs, to which we have owed this good harmony that reigns between your soldiers and our Citizens." In Cambrai, the police commissioner commended to the French king the British and Russian commanders, lauding even the Cossacks, who, despite their reputation as "*anthropophages*" had exhibited perfect behavior: "The inhabitants with whom they were lodged had only praise to offer for their gentleness and their probity." Even in Wissembourg, where relations between French inhabitants and occupying Württemberger troops were notoriously difficult, a local authority sent a letter to the commanding officer praising his efforts to "maintain good order and assure exact discipline," which had earned him "Rights to the recognition of the inhabitants of the arrondissement." As the Danish Prince Frederick departed from Bouchain, he received thanks from the mayor and local notables. Wearing a French decoration "for military merit," he was acclaimed by cries of "Vive le Prince Frédéric" and met by two young men bearing garlands of flowers, plus an old man, who gave him a bouquet and asked the benediction of God on him and his country.[45] In Landrecies, where the evacuating Russian troops were also accompanied out of town by inhabitants exchanging with them signs of friendship, the municipality offered the general Loewenstern and the regimental colonel Alexiopolsky a sword of honor as an "authentic testimony of its recognition and high consideration." The Russian commander Vorontsov and his adjunct, General Alexeieff, were given medals with effigies of Louis XVIII in gratitude for their "good understanding" with the inhabitants of Rethel and Vouziers.[46] In Colmar, where the schoolteacher Georges Ozaneaux noted that the Austrian commander Baron de Frimont would take with him "universal affection," in a meeting on October 23, 1818, the mayor offered a box containing various precious objects to the Austrian captain Schluderer and two watches to his secretary and barracks guard; all of these gifts had been purchased by the mayor himself at a jeweler in Paris, for 2,000 francs.[47] In the months after the evacuation, the foreign ministry arranged to confer some of France's highest decorations on a number of Saxon officers who had overseen the occupation of the region around Tourcoing: given that they were all Protestant, they were awarded the Royal Order of Military Merit, as opposed to the Order of Saint Louis, reserved only for Catholics.[48]

In exchange for such testimonials, foreign officers paid their compliments to local officials. Loewenstern sent the mayor of Landrecies a letter celebrating the "fraternal union" between their two peoples: "You have treated us as friends and as brothers," he wrote. "We soon felt as if we were compatriots. . . . Our hearts tighten at the very idea of leaving such true allies. . . . The joy of seeing again our homeland and our families is mixed with a sincere regret to abandon friends who have earned so many rights to our attachment and our recognition." In Colmar, the mayor and parish priest were named knights of the Austrian Imperial Order of Leopold by the imperial government in Vienna. Before leaving Sedan, the commanding officer of the Prussian garrison sent the mayor not one, but two, letters thanking the inhabitants for their "good conduct" toward his troops. He wrote, "If we have lived in Sedan for three years tranquilly and cordially, as in a city of our own homeland, we owe the greatest thanks to the inhabitants and principally to you along with the authorities of the city who have regulated by your wise hands the conduct of the inhabitants." Complimenting the behavior of the local inhabitants toward his troops and expressing his own regret at leaving France, Prussian commander von Zieten reportedly said, with tears in his eyes, "It is impossible for me to express my current state; I would never have imagined that I would contract so much attachment for a nation that is not mine, and for a sovereign whom I do not serve: I am shaken by this separation."[49]

By early 1819, almost all of the Allied troops—and many accompanying foreign civilians—had left France. Aside from a few officers charged with overseeing the transition from foreign occupation to national self-defense, including the Russian general Loewenstern, of the hundreds of thousands of troops who had invaded France in 1815 there remained only a few thousand sick and deserters. In late 1818, there was much correspondence between Allied and French authorities to arrange care of sick foreign troops after the evacuation. The French agreed to keep them in their own hospitals, in exchange for payment of 2.75 francs per soldier per day from the national governments. The British alone left behind some 1,600 sick soldiers. Most sick soldiers were repatriated within a few months, but hundreds, perhaps thousands, of deserters remained in France indefinitely.[50]

As the occupying army departed, the French army repossessed the fortresses inside the northeastern frontier. In the weeks leading up to the evacuation, the army sent engineers to verify the condition of these fortresses and inventory their equipment, to ensure that the occupiers had not damaged or taken anything. In the Nord, French troops entered Valenciennes and Cambrai the day after they were evacuated by the British. As they moved from assignments in other parts of the country back into these frontier garrisons, French soldiers caused some disorder, often connected to the revival of recruiting in this area. In addition to brawling, they terrorized more than a few remaining Allied soldiers and local civilians in the former occupied zone. In the Meuse, one landowner complained that on its passage through his commune the Thirteenth Regiment of Chasseurs had stolen hay and straw; demanding 45 francs as recompense from the war ministry, he asserted that such disorders had never been committed (at least against him) by the occupying Prussians and Russians.[51] Once these soldiers were settled in the northeastern garrisons, they were welcomed by the inhabitants with ceremonies and parties. In Thionville, where a Prussian corps was due to be replaced by a French one, already in late October a butcher planned to donate a steer, and a brewer promised to distribute beer to the returning troops. In Colmar, the return of the French garrison prompted grand festivities. Once the celebration was over, however, these garrison towns often suffered from the replacement by French troops, who tended to have less money to spend.[52]

By the end of November, evacuation of the occupying army was complete. Remarkably quickly and peacefully, Allied and French authorities had coordinated the movement of more than one hundred thousand men out of the northeast. As the prefect of the Haut-Rhin reported to the war ministry in mid-November, "Everywhere the departure of the occupation troops, the absence of any foreign flag filled the inhabitants of the Haut-Rhin with joy, and I could not applaud too much the sentiments they demonstrated in this circumstance, even more since this joy did not explode until after the departure of the allies, and no insult, no provocation took place in any part of the Department," aside from the death of a drunk Austrian chasseur who provoked a fight with a guardsman.[53]

Following the completion of the evacuation, the commander in chief of the army of occupation, the Duke of Wellington, took leave of his troops, thanking them for their "uniform good conduct" and assuring them that he would "always reflect with satisfaction upon the three years which have passed and will be always happy to hear of their success."[54] In turn, the Iron Duke received countless trophies and decorations from a number of foreign states, including one-of-a-kind porcelain dish sets, often featuring battles from the Napoleonic Wars, from the monarchs of Prussia, Austria, and Saxony, for which he created a separate "museum" room in Apsley House, his home in London. From the king of France, whose proposal to offer him an estate near Paris called Grosbois was rebuffed by the ministry, the duke ultimately received the medal of the Ordre du Saint-Esprit and a number of priceless gifts, including forty-four dessert plates in blue Sèvres porcelain, also now on display at Apsley House.[55]

Back home, some of the Allied troops were reassigned. In Britain, many were garrisoned at home, especially in Scotland and Ireland, to fight civil disturbance. After evacuating France, Lieutenant Colonel Leach recorded how his battalion was "despatched, post haste, from England to Scotland, for the purpose of keeping in order the radicals of Glasgow, Paisley, and the vicinity. It was by no means a delectable service, for we found them a most nefarious crew." Other British troops were shipped out again to the Caribbean, India, or Australia. As Christine Wright has documented, many British veteran officers emigrated to Australia, where they became estate owners and government leaders in the new colony. Among the Saxon contingent were a number of men who would assume positions of leadership in their home military and government, including General von Gablenz, who would be responsible for the "pacification" of Dresden after a revolution in 1830, and Lieutenant Eduard von Treitschke, future father of the great German historian Heinrich von

Treitschke. The Austrian commander, Baron de Frimont, would go on to direct the imperial army against revolutionaries in Italy, from where he would continue to correspond with the mayor of Colmar. While the Russian commander, Vorontsov, was transferred to the civil service in Odessa, where he remained governor-general for thirty years, most Russian officers and soldiers remained in military service. Other Allied troops were demobilized, put on half pay or a small pension, if they were lucky, or forced to find other employment. In the German lands, while demobilization was gradual, a number of men who had served in France found themselves back at home by mid-1819. Disillusioned by their treatment by the state, demobilized soldiers struggled to reintegrate in civilian life. In Britain, many of these soldiers fought on both sides of the civil disturbances of the late 1810s and 1820s.[56]

Many of these Allied troops were not happy to leave their posts in France. From late 1818, there are reports of soldiers and officers, especially from Russia, shedding tears as they departed. Referring to reports that some Russians cried at the idea of returning home, historian Marc Blancpain acknowledges that they had reason not to want to leave the good life and relative freedom they had enjoyed in France. According to him, around Bazuel and Fontaine-au-Pire in the Nord, some Russian troops even hid in the forest of Thiérache to avoid leaving.[57] From the British port of embarkation in Calais, a French police informant reported that the departing troops were actually quite sad. After having lived for three years on their usual salary far better in France than they could in England, these soldiers had exchanged the old popular prejudices against the French for "more just and reasonable ideas" about them, to such an extent that the informant feared that, after demobilization, many of them would return to take up residence in the villages where they had been garrisoned.[58] One British officer, who noted that the French were now free to engage in "what plots they please," emphasized that the period of the occupation of France "ought not to be that of his existence to which he is most reluctant to look back."[59] Lieutenant Colonel Leach, transferred first to Scotland and then to Ireland, recalled:

> It was the breaking up of a large family, which was, or ought to have been, bound together by those ties which the various scenes inseparable from the life in which they had been actors, might naturally be expected to create. It

> was impossible to witness, without feelings of regret, this thorough dispersion of regiments and of individuals so long known to each other; and who, in all human probability, would not be reassembled under similar circumstances of interest and excitement.[60]

The break-up of the army of occupation generated very mixed feelings, at least among the Allies.

Celebration

Within France, the end of the occupation of guarantee was celebrated with great pomp. While some individual men and, especially, women regretted the departure of foreign soldiers of whom they had grown fond, most experienced only relief at the end of the material burden and physical violence. As the occupying troops departed, many towns, particularly but not only in the northeast, organized banquets, parades, balls, and illuminations. Some of these were attended by members of the royal family, especially the Duc d'Angoulême, who at the behest of the police minister toured the liberated departments between late October and early December. He was welcomed in town after town with military receptions, official ceremonies, and other festivities, all meticulously recorded in local histories.[61] Coinciding with an exceptionally good *vendange,* dubbed "the liberation wine," the evacuation inspired a popular refrain, "Ah! We drink our wine among our own family." To fête the liberation, artists produced numerous prints, poems, and plays. While most had a nationalist tinge, they also extolled the return of peace in Europe.

Despite the fact that their budgets had already been hard hit by the occupation and evacuation, municipalities throughout the occupation zone went to great expense to mark the liberation with public illuminations, parades, banquets, and balls. Typical was the celebration in Valenciennes on its day of "deliverance" on November 19, chronicled in the *Moniteur:*

> It was yesterday at noon that the English troops left Valenciennes. The national guard was under arms; this departure gave place to no brawl, to no provocation. The inhabitants were in a state of drunkenness and made the air resound with cries a thousand times repeated of Vive le Roi! Vivent les Bourbons! All the houses, without exception, were adorned with white flags, strewn with fleurs-de-lys. The night of the 19th to 20th was consecrated to dances,

games, and celebrations. The inhabitants covered with white ribbons the carriage of the courier Languet who carried this good news to Paris. One awaits at Valenciennes a regiment of the royal guard, and everyone is fighting each other for the pleasure of lodging the officers. The town will throw them a party on the day of their arrival.

This pattern was repeated in town after town. As the *Nouvel homme gris* remarked in late 1818, "Everywhere in France one has celebrated with enthusiasm the departure of the allies; we receive every day new details on the patriotic banquets given on this occasion." The paper singled out the town of Bar-le-Duc, "whose inhabitants are animated with the most pure patriotism."[62]

Amateur as well as professional writers composed poems and songs for the occasion. In Bar-le-Duc, the departure of the Prussian contingent inspired these couplets for a local theater production: "During three years of suffering/The austere laws of a foreign army/This France to my heart so dear,/Seemed to have lost its rights; (bis)/Today is her deliverance,/Do not blush anymore from peace;/Celebrate our independence. . . . /France is returned to the French."[63] In a more satirical vein, a song bemoaned the departure of so many consumers who had spurred commerce: "What a shame,/Dear allies!/What! You are leaving with your arms and baggage!/What a shame,/Dear allies!/It is thus that you leave us?/To what regrets is France going to deliver herself,/Worthy friends, whom she received so well!/You who, fulfilling her most cherished hope,/With your generosity crushed the defeated./What a shame,/Dear allies!"[64]

The liberation was also commemorated in pictures, circulated in Paris and across the country in late 1818 and early 1819. Most of these celebrated the end of occupation as a much-anticipated liberation from a hated foreigner. In *The Departure of the Prussians,* representing a corps marching through a city gate as the townspeople wave goodbye, the caption reads, "Bon voyage, Messieurs the Prussians, and do not ever return at the same price." Another, *Bon Voyage,* captures the popular mood with its depiction of a wounded French veteran and his female companion sweeping debris from their home as dancing foreign soldiers depart, taking a basket of food, bottles of wine, and a bag of loot. In the background is a gate on which are engraved the words, "To Hope.

Bon Voyage. Anonymous lithograph, 1818. BNF.

Pavilion of Peace." In that pavilion, behind a poster advertising "New Wine of 1818," sit the town's inhabitants at long tables, fêting the definitive end of war.[65]

The relief at liberation was conveyed in many theater pieces created to mark the end of occupation. A typical example is *One Hour on the Frontier,* performed at the Théâtre de la Gaîté in Paris, which featured two demobilized soldiers transitioning into farming. At the beginning of the piece, the two men plan to enter *en campagne* (a play on words meaning both "on campaign" and "in the countryside") by marrying local girls in the main square of a village near the fortress of Valenciennes; once that fortress is returned to the French, the now-married soldiers resume active duty. Following scenes of dancing to Russian, German, and English airs, the piece concludes with a vaudeville sung by one of the soldiers: "No more Polish mode,/Nor any more German style;/Let us give up the English appearance,/And the Russian dress./Let's go, my good friends,/Display ourselves à la française;/Let us prove, my dear friends,/That we are worthy of our country." Reviewing this piece, the English-language Parisian newspaper *Galignani's Messenger* noted, "Although the plot is almost nothing, being just a little piece got up for the moment upon the evacuation of France, yet its dialogue is so sprightly, and its minor details so true to life, that it met with a highly favorable reception."[66]

Also applauded by audiences in late 1818, according to *Galignani's Messenger,* was a one-act vaudeville at the Théâtre Saint-Martin, *The Return to Valenciennes, or Let Us Go Back Home.* Featuring a local hotelkeeper named Robert, his daughter, Rose, and their servant, Jeanette, it is set at the moment when the occupying soldiers prepared to depart and the French began to return. Bidding farewell to Rose, whom they have been courting, are a cast of foreign troops: Timidoff, a young Russian officer, who speaks perfect French; Sterling, an administrative officer of the English army whose futile efforts to learn the language have left him incomprehensible to the locals; and Trinquemann, a Saxon officer. Rose's servant, Jeanette, has been wooed by a German trumpeter, Tantaratingting, who served as jockey to the three officers. When Tantaratingting invites her to a ball planned by the foreign officers, Jeanette responds, "Excuse me, but I dance/Never! . . . (Aside) Except with Frenchmen." When the German complains that, even though she declares him to be honest and likable, she would be pleased if he moved far away, the servant girl sings, "Listen here. At your home we have taken shelter/For a long time,/And you were, with our visits,/Not too content./Like you, we will see reborn/More gentle times;/For that, my dear, we must be/Each one at home." When the officers appear, lauding French wine and women, the hotelkeeper says he will offer his daughter's hand to the first one who announces their departure date. However, Rose and her servant are waiting for the return of their French boyfriends, soldiers Victor and Leveillé, who have been stationed far away for the last three years. When they suddenly appear, announcing the liberation, Robert bids adieu to the foreign officers, who in turn drink to the prosperity of France, to peace, and to their own voyage home. Warning the French against further aggression, the Russian officer Timidoff proclaims, "We have had laurels,/Each one in the homeland of the other,/We are returning to our hearths,/You stay at your own." To this, Victor replies, "[Here in France], only lovers,/Will make conquests," and Rose adds, "To marry an Englishman,/I am too French." Urging everyone to dance, Jeanette ends the vaudeville by singing, "Vive le Roi!/Et vive la France!"[67]

One Hour on the Frontier and *The Return to Valenciennes* are representative of the nationalist message of most of the plays—as well as songs, poems, and images—produced on the occasion of the liberation. In a few instances, however, this sort of blatant patriotism was mixed with a more subtle message of international reconciliation and peace. This mix of nationalism and internationalism is seen in another one-act tableau, *The Route to Aix-la-Chapelle,* first performed at the Théâtre du Vaudeville in early November 1818, even before the conclusion of the peace congress. Using the same basic plot of a young French girl (in this case named Victoire, or Victory) rebuffing the attentions of foreigners, out of fidelity to a French soldier (here named Tout Coeur, or All Heart), *The Route to Aix-la-Chapelle* emphasizes the importance of this moment for the destiny of Europe, predicted here by a fortune-teller on her way to the Congress. To a Russian officer, Tertef, who proclaims his love of French women, Victoire retorts, "How I love you, . . . do not stay for that, I would like even better to miss you a little than to see you so near to me," and "Adieu! monsieur Tertef, bon voyage, and do not come back again." In this case, however, the play ends with everyone drinking to the Congress of Aix-la-Chapelle, and Victoire's mother proclaiming, "No more enemy discord,/Peace succeeds fear;/Good faith,/Voilà the law;/And all of Europe exclaims:/Everyone must stay at home," except, as Victoire adds at the end, "to go to the theater."[68] With the conclusion of the Congress of Aix-la-Chapelle, it was time for reconciliation—and amusement.

Crisis and Reaction

Before the wine of liberation had been drunk, however, the peace negotiated at Aix-la-Chapelle was threatened by a number of developments in France and abroad. The ink had barely dried on the settlement for the loan with which the French government intended to fulfill its indemnity, when a stock market crash caused a sharp drop in the rate of bonds and in the price of goods in agriculture and industry. By early 1819, most of Europe was in an economic slump. The economic crisis was accompanied by political crisis. Following the liberation, many of the statesmen who had steered the ship of Europe through the wake of the Napoleonic Wars were sidelined in favor of new political leaders. The change in leadership was followed by a wave of political unrest, which made 1819 one of the most revolutionary years in three decades.

Soon after the negotiation of the loan that allowed France to meet its last reparation payments, there was a crisis at the Paris Bourse. Provoked by excessive speculation and currency shortage, this crisis caused a drop in the *rente* from 80 to 60 percent. As a result, in mid-November Baring Brothers and Hope & Co. renegotiated their loan to stretch payments over eighteen months instead of nine, with an option to pay half of each monthly installment in drafts, redeemable in the major banking cities of Europe, and an interest charge of 5 percent for the delay. When this failed to stop the slide in rates, in a final arrangement dated February 2, 1819, the Allied powers agreed to hold the bonds delivered to them as payment for the last 100 million francs of the indemnity in a trust until June 1, 1820, at which date they would be returned to the French government in exchange for treasury notes payable over nine months.[69] Meanwhile, across France, the sudden shortage of money and drop in prices threatened the income of merchants and farmers. From Lille, Nantes, Bordeaux, Lyon, and a number of other towns came reports of commercial "inactivity" and bankruptcy. Around Calais, cultivators complained that the price of grain was too low; if the decrease continued, they complained, they would not be able to pay their taxes. This crisis was not isolated to France but hit much of the rest of Europe. In Great Britain, still dealing with heavy debts and taxes from the last years of the Napoleonic Wars, the price of grain plunged in late 1818 and early 1819, provoking landowners to demand the Corn Laws, imposing steep tariffs against imports. In late 1818, the Saxon representative in Paris telegraphed home that, because almost all liquid money in Europe had been employed to pay the governments of the victorious powers, especially England and Russia, "The transmission of money from [the French capital] to Leipzig was becoming everyday more onerous and menaced Saxon commerce with a very dangerous crisis." Although the economic crisis was short-lived, it provoked considerable anxiety among populations still recovering from the wars, as well as the grain crisis of 1816–1817.[70]

The accompanying political crisis was already brewing before the Congress of Aix-la-Chapelle had adjourned. While Richelieu was at Aix-la-Chapelle, elections were held for the Chamber of Deputies, in which the liberal opposition prevailed over both moderate and ultraroyalist candidates. In the cabinet reshuffle that followed, Richelieu and Corvetto, the architects of the liberation, were forced to resign in favor of police minister Decazes. Richelieu, who donated a pension offered by the Chamber of Deputies to the hospitals of Bordeaux so as not "to see myself the cause of adding anything to the burdens of the nation," was left almost penniless; returning to lead the ministry briefly between February and December 1821, he would die within a few short years of the liberation, in May 1822.[71] Across the Channel, Wellington received more recognition as a military hero but was nonetheless marginalized until 1828, when he became prime minister.[72] Within months of the congress, the major players in the postwar settlement had been driven from power, at least temporarily, to the chagrin of other Allied authorities. Tsar Alexander, for instance, reportedly saw in the change in ministry "threatening omens for the future tranquillity of France."[73]

Meanwhile, their subjects grew more restless. In the last months of 1818 and the first months of 1819, peoples across Europe spread alarming rumors, shared seditious pamphlets and prints, formed secret societies, and organized demonstrations in protest against their governments. Throughout France, anti-Bourbon "noises" and propaganda circulated widely, causing one British observer to fear that the "Jacobin faction will gain ground rapidly & the Peace of France & Europe again be disturbed." In Paris, where the play *One Hour on the Frontier* was shut down for being more "national" than "monarchist," the general secretary of the prefecture of police regretted how the change in ministry had unleashed unrest: "One believed that the evacuation of the French territory would be the signal for interior peace, of union between the French and prosperity of commerce. Since that instant, which should be an epoch of happiness, a muffled agitation makes itself known, parties are forming, they receive a push from avowed leaders, they concert among themselves, and if the superior authority does not pay serious attention, some events are brewing."[74]

Within months, events were indeed brewing, not just in France, but across the Continent. In Germany, associations of students called *Bur-*

schenschaften became increasingly restive. In March 1819, in Mannheim, radical student Karl Sand assassinated August von Kotzebue, a German dramatist who had spent time in Russia. Later that year, beginning with the anti-Semitic Hep-Hep riots in Bavaria in August, economically motivated protests spread across Germany into the Netherlands and Denmark. Over the next year, revolution erupted in Naples and Spain, as well as its colonies. Fed by officers returning from the occupation of France, secret societies formed in Russia, contributing both to the mutiny of the Semenovsky Regiment in 1820 and to the Decembrist plot against Tsar Nicholas I in 1825.[75] In the United Kingdom, there was an outburst of pamphlets, speeches, and demonstrations calling for economic and political liberty. On August 16, 1819, on St. Peter's Field outside of Manchester, a crowd of some sixty thousand workers demonstrating in favor of parliamentary reform was charged by mounted troops, killing eleven and wounding hundreds more. In what was henceforth known (in an ironic allusion to the battle of June 18, 1815) as the "Peterloo Massacre," soldiers—some of whom had just returned from the occupation of France—fought on both sides.[76]

In the face of this unrest, governments across the Continent began to crack down on political activity. In September 1819, at the instigation of Metternich, German rulers issued the so-called Carlsbad decrees, severely restricting the activities of universities, secret societies, and periodicals. In November, the British government passed the Six Acts, repressing radical organizations and publications. By the first anniversary of the liberation of France, a wave of reaction had blanketed Europe, in the wake of the return of the army of occupation. However, over the long term this reaction would prove futile, as liberal ideas continued to spread—often with returning soldiers—from France to other regions of the Continent.[77]

In October 1818, as the Congress of Aix-la-Chapelle concluded its work and the Allied armies prepared to evacuate, a painter of fabric and artificial flowers in Colmar, Henri Lebert, commemorated the liberation of his country by designing a silk scarf depicting "The Departure of the Allies in 1818." Inspired by an experiment with steam-printing on silk by a local fabricant, the artist approached a textile manufacturer in

Munster, André Hartmann & Sons, who agreed to undertake the project. Lebert made numerous sketches for the piece, especially the medallion in the center depicting the new royal army around a column celebrating the victories of the old imperial one. This particular sketch he shared with the artist Horace Vernet, who added a few touches to the figures of the soldiers, to give them a "more severe aspect." The final piece was transferred to planks of wood by the lithographer Godefroy Engelmann and printed on silk by Hartmann.

The resulting scarf, which Lebert later remembered was sold in shops in Paris and displayed on walls in French homes, was spectacular. Printed in fourteen colors on a piece of silk about one meter square, the scarf depicts both the reconstruction of a peaceful army in France and the return home of the Allied armies. In the center, surrounded by laurel leaves and flowers, is a band of French troops in a mix of blue and green uniforms. Some hold musical instruments; others, swords; another, a book. But their guns are gathered behind them, bundled in a fasces (a bundle of rods around a projecting ax blade, carried by a Roman lictor, or bodyguard to a magistrate with the right of imperium, and thus symbolic of the defense of imperial authority), with the names of military victories written on the side and more laurel leaves on the top. In front, one weary veteran sits rubbing his eye, while another stands looking down at a child, apparently recounting stories of former glory. To the right, a man in civilian dress leads a crowd of men, presumably new recruits, to join the scene. From this center medallion radiate outward twenty spokes, each depicting a different Allied contingent departing France for Russia, Prussia, Austria, England, and numerous other countries. Modeled after the caricatures of these foreign troops by Horace Vernet's father, Carle, which circulated widely after the invasions of 1814 and 1815, these representations of the Allied troops detail the uniforms, horses, wagons, baggage, and accoutrements of each contingent. Around these twenty spokes, there is a border containing gold coins (complete with portraits of the restored king Louis XVIII) and tricolor *fleurs de pensée,* literally "thinking flowers," or pansies. Whereas the former symbolized the monetary contributions paid by the French to the Allied powers under the restored monarchy, the latter, closely related to the Bonapartist emblem of the violet, symbolized desire for liberty and even hope for another return by Napoleon.[78]

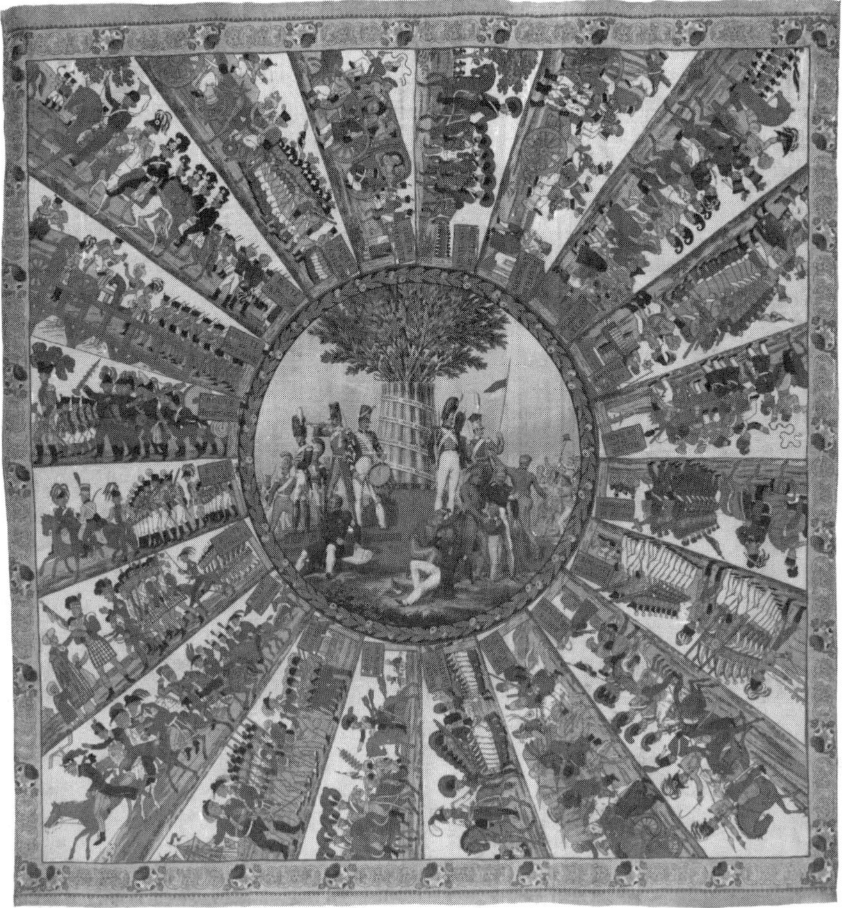

Le départ des Alliés en 1818. Silk scarf by H. Lébert (designer), G. Engelman (lithographer), and Fabrique Hartmann et Fils of Munster (printer), 1818. Musée de l'Impression sur Étoffes, Mulhouse, France.

As the symbolism indicates, this scarf was anti-royalist. In his journal, Lebert admitted that he, like many others, was humiliated by the presence of foreign soldiers in France and resigned, at best, to the return of monarchy. Quoting from a letter to his mother from Paris, where crowds cheered plays about Henri IV, he wrote in February 1816, "I do not feel myself to be royalist: there is in the bottom of my heart something that suffers and cries 'Vive Napoleon!'" Such sentiments are broadcast loud and clear in the scarf celebrating the departure of the Allies, not just in the overtly imperial symbolism, but in the more subtle expressions on the faces of the soldiers, many of whom seem to long for their old imperial army. In vivid fashion, the scarf foreshadows the overthrow of the Bourbon monarchy less than twelve years later.

However, the spokes radiating out from the central medallion suggest a different message about the occupation of guarantee. To be sure, like Carle Vernet, Lebert caricatures the departing soldiers, thereby reinforcing national stereotypes. But the brilliantly colored uniforms and expressions also work to celebrate the diversity of these troops, who had contributed to a cosmopolitan mix of peoples and cultures in France. In some spokes—for instance, the route of Austria, Bohemia, and Hungary—the soldiers are bid a more or less friendly adieu by local women. On the route to Russia, Lebert recycles a standard trope of a genteel officer bowing before a Frenchwoman. On the route to Pomerania, he depicts a scantily clad woman with a barrel of beer on her back on horseback clinking glasses with a soldier mounted on a cannon, while behind them another soldier embraces a peasant woman on top of a covered wagon. In a few cases, the women even depart with the troops, for instance to Silesia (seemingly willingly) and Hanover (perhaps less so). Like Pierre-Jean de Béranger's song "Our Friends, the Enemies," this scarf encapsulates the contradictions of the occupation of guarantee: while it fueled Bonapartism as a political movement, it also provided the context for political reconciliation and reconstruction, within France and across Europe. While it provoked intense nationalism not just among the French but also among the Allied troops, it also promoted significant cosmopolitanism, cross-cultural exchange, and, in some cases at least, genuine amity. Lebert's masterpiece suggests that, long after the twenty-some Allied contingents followed their routes home, the occupation of guarantee left a legacy to a generation of French men and women, as well as the troops who had spent up to three years in their country and, as they marched off, took memories of their experiences with them.

Conclusion

LIKE THE COMMUNITIES in which they had been stationed, the occupying troops that dispersed across Europe retained memories of the occupation of guarantee for decades afterward. Individuals preserved their memories in souvenirs, memoirs, legends, and regimental and local histories. But the experience was increasingly forgotten in the public cultural memory of the nations involved. Except in moments of subsequent conflict between these nations, such as the Franco-Prussian War, World War I, and World War II, it was neglected in national histories and legends, especially in France, where it constituted a painful reminder of the trauma of defeat.

Foreign troops left only sparse and scattered evidence of their memories of the occupation. But they certainly took souvenirs of their experiences in France. As the Danish contingent was departing, Prince Frederick commissioned prints of the towns of Bouchain and Lewarde as mementos for his troops, and he organized a competition for a Danish national anthem. The ultimate winner, "Der er et yndigt land" ("There Is a Lovely Country") would forever be associated with the moment of the occupation, when the Danes first noticed the anthems of other nations.[1] Like the Danes, other contingents exported French products and customs—food, fashions, amusements, books, expressions—as well as French partners, back home. Sir Harry Smith, who had served in the Peninsular Campaign and the War of 1812 before participating in the Battle of Waterloo and the occupation of France, recalled how when the British army embarked from Calais in November 1818, his wife transported home an "immense box" of French dresses with large flounces.[2] German and Russian troops exported quantities of French food and wine, as well as books and periodicals. Such French exports influenced culture in Britain, Germany, Russia, and elsewhere for decades.

The occupation of guarantee was also remembered in an unprecedented wave of memoirs of the Napoleonic Wars by ordinary soldiers as well as elite officers. Often following the genre of the picaresque, travelogue, Gothic, or bildungsroman, these memoirs share a number of tropes regarding the occupation, which they characterized as a formative experience: identification of France with "civilization"; curiosity, but also anxiety, regarding foreign peoples; and criticism of French inconstancy, tyranny, and decadence, often identified with the Palais-Royal in Paris, whose bookshops, gambling houses, restaurants, and prostitutes remained legendary as far east as Russia.[3] Taken together, these memoirs highlight the role of the multinational occupation in promoting international exchange but also patriotism and nationalism.

For many foreign troops, the invasion of France was remembered as an initiation into civilization. As Russian Baron Andrei Rozen later recollected of his time in France:

> Under a milder sky, in fresh surroundings, which bore the stamp of a higher civilization, under the influence of softer manners and a more humane outlook on life, many of the Russian officers acquired some new ideas about the government of their own country. To the young men who had spent the greater part of their lives in the monotony of distant Russian country towns, or in the bacchanalian uproar of St. Petersburg feasts, a new and beautiful world opened upon the sunny banks of the Loire and the Garonne, to whose charms they yielded with delight.[4]

Similar sentiments were expressed by German and British participants in the occupation, many of whom later remembered their time in France as among the happiest days of their lives. Although not overjoyed about his assignment in France for the occupation of guarantee, Prussian officer Carl Friedrich von Blumen later recalled his stay in Bar-le-Duc as "ein zivilisierten Leben," or civilized life.[5]

In addition to food, drink, and women, the foreign troops appreciated the liberalism of France. Of his three-year stay at British headquarters in Cambrai, which he regretted having to leave in 1818, Lieutenant General Sir Harry Smith recalled, "We had saved Europe, and now we were thanked for our conduct in quarters, when in occupation of the country of our enemy, who had been the oppressors of the world; although, as good does come out of evil, so has Europe been wonderfully improved owing to the liberal principles moderately derived from the madness of French democracy." (In 1824, Smith returned to visit Paris, which he found still marked by the events of 1815, but quieter.)[6] The embrace of liberalism was especially pronounced among Russian officers, who dated their political education from their stay in France. According to Baron Rozen, "The most zealous and most active spirits of the Russian Guards enthusiastically imbibed the concepts of liberty, citizenship and constitutional right, and threw themselves with energy into the life of the people for whose conquest they had come from the distant east." As Marie-Pierre Rey has shown, many of the officers involved in the failed Decembrist plot noted during the investigation that they had been "infected" with the ideal of liberty during the invasions of France. For instance, Kondrati Ryleyev, hanged in July 1826 for participating in the plot, acknowledged, "That freedom of spirit, I first contracted during the campaigns in France in 1814 and 1815."[7]

But memories of the occupation also reinforced a sense of *patrie,* if not always outright nationalism. For Russians, this sense of identity centered on a critique of French "decadence" and "false Enlightenment." It involved a reaction against the use of French language and the adoption of French cuisine among the Russian aristocracy. In Britain, where there was a renewed mania for France in the aftermath of the Napoleonic Wars, the occupation nonetheless left many troops with a sharper sense of national difference. On top of their victory at Waterloo, the exposure to a wide variety of peoples, including the French, reinforced their sense of national superiority.[8] For the German contingents, the relationship between occupation and nationalism was more complicated. As numerous scholars have emphasized, in the German lands the "wars of liberation" against Napoleon tended to promote attachment to region, or *patrie,* rather than unified national identity, especially in those states allied with Napoleon until late in the wars. Nonetheless, from this experience, including the occupation of France, German troops did develop *Feindbilder,* or pictures of the enemy, which shaped their identity well into the nineteenth century and beyond.[9] As Karen Hagemann has argued, anti-French feelings among German troops were fueled by the campaigns beginning in 1813, especially among Prussian troops who participated in the occupations of 1814 and 1815–1818: "Their disdain for France and its population was more marked than that of any other country's occupation troops. A strictly anti-French stance dominated not just at Prussian army headquarters but also in the ranks after the final victory over Napoleon. Presumably, anti-French attitudes also persisted after the war in parts of the civilian population. These anti-French sentiments were easy to mobilize again in later years of national crisis and conflict."[10] The memory of occupation endured among Allied troops, providing a fountainhead for nationalism.

Back in France, the occupiers left behind a number of mementos of their stay, including equipment, landmarks, recipes, expressions, stories, and horses, as well as deserters. In Valenciennes, for instance, the British left benches they had constructed on the city ramparts, which continued to be used by local inhabitants, and a path alongside the fortification wall to the north of the town long remained known as the "Trail of the Allies."[11] In Walcourt, in modern-day Belgium, where a Catholic church dedicated to "Notre-Dame" had been converted to Orthodox for the use of the occupying contingent, it remained known as the "Russian chapel." In the surrounding region, there also remained a site referred to as the "Four Russians," where four soldiers who had killed their sergeant had been executed in 1817. In the Ardennes, the Russians also left a number of *versts,* or markers, noting in Russian the distance between their camp and various towns. Of the various souvenirs left by the occupiers, one of the most curious is a series of posts that had marked the encampments of the Russians in the area around Givet. Under these pyramid-shaped stones, local legend has it, the commander Loewenstern left some Russian coins, imported by Jews from Poland, as a surprise for "the savants of the year 2018."[12]

In their wake, Allied troops left considerable ruins, which served to remind local inhabitants of the events of 1814 to 1818. For many communities, the process of burying the dead, clearing the rubble, and rebuilding their infrastructure took years, even decades. In the meantime, the remains themselves constituted daily reminders—and even semiofficial memorials—of the trauma of invasion and occupation. In Soissons, for instance, the edifices of the city hall and court, burned in 1814, were not removed until 1822. In Nogent, where already in 1819 local authorities complained about "afflicting, unhealthy [and] dangerous" ruins, the remains of a damaged municipal building were not destroyed until 1826–1829. As late as the 1850s, traces of the destruction of 1814–1815 were still visible in Chaumont and Nogent, now interpreted as signs of the bravery of the French in defending themselves. More morbidly, at mid-century in the Lorraine, at a *guinguette*, or open-air dancehall, on Sundays some patrons played "quills" with the tibias and crania of foreign as well as French soldiers from the Napoleonic Wars, while others danced. As Jacques Hantraye has eloquently argued, "In the absence of commemorative edifices, ruins constituted supports for the construction—literally as well as figuratively—of a memory of the wars of the Empire."[13]

Supplementing such traces of invasion and occupation were structures erected by the French themselves as they recovered from the destruction wrought on their communities. In Vouziers, a number of buildings destroyed by a fire set by invading Hessian soldiers in 1815 were marked by plaques acknowledging the generosity of the royal family, with whose aid they had been reconstructed. On one such structure, still standing in 1890, the plaque read: "This house burned in 1815 was reconstructed in 1817 by the munificence of His Royal Highness Monseigneur the Duc de Berri. The Dear M. Levasseur, mayor, The Dear M. Coster, subprefect." With or without such plaques, the material reconstruction from war provided numerous physical landmarks for local memory of the occupation.[14]

On the local level, the memory of the occupation was constructed largely through the process of state indemnification for the damages and expenses incurred from invasion and occupation, which continued into the 1820s and beyond. By pushing citizens to declare their losses, this process cemented their "experience" of these events. As Hantraye has shown, "These declarations of losses, as well as the whole process of indemnificiation, played an important role in the elaboration of the representations of events for the victims. These procedures thus constituted a time for self-reflection that was an occasion for evoking suffering linked to the invasion and the occupation, but also for beginning to mourn."[15] In many cases, this mourning was ultimately embodied in a local structure—such as the city hall in Méry and probably in Songeons, in the Oise—reconstructed with funding provided by the state. For example, in the town of Boinville, whose inhabitants decided in December 1817 to devote a part of their indemnity to replace the bell of the municipality, "The memory of the origin of this bell remained under the July Monarchy, when the subprefect wrote that it had been purchased 'with the money from the rations for the Prussians.' The symbolism surrounding this bell was very rich." The association between church bells and state indemnities for war claims was common in villages that had experienced invasion and occupation.[16] Even when demands for indemnities were not satisfied, the process of petitioning kept the memory of the occupation alive as late as the 1850s, when the declaration of another, Second Empire renewed the hope of some determined claimants. Still in December 1852, one Jacques Elloy, a shepherd in the Moselle, was demanding (in vain) that the government compensate him for being "totally ruined" by Allied pillaging of livestock and forage during the "disastrous epoch" of 1814 and 1815.[17]

Through the stories and the petitions of such victims, the memory of occupation was kept alive in local communities, especially in the northeast, which bore the brunt of the events of 1814 and 1815–1818. In this region, the memory of occupation persisted in oral traditions and local histories—including the monographs prepared for each commune by its head teacher for the centennial of the Revolution in 1889—through the nineteenth century and, reinterpreted through the lens of later conflicts, even into the twentieth. Beginning in 1830, during each successive domestic revolution and international crisis, anxieties about foreign invasion resurfaced among inhabitants of the northeast. From generation to generation, the memory of the occupation of 1815–1818 was passed down in stories and idioms. In his memoirs about the revolutions of 1848 and 1870, for instance, Ernest Denormandie recalled, "During my childhood, I had heard the stories of the elders, recounting with a still great emotion, the details of the occupation of 1815 and prolonged cohabitation inside as well as outside of Paris."[18] For a long time, in local parlance this period was referred to as "the time of the enemy." It was memorialized in colloquial expressions, such as the term "blücher," meaning a ferocious dog, or the phrase "Here is something the Cossacks (or Germans) will not have," to compliment a chef.[19] Employing the records of the indemnification process in municipal and departmental archives, amateur historians also began to recount the events of 1814–1818 in local historical societies and journals, especially in the wake of subsequent invasions and occupations, in the late nineteenth and early twentieth centuries.[20]

Outside the local communities that had experienced it, however, the occupation of guarantee was soon forgotten. On the national level, it was quickly erased from public memory. In its struggle to maintain legitimacy, the Bourbon monarchy was loath to remind its subjects that it had returned to power under the protection of foreign armies. To the extent that the occupation was discussed, it was blamed on Napoleon. When this regime was overthrown in 1830, successive governments—especially the Second Empire of Napoleon's nephew, Louis Napoleon—commemorated the glory, not the demise, of the First Empire. Already in 1840, the July Monarchy orchestrated the return of Napoleon's body from Saint Helena to Paris, where it has remained in a lavish casket in the Hôtel des Invalides. But in contrast to the commemoration of the "wars of liberation" in Germany, there were few official monuments to ordinary citizens or ceremonies on battle anniversaries related to the Napoleonic Wars in France. For most of the nineteenth century, successive governments sought more or less consciously to forget the end of the Empire, including the occupation of guarantee.[21]

The memory of the occupation of 1815–1818 was revived only as a result of the Franco-Prussian War of 1870–1871, after which northeastern France was again occupied, by the army of the newly unified Germany. This new conflict provoked a slew of legends, memoirs, and histories of the occupation of 1815–1818, in which the enemy was refigured from a generic "Cossack" barbarian to a German "Teuton," later "Boche." Retroactively, the Franco-Prussian War constructed a "historic" enmity between France and Germany. In the aftermath of this war, numerous memoirists and historians called for a "double revenge" against the Germans, for 1815 as well as for 1870.[22] The stereotype of this enemy, through which the earlier multinational occupation was viewed, would condition expectations of subsequent conflicts in the twentieth century. Following another war with Germany between 1914 and 1918, this stereotype colored the first real history of the occupation of 1815, written by Roger André in 1924. Asserting that the French had long nursed memories as victims of an "unjustified aggression" during the initial occupation, especially against the Germans, André concluded, "The foreigners presented themselves as allies; they behaved as true enemies." Reinforced by yet another occupation by Germany during World War II, this interpretation has prevailed in most subsequent histories of the occupation of 1815–1818, as late as 1983, in a study that explicitly compares the occupations of 1814/1815, 1871–1873, 1914–1918, and 1940–1944 in the department of the Nord. As a result, to the extent that this occupation has been remembered at all in France, it has usually been characterized as a brutal, largely German, conquest. Its more multinational and accommodationist aspects have been largely forgotten.[23]

This historical amnesia regarding the first Allied occupation of France has foreshortened our understanding not just of Franco-German relations but also of war termination and postwar reconstruction. The occupation of guarantee was forgotten at great cost in 1919, when—despite a proposal from a British working committee chaired by Sir Walter Phillimore, who had studied the post-1815 Congress System, for a permanent council representing the Great Powers—the victorious powers, themselves divided in their aims, excluded the vanquished from the negotiations. Focused on the "German problem," itself a legacy of the Napoleonic era, they took a more punitive approach to the defeated, thereby provoking the rise of fascism and the outbreak of another war within two decades.[24] In the aftermath of this Second World War—which, like the Napoleonic Wars, united disparate nations in a total, ideological war—a new group of Allies again faced the problem of how to ensure total peace. Although their reference tended to be the peace settlement of 1919 rather than 1815, the military planners and diplomatic representatives arrived at many of the same solutions as had the Allies against Napoleon. Reacting against the Versailles Settlement, they insisted on reincorporating the defeated powers into the community of nations. In ad hoc fashion, they employed military occupation as a main tool of postwar reconstruction. But this parallel between 1945 and 1815 was not recognized until later, most notably by Henry Kissinger, following the outbreak of the Cold War.[25]

In retrospect, the occupation of guarantee of 1815–1818 was one of the most successful cases of war termination ever. In comparison even to 1945, when Allied cooperation degenerated into Cold War within four years, this first modern peacekeeping mission succeeded in reconciling the powers of Europe over the long term. Aside from a handful of short conflicts between individual powers, the Continent was free of "total" war for a century, until the outbreak of the Great War in August 1914. The reasons for this are multiple. Some analysts, especially in political science and international relations, attribute the success of the settlement of 1815 to its comparatively moderate and multilateral nature, its focus on encouraging the defeated nation to fulfill its financial obligations and stabilize its political institutions, and the relative unity among the victorious powers to prevent additional revolution.[26] According to the study of the British role in this occupation by Thomas Dwight Veve, its success was due above all to the leadership of the commander in chief, the Duke of Wellington, on the one hand, and the French foreign minister, the Duc de Richelieu, on the other.[27]

As this book has shown, however, the success of the occupation also depended on the cooperation of thousands of Allied officers and soldiers and French authorities and inhabitants on the ground, in towns such as Cambrai, Valenciennes, Tourcoing, Bouchain, Maubeuge, Sedan, Bar-le-Duc, Sarreguemines, Wissembourg, and Colmar, and surrounding villages and hamlets. To the extent that the occupation succeeded in reconciling the peoples of Europe, it was due to the efforts of Allied officers such as the Austrian Baron de Frimont and the Russian Baron Loewenstern, who became renowned for their moderation and generosity toward the occupied, and their French interlocutors, such as the prefect of the Haut-Rhin or the mayor of Valenciennes, who were particularly conciliatory toward the occupiers. Even more, it was due to the thousands of French men and women who housed, fed, and supplied the Allied soldiers for three years, with relatively little violence and sometimes even remarkable kindness and sympathy. These men and women, whose contact with the occupiers can only be glimpsed in the official records, were the true heroes of the occupation of 1815–1818.

Little more than three years after he warned his fellow citizens against relations with "Our Friends, the Enemies," Pierre-Jean de Béranger wrote another, more serious song for a party to celebrate the liberation of France, hosted by the Duc de Rochefoucauld at Liancourt. Entitled "The Holy Alliance of Nations," this new song evoked more positive effects of the foreign occupation. In contrast to the earlier tune, it was a genuine celebration of peace and reconciliation between the nations of Europe. The first verse reads, "Peace has been seen to come down amidst us here,/Bidding Earth teem with corn, with flowers, with gold/Calm were the heavens, for lo as Peace drew near,/Mars' lurid bolts became extinct or cold./French, English, Belgian, thus heard her call,/German, and Russ, in prowess equal all,/Nations, unite to form one holy band,/And join ye hand in hand." Calling on the peoples of Europe to forsake their swords for ploughs and to unite together, the song lauded the fruits of peace, concluding, "Good wines of France, flow, freely flow to-day/Back to his land the alien takes his way/Let us, Nations, form one holy band,/And join we hand in hand."[28] To supplement the official Holy Alliance created in September 1815 and re-invoked at the Congress of Aix-la-Chapelle, Béranger demanded a confederation of nations, or peoples, united in security, plenty and, presumably, liberty. Still hopeful that the Restoration would serve the popular interest, he expressed optimism about the future of France and Europe.

Following the liberation of France, this hope for international unity and liberty would be challenged on many fronts. As the Holy Alliance shifted from buttressing the constitutional monarchy in France against ultraroyalists, on the right, and Jacobins, on the left, to suppressing revolutionary ideas across Europe, it stifled any chance of truly popular international cooperation for the foreseeable future. However, from the perspective of late 1818, this reaction against liberalism and cosmopolitanism was by no means a foregone conclusion. Moreover, it ultimately failed to stamp out ideals of freedom and fraternity.

Over the succeeding months, Béranger's song inspired a bas-relief, now in the museum of Valenciennes, as well as a color lithograph produced in Brussels featuring a Briton, a Belgian, a Russian, and a Prussian shaking the hand of a French grenadier, while in the background some mounted troops depart, preceded by a wheelbarrow full of monks. The song quickly became popular outside of France, too. In 1819, a French periodical, *Le nouvel homme gris,* reported that, according to letters coming from the German lands, the song was sung at all social gatherings there. According to this paper, "It is no longer just the grave Teuton who knows today what is signified by [this phrase] '*la sainte alliance*' and what is its true goal."[29] The song was exported with returning troops as far east as Russia, where it and other liberal ballads by Béranger became popular, including among the officers involved in the Decembrist uprising. It remained one of his most successful songs through at least 1848, when it was sung by British Chartists, as well as revolutionaries across the Continent.[30]

Following the rise of nationalism in the second half of the nineteenth century, Béranger's dream of international cooperation was repeatedly quashed, most brutally in the two world wars of the twentieth century. Revived in the aftermath of World War II, in the United Nations and European Union, this dream is once again under widespread threat by virulent nationalism. But two centuries after the Allied occupation of guarantee brought the first total war of the French Revolution and Napoleonic Empire to a close, Béranger's hope for total peace bears repeating: "Yes, free at last, let the world breathe;/Over the past throw a thick veil./Sow your field to the tunes of the lyre;/The incense of the arts must burn for peace./Hope, laughing, in the breast of abundance,/Will welcome the sweet fruits of Hymen [god of marriage]./Peoples, form a saint alliance,/And give each other your hand."

Notes

ABBREVIATIONS

AAE	Archives des Affaires Étrangères (Courneuve)
AN	Archives Nationales
AD	Archives Départementales
AM	Archives Municipales
APP	Archives de la Préfecture de Police (Paris)
AVES	Archives de la Ville et de l'Eurométropole de Strasbourg
BL	British Library
BMV	Bibliothèque Multimédia de Valenciennes
BNA	British National Archives (Kew)
BNF	Bibliothèque Nationale de France (Paris)
BHVP	Bibliothèque Historique de la Ville de Paris
Bay. HStA Kriegsarchiv	Bayerisches Hauptstaatsarchiv Kriegsarchiv (Munich)
CAC	Centre des Archives Contemporaines (Fontainebleau)
CAD	Centre des Archives Diplomatiques (Nantes)
HStA Dresden	Hauptstaatsarchiv Dresden (Sächisches Staatsarchiv)
HStA Stuttgart	Hauptstaatsarchiv Stuttgart (Landesarchiv Baden Württemberg)
JF	*Journal général de France*
JP	*Journal de Paris*
MU	*Moniteur universel*
NAM	National Army Museum, Templer Study Centre (London)

NLS	National Library of Scotland (Edinburgh)
SHD	Service Historique de la Défense (Vincennes)
WD	*The Dispatches of Field Marshal the Duke of Wellington*, ed. Lt. Col. Gurwood, 12 vols. (London: John Murray, 1836–1839)
WSD	*The Supplementary Despatches, Correspondence and Memoranda of Field Marshal, Duke of Wellington, K. G.*, ed. by his son, the Duke of Wellington, 15 vols. (London: John Murray, 1858–1872)

INTRODUCTION

Epigraph: From François-Simon Cazin, *Les Russes en France: Souvenirs des années 1815, 1816 et 1817* (Avranches: J. Durand, 1880), 2.

1. P.-J. de Béranger, *Oeuvres complètes,* new ed. (Paris: Perrotin, 1851), 1:171–173. Unless otherwise noted, all translations from non-English sources are my own. In quotations from primary sources, I have retained the original spelling, capitalization, and punctuation, except where it hinders meaning.
2. The classic accounts are Henry Kissinger, *A World Restored: Metternich, Castlereagh and the Problem of Peace, 1812–1822* (Boston: Houghton Mifflin, 1957), and Gordon A. Craig, "Problems of Coalition Warfare: The Military Alliance against Napoleon, 1813–1814," in *War, Politics, and Diplomacy: Selected Essays* (London: Weidenfeld and Nicolson, 1966), 22–46. This approach is also taken by the historiography on the Restoration in France, such as: Guillaume de Bertier de Sauvigny, *The Bourbon Restoration,* trans. Lynn M. Case (Philadelphia: University of Pennsylvania Press, 1966); André Jardin and André-Jean Tudesq, *Restoration and Reaction, 1815–1848,* trans. Elborg Forster (Cambridge: Cambridge University Press, 1983); Emmanuel de Waresquiel and Benoît Yvert, *Histoire de la Restauration, 1814–1830* (Paris: Perrin, 1996); Francis Démier, *La France de la Restauration, 1814–1830: L'impossible retour du passé* (Paris: Gallimard, 2012).
3. Paul W. Schroeder, *The Transformation of European Politics, 1763–1848* (Oxford: Clarendon Press, 1994); Alan Sked, *Metternich and Austria: An Evaluation* (New York: Palgrave Macmillan, 2008); Michael Howard, *The Invention of Peace: Reflections on War and International Order* (New Haven, CT: Yale University Press, 2000); G. John Ikenberry, *After Victory: Institutions, Strategic Restraint, and the Rebuilding of Order after Major Wars* (Princeton, NJ: Princeton University Press, 2001); Mark Mazower, *Governing the World: The History of an Idea* (New York: Penguin, 2012); Adam Zamoyski, *Rites of Peace: The Fall of Napoleon and the Congress of Vienna* (New York: Harper Perennial, 2007); Mark Jarrett, *The Congress of Vienna and Its Legacy: War and Great Power Diplomacy after Napoleon* (London: I. B. Tauris, 2013); Brian E. Vick, *The Congress of Vienna: Power and Politics after Napoleon* (Cambridge, MA: Harvard University Press, 2014).

4. There have been a few specialized studies of particular armies and/or regions involved in the occupation, including Marc Blancpain, *La vie quotidienne dans la France du Nord sous les occupations, 1814–1944* (Paris: Hachette, 1983); Thomas Dwight Veve, *The Duke of Wellington and the British Army of Occupation in France, 1815–1818* (Westport, CT: Greenwood Press, 1992); Volker Wacker, *Die allierte Besetzung Frankreichs in den Jahren 1814 bis 1818* (Hamburg: Dr. Kovac, 2001); and Jacques Hantraye, *Les Cosaques aux Champs-Élysées: L'occupation de la France après la chute de Napoléon* (Paris: Belin, 2005). As I was completing this manuscript, I discovered another recent book on the aftermath of the Napoleonic Wars in France: Yann Guérin, *La France après Napoléon: Invasions et occupations, 1814–1818* (Paris: L'Harmattan, 2014). It includes one section on the occupation of guarantee and one on the liberation of 1818. Based on a limited number of national police and military records, it provides only a cursory analysis of the experience of occupation on the ground in the northeast. Focused on the humiliation of the French in the wake of Waterloo, it also underappreciates the significance of this novel type of occupation in promoting international reconciliation.
5. Gregory P. Downs, *After Appomattox: Military Occupation and the Ends of War* (Cambridge, MA: Harvard University Press, 2015); Eyal Benvenisti, *The International Law of Occupation* (Princeton, NJ: Princeton University Press, 1993); Peter Hagenmacher, "L'occupation militaire en droit international: Genèse et profil d'une institution juridique," *Relations internationales* 79 (1994): 285–301; Karma Nabulsi, *Traditions of War: Occupation, Resistance, and the Law* (Oxford: Oxford University Press, 1999); and Stephen C. Neff, *War and the Law of Nations* (Cambridge: Cambridge University Press, 2005). Notable exceptions to this oversight of the occupation of 1815–1818 include David M. Edelstein, *Occupational Hazards: Success and Failure in Military Occupation* (Ithaca, NY: Cornell University Press, 2008); Peter M. R. Stirk, "The Concept of Military Occupation in the Era of the French Revolutionary and Napoleonic Wars," *Comparative Legal History* 3, no. 1 (2015): 60–84; and Stirk, *The Politics of Military Occupation* (Edinburgh: Edinburgh University Press, 2009). For new approaches to the aftermath of war in the twentieth century, see especially Stéphane Audoin-Rouzeau and Annette Becker, *14–18: Understanding the Great War,* trans. Catherine Temerson (New York: Hill and Wang, 2002); Antoine Prost, *In the Wake of War: "Les Anciens Combattants" and French Society, 1914–1939,* trans. Helen McPhail (London: Bloomsbury Academic, 2002); Bruno Cabanes, *La victoire endeuillée: La sortie de guerre des soldats français (1918–1920)* (Paris: Seuil, 2004); Stéphane Audouin-Rouzeau and Christophe Prochasson, *Sortir de la Grande Guerre: Le monde et l'après-1918* (Paris: Tallandier, 2008); John Horne, "Demobilizing the Mind: France and the Legacy of the Great War, 1919–1939," *French History and Civilization* 2 (2009): 101–107; Bruno Cabanes and Guillaume Piketty, eds., *Retour à l'intime au sortir de la guerre* (Paris: Tallandier, 2009); and Richard Bessel, *Germany 1945: From War to Peace* (New York: Harper Perennial, 2010). For recent studies of military

occupation in the twentieth century, see Norman M. Naimark, *The Russians in Germany: A History of the Soviet Zone of Occupation, 1945–1949* (Cambridge, MA: The Belknap Press, 1995); John W. Dower, *Embracing Defeat: Japan in the Wake of World War II* (New York: W. W. Norton/The New Press, 1999); Helen McPhail, *The Long Silence: Civilian Life under the German Occupation of Northern France, 1914–1918* (London: I. B. Tauris, 1999); Ronald C. Rosbottom, *When Paris Went Dark: The City of Light under German Occupation, 1940–1944* (New York: Little, Brown, 2014); Susan Caruthers, *The Good Occupation: American Soldiers and the Hazards of Peace* (Cambridge, MA: Harvard University Press, 2016); and Philippe Burin, "Writing the History of Military Occupations," in *France at War: Vichy and the Historians,* ed. Sarah Fishman et al. (Oxford: Berg, 2000): 77–90.

6. David A. Bell, *The First Total War: Napoleon's Europe and the Birth of Warfare As We Know It* (Boston: Houghton Mifflin, 2007); Roger Chickering and Stig Förster, *War in an Age of Revolution, 1775–1815* (Cambridge: Cambridge University Press, 2007).
7. Geoffrey Best, *Humanity in Warfare: The Modern History of the International Law of Armed Conflicts* (London: Weidenfeld and Nicolson, 1980).
8. In addition to the works of Benvenisti, Hagenmacher, Nabulsi, and Stirk cited above, see Christy Pichichero, *The Military Enlightenment: War and Culture in the French Empire from Louis XIV to Napoleon* (Ithaca, NY: Cornell University Press, 2017); Yves-Marie Bercé, ed., *La fin de l'Europe napoléonienne, 1814: La vacance du pouvoir* (Paris: Henri Veyrier, 1990); G. Jacquemyns, ed., *Occupants, occupés, 1792–1815: Colloque de Bruxelles, 29 et 30 janvier 1968* (Brussels: Université Libre de Bruxelles, 1969); Jean-François Chanet, Annie Crépin, and Christian Windler, eds., *Le temps des hommes doubles: Les arrangements face à l'occupation, de la Révolution française à la guerre de 1870* (Rennes: Presses Universitaires de Rennes, 2013); Robert Ouvrard, *1809: Les Français à Vienne: Chronique d'une occupation* (Paris: Nouveau Monde Éditions/Fondation Napoléon, 2009); Michael Rowe, *From Reich to State: The Rhineland in the Revolutionary Age, 1780–1830* (Cambridge: Cambridge University Press, 2003); T. C. W. Blanning, *French Revolution in Germany: Occupation and Resistance in the Rhineland* (Oxford: Clarendon, 1983); and Karen Hagemann, *Revisiting Prussia's Wars against Napoleon: History, Culture, and Memory,* trans. Pamela Selwyn (Cambridge: Cambridge University Press, 2015).
9. Wellington to Viscount Castlereagh, K. G., Paris, 11 Aug. 1815, in *WD,* 12:599. On the Central Administration of 1813–1814, see Stirk, "Concept of Military Occupation," 78.

CHAPTER ONE ✣ EXITING WAR, TWICE

1. François Baudez, ed., *Pierre-Jean de Béranger: Poète national* (Montigny le Bretonneux, France: Le Dormeur du Val, 2005), 1:82; Jean Touchard, *La gloire de Béranger* (Paris: Librarie Armand Colin, 1968), 1:183.

2. David A. Bell, *The First Total War: Napoleon's Europe and the Birth of Warfare as We Know It* (Boston: Houghton Mifflin, 2007).
3. Alan Forrest and Peter H. Wilson, eds., *The Bee and the Eagle: Napoleonic France and the End of the Holy Roman Empire, 1806* (New York: Palgrave Macmillan, 2009), esp. the essay by Karen Hagemann, "'Desperation to the Utmost': The Defeat of 1806 and the French Occupation in Prussian Experience and Perception"; Hagemann, *Revisiting Prussia's Wars against Napoleon: History, Culture and Memory,* trans. Pamela Selwyn (Cambridge: Cambridge University Press, 2015); G. Jacquemyns, ed., *Occupants, occupés, 1792–1815: Colloque de Bruxelles, 29 et 30 janvier 1968* (Brussels: Université Libre de Bruxelles, 1969); Jean-François Chanet, Annie Crépin, and Christian Windler, eds., *Le temps des hommes doubles: Les arrangements face à l'occupation, de la Révolution française à la guerre de 1870* (Rennes: Presses Universitaires de Rennes, 2013); Robert Ouvrard, *1809: Les Français à Vienne: Chronique d'une occupation* (Paris: Nouveau Monde Éditions/Fondation Napoléon, 2009); Katherine Aaslestad, "Paying for War: Experiences of Napoleonic Rule in the Hanseatic Cities," *Central European History* 39 (2006): 641–675; Ute Planert, "From Collaboration to Resistance: Politics, Experience, and Memory of the Revolutionary and Napoleonic Wars in Southern Germany," *Central European History* 39 (2006): 676–705.
4. Dominic Lieven, *Russia against Napoleon: The True Story of the Campaigns of War and Peace* (New York: Viking, 2010); Marie-Pierre Rey, *L'effroyable tragédie: Une nouvelle histoire de la campagne de Russie* (Paris: Flammarion, 2012); Jacques-Olivier Boudon, *Napoléon et la campagne de Russie: 1812* (Paris: Armand Colin, 2012); Michael Leggiere, *Napoleon/Berlin: The Franco-Prussian War in North Germany, 1813* (Norman: University of Oklahoma Press, 2002); Alexander Mikaberidze, *The Napoleonic Wars: A Global History* (Oxford: Oxford University Press, forthcoming in 2019).
5. Michael V. Leggiere, *The Fall of Napoleon: The Allied Invasion of France, 1813–1814* (Cambridge: Cambridge University Press, 2007); Leggiere, *Blücher: Scourge of Napoleon* (Norman: University of Oklahoma Press, 2014); and Gordon Craig, "Problems of Coalition Warfare: The Military Alliance against Napoleon, 1813–14," in *War, Politics, and Diplomacy: Selected Essays* (New York: Praeger, 1966), 22–45.
6. Sir Hudson Lowe Papers, BL, Add Mss. 37,051 (War in Germany and France, 1813–1814); Philip Mansel, *Paris between Empires, 1814–1852: Monarchy and Revolution* (London: Phoenix Press, 2003), 35–36.
7. AN, F 1a/583. On this invasion, see also André Jardin and André-Jean Tudesq, *Restoration and Reaction, 1815–1848,* trans. Elborg Forster (Cambridge: Cambridge University Press, 1983); Marc Blancpain, *La vie quotidienne dans la France du Nord sous les occupations, 1814–1944* (Paris: Hachette, 1983); François Cochet, ed., *Les occupations en Champagne-Ardenne: 1814–1944* (Reims: Presses Universitaires de Reims, 1996); Emmanuel de Waresquiel and Benoît Yvert, *Histoire de la Restauration, 1814–1830* (Paris: Perrin, 1996); Jacques Hantraye, *Les Cosaques aux Champs-Élysées: L'occupation de la France après la chute de Napoléon* (Paris: Belin, 2005).

8. [Prince Golitsyn], *Souvenirs et impressions d'un officier russe pendant les campagnes de 1812, 1813 et 1814, avec la relation de la bataille de Borodino* (St. Petersburg: Imprimerie française Troïtzkoy Péréoulok, 1849), 115; *Extracts of the Journals and Correspondence of Miss Berry: From the Year 1783 to 1852*, ed. Lady Theresa Lewis (London: Longmans, Green, 1865), 3:13–19; Alfred Nettement, *Histoire de la Restauration* (Paris: Jacques Lecoffre, 1860), 1:129.
9. Waresquiel and Yvert, *Histoire de la Restauration,* 21; Jardin and Tudesq, *Restoration and Reaction,* 6–8; and Leggiere, *Fall of Napoleon,* esp. ch. 17, "The Protocols of Langres."
10. Waresquiel and Yvert, *Histoire de la Restauration*, 63–64.
11. David Andress, *The Savage Storm: Britain on the Brink in the Age of Napoleon* (New York: Little, Brown, 2012), 348–353, and Jenny Uglow, *In These Times: Living in Britain through Napoleon's Wars, 1793–1815* (New York: Farrar, Strauss and Giroux, 2014), 602–608. On the Congress of Vienna, see Adam Zamoyski, *Rites of Peace: The Fall of Napoleon and the Congress of Vienna* (New York: Harper Perennial, 2007); Mark Jarrett, *The Congress of Vienna and Its Legacy: War and Great Power Diplomacy after Napoleon* (London: I. B. Tauris, 2013); and Brian E. Vick, *The Congress of Vienna: Power and Politics after Napoleon* (Cambridge, MA: Harvard University Press, 2014).
12. [Abbé François Épineau], *Mémoires d'un vicaire de campagne, écrits par lui-même,* ed. M. Ant. Aumétayer, 2nd ed. (Paris: A. Royer, 1843), 17.
13. For evidence of such unrest in 1814, see AN, F7/3147.
14. See, for example, Prussian general Müffling to British general Sir Hudson Lowe, Aix-la-Chapelle, 21 Nov. 1814, in favor of British-Prussian alliance against Russia and Austria, insisting on right to Saxony and the country between the Rhine and the Meuse, BL, Add. Mss., 37,051 (War in Germany and France, 1813–1814).
15. Emmanuel de Waresquiel, *Cent Jours: La tentation de l'impossible, mars-juin 1815* (Paris: Fayard, 2008).
16. Waresquiel and Yvert, *Histoire de la Restauration,* 134–135, and Jardin and Tudesq, *Restoration and Reaction,* 20–21.
17. *Journal du Lieutenant Woodberry: Campagnes de Portugal et d'Espagne, de France, de Belgique et de France (1813–1815),* trans. Georges Hélie (Paris: Plon, Nourrit et Cie., 1896), 319 and 326; *The Letters of Private Wheeler,* ed. B. H. Liddell Hart (Witney, UK: Windrush Press, 1998), 177; Field Marshal Blücher, quoted in Waresquiel and Yvert, *Histoire de la Restauration,* 147.
18. Fournel to Pierre Vitet, [Paris], 9 July 1815, AM Lyon 84 II 10 (generously shared with me by Denise Davidson); *JP,* 6 July 1815; Chabrol de Volvic, prefect of Seine, to Commission on Requisitions, Paris, 14 Aug. 1815, BHVP, mss. CP 06 527–06531; Louis de Viel-Castel, *Histoire de la Restauration* (Paris: Michel Lévy Frères, 1861), 3:488; Waresquiel and Yvert, *Histoire de la Restauration,* 148; Helen Maria Williams, *A Narrative of the Events Which Have Taken Place in France from the Landing of Napoleon Bonaparte on the*

First of March, 1815, till the Restoration of Louis XVIII (Cleveland: Burrows Brothers, 1895), 168.

19. Note (in German) in "Registre des mercuriales de la ville de Wissembourg commencé le 3 novembre 1814 geendigt le 31 décembre 1822," AM Wissembourg, A-12–285; Octave Beuve, ed., *L'invasion de 1814–1815 en Champagne: Souvenirs inédits* (Nancy: Berger-Levrault, 1914), 155.
20. [Étienne-Denis Pasquier], *Histoire de mon temps: Mémoires du Chancelier Pasquier,* ed. Duc d'Audiffret-Pasquier, 2nd ed. (Paris: Librairie Plon, 1894), 3:345.
21. Roger André, *L'occupation de la France par les Alliés en 1815 (juillet-novembre)* (Paris: Boccard, 1924), 49–51.
22. Waresquiel and Yvert, *Histoire de la Restauration,* 147; Blancpain, *La vie quotidienne,* 42; report from stagecoach driver from Chalon-sur-Saône, departing 30 July 1815, AN, F7/3824, as well as AN, F7/3823; E. Lafforgue, *Belfort, ses environs et l'Alsace de 1813 à 1834, d'après un livret de famille* (Tarbes: Lesbordes, 1920), 7; Éléonore-Adèle d'Osmond, Comtesse de Boigne, *Mémoires de la Comtesse de Boigne, née d'Osmond: Récits d'une tante,* ed. Jean-Claude Berchet, vol. 1, *Du règne de Louis XVI à 1820* (Paris: Mercure de France, 1999), 500.
23. Alphonse F*******, *Lettre d'un Français aux monarques alliés* (Paris: Chez les Marchands de Nouveautés, 1815); George Canning quoted in Waresquiel and Yvert, *Histoire de la Restauration,* 147; and Guillaume de Bertier de Sauvigny, *The Bourbon Restoration,* trans. Lynn M. Case (Philadelphia: University of Pennsylvania Press, 1966), 120.
24. AN, F7/3824; Paul Gaffarel, *La Seconde Restauration et la seconde occupation autrichienne à Dijon, juin-décembre 1815* (Dijon: Darantière, 1896), 93; Achille de Vaulabelle, *Histoire des deux Restaurations jusqu'à l'avénement de Louis-Philippe (de janvier 1813 à octobre 1830),* 5th ed. (Paris: Perotin, 1860), 3:386–387.
25. Waresquiel and Yvert, *Histoire de la Restauration,* 146–147, and André, *L'occupation,* chs. 6 and 7, "Les alliés et les administrations françaises" and "suite."
26. André, *L'occupation,* ch. 4, "La note du 24 juillet et l'extension de l'occupation," and ch. 5, "La note alliée du 6 août et l'ordonnance royale du 16." See also Jardin and Tudesq, *Restoration and Reaction,* 23, and Waresquiel and Yvert, *Histoire de la Restauration,* 148.
27. André, *L'occupation,* 70–73.
28. *Correspondance d'un préfet avec les généraux, intendans et commissaires de l'Armée autrichienne d'Italie, stationnée à Lyon, pendant l'occupation de 1815* (Tours: Mame, 1828), 25–26.
29. Henri Tournoüer, *Les Prussiens dans l'Orne en 1815: Lecture faite à l'Assemblée générale tenue à Alençon le 28 sept. 1920* (Alençon: Imprimerie Alençonnaise, 1921), excerpted from *Bulletin de la Société historique et archéologique de l'Orne* 40 (1921): 16.

30. Mayor of Issenheim to prefect of Haut-Rhin, 16 Sept. 1815, AD Haut-Rhin, 8R/33; *JP*, 18 Nov. 1815.
31. Denis Michel, "Les 'alliés' en Haute-Loire, l'occupation et ses problèmes, 1814–1815," *Cahiers de la Haute-Loire* (1968): 53.
32. André, *L'occupation,* 70–71 and 157–161, based on reports by prefects in CAC, F5/II (Comptabilité départementale). The magnitude of these costs may be realized in comparison to the average daily wage for a worker in the construction or textile industies around 1815, which was declining to between two and three francs (Jacques Rougerie, "Remarques sur l'histoire des salaires à Paris au XIXe siècle," *Le mouvement social* 63 [1968]: 71–108).
33. Records of the Commission des Réquisitions, July 1815–Feb. 1816, CAD, 8 ACN, cartons 1–51; André, *L'occupation,* 100; Hantraye, *Les Cosaques,* 31–34; correspondence of local French officials around Meaux and Auxerre with Bavarian military authorities, summer 1815, Bay. HStA Kriegsarchiv, B 570 and 592.
34. Waresquiel and Yvert, *Histoire de la Restauration,* 147; André, *L'occupation,* 85–95; Jardin and Tudesq, *Restoration and Reaction,* 22–23.
35. Jacques Hantraye, "Le Camp de Vertus: Un épisode révélateur des relations entre la Russie et les autres puissances européennes, septembre 1815," *Revue des études slaves* 83, no. 4 (2012): 1023–1033.
36. Blancpain, *La vie quotidienne,* 47–57; Marie-France Barbe, "Rocroi, après Waterloo," *L'Hobbette* 9 (2001): 9–23; Paul Leuilliot, *L'Alsace au début du XIXe siècle: Essais d'histoire politique, économique et religieuse (1815–1830),* vol. 1, *La vie politique* (Paris: SEVPEN, 1959), 63–65; report from Bordeaux, departing 28 July 1815, AN, F7/3824.
37. Jardin and Tudesq, *Restoration and Reaction,* 23–25; Bertier de Sauvigny, *Bourbon Restoration,* 117–119; Julie Pellizzone, *Souvenirs: Journal d'une Marseillaise,* ed. Pierre and Hélène Échinard and Georges Reynaud, vol. 2, *1815–1824* (Paris: Indigo/Côté-Femmes Éditions and Université de Provence, 2001), 79–80; Ian Coller, *Arab France: Islam and the Making of Modern Europe, 1798–1831* (Berkeley: University of California Press, 2011), ch. 5, "Massacre and Restoration." On the White Terror in the Midi, see also Pierre Triomphe, *1815: La Terreur blanche* (Toulouse: Privat, 2017).
38. Waresquiel and Yvert, *Histoire de la Restauration,* 149–154; Ernest Daudet, *La Terreur blanche: Épisodes et souvenirs de la réaction dans le Midi en 1815 d'après des souvenirs contemporains et des documents inédits* (Paris: A. Quantin, 1878); Daniel Resnick, *The White Terror and the Political Reaction after Waterloo* (Cambridge, MA: Harvard University Press, 1966); Duc de Castries, *La Terreur blanche: L'épuration de 1815* (Paris: Perron, 1981).
39. Jules Michelet, *Ma jeunesse* (Paris: Calmann Lévy, 1884), 139–140.
40. Williams, *Narrative,* 216–217; *Mémoires complets et authentiques de Laure Junot, Duchesse d'Abrantès* (Paris: Jean Bonnot, 1968 and 1969), 13:iii and 14:224.
41. Report from Amiens, departing 5 Aug. 1815, AN, F7/3824; Blancpain, *La vie quotidienne,* 37 and 46.
42. Reports from prefect of Ardennes, 4 Nov. and 19 Dec. 1815, AN, F7/3823; report on the "political situation" during Jan. 1816 in the departments of the

Moselle, Meuse, Marne, and Ardennes, forming together the Twenty-Third Legion of the Gendarmerie Royale, Metz, 2 Feb. 1816, SHD, 3D/20.

43. Madame de Montbrison and Madame de Berckheim, quoted in Leuilliot, *L'Alsace,* 1:68 and 66; [Épineau], *Mémoires,* 19–20.

44. [Duc d'Otrante], *Rapport au Roi, sur la situation de la France et sur les relations avec les armées étrangères, fait dans le Conseil des Ministres, le 15 août 1815* (Paris: Plancher, Eymery, Delaunay, 1815), 3–4; Wellington, quoted in Blancpain, *La vie quotidienne,* 50.

45. E. de Vorges, "Projet de démembrement de la France par les Alliés en 1815, avec la carte dressée par le général Knesebeck," *Revue d'histoire diplomatique* 2 (1888): 402–405, and Blancpain, *La vie quotidienne,* 58–59. On these negotiations, see also *WD,* vol. 12; *WSD,* vol. 11; Thomas Dwight Veve, *The Duke of Wellington and the British Army of Occupation in France, 1815–1818* (Westport, CT: Greenwood Press, 1992), ch. 2, "Establishment of the Army of Occupation"; and Emmanuel de Waresquiel, *Le Duc de Richelieu, 1766–1822* (Paris: Perrin, 1990), ch. 8, "Une paix difficile."

46. Wellington to Viscount Castlereagh, K. G., Paris, 11 Aug. 1815, *WD,* 12:596–600.

47. "Memorandum: On the temporary Occupation of part of France, To Viscount Castlereagh, K. G., Paris, 31st August 1815," in *WD,* 12:622–625.

48. Veve, *Duke of Wellington,* 13–14.

49. Blancpain, *La vie quotidienne,* 58–62, and Veve, *Duke of Wellington,* 15–18.

50. Blancpain, *La vie quotidienne,* esp. 60 and 63; Bertier de Sauvigny, *Bourbon Restoration,* 128–130; and Veve, *Duke of Wellington,* 18–21.

51. Bertier de Sauvigny, *Bourbon Restoration,* 129–130; Jardin and Tudesq, *Restoration and Reaction,* 28; Veve, *Duke of Wellington,* 18–19 and ch. 7, "Wellington and the Barrier Fortresses"; and Pierre Rain, *L'Europe et la Restauration des Bourbons, 1814–1818* (Paris: Perrin, 1908). For the text of the treaty, see Veve, *Duke of Wellington*, Appendix A.

52. Veve, *Duke of Wellington,* 18–20.

53. André Nicolle, "The Problem of Reparations after the Hundred Days," *Journal of Modern History* 25, no. 4 (1953): 343–354, and Eugene N. White, "Making the French Pay: The Costs and Consequences of the Napoleonic Reparations," *European Review of Economic History* 5, no. 3 (2001): 337–365. On the historical development of war reparations, see Stephen C. Neff, *War and the Law of Nations* (Cambridge: Cambridge University Press, 2005), 211–214; John Torpey, "'Making Whole What Has Been Smashed': Reflections on Reparations," *The Journal of Modern History* 73, no. 2 (2001): 333–358; and Luc Somerhausen, *Essai sur les origines et l'évolution du droit à réparation des victimes militaires des guerres* (Brussels: Musée Royal de l'Armée, 1974).

54. Quoted in Bertier de Sauvigny, *Bourbon Restoration,* 128–129.

55. Quoted in Veve, *Duke of Wellington,* 21.

56. Reports from Quartier de la Paix, 3 Dec. 1815, and Palais de Justice, 27 Nov. 1815, AN, F7/3838; reports from departments of Aveyron, 14 Dec., and Dordogne, 16 Dec., 1815, AN, F7/3823.

57. Comte d'Haussonville, *Ma jeunesse: Souvenirs, 1814–1830* (Paris: Calmann Lévy, 1885), 114; print *Adieux d'un Russe à une Parisienne*, designed by Carle Vernet and engraved by Debucourt, in Armand Dayot, *La Restauration (Louis XVIII–Charles X), d'après l'image du temps* (Paris: Revue Blanche, 1900), 21.
58. Wellington to Bathurst, 14 and 23 Oct. 1815, in *WD,* vol. 12; poem "The Hussars in Occupation, or a Souvenir of the Old Eighteenth" from Colonel Harold Malet, *The Historical Memoirs of the XVIII (Princess of Wales's Own) Hussars* (London: Simpkin, 1907), quoted in Veve, *Duke of Wellington,* 70.
59. Report from Meurthe, 22 Dec. 1815, AN, F7/3823; state of regiments and detachments of English army embarked at Calais from 14 Dec. 1815 to 4 Feb. 1816, SHD, 3D/20; report from Brussels, departing 27 Nov. 1815, AN, F7/3824; report from Laon, departing 30 Nov. 1815, AN, F7/3825.
60. Paris police report, 17 Nov. 1815, AN, F7/3838; Richelieu to Osmond, 30 Jan. 1816, in *Lettres du Duc de Richelieu au Marquis d'Osmond, 1816–1818,* ed. Sébastien Charlety, 7th ed. (Paris: Gallimard, 1939), 4; report on visit to temporary barracks on site of abattoir of Montmartre, in which remained weapons of English troops, signed by general secretary of Prefecture of the Seine, Walckenauer, 6 Feb. 1816, Bibliothèque de l'Hôtel de Ville, ms. 1237, f. 53.
61. AN, F7/3823, esp. report from Ain, 12 Dec.; report from Isère, 20 Oct.; and report from Haute-Saône, 26 Dec. 1815.
62. Blancpain, *La vie quotidienne,* 68–69.
63. Veve, *Duke of Wellington,* 34–35.
64. Olivier Podevins, "L'occupation de Tourcoing par les troupes saxonnes entre 1816 et 1818: Un épisode peu connu de l'histoire de la ville" (article for research group on French-Saxon relations, Technical University, Dresden), 13–14, AM Tourcoing.
65. Jules Duvivier, "La ville de Bouchain et l'Ostrevant de 1814 à 1818: L'occupation danoise," in *Bulletin de la Commission historique du Nord* 34 (1933): 327–329.
66. Blancpain, *La vie quotidienne,* 68; André Sacrez, "Les russes en 'Ardenne wallonne' (1814–1818)," *Ardenne wallonne* 97 (2004): 2–11; Natacha Naoumova, "Le Corps d'armée russe en France, 1815–1818," in Cochet, *Les occupations,* 11–22.
67. H. Jadart, "Le casernement des troupes russes dans le canton d'Asfeld, en 1817," *Revue historique ardennaise* 9 (1902): 300–304.
68. Emmanuel Boudot, "L'occupation alliée de 1815–1818 dans le département de la Moselle" (master's thesis, Université de Metz, 1995), 10–13, AD Moselle; "État des troupes prussiennes qui doivent être cantonnés dans le Département de la Meuse," n.d., AD Meuse, 8R/68. Population statistics from AN, F20/408/2.
69. Correspondence regarding maintenance of Allied troops remaining in France, late 1815, AD Haut-Rhin, 8R/1175; Paul Leuilliot, "L'occupation alliée à Colmar et dans le Haut-Rhin, 1815–1818," *Annuaire de Colmar* 3 (1937): 160, and Leuilliot, *L'Alsace,* 1:78.
70. André, *L'occupation,* 161–162; Blancpain, *La vie quotidienne,* 61; and Veve, *Duke of Wellington,* 22.

71. Maurice de Bonnard, Avallon, to Augustin de Bonnard, Montferrat, 11 June 1816, AN, AP 352/44 (shared with me by Dena Goodman).

CHAPTER TWO ✣ A BURDEN SO ONEROUS

1. Note from prefect of Nord, 28 Jan. 1816, AM Tourcoing, 5/H8 (Cantonnement de troupes saxonnes); prefect of Nord to ministry of war, Lille, 16 Jan. 1816, and memorandum from mayors of rural communes of canton of Givet to ministry of war, 17 Jan. 1816, in SHD, 3D/19.
2. Municipal council of Ligny to prefect of Meuse, 1 Feb. 1816, AD Meuse, 8R/31. On the women who accompanied such armies, see John A. Lynn II, *Women, Armies, and Warfare in Early Modern Europe* (Cambridge: Cambridge University Press, 2008).
3. On the early modern tradition of making war feed war, see John A. Lynn, ed., *Feeding Mars: Logisitics in Western Warfare from the Middle Ages to the Present* (Boulder, CO: Westview Press, 1993).
4. Jacques Hantraye, *Les Cosaques aux Champs-Élysées: L'occupation de la France après la chute de Napoléon* (Paris: Éditions Belin, 2005), 71–82, and Hantraye, "Guerre et monde rural: Les réquisitions dans les environs de Paris (1814–1816)," *Histoire et Sociétés Rurales* 16 (2001/2): 117–139; Jean-Louis Schlienger and André Braun, *Le mangeur alsacien: Histoire de l'alimentation en Alsace de la Renaissance à l'annexion* (Bar-le-Duc: La Nuée Bleue/Dernières Nouvelles d'Alsace, 1990); Françoise Waro-Desjardins, *La vie quotidienne dans le Vexin au XVIIIe siècle, d'après les inventaires après décès de Genainville, 1736–1810* (Colombelles: Valhermeil/Société Historique de Pontoise, 1992).
5. General Order of 20 June 1815, *WD,* 12:493–494.
6. Chef de bataillon en mission in Ardennes, Meuse, and Moselle, to ministry of war, Sedan, 16 Jan. 1816, SHD, 3D/19.
7. Records of the Commission dite des requisitions, CAD, 8 ACN, esp. cartons 1, 5, 43 and 44. On this Commission, see also Roger André, *L'occupation de la France par les Alliés (juillet-décembre 1815)* (Paris: Boccard, 1924), esp. 31–32, 40–43, and 70.
8. On the transition to contracting, see printed circular letter from prefect of Nord to subprefects, Lille, 12 Dec. 1815, explicating measure regarding subsistence of Allied troops published in *Gazette officielle* on 29 Nov., SHD, 3D/16, and correspondence related to "Dispositions générales" for the occupying troops, SHD, GR 19 C/86.
9. Emmanuel Boudot, "L'occupation alliée de 1815–1818 dans le département de la Moselle" (master's thesis, Université de Metz, 1995), 31, AD Moselle; AD Bas-Rhin, RP/1254 and bis.
10. See, for instance, A.P., ancien directeur des vivres dans l'intérieur et aux armées, Strasbourg, *Opinion d'un ancien agent des subsistances militaires sur les moyens d'administrer les vivres de l'intérieur dans l'intérêt du trésor, du peuple et de*

l'armée (Paris: Magimel, Anselin et Pochard, 1817), and G. Gaultier, ancien employé supérieur des vivres, ex-secrétaire-général de la régime des sels et tabacs d'Illyrie, *Mémoire sur les économies très-importantes que le gouvernement peut faire sur le service manutentionnaire des vivres-pain à distribuer aux troupes des alliés, cantonnés en France* (Paris: Le Normant, 1817).

11. On the negotiation over and transition to this system of requisitioning, see AAE, Fonds France 692. For the *tarif,* see copy accompanying letter from prefect of Nord to subprefects, Lille, 12 Dec. 1815, in SHD, 3D/16.
12. Thomas Dwight Veve, *The Duke of Wellington and the British Army of Occupation in France, 1815–1818* (Westport, CT: Greenwood Press, 1992), Appendix B.
13. Duke of Wellington to Earl of Bathurst, Paris, Dec. 18, 1815, BNA, WO 1/208 (British Army in Flanders and France, 1815), vol. 3 (Oct.–Dec.); "Observations faites par ordre de Monseigneur le Duc de Wellington sur le Tarif proposé en ce qui regarde le Corps russe," Sir George Murray Papers, NLS, 46.6.7; "Statement of Allowances to Officers serving with the British Contingent of the Allied Army of Occupation in France, under the Command of Field Marshal the Duke of Wellington, as approved by His Grace, the 12th day of November 1816," BNA, WO 1/209; "Division of the 2/5th of 1,080,000 francs per month allotted to the British and the four smaller Contingents, in lieu of Rations to Officers, calculated on the actual numbers accounted for in the States of those Corps," Sir George Murray Papers, NLS, 46.7.4.
14. Returns of chief of staff's allowances, 1815–1818, Sir George Murray Papers, NLS, 46.7.22; Hantraye, "Guerre et monde rural," 128, and Hantraye, *Les Cosaques,* 74.
15. Contract with Eugène Rouffio [early 1816], SHD, 3D/14; proposals and accounts for supplies from Rouffio and Cassabois, SHD, GR 19 C / 88; treaty with Leleu & Cie., 29 Jan. 1816, SHD, GR 19 C/86; and file regarding liquidation of Leleu's bills for supplies, SHD, GR 19 C/99.
16. SHD, GR 19 C/96 and 99 (Leleu), and 88 (Rouffio).
17. Extract of minutes by mayor of Ligny, 3 Feb. 1816, in dossier "Ministère de la Guerre: Subsistances: Observations sur les comptabilités des fournisseurs de l'occupation de 1815 et 1816," AD Meuse, 8R/29.
18. Quote from Max Bruchet, "L'invasion et l'occupation du département du Nord par les alliés, 1814–1818 (suite)," *Revue du Nord* 6 (1921): 60; and Marc Blancpain, *La vie quotidienne dans la France du Nord sous les occupations, 1814–1944* (Paris: Hachette, 1983), 89. For examples of complaints by Allied contingents regarding provisions, see AN, F7/9899.
19. On the struggle over tobacco, see correspondence of the Conseil Administratif des Armées Alliées, CAD, 8 ACN, carton 1 and 7, esp. director of indirect contributions to minister of finances, Paris, 7 Nov. 1815, requesting decrease in supply of tobacco by department of Ardennes to Prussian corps under Gen. Hake, to compensate for appropriation they took from state warehouse, as well as letter from same to prefect of Meuse, 2 Oct. 1815 (both in carton 7). On the

arrangements for supplying tobacco, see "Dispositions générales" regarding provisioning of occupying troops in SHD, GR 19 C/86.

20. Jean-Baptiste Lépine, *Histoire de la ville de Rocroi depuis son origine jusqu'en 1850* (Rocroi: Mme. Veuve Lenoir, 1860), 236. For examples of lodging billets, see those addressed to mayor of Lacroix-sur-Meuse by Prussian commander, Feb. 1817, AD Meuse, 1J/422.
21. Memorandum from Ministère de la Guerre, 7e Division: Bureau du Génie, Paris, 2 Jan. 1816, SHD, 3D/134.
22. AD Meuse, 8 R/29.
23. AD Nord, 8 R/21 (Baraquements, projet de construction: Rapport, Lille, 6 Jan. 1816).
24. AD Bas-Rhin, RP/1266 (Liquidation des charges de guerre: Entreprises: Arrondissement de Wissembourg).
25. Olivier Podevins, "L'occupation de Tourcoing par les troupes saxonnes entre 1816 et 1818: Un épisode peu connu de l'histoire de la ville" (article for research group on French-Saxon relations, Technical University, Dresden), 14–16, AM Tourcoing; Registre des délibérations du Conseil municipal, 1799–1821 (entry from 4 June 1817), AM Tourcoing, 1D/1.
26. Bruchet, "L'invasion et l'occupation," 33.
27. Jean Desgranges, "L'occupation étrangère dans le Cambrésis de 1815 à 1818: Quelques aspects des rapports de la population avec les occupants," *Études cambrésiennes de la Société d'émulation* 1 (1981): 17.
28. Gustave Groeber, "L'occupation d'Oberbronn par des troupes Würtembergeoises de 1816 à 1818," *Bulletin de la Société niederbronnoise d'histoire et d'archéologie* 8 (1960): 186.
29. AD Meuse, 8R/36, and AD Ardennes, EDEPOT/Charleville/5H/6 (Lettre d'une veuve sage femme au maire et membres de la municipalité de Charleville, 7 July 1815).
30. Printed circular from Ministère de la Guerre, 7e Division: Bureau du Casernement, to prefects and "Commissaires ordonnateurs des Commissions mixtes," Paris, 9 Apr. 1816, SHD, 3D/23; Podevins, "L'occupation de Tourcoing," 19; AM Tourcoing, 5H/30 (Indemnités dues pour le logement des troupes: États de dépenses, correspondance, reçus, listes de particuliers qui ont refusé l'abandon de leur indemnités, 1817–1822). For complaints by local mayors and subprefects of delays in payment of indemnities for lodging, see for instance AD Nord, 8 R/12 and 17.
31. Memorandum from Ministère de la Guerre, 7e Division: Bureau du Casernement, Paris, 26 Mar. 1816, SHD, 3D/134.
32. Ministry of war, Fourth Division, to minister of police, Paris, 14 May 1817, AN, F7/9900.
33. Note from general secretary of prefecture of Bas-Rhin, 24 Jan. 1817, quoted in Daniel Peter, "Les occupations alliées dans l'arondissement de Wissembourg, 1814–1818," *L'Outre-Forêt: Revue d'histoire de l'Alsace du nord* 58 (1987): 50; Paul Leuilliot, *L'Alsace au début du XIXe siècle: Essais d'histoire politique,*

économique et religieuse, 1815–1830, vol. 1, *La vie politique* (Paris: SEVPEN, 1959), 80.

34. AM Tourcoing, 5H/5 and 9, and report from Lille to ministry of police, 16 Mar. 1817, AN, F7/9901.
35. AD Nord, 8 R/10; CAC, F6/I/22 (Loyers d'occupation de lits militaires).
36. Subprefect of Commercy to prefect of Meuse, 16 Dec. 1815, AD Meuse, 8 R/34.
37. Groeber, "L'occupation d'Oberbronn," 188.
38. Maréchal de Camp, Chef de la 7e Division, to Monsieur le Marquis de Brossard Lieutenant Colonel Officier d'État Major de S. E. le Ministre de la Guerre à Maubeuge, Paris, 3 Feb. 1816, and Ministère de la Guerre, 7e Division: Bureau du Casernement, to same, both in SHD, 3D/134.
39. Groeber, "L'occupation d'Oberbronn," 192.
40. BMV, D1/22 (Régistre des délibérations du Conseil municipal, 21 May 1816).
41. AM Tourcoing, 5H/17.
42. Groeber, "L'occupation d'Oberbronn," 188–189.
43. Waro-Desjardins, *La vie quotidienne dans le Vexin au XVIIIe siècle,* esp. ch. 1, "Le cadre de vie et le décor du quotidien," and ch. 4, "Le corps et la maison: Hygiène et entretien."
44. Minutes of Conseil Municipal, 29 Nov. 1815, BMV, D1/22.
45. SHD, 3D/134. For a complaint about the devastation of forests in the Ardennes, see report from chef en mission to minister of war, Sedan, 16 Jan. 1816, SHD 3D/19.
46. AD Meuse, 8 R/39 and 29.
47. AD Haut-Rhin, 8 R/1179; mayor of Autrécourt, 3 Mar. 1816, AD Meuse, 8R/31.
48. *Tarif,* appended to circular letter from prefect of Nord to subprefects, Lille, 12 Dec. 1815, SHD, 3D/16; war ministry to prefect of Meuse, Paris, 7 Feb. 1816, regarding forage contract entrusted to Boubée, and circular from ministry of war, Service des Fourrages pour les Troupes alliées, Départements de la Meuse et de la Moselle, to mayors of communes regarding "L'Entrepreneur du Service des Fourrages pour les Troupes alliées," Verdun, 23 Mar. 1816, both in AD Meuse, 8R/31, plus bilingual printed instruction regarding lodging of Prussian army, according to *Tarif* of 20 Nov. 1815, in AD Meuse, 8R/37; and AD Meurthe-et-Moselle, 8R/7.
49. Report from subprefect of Verdun to minister of police, 28 Feb. 1816, AN, F7/9900. On requisitions of transports, see also Groeber, "L'occupation d'Oberbronn," 196–197; AD Meuse, 8R/29 and 37; AD Haut-Rhin, 8R/1177.
50. AD Nord, 8R/20 (Champs de manoeuvres utilisés par les Alliés: Indemnité, 1817); AD Moselle, 1R/491 (Champs de manoeuvre pour les troupes alliées); report from chef en mission to minister of war, Sedan, 16 Jan. 1816, SHD, 3D/19; Sr. Ratisbonne to prefect, Strasbourg, 2 Sept. 1818, AD Bas-Rhin, RP/55a (Logement); correspondence regarding new lodging for [Saxon] chaplain for practice of sect, Mar. 1818, AM Tourcoing, 5H/15; Wells, captain of Royal Engineers, to Lieutenant General Charles Colville, Valenciennes, 5 Mar. 1816, with plan and estimate for cooking house in courtyard of bar-

racks called Grand Hôpital, BMV, H7/38; R. Wauthier, "Les Russes à Givet, 1816–1818," *Revue historique ardennaise* 19 (1912): 155–161; instruction from prefect of Bas-Rhin to subprefects and mayors, Strasbourg, 3 Aug. 1816, AD Bas-Rhin, 3K/17; Boudot, "L'occupation alliée," 56.

51. Von der Marck, commissaire ordonnateur en chef près l'armée prussienne, to prefect of Ardennes, Sedan, 6 Nov. 1815, AD Ardennes, 1J/17 (Sedan: Occupation 1815); "Place de Givet: État des effets et habillement nécéssaires dans l'hôpital militaire de Givet dont l'établissement vient d'être ordonné pour 200 hommes," 7/19 Feb. 1816, SHD, 3D/134; correspondence and reports regarding the Hôpital-Hospice de Mézières, 1816–1818, AD Ardennes, EDEPOT/Mezieres-Hospice/2V1, 2V2, and 2V3; subprefect of Wissembourg to prefect, regarding hospitals [n.d.], AD Bas-Rhin, RP/74. On military medicine in this period, see John S. Haller, Jr., *Battlefield Medicine: A History of the Military Ambulance from the Napoleonic Wars through World War I* (Carbondale, IL: Southern Illinois University Press, 2011).
52. Podevin, "L'occupation de Tourcoing," 19; Francis Lichtle, "L'occupation autrichienne à Colmar de 1815 à 1818," *Mémoire colmarienne: Bulletin trimestriel de liaison de la Société d'histoire et d'archéologie de Colmar*, 123 (2011): 5; Bruchet, "L'invasion et l'occupation," 60–61.
53. On the settlement process, see Chapter 6, as well as Jacques Hantraye, "Rebâtir après les défaites napoléoniennes: Les enjeux de la reconstruction immobilière dans la France du Nord et de l'Est, 1814–1860," *Annales historiques de la Révolution française* 2 (2007): 185–198, and Thomas Gauchet, "Restaurer le régime, restaurer la confiance: Les charges de guerre, leur processus de liquidation et de remboursement dans le Haut-Rhin (1815-années 1820)" (master's thesis, Institut d'Etudes Politiques, Paris, 2015).
54. Hantraye, *Les Cosaques,* 88, and Hantraye, "Guerre et monde rural," 128.
55. SHD, 19C/92, dossier 6, Maubeuge, 31 Jan. 1817, quoted in Jean Breuillard, "L'occupation russe en France, 1816–1818," 1st part, typescript ms. for *Revue des Etudes Slaves,* AD Ardennes, 1J/486; reports from Avesnes, spring and summer 1817, AN, F7/9901.
56. Weekly report from Saint-Pol, 11 May 1817, AN, F7/9903.
57. Report from subprefect in Hazebrouck to minister of police, 1 Mar. 1817, AN, F7/9902.
58. Prussian quartermaster Hesse to mayor of Sedan, 19 Dec. 1816, AM Sedan, H/68.
59. Prefect of Meuse to ministers of finance and war, 9 Jan. 1816, AD Meuse, 8R/29.

CHAPTER THREE ✣ VIOLATION

1. All reports in AN, F7/3826. Emphases added.
2. Subprefect of Bar-le-Duc to prefect of Meuse, 13 and 17 Aug. 1815, and general director of military police of Russian imperial troops to prefect of Marne, 20 Aug. 1815, AD Meuse, 8R/34.

3. Complaint by juge d'instruction, arrondissement of Cosne (Nièvre), Aug. 1815, AN, BB30/191.
4. Subprefect of Rethel to prefect of Ardennes, 29 Nov. 1815, CAD, 8 ACN, carton 11.
5. Report from Brussels, departing 1 Dec. 1815, AN, F7/3825.
6. Subprefect of Hazebrouck to minister of police, 1 Mar. 1817, AN, F7/9901.
7. Note to ministry of police regarding Russians at Landrecies, Cambrai, 30 Mar. 1817, AN, F7/9901.
8. Report from Gendarmerie Royale, Compagnie de la Meuse, to prefect of Meuse, 3 May 1816, AD Meuse, 8 R/32; Thomas Dwight Veve, *The Duke of Wellington and the British Army of Occupation in France, 1815–1818* (Westport, CT: Greenwood Press, 1992), 85, based on AAE, MD France 702 (minister of interior to Richelieu, 1 May 1816); commissaire général de police à Cambrai to minister of police, Valenciennes, 27 Mar. 1817, AN, F7/9901; report from subprefect of Sarreguemines to minister of police, 6 Mar. 1817, AN, F7/9900.
9. Report from Lille, departing 4 Oct. 1816, AN, F7/3826. For similar complaints, see reports on British contingent in the Nord in AN, F7/9899 and 9901.
10. André Sacrez, "Les russes en 'Ardenne wallonne' (1814–1818) (suite et fin)," *Ardenne wallonne* 98 (2004): 10–17, based on commander in chief of Russian army corps in France to French royal commissioner to Russian army, Maubeuge, 25 Sept. 1816, and subprefect of arrondissement of Avesnes to same, 22 Oct. 1816, both in SHD, 3D/134.
11. Prefect of Pas-de-Calais to minister of police, 1 Mar. 1817, AN, F7/9903.
12. Subprefect of Douai to prefect of Nord, 13 Aug. 1817, AD Nord, 8R/10, as well as Wellington to prefect of Pas-de-Calais, regarding his prohibition against hunting on planted fields, Cambrai, 30 Nov. 1817, in *WSD* 12:148–149. On the restriction of hunting, see also Veve, *Duke of Wellington,* 76.
13. Gendarmerie Royale, Compagnie de la Meuse, to prefect, Bar-le-Duc, 10 Mar. 1816, AD Meuse, 8R/31.
14. Prefect of Nord to minister of police, Lille, 11 Sept. 1817, AN, F7/9901.
15. Report from Mézières, departing 2 June 1816, AN, F7/3826.
16. Correspondence and report regarding "excesses" of Austrian cannoneers toward two children of village of Perouse, 24 Dec. 1815, AD Haut-Rhin, 8R/1172–1173.
17. Subprefect of Verdun to prefect, 2 May 1816, AD Meuse, 8R/32.
18. Report from Mons, departing 18 June 1816, AN, F7/3826.
19. Complaint from Monsieur Boillet, merchant inhabiting commune of Commercy, against Prussian soldier, forwarded to ministry of war, 14 Feb. 1816, and "Rapport sur la situation politique pendant le mois de Janvier 1816: Des Départemens de la Moselle, la Meuse, la Marne, et les Ardennes formant ensemble la 23e Légion de Gendarmerie Royale," Metz, 2 Feb. 1816, SHD, 3D/20.
20. Subprefect of Belfort to prefect of Haut-Rhin, 2 Apr. 1816, with accompanying letter from mayor of Dannemarie to subprefect and report on incident, both 1 Apr. 1816, in AD Haut-Rhin, 8R/1172–1173.

21. Report from Sedan, departing 18 June 1816, AN, F7/3826, and "Rapport sur la situation politique pendant le mois de Janvier 1816: Des Départements de la Moselle, la Meuse, la Marne, et les Ardennes formant ensemble la 23e Légion de Gendarmerie Royale," Metz, 2 Feb. 1816, SHD, 3D/20.
22. Report from Bas-Rhin, 3 Nov. 1815, AN, F7/3823; report from Fifteenth Military Division, 6 Feb. 1816, SHD, 3D/20; AN, F7/3824 and 3825.
23. Veve, *Duke of Wellington,* 84; report from Pas-de-Calais, departing 6 Jan. 1816, AN, F7/3823; Jules Deschamps, "En Belgique avec les Anglais après Waterloo," *Société belge d'études napoléoniennes: Bulletin* 51 (1965): 50–57; Jean Desgranges, "L'occupation étrangère dans le Cambrésis de 1815 à 1818: Quelques aspects des rapports de la population avec les occupants," *Études cambrésiennes de la Société d'émulation* 1 (1981): 20–21.
24. Report on seditious writings found in streets of Forbach, Sept. 1818, AN, F7/9900, and correspondence, reports, and instructions regarding *bruits* about return of Napoleon, 1816–1818, AD Meurthe-et-Moselle, 1M/655 (Opinion Publique/Esprit Public: Premier Empire et Restauration).
25. Report from Mézierès, April 1816, AN, F7/9899.
26. Report to subprefect of Colmar, 12 Dec. 1815, AD Haut-Rhin, 8R/33.
27. Report from diverse posts of National Guard of Paris, 7 Dec. 1815, SHD, 3D/16.
28. Bucher, commander of Saxon headquarters, to mayor of Tourcoing, 21 Sept. 1816, AM Tourcoing, 5H/7.
29. Report from prefecture of Pas-de-Calais, 2 Dec. 1817, AN, F7/9903.
30. *JP,* 22 Sept. 1815.
31. Ch. Roussel-Defontaine, *Histoire de Tourcoing* (Brussels: Culture et Civilisation, 1976), 224–226, and Olivier Podevins, "L'occupation de Tourcoing par les troupes saxonnes entre 1816 et 1818: Un épisode peu connu de l'histoire de la ville" (article for research group on French-Saxon relations, Technical University, Dresden), 17, AM Tourcoing.
32. Report from subprefect of Douai, 30 May 1817, AN, F7/9901.
33. Correspondence and reports regarding *rixe* at Cassel, arrondissement of Hazebrouck, 15 May 1817, AN, F7/9901.
34. Weekly report from Saint-Pol, 25 May 1817, AN, F7/9903.
35. Prefect of Bas-Rhin to minister of police, Strasbourg, 4 Jan. 1818, regarding *rixe* of 28 Dec. 1817 in Scheibenhardt, AN, F7/9904.
36. Instruction from subprefect of arrondissement of Douai to mayors of communes of arrondissement, 15 Apr. 1818, quoted in Jules Duvivier, "La ville de Bouchain et l'Ostrevant de 1814 à 1818," *Bulletin de la Commission historique du Nord* 34 (1933): 333, as well as AD Nord, 8R/12, and AN, F7/9899.
37. Sacrez, "Les russes," 11–12; subprefect of Hazebrouck to prefect of Nord, 18 Nov. 1817, AD Nord, 8R/12.
38. Emmanuel Boudot, "L'occupation alliée de 1815–1818 dans le département de la Moselle" (master's thesis, Université de Metz, 1995), 59–60, AD Moselle.

39. Subprefect of Wissembourg to prefect of Bas-Rhin, 27 Apr. 1816, AD Bas-Rhin, RP/1247.
40. On the conflicts between French customs officials and Württemberger troops, see AD Bas-Rhin, RP/1247, esp. minister of interior to prefect, 13 July 1816, as well as correspondence between General Murray and Baron von Woellwarth, May–June 1816, HStA Stuttgart, E 270 a/Bü472 (Geheime Kriegskanzlei: Occupationkorps im Elsaβ: Korrespondenz mit dem Hauptquartier des Feldmarschalls Herzog v. Wellington während der Okkupation Frankreichs durch die Allierten, 1816–1818).
41. On the role of rape in military occupation, see Georges Vigarello, *Histoire du viol, XVIe-Xxe siècle* (Paris: Seuil, 1998), esp. 22, as well as Jacques Hantraye, *Les Cosaques aux Champs-Élysées: L'occupation de la France après la chute de Napoléon* (Paris: Belin, 2005), 41–42.
42. Correspondence regarding "seduction" of young village girls by British soldiers in Nord and Pas-de-Calais, Jan. 1818, AN, F7/9899; bulletin of Police de Paris, 22 and 23 Jan. 1817, AN, F7/3837; commissaire général in Cambrai to minister of police, 17 Mar. 1817, AN, F7/9901; copy minister of justice Séguier, to Comte d'Hauterive, ambassador in London, 6 Oct. 1818, AN, F2(I)/1183.
43. Minister of interior to prefect of Nord, Paris, 8 Jan. 1818, AD Nord, 8R/10; Desgranges, "L'occupation étrangère," 19.
44. *Morning Chronicle,* 16 Nov. 1818, cited in Veve, *Duke of Wellington,* ch. 5, n. 59; *JP,* 12 Nov. 1818.
45. Hantraye, *Les Cosaques,* 41–42.
46. *JP,* 13 July 1815.
47. Report from Chalon-sur-Saône, arriving 15 Aug. 1815, AN, F7/3824.
48. Roger André, *L'occupation de la France par les Alliés en 1815 (juillet-novembre)* (Paris: Boccard, 1924), 133–134.
49. Procès-verbal, 23e Légion de Gendarmerie des Ardennes, 18 Jan. 1816, SHD, 3D/19.
50. Weekly report from Saint-Pol, 27 Apr. 1817, AN, F7/9903.
51. Report from Moselle, 8 July 1818, AN, F7/9900.
52. Report from Meuse, Sept. 1818, AN, F7/9900.
53. Report from Bar-le-Duc, 27 June [1817 or 1818], AN, F7/9900.
54. Hantraye, *Les Cosaques,* 40–41.
55. *Les meringues du perron, ou Milord la gobe* and *Les Alliés à Paris,* both in BNF.
56. This recounting of the story of the "rape" of the Louvre is based on Charles Saunier, *Les conquêtes artistiques de la Révolution et de l'Empire: Reprises et abandons des Alliés en 1815: Leurs conséquences sur les musées d'Europe* (Paris: H. Laurens, 1902); Ferdinand Boyer, "Comment fut décidé en 1815 la restitution par la France des oeuvres d'art de la Belgique," *Société belge d'études napoléoniennes: Bulletin* 53 (1965): 9–17; André Chuquet, "Variétés: Les Prussiens et le Musée du Louvre en 1815," *Revue des sciences politiques* 36 (1916): 264–294; and André, *L'occupation,* esp. 106–116 and Appendix IV, "Etat général des objets d'art enlevés en 1815" (based on AN, O3/1429 and F21/574).

57. *Cogitations of a Vagabond, by Authority of the King's Commission, during the Occupation of Paris, and Subsequently, collated by the Author of "Frank Orby" and Dedicated to His Friends in the Army* (London: Thomas & William Boone, 1838), 175–179.
58. Report to Comte de Pradel, 23 Nov. 1815, AN, O3/1430; Vivant Denon to Bettine (Isabella Teotochi Albrizzi), 11 Sept. 1815, in Denon, *Lettres à Bettine* (Arles: Actes Sud, 1999), 573–574. The definitive history of the original appropriations is Bénédicte Savoy, *Patrimoine annexé: Les biens culturels saisis par la France en Allemagne autour de 1800,* 2 vols. (Paris: Maison des sciences de l'homme, 2004). On nationalism under the guise of universalism with regard to scientific war booty, see Elise S. Lipkowitz, "Seized Natural-History Collections and the Redefinition of Scientific Cosmopolitanism in the Era of the French Revolution," *British Journal for the History of Science* 47, no. 1 (2014): 15–41.
59. Vicomtesse de Chastenay, quoted in Ferdinand Boyer, "Metternich et la restitution par la France des oeuvres d'art de l'étranger, 1814–1815," *Revue d'histoire diplomatique,* 84 (1970): 65–66; Saunier, *Les conquêtes artistiques,* esp. 85.
60. AN, O3/1429–1431, 1585 bis, and 2200. On the role of Alexander von Humboldt in saving the collections of the Musée d'Histoire Naturelle, see Lipkowitz, "Seized Natural-History Collections," 14–17.
61. *Cogitations,* 181–184.
62. William Hamilton, *Considerations [on the restitution of the works of art removed to France during the Revolutionary Wars] in the form of a letter intended to be submitted to the king of France* (London: R. G. Clarke, [1815]); Philip Mansel, *Paris between Empires, 1814–1852: Monarchy and Revolution,* 2nd ed. (London: Phoenix, 2003), 327–328.
63. *WD,* 12:641–646; Boyer, "Metternich," 79.
64. M. Hippolyte ***, *Observations d'un Français sur l'enlèvement des chefs-d'oeuvre du Muséum de Paris, en réponse à la lettre du Duc de Wellington au Lord Castlereagh, sous la date du 23 septembre 1815, et publiée, le 18 octobre, dans le* Journal des débats (Paris: Pélicier, 1815); Chuquet, "Les Prussiens," 290.
65. Denon to Pradel, Paris, 1 Oct. 1815, in AN, O3/1429; Denon to Bettine, 28 Mar. 1816, in *Lettres à Bettine,* 575.
66. *JP,* 18 Dec. 1815; *Le conservateur impartial* (St. Petersburg), no. 1 (4/16 Jan. 1816); *Le mercure de France,* Feb. 1816; Boyer, "Metternich," 72; Saunier, *Les conquêtes artistiques,* 111.
67. *The Annual Register for the Year 1815* (London: T. Bensley & Sons, n.d.), 89–90; prince Wilhelm quoted in Chuquet, "Les Prussiens," 289; Peter Hervé, *How to Enjoy Paris: Being a Guide to the Visitor of the French Metropolis in Two Volumes* (London: Egerton; Hoitt; Sherwood, Neely & Jones, 1816), 1:81.
68. AN, O3/1429–1430 and F21/574, summarized in André, *L'occupation,* Appendix IV.
69. AN, O/3/1430.
70. Fournet in Paris to Pierre Vitet in Rouen, 30 Sept. 1815, AM Lyon, 84 II 10 (obtained from Denise Davidson).

71. See, for instance, P. Villiers, *Les Cosaques, ou le jeune Dodiski, mélodrame-historique en trois actes et en prose . . . , mis en scène par M. Ribié, représenté pour la première fois au Théâtre de la Gaîté, 13 vendémiaire an 14 (5 oct. 1805)* (Paris: Ducrocq, 1805); M. Frédéric, *Soubakoff, ou la révolte des Cosaques: Scènes: Pantomimes équestres en trois parties, à grand spectacle; . . . représentées pour la première fois au Cirque Olympique, 9 juin 1810* (Paris: Barba, 1810); L. J. Karr, *Des Cosaques, ou détails historiques sur les moeurs, coutumes, vêtemens, armes, et sur la manière dont ce peuple fait la guerre, recueillis de l'allemand* (Paris: Lebégue/Petit/Gabriel Warrée, 1814); Charles-Louis Lesur, *Histoire des Kosaques, précédée d'une Introduction, ou Coup d'oeil sur les peuples qui ont habité le pays des Kosaques avant l'invasion des Tartares,* 2 vols. (Paris: H. Nicolle, 1814); *Tableau historique des atrocités commises par les Cosaques en France* (Paris: Aubry, n.d. [early 1814]). The *Bibliographie de la France* mentions a number of other representations of Cossacks between 1812 and 1814, including *Lodoiska ou les Tartares; Tableau historique des atrocités commises par les Cosaques en France; L'élan parisien, chant national, suivi d'un chant guerrier, traduit du russe, et d'une Notice sur diverses peuplades qui fournissent à la Russie les troupes indisciplinées, connues sous le nom de <<Cossaques>>.*
72. On this shift in the image of the enemy, see Hantraye, *Les Cosaques,* ch. 6, "La figure du Cosaque," and Maurice Jacob, "Cosaques, Prussiens, Boches: Les mots et les mentalités," *Le texte et l'idée* 4 (1989): 129–146.
73. General Alexander Cavalié Mercier, *Journal of the Waterloo Campaign* (London: Blackwood, 1870), 2:58–59; prefect of Meuse to minister of finances, 9 Jan. 1816, AD Meuse, 8R/29; report from Chevalier Rodolph de Gournay, chef de batallion en mission, to unnamed general (probably head of a division for the ministry of war), Sedan, 16 Jan. 1816, SHD, 3D/19. On the hiding of persons and goods during the initial invasion and occupation, see Hantraye, *Les Cosaques,* 99–114.
74. Report from subprefect of Verdun to minister of police, 28 Feb. 1816, AN, F7/9900.
75. Cavalié Mercier, *Journal,* 2:175–176 and 179.
76. Report of lieutenant at Calais, 30 Dec. 1815, SHD, 3D/17; Podevins, "L'occupation," 17.
77. Subprefect of Wissembourg to prefect, 27 Apr. 1816, AD Bas-Rhin, RP/1247. This point is made by Boudot, "L'occupation," 66–76.
78. Printed bilingual warning from mayor of Strasbourg, Kentzinger, 26 Oct. 1815, AD Bas-Rhin, RP/1247.
79. AM Tourcoing, 5H/29 (Trouble des cérémonies religieuses saxonnes par les tourquenois: Plaintes et sanctions: Correspondance, ordonnance municipale, Apr. 1816), and Podevins, "L'occupation de Tourcoing," 17.
80. Report from Rhétel [*sic*] (Ardennes), 15 Jan. [no year], and correspondence regarding "scène tumultueuse" at spectacle in Mézières, late Apr. to early May 1818, both in AN, F7/9899.
81. Reports from Valenciennes, arriving 2 Aug., and from Lyon, arriving 3–4 Aug. 1815, both in AN, F7/3824.

82. Gendarmerie to prefect, Bar-le-Duc, 19 Aug. 1816, AD Meuse, 8R/33; subprefect of Hazebrouck to minister of police, 1 Mar. 1817, AN, F7/9901; report from police station at Luxembourg, 10 Apr. 1818, AN, F7/3839. For more examples, see SHD, 3D/52, which includes reports on several attacks on Prussian soldiers, among others, in the Meuse and Ardennes.
83. Report on arrondissement of Boulogne, 3 Mar. 1817, AN, F7/9903; report from Lille, departing 28 July 1816, AN, F7/3826; report from Metz, departing 1 June 1818, AN, F7/3827; report from Sedan, departing 16 Sept. 1818, AN, F7/3827.
84. Report from Sedan, departing 6 June 1816, AN, F7/3826; report from Valenciennes, departing 16 Nov. 1816, AN, F7/3826; and report from Mézières, 11 Dec. [no year], AN, F7/9899. For another example, see report from subprefecture of Sedan, 28 Feb. 1817, AN, F7/9899.
85. French translation of letter from Col. von Zerschwitz, Commandt. ad intérim le Contingent Saxon to Major de Schreibershofen, Tourcoing, 15 Feb. 1817, AN, F7/9901; report from subprefect of Verdun to ministry of police, 5 Feb. 1818, AN, F7/9900.
86. "Cabinet" to prefect of Nord, Paris, 6 Oct. 1817, AD Nord, 8R/10.

CHAPTER FOUR ✣ PEACEKEEPING

1. Report from mayor of Dannemarie, Baumann, 29 Feb. 1816; subprefect of Belfort to prefect of Haut-Rhin, 1 Mar. 1816; mayor of Dannemarie, Baumann, to subprefect, 1 Apr. 1816; and subprefect of Belfort to prefect of Haut-Rhin, 2 Apr. 1816, with accompanying report dated 1 Apr. 1816 on incident in which mayor was insulted by commander, all in AD Haut-Rhin, 8R/1172–1173.
2. Mayor of Dannemarie, Baumann, to subprefect, 1 Apr. 1816, and subprefect of Belfort to prefect of Haut-Rhin, 2 Apr. 1816, AD Haut-Rhin, 8R/1172–1173.
3. On this shift, in which the role of the occupation of guarantee is generally overlooked, see Geoffrey Best, *Humanity in Warfare: The Modern History of the International Law of Armed Conflicts* (London: Weidenfeld, 1980); Michael Howard, *The Invention of Peace: Reflections on War and International Order* (New Haven, CT: Yale University Press, 2000); Stephen C. Neff, *War and the Law of Nations* (Cambridge: Cambridge University Press, 2005); Mark Mazower, *Governing the World: The History of an Idea* (New York: Penguin, 2012); Rachel Chrastil, *The Siege of Strasbourg* (Cambridge, MA: Harvard University Press, 2014), 74–78.
4. Cte de Vignolle, lt. gen. commanding the Eighteenth Military Division, Dijon, 6 Aug. 1815, SHD 3D/4.
5. Royal court of Amiens to ministry of justice, 29 Aug. 1815, AN, BB30/191.
6. Police Administration: Nord to prefect of Meuse, Paris, 2 Sept. 1815, and subprefect of Bar-le-Duc to prefect of Meuse, 20 Aug. 1815, both in AD Meuse, 8R/34.
7. Thomas Dwight Veve, *The Duke of Wellington and the British Army of Occupation in France, 1815–1818* (Westport, CT: Greenwood Press, 1992),

Appendix A, "The Treaty of Paris, November 20, 1815," and Appendix B, "Military Convention of the Second Treaty of Paris."

8. Correspondence between Gendarmerie Royale, Compagnie des Ardennes, and ministry of war, 20 and 22 Jan. 1816, SHD 3D/19.
9. Subprefect of Cambrai to Marquis de Brossard, lt. col. attaché to the État-Major of the minister of war, sent on mission to the division occupied by foreign troops, 3 Jan. 1816, SHD, 3D/134.
10. Order by Vorontsov printed in *MU,* 10 May 1816; subprefect of Sarreguemines to minister of police, 6 Mar. 1817, AN, F7/9900.
11. Report from prefect of Meuse to ministry of war, 2 Jan. 1816, and circular from director of Prussian military police, Count von Loucey, 12 Jan. 1816, SHD 3D/18; French lt. gen. to prefect of Meuse, 14 Feb. 1816, AD Meuse, 8R/31.
12. Report from Mons, departing 24 June 1816, AN, F7/3826.
13. Chevalier Rodolph de Gournay, Chef de bataillon en mission, to Gal (general of a division of the ministry of war), Sedan, 16 Jan. 1816, SHD, 3D/19; Richelieu to minister of war, Paris, 4 Mar. 1816, SHD, 3D/22; report from Saint-Pol to ministry of police, regarding order to British troops in Moulle, Dec. 1817, AN, F7/9903.
14. CAD, 8 ACN, carton 7, file 4 (Correspondence between Commission des Réquisitions and Administration des Douanes).
15. Report from prefecture of Pas-de-Calais, Arras, to ministry of police, 20 Nov. 1817, with accompanying report, 11 Nov. 1817, AN, F7/9903.
16. Subprefect of Hazebrouck to minister of police, 18 Nov. 1817, AN, F7/9902. For examples of orders upholding the French customs regime, see *Articles réglementaires pour l'exécution des traités et conventions du 20 novembre 1815 en ce qui concerne les douanes françaises* (Paris, March 1816), reprinted in *WSD,* 11:321–322.
17. Circular from minister of police to twenty-eight prefects and subprefects of occupation zone, Paris, 26 Feb. 1817, AN, F7/6834. For an example of the difficulty of filing such reports during the initial invasion of 1815, see prefecture of Haut-Rhin to ministry of police, Colmar, 8 Feb. 1816, AN, F7/9694.
18. Quoted in Paul Leuilliot, *L'Alsace au début du XIXe siècle: Essais d'histoire politique, économique et religieuse, 1815–1830,* vol. 1, *La vie politique* (Paris: SEVPEN, 1959), 85.
19. AD Ardennes, EDEPOT/Charleville 5H/4 (Occupation de la ville/Événements de 1815–1816).
20. Anthony L. H. Rhinelander, *Prince Michael Vorontsov: Viceroy to the Tsar* (Montreal: McGill-Queen's University Press, 1990), esp. ch. 3, "Commanding the Occupation Army"; Vorontsov circular to deputies of arrondissement of Rocroy [*sic*], 17 Jan. 1816, SHD, 3D/19; André Sacrez, "Les russes en 'Ardenne wallonne' (1814–1818) (suite et fin)," *Ardenne wallonne* 98 (2004): 10; Natacha Naoumova, "Le Corps d'armée russe en France, 1815–1818," and Georges Clause, "Les Russes dans la Marne en 1814 et de 1815 à 1818," in

Les occupations en Champagne-Ardenne, 1814–1944, ed. François Cochet (Reims: Presses Universitaires de Reims, 1996), 11–22 and 23–50. On the "discipline" imposed by Russian officers, see also Marc Blancpain, *La vie quotidienne dans la France du Nord sous les occupations, 1814–1944* (Paris: Hachette, 1983), 69–70, and R. Wauthier, "Les Russes à Givet," 1816–1818," *Revue historique ardennaise* 19 (1912): 155–161.

21. Veve, *Duke of Wellington,* 71–75; minister of police to prefect of Nord, 21 Jan. 1818, AD Nord, 8R/12.
22. Royal Gendarmerie Company of the Meuse, No. 345, to prefect of Meuse, Bar-le-Duc, 4 Mar. 1816, AD Meuse, 8R/31.
23. "Coup d'oeil sur la conduite des troupes autrichiennes cantonnées dans l'est de la France" [n.d.], AN, F7/9899.
24. Max Bruchet, "L'invasion et l'occupation du département du Nord par les Alliés, 1814–1818 (suite)," *Revue du Nord* 7 (1921): 42; Finn Nerland, "Danish Troops in France following Napoleon's Fall," in *Danmark og Napoleon,* ed. Eric Lerdrup Bourgois and Niels Høffding (Gjern: Forlaget Hovedland, 2007) (translated from Danish for me by Willem Osuch), 242; subprefect of Avesnes to minister of police, 1 Mar. 1817, AN, F7/9901; "Police Général" to prefect of Bas-Rhin, Paris, 29 Dec. 1817, and report from subprefect of Wissembourg, Feb. 1818, AD Bas-Rhin, RP/1247. The practice of such joint patrols with the Russians but not other foreign troops is noted by Jean Desgranges, "L'occupation étrangère dans le Cambrésis de 1815 à 1818: Quelques aspects des rapports de la population avec les occupants," *Études cambrésiennes de la Société d'émulation* 1 (1981): 18.
25. See, for instance, circular letter from Richelieu to prefects of occupied departments, Paris, 14 Mar. 1816, and copy Vorontsov to prefect of Aisne, Maubeuge, 2 Nov. 1817, both in AN, F7/9899.
26. William Lawrence, *Mémoires d'un grenadier anglais, 1791–1867,* trans. Henry Gauthier-Villars (Paris: Plon, 1897), 259–262; *JP,* 25 Oct. 1815; *JF,* 11 Aug. 1817.
27. A. Deloffre, *Landrecies de 1814 à 1818: Fragments d'histoire locale suivis de notes biographiques et historiques sur le Maréchal Clarke, duc de Feltre, né à Landrecies (1765–1818)* (Lille: L. Danel, 1910), 86.
28. Subprefect of Belfort to prefect of Haut-Rhin, 27 Oct. 1817, AD Haut-Rhin, 8R/1174.
29. AD Meuse, 8R/29.
30. Report from Saint-Pol, 29 June 1817, AN, F7/9903.
31. Wellington to Bathurst, Cambrai, 5 May 1816, regarding fire in Fontaine-Notre-Dame, BNA, WO 1/210; Wellington to Bathurst, Cambrai, 28 Oct. 1816, regarding report on same fire, BNA, WO 1/211; Wellington to Bathurst, Paris, 1 Jan. 1817, regarding payment of indemnity to Fontaine-Notre-Dame; and Wellington to Bathurst, Cambray [*sic*], 19 Dec. 1817, regarding indemnity for villages devastated during invasion of 1815, BNA, WO 1/214.

32. Prefect of Nord to ministry of police, 5 Apr. 1818, AN, F7/9902; Russian intendant of department of Meuse and of district of Wassy to prefect of Meuse, 1/13 Sept. 1815, AD Meuse, 8R/34.
33. AAE, Fonds France 700, esp. Barbé-Marbois to Richelieu, 2 Feb. 1816, and Richelieu to Wellington, 10 Feb. 1816, plus subsequent discussion by Wellington and Barbé-Marbois of procedures regarding witnesses, 29 Feb., 15 Mar., and 1 Aug. 1816; report by Barbé-Marbois to king [early 1816], AN, BB30/191; *MU,* 27 Feb. 1816; translation in *Times* (London), 4 Mar. 1816. This policy, which was not communicated to the Council of Allied Ambassadors until the notice in the *Moniteur universel,* was discussed in their meeting of 28 Feb. 1816 (BNA, FO 146/6). On the struggle between von Zieten and Barbé-Marbois over the "mixed commissions," see Volker Walker, *Die allierte Besetzung Frankreichs in den Jahren 1814 bis 1818* (Hamburg: Dr. Kovač, 1999), 237–245. On justice minister Barbé-Marbois, see E. Wilson Lyon, *The Man Who Sold Louisiana: The Career of François Barbe-Marbois* (Norman: University of Oklahoma Press, 1942).
34. AN, BB18/1029, no. 1306; Naoumova, "Le Corps d'armée russe," 19.
35. Protocol of 23 June 1816, with attached letters [in French] from Wellington to Richelieu (22 June 1816) and vice versa (25 June 1816), BNA, FO 146/6.
36. Commissaire général in Cambrai to minister of police, 13 July 1817, AN, F7/9901, and copy Wellington to prefect of Pas-de-Calais, 24 Nov. 1817, BNA, WO 1/214.
37. Jean Breuillard, "L'occupation russe en France (1816–1818)," typescript ms. for *Revue des études slaves*, AD Ardennes, 1J/486.
38. Report from Gendarmerie Royale, Twenty-Third Legion, on political situation during Nov. 1815 in departments of Moselle, Meuse, Marne, and Ardennes, 4 Dec. 1815, SHD, 3D/16; note from Mézières to ministry of police, 11 [Dec. 1817?], AN, F7/9899; bulletin from Arras, 17 Mar. [1817], AN, F7/9903.
39. Royal prosecutor at Tribunal Civil of Cambrai to minister of police, 6 Sept. 1817, AN, F7/9901; report from interim commandant of Second Military Division to minister of war, Clermont, 28 Feb. 1818, SHD, 3D/50; report on decision of court of assizes against customs officials accused of killing Russian Cossack, Oct. 1818, AN, F7/9902; AN, BB/22/30–38, No. 2573 (Recours en grace: Valentin Gerard et Antoine Guillaumot).
40. BNA, WO 90/1, 71/245, and 28/44; entry dated 20 Nov. 1815, Order Book of 27th Regt., 1808–1816, NAM (19)7204–18–5; and Veve, *Duke of Wellington,* 71.
41. Report on "excesses" by Bavarian troops, June–Aug. 1818, AN, F7/9900; Naoumova, "Le Corps d'armée russe," 19.
42. BNA, WO 90/1 (Register of Courts-Martial, 1814–1818); report from Cambrai, 24 Mar. 1817, AN, F7/9901.
43. Veve, *Duke of Wellington,* 85 and 89–90.
44. BNA, WO 71/245/172.
45. Ibid.

46. Report from prefecture of Nord to ministry of police, 23 Mar. 1817, AN, F7/9901.

CHAPTER FIVE ✣ ACCOMMODATION

1. Minister of interior to prefect of Nord, Cte de Rémuzat, Paris, 1 Apr. 1818, AD Nord, 8R/10 (my emphasis).
2. Circular letter from prefect of Pas-de-Calais to mayors of department, Arras, 27 Feb. 1817, AN, F7/9903; report from subprefect of Sedan to minister of police, Sedan, 28 Feb. 1817, AN, F7/9899. My emphases.
3. François-Simon Cazin, *Les Russes en France: Souvenirs des années 1815, 1816 et 1817* (Avranches: J. Durand, 1880), 2.
4. See, for instance, Ronald C. Rosbottom, *When Paris Went Dark: The City of Light under German Occupation, 1940–1944* (Boston: Little, Brown, 2014); Norman M. Naimark, *The Russians in Germany: A History of the Soviet Zone of Occupation, 1945–1949* (Cambridge, MA: Belknap Press, 1995); and John W. Dower, *Embracing Defeat: Japan in the Wake of World War II* (New York: W. W. Norton, 1999). On moving beyond the collaboration-resistance dichotomy, see Sarah Fishman et al., eds., *France at War: Vichy and the Historians* (Oxford: Berg, 2000), esp. the essay by Philippe Burin, "Writing the History of Military Occupations."
5. This is true of the most recent work on the subject, Yann Guerrin's *La France après Napoléon: Invasions et occupations, 1814–1818* (Paris: L'Harmattan, 2014). An important exception is Jacques Hantraye, *Les Cosaques aux Champs-Elysées: L'occupation de la France après la chute de Napoléon* (Paris: Belin, 2005), which through the case of the Seine-et-Oise in 1814 and 1815 elucidates the role of occupation in "apprenticeship of the Other."
6. M. X. V. Draparnaud, *À Sa Majesté l'Empereur de Russie, Libérateur: Épître* (Paris: Dehansy, 1814); *Portrait d'Attila, par Mme la baronne de Staël-Holstein, suivi d'un Épître à M. de Saint-Victor sur les sujets que le règne de Buonaparte offre à la poésie par Louis-Aimé Martin* (Paris: n.p., 1814), 23, quoted in Marie-Pierre Rey, *1814: Un Tsar à Paris* (Paris: Flammarion, 2014), 208. For portraits of Alexander, see for instance Bibliothèque Thiers (Paris), Collection Doisne, 34/8006 and 8007.
7. *Alexandrana, ou Bons mots et paroles remarquables d'Alexandre Ier, pendant son séjour dans Paris, précédé d'un précis des opérations de l'Empereur de Russie et de ses augustes alliés, pour rétablir Louis XVIII sur le trône de ses ancêtres; et suivi de détails sur les derniers momens du général Moreau* (Paris: Lemercier, 1815), 73.
8. *JP*, 12 July 1815.
9. AD Nord, M/135, file 38, cited in Max Bruchet "L'invasion et l'occupation du département du Nord par les alliés, 1814–1818 (suite)," *Revue du Nord* 7, no. 25 (1921): 44, n. 2.
10. *MU*, 11 July 1815.
11. *JP*, 13 July 1815.

12. *JP*, 15 and 19 July 1815.
13. *JP*, 17 July 1815.
14. Philip Mansel, "Wellington et la Restauration," *Revue de la Société d'histoire de la Restauration* 2 (1988): 45–53.
15. Jean-Louis Renteux, "Les Anglais à Valenciennes, 1815–1818," *Valentiana* 49 (2012): 10; mayor of Tourcoing to commanding general of Saxon army, 7 July 1816, AM Tourcoing, 5H/2; report from commissariat spécial des Ardennes to ministry of police, Mézières, 5 Sept. 1817, AN, F7/9899.
16. Paul Leuilliot, "L'occupation alliée à Colmar et dans le Haut-Rhin, 1815–1818," *Annuaire de Colmar* 3 (1937): 157–164; Georges Ozaneaux, *La vie à Colmar sous la Restauration*, ed. Jules Joachim (Colmar: Paul Hartmann, 1929), 10 Feb. 1818; *MU*, 25 Feb. and 9 Aug. 1818; Jules Duvivier, "La ville de Bouchain et l'Ostrevant de 1814 à 1818," *Bulletin de la Commission historique du Nord* 34 (1933): 332 and 334.
17. AD Nord, M/135, files 37 and 38, cited in Bruchet, "L'invasion et l'occupation," 44–45; also reported in *JP*, 13 July 1816.
18. *JP*, 30 July 1816.
19. Cited in Leuilliot, "L'occupation alliée," 160; Bruchet, "L'invasion et l'occupation," 43–44; commanding colonel of Seventh Division of Prussian Lancers to mayor of Charleville, Jan. 1816, AD Ardennes, EDEPOT/Charleville/5H / 4.
20. [Prefect] to Commissaire du Gouverneur en Alsace, Colmar, 7 Sept. 1815, AD Haut-Rhin, 8R/33; Francis Lichtle, "L'occupation autrichienne à Colmar de 1815 à 1818," *Mémoire colmarienne* 123 (2011): 7; *JP*, 12 July 1816.
21. Subprefect of Verdun to minister of police, 28 Feb. 1816, AN, F7/9900.
22. Subprefect of Avesnes to minister of police, 1 Mar. 1817, AN, F7/9901; R. Wauthier, "Les Russes à Givet, 1816–1818," *Revue historique ardennaise* 19 (1912): 155–161.
23. Regulation of "military economy" of Russian troops issued by Barclay de Tolly [n.d., prob. late 1815], AD Meuse, 8R/29.
24. Duvivier, "La ville de Bouchain," 337.
25. *MU*, 31 July and 1 Aug. 1815; General Alexander Cavalié Mercier, *Journal of the Waterloo Campaign, Kept throughout the Campaign of 1815* (Edinburgh: William Blackwood, 1870), 2:224–226.
26. Subprefect of Verdun to prefect of Ardennes, 9 Aug. 1816, and subsequent letters from prefect to General von Zieten and vice versa, AD Meuse, 8R/32.
27. Report from subprefect of Sedan to minister of police, 28 Feb. 1817, AN, F7/9899; *Mémoires du Général-Major russe Baron de Löwenstern (1776–1858), d'après le manuscrit originel et annotés par M.-H. Weil* (Paris: Albert Fontemoing, 1903), 2:455–456; Wauthier, "Les Russes à Givet," 155–161; and Jean Breuillard, "L'occupation russe à Givet de 1816 à 1818, d'après les mémoires du Gén.-Baron V. I. Loewenstern," *Revue historique ardennaise* 12 (1977): 57–77.
28. Mayor of Soultz to prefect of Haut-Rhin, AD Haut-Rhin, 8R/33; A. Deloffre, *Landrecies de 1814 à 1818: Fragments d'histoire locale suivis de notes biographiques et historiques sur le Maréchal Clarke, duc de Feltre, né à Landrecies (1765–1818)* (Lille: L. Danel, 1910), 77; general-major and chef de brigade

Heuckel de Donnersmarck to prefect of Meuse, Ligny, 26 June 1817, and subprefect of Verdun to prefect of Meuse, 28 June 1817, AD Meuse, 8R/29; correspondence regarding the collection of funds for the victims of fires in Alsace, AD Meuse, 8R/31.

29. Report from arrondissement of Béthune to ministry of police, 1 Mar. 1817, AN, F7/9903; *JP,* 1 Nov. 1818; subprefect of Avesnes to prefect of Nord, 6 Aug. 1817, AD Nord, 8R/12; Olivier Podevins, "L'occupation de Tourcoing par les troupes saxonnes entre 1816 et 1818: Un épisode peu connu de l'histoire de la ville" (article for research group on French-Saxon relations, Technical University, Dresden), 17, AM Tourcoing; letter regarding rejection of indemnity by von Gablenz, 4 [month illegible] 1818, AM Tourcoing, 5H/7.

30. *JP,* 3 Dec. 1815; decree of prefect of Haut-Rhin, Colmar, 8 Jan. 1816, *Recueil des actes de la préfecture du département du Haut-Rhin,* vol. 1 (1815), no. 6, pp. 32–32. On the legend of Soeur Marthe, see Gaétan Brianchon, *Biographie de la Soeur Marthe, surnommée la Mère du peuple: Extrait de sa vie* (Lyon: J.-B. Porte, 1867), as well as report on medals given to her by Prince von Hardenberg and Tsar Alexander, *MU,* 7 Sept. 1815.

31. Hantraye, *Les Cosaques,* ch. 7, "Guerre, mort et absence (1814–1816)," esp. 257 and 250, as well as Hantraye, "Questions autour de la mort et de la sépulture des militaires en Lorraine lors des occupations de la fin du Premier Empire et du début de la Restauration (1813–1817)," *Empreinte militaire en Lorraine,* August 2013, https://lorexplor.istex.fr/Wicri/Europe/France/Lorraine/fr/index.php?title=Empreinte_militaire_en_Lorraine_(08-2013)_Jacques_Hantraye&oldid=7661; Wauthier, "Les Russes à Givet," 155–161.

32. Marie-Pierre Rey, *Alexandre Ier* (Paris: Flammarion, 2009), 338–339; Jacques Hantraye, "Les relations entre le clergé français et les militaires des armées d'invasion et d'occupation en France entre 1814 et 1818: Le cas du diocèse de Metz," in *Le temps des hommes doubles: Les arrangements face à l'occupation, de la Révolution française à la guerre de 1870,* ed. Jean-François Chanet, Annie Crépin, and Christian Windler (Rennes: Presses Universitaires de Rennes, 2013), 271; D. Michel, "Les 'alliés' en Haute-Loire: L'occupation et ses problèmes, 1814–1815," *Cahiers de la Haute-Loire* (1968): 40.

33. Hantraye, *Les Cosaques,* 238–239, and Hantraye, "Les relations," 270.

34. Hantraye, "Les relations," 266–270; Ozaneaux, *La vie à Colmar,* 2 Feb. 1818; Paul Leuilliot, *L'Alsace au début du XIXe siècle: Essais d'histoire politique, économique et religieuse, 1815–1830,* vol. 1, *La vie politique* (Paris: SEVPEN, 1959), 203.

35. Duvivier, "La ville de Bouchain," 334; "Lecture par M. Duvivier d'un mémoire sur l'occupation étrangère de la region du Nord de 1816 à 1818: Journal du lt. danois Muller," 24 Oct. 1938, in *Bulletin de la Commission historique du Département du Nord* 36 (1948): 47–79; F. V. Nerland, "Danske fredsbevarende tropper I Frankrig, 1815–1818," *Krigshistorisk Tidsskrift* 39, no. 1 (2003): 18 (translation by Willem Osuch); J. Breuillard, "L'occupation russe en France (1816–1818)," typescript ms., for *Revue des études slaves,* AD Ardennes, 1J/486, Part I, p. 15; Lichtle, "L'occupation autrichienne," 8.

36. Hantraye, "Les relations," 272–276.
37. *JP,* 17 Sept. 1815; report from Cambrai to ministry of police, 1 July 1818, AN, F7/9901; invitations from local authorities to British officers, BNA, WO 28/17 (Records of Military Headquarters in Calais, France).
38. Marc Blancpain, *La vie quotidienne dans le Nord sous les occupations, 1814–1944* (Paris: Hachette, 1983), 78–79; Jean-Baptiste Lépine, *Histoire de la ville de Rocroi depuis son origine jusqu'en 1850* (Rocroi: Mme. Veuve Lenoir, 1860), 235–236; Breuillard, "L'occupation russe à Givet," 60; Ch. Roussel-Defontaine, *Histoire de Tourcoing* (Brussels: Culture et Civilisation, 1976), 224; commissaire général at Cambrai to minister of police, 5 June 1818, AN, F7/9902.
39. Breuillard, "L'occupation russe à Givet," 62.
40. *MU,* 11 July 1815; *JP,* 17 July 1815, 16 Sept. 1815, and 3 Feb. 1816; Renteux, "Les Anglais à Valenciennes," 10; Breuillard, "L'occupation russe à Givet," 60.
41. Peter Hervé, *How to Enjoy Paris: Being a Guide to the Visitor of the French Metropolis in Two Volumes* (London: Egerton; Hoitt; Sherwood, Neely & Jones, 1816), 1:77; Ozaneaux, *La vie à Colmar,* 41–42; Cazin, *Les Russes en France,* excerpted in "Rocroi en 1816: Des Prussiens aux Russes," *Études ardennaises* 43 (1965): 27–28; Blancpain, *La vie quotidienne,* 79.
42. Michel Lefebvre, *Les francs-maçons à Cambrai: Bicentenaire de la loge Thémis, 1786–1986* (Dunkirk: Imprimerie Landais, 1986), cited in Arnaud Gabet and Christianne Lepie, "La présence britannique à Cambrai de 1815 à 1848," *Cambrésis terre d'histoire* 7 (1993): 21–30; correspondence between personnel of ministry of police and police chief of Prussian army, Loucey, AN, F7/6837; Blancpain, *La vie quotidienne,* 73–74 and 95; and Breuillard, "L'occupation russe en France," Part 2, pp. 1–9.
43. Renteux, "Les Anglais à Valenciennes," 10; Gabet and Lepie, "La présence britannique," 22.
44. Deloffre, *Landrecies,* 78 and 86.
45. This point was emphasized by Jean Garand in a series of articles on "Russes et Prussiens dans l'arronndissement de Rocroi," *L'Union,* 9, 12, 14, 19, 20, 21 Jan. and 1 Feb. 1960, AD Ardennes.
46. Blancpain, *La vie quotidienne,* 99.
47. Cavalié Mercier, *Journal,* 2:224–226.
48. Printed decrees regarding policing of cabarets, 1 Apr. 1816 and 8 Oct. 1817, AM Tourcoing, 8D/1–2 (Arrêtés du maire); Duvivier, "La ville de Bouchain," 329–331; Blancpain, *La vie quotidienne,* 78; Breuillard, "L'occupation russe à Givet," 68.
49. On sex in other occupations, see Mary Louise Roberts, *What Soldiers Do: Sex and the American G.I. in World War II France* (Chicago: University of Chicago Press, 2013).
50. Paul Gaffarel, *La Seconde Restauration et la seconde occupation autrichienne à Dijon (juil.-déc. 1815)* (Dijon: Darantière, n.d.), 95; Leuilliot, *L'Alsace,* 1:79; commissaire municipal de police en service extraordinaire, Cathelin, to minister of police, Sélestat, 3 Aug. 1817, AN, F7/9904; Blancpain, *La vie quotidienne,* 83.

51. Austrian general-in-chief to prefect of Haut-Rhin, Colmar, 4 Mar. 1816, AD Haut-Rhin, 8R/1172–1173.
52. Philip Mansel, *Paris between Empires, 1814–1852: Monarchy and Revolution,* 2nd ed. (London: Phoenix Press, 2003), 47.
53. Correspondence of Bucher, Commandant du Quartier Général, to mayor of Tourcoing, 1816–1818, AM Tourcoing, 5H/7; correspondence between Allied commanders, local authorities, and minister of police, regarding spread of venereal disease by *femmes publiques,* AN, F7/9901.
54. Mayor of Niederbronn to prefect, 6 May 1816, AD Bas-Rhin, RP/1247; Daniel Peter, "Les occupations alliées dans l'arrondissement de Wissembourg, 1814–1818," *L'Outre-Forêt: Revue d'histoire de l'Alsace du nord* 58, no. 2 (1987): 51.
55. Blancpain, *La vie quotidienne,* 83.
56. For discussion of the problem of the seduction and abandonment of Frenchwomen by British troops, see correspondence between prefecture of Pas-de-Calais and ministers of police and interior, Jan. 1818, AN, F7/9899.
57. Hantraye, "Les relations," 266–267; Podevins, "L'occupation de Tourcoing," 17; J. Joliot, "Les troupes alliées à Sedan de 1815 à 1818: Occupation ennemie ou stationnement de troupes ayant vaincu l'Empereur?" *Annales sedanaises* 21 (1954): 19–22.
58. Rev. G. G. Stonestreet Papers, BL, Add. Mss. 61805; Thomas Dwight Veve, *The Duke of Wellington and the British Army of Occupation in France, 1815–1818* (Westport, CT: Greenwood Press, 1992), 77; Saxon minister Wilke to mayor of Tourcoing, 15 Feb. 1818, AM Tourcoing, 5H/3; Hantraye, "Les relations," 266–267; subprefect of Belfort to curé of Thann, Mar. 1817, AD Haut-Rhin, 54M/11, quoted in Leuilliot, *L'Alsace,* 1:197.
59. William Lawrence, *Mémoires d'un grenadier anglais (1791–1867),* trans. Henry Gauthier-Villars (Paris: Plon, 1897), 251–253; Gabet and Lepie, "La présence britannique," 25–26; Podevins, "L'occupation de Tourcoing," 17; Lichtle, "L'occupation autrichienne à Colmar," 8; Duvivier, "La ville de Bouchain," 331; and "Lecture par M. Duvivier," 47–49.
60. Mansel, *Paris between Empires,* Appendix IV, "Franco-British and Franco-Irish Marriages"; Wauthier, "Les Russes à Givet," 155–161, and André Sacrez, "Les Russes en 'Ardenne wallonne' (1814–1818) (suite et fin)," *Ardenne wallonne* 98 (2004): 3; Deloffre, "Landrecies de 1814 à 1818," 87; Joliot, "Les troupes alliées."
61. Georges Clause, "Les Russes dans la Marne en 1814 et de 1815 à 1818," in *Les occupations en Champagne-Ardenne: 1814–1944,* ed. François Cochet (Reims: Presses Universitaires de Reims, 1996), 35; Breuillard, "L'occupation russe à Givet," 74; Hantraye, *Les Cosaques,* 202–203. For other evidence of foreign deserters, especially Austrians and Hungarians, in 1817 and 1818, see AD Haut-Rhin, 4M/199.
62. Hantraye, *Les Cosaques,* 202–203, and APP AA/419.
63. Report on desertions by Prussians in Sept. 1818, AN, F7/3827; Leuilliot, *L'Alsace,* 1:202.

64. Prefect of Nord to minister of interior, Lille, 9 Jan. 1819, and related correspondence, including with prefect of Meuse, AN, F7/9904. On immigration policy in this period, see Jennifer Ngaire Heuer, *The Family and the Nation: Gender and Citizenship in Revolutionary France, 1789–1830* (Ithaca, NY: Cornell University Press, 2005).
65. Hantraye, *Les Cosaques,* 212; Gabet and Lepie, "La présence britannique," 28–30.
66. Reports from stagecoach drivers received 1 June 1816, AN, F7/3826; report from subprefect of Avesnes to minister of police, 12 July 1817, AD Nord, 8R/12.
67. Minutes of Conseil municipal of Valenciennes, 25 Apr. 1817, BMV, D1/22.
68. AVES, esp. 1M/130 (Arrêtés du maire, 1815–1816) and 1M/131 (Publications imprimées, 11 Jan. 1817–27 Dec. 1821). For other examples, see AM Nancy, 1D/23 and 25 (Procès-verbaux du Conseil municipal, 1815+), and AM Sarreguemines, Section II, 2D1–5D9, carton 61 (Register der Verfügung des Bürgermeisters, 1811–1815, and Correspondenz-Journal vom 21 Sept. 1814 bis 4 März 1816).
69. Report from subprefect of Thionville to ministry of police, 7 Nov. 1817, AN, F7/9900.

CHAPTER SIX ✣ COSMOPOLITANISM

1. Marquise de Montcalm, *Mon journal, 1815–1818, pendant le premier ministère de mon frère,* ed. Sébastien Charléty (Paris: Bernard Grasset), 198; [Eugène Scribe et Henri Dupin], *Le combat des montagnes, ou La Folie Beaujon, folie-vaudeville en un acte, représentée, pour la première fois, à Paris, sur le Théâtre des Variétés, le 12 juillet 1817* (Paris: Mlle. Huet-Masson, 1817).
2. On cosmopolitanism before and during the revolutionary era, see Margaret Jacob, *Strangers Nowhere in the World: The Rise of Cosmopolitanism in Early Modern Europe* (Philadelphia: University of Pennsylvania Press, 2006); Ellen Welch, "'Paris cosmopolite': Le mythe de la 'capitale du monde' dans les guides de Paris," *Littératures classiques* 76 (2011): 53–62; Steven Vertovec and Robin Cohen, eds., *Conceiving Cosmopolitanism: Theory, Context and Practice* (Oxford: Oxford University Press, 2002). On Francophilia in England, see Robin Eagles, *Francophilia in English Society, 1748–1815* (New York: St. Martin's, 2000), and Gerald Newman, *The Rise of English Nationalism: A Cultural History, 1740–1830* (New York: St. Martin's, 1987). On travel during the wars, see Catriona Kennedy, *Narratives of the Revolutionary and Napoleonic Wars: Military and Civilian Experience in Britain and Ireland* (New York: Palgrave Macmillan, 2013); Leighton S. James, *Witnessing the Revolutionary and Napoleonic Wars in German Central Europe* (New York: Palgrave Macmillan, 2013); and Nicolas Bourguinat and Sylvain Venayre, ed., *Voyager en Europe de Humboldt à Stendhal: Contraintes nationales et tentations cosmopolites, 1790–1840* (Paris: Nouveau Monde, 2007).
3. Brian Vick, *The Congress of Vienna: Power and Politics after Napoleon* (Cambridge, MA: Harvard University Press, 2014).

4. On these refugees, see Christopher J. Tozzi, "Soldiers without a Country: Foreign Veterans in the Transition from Empire to Restoration," *The Journal of Military History* 80, no. 1 (2016): 93–120.

5. On nationalism in Great Britain, see, in addition to the works by Newman and Eagles cited above, Linda Colley, *Britons: Forging the Nation, 1707–1837* (New Haven, CT: Yale University Press, 1992). On romanticism and historicism, see James Chandler, *England in 1819: The Politics of Literary Culture and the Case of Romantic Historicism* (Chicago: University of Chicago Press, 1998); J. R. Watson, *Romanticism and War: A Study of British Romantic Period Writers and the Napoleonic Wars* (New York: Palgrave Macmillan, 2003); and Peter Fritzsche, *Stranded in the Present: Modern Time and the Melancholy of History* (Cambridge, MA: Harvard University Press, 2004). On the rise of consumer culture and mass spectacle, see Rosalind Williams, *Dream Worlds: Mass Consumption in Late Nineteenth-Century France* (Berkeley: University of California Press, 1982); Charles Rearick, *Pleasures of the Belle Époque: Entertainment and Festivity in Turn-of-the-Century France* (New Haven, CT: Yale University Press, 1985); Vanessa Schwartz, *Spectacular Realities: Early Mass Culture in Fin-de-Siècle Paris* (Berkeley: University of California Press, 1998); Lisa Tiersten, *Marianne in the Market: Envisioning Consumer Society in Fin-de-Siècle France* (Berkeley: University of California Press, 2001); Patricia T. Tilburg, *Colette's Republic: Work, Gender, and Popular Culture in France, 1870–1914* (New York: Berghahn, 2009); H. Hazel Hahn, *Scenes of Parisian Modernity: Culture and Consumption in the Nineteenth Century* (New York: Palgrave Macmillan, 2009). On Paris as world capital in the nineteenth century, see Patrice Higonnet, *Paris: Capital of the World* (Cambridge, MA: Belknap Press, 2002), and Pascale Casanova, *The World Republic of Letters* (Cambridge, MA: Harvard University Press, 2004). More recently, scholars have begun to note the importance of the postwar context for the revival—or reconfiguration—of cosmopolitanism. In addition to Vick, *Congress of Vienna,* see for example, Richard Stites, *The Four Horsemen: Riding to Liberty in Post-Napoleonic Europe* (Oxford: Oxford University Press, 2014); Ian Coller, *Arab France: Islam and the Making of Modern Europe, 1793–1831* (Berkeley: University of California Press, 2011); Michael Scrivener, *The Cosmopolitan Ideal in the Age of Revolution and Reaction, 1776–1832* (London: Pickering and Chatto, 2007); and Victoria Thompson, "Foreign Bodies: British Travel to Paris and the Troubled National Self, 1789–1830," *Studies in Travel Writing* 15, no. 3 (2011): 243–265.

6 "Soutz-sous-Forêts: Les événements de 1815–1817 relatés par le Pasteur Weissmann," *L'Outre-Forêt: Revue du Cercle d'histoire et d'archéologie de l'Alsace du Nord* 122, no. 2 (2003): 15–18; Julie Pellizzone, *Souvenirs: Journal d'une Marseillaise*, ed. Pierre and Hélène Échinard and Georges Reynaud, vol. 2, *1815–1824* (Paris: Indigo/Côté-Femmes Éditions and Université de Provence, 2001), 104; Edgar Quinet, *Histoire de mes idées: Autobiographie,* ed. Simone Bernard-Griffiths (Paris: Flammarion, 1972), 155.

7. *The Reminiscences and Recollections of Captain Gronow, Being Anecdotes of the Camp, Court, Clubs and Society, 1810–1860,* ed. John Raymond (New York: Viking Press, 1964), 87; *Letters of Harriet Countess Granville, 1810–1845,* ed. by her son the Hon. F. Leveson Gower (London: Longmans, Green, 1894), 1:72; Leonid I. Strokhovsky, *Alexander* (New York: W. W. Norton, 1947), 167. On the review at Vertus, see Octave Beuve, ed., *L'invasion de 1814–1815 en Champagne: Souvenirs inédits* (Paris/Nancy: Berger-Levrault, 1914), 155, and Jacques Hantraye, "Le Camp de Vertus: Un épisode révélateur des relations entre la Russie et les autres puissances européennes, Septembre 1815," *Revue des études slaves* 83, no. 4 (2012): 1023–1033.
8. "L'occupation russe de 1816 à 1818: Les mémoires du général-baron V. I. Loewenstern," typescript transcription by Jean Breuillard, AD Ardennes, 1J/486, pp. 10 and 13.
9. Nina Maria Athanassoglou-Kallmyer, *Eugène Delacroix: Prints, Politics and Satire, 1814–1822* (New Haven, CT: Yale University Press, 1991), esp. ch. 2, "Our Friends, the Enemies."
10. Armand Dayot, ed., *La Restauration d'après l'image du temps* (Paris: La Revue Blanche, 1900), 21–23.
11. *Reminiscences and Recollections of Captain Gronow,* 76; Pellizzone, *Souvenirs,* 2:86.
12. Excerpt from *MU,* 12 Sept. 1815, in APP, AA 419; Pellizzone, *Souvenirs,* 2:88; Ch. Roussel-Defontaine, *Histoire de Tourcoing* (Brussels: Culture et Civilisation, 1976), 224; "The English at Valenciennes, by the author of Waterloo" *The United Service Journal and Naval and Military Magazine* 1829: 321–322; Georges Ozaneaux, *La vie à Colmar sous la Restauration: Lettres de 1817 à 1820,* ed. Jules Joachim (Colmar: Paul Hartmann, 1929), 129.
13. On the image of the Cossack in this period, see Jacques Hantraye, *Les Cosaques aux Champs-Élysées: L'occupation de la France après la chute de Napoléon* (Paris: Belin, 2005), ch. 6, "La figure du Cosaque."
14. *Letters of Harriet Countess Granville,* 1:64; A. F. . . . .s, *Anglaisiana, ou Les Anglais, les Écossais et les Irlandais à Londres et à Paris; Ouvrage curieux et amusant par les anecdotes, les bons mots, les plaisanteries, les gaîtés, les originalités, les facéties, les naïvetés, les jeux de mots et les calembourgs des habitans des trois royaumes* (Paris: Corbet, 1815), 98–99. For examples of the mania for Scotland, see *Le chef écossais, ou la caverne d'Ossian: Pantomime en deux actes, à grand spectacle, avec un prologue,* performed at the Théâtre du Cirque Olympique, Paris, 25 Sept. 1815 (Paris: J. N. Barba, 1815); M. de Montmaur, *Le brigadier écossais* (Paris: Louvard, 1815); Leblanc and Charles, *La coutume écossaise, ou Le mariage sur la frontière* (Paris: Maugeret, 1813); and the *Contes d'Écosse* as well as the edition of *Ossian* listed in the *Bibliographie de la France* in 1817 and 1818, respectively.
15. Hon. J. W. Ward to Miss Berry, Paris, 11 May 1814, in *Extract of the Journals and Correspondence of Miss Berry from the Year 1783 to 1852,* ed. Lady Theresa Lewis (London: Longmans, Green, 1865), 3:13–14.

16. "Précis des événements qui se sont passés à Châlons depuis le retour de Napoléon en France . . ." (1818), in Beuve, ed., *L'invasion,* 155.
17. *JP,* 1 and 2 Aug. 1815.
18. *JP,* 17 July 1815; John Bew, *Castlereagh: A Life* (Oxford: Oxford University Press, 2012), 402–403.
19. *JP,* 30 July 1815.
20. *JP,* 11 Aug., 16 Aug., and 18 Sept. 1815.
21. Hantraye, *Les Cosaques,* 190.
22. Marquise de Montcalm, *Mon journal,* entry for 26 Aug. 1817, pp. 290–292.
23. Quoted in Philip Mansel, "La France de la Restauration vue par les Anglais," trans. Guillaume de Bertier de Sauvigny, *Revue de la Société d'histoire de la Restauration* 1 (1987): 11.
24. General Alexander Cavalié Mercier, *Journal of the Waterloo Campaign, Kept throughout the Campaign of 1815* (Edinburgh: William Blackwood, 1870), 1:56; Margery E. Elkington, *Les relations de société entre l'Angleterre et la France sous la Restauration (1814–1830)* (Paris: Honoré Champion, 1929), 11.
25. Hon. J. W. Ward to Miss Berry, Paris, 11 May 1814, in *Extract of the Journals and Correspondence of Miss Berry,* 3:18.
26. Guillaume de Bertier de Sauvigny, *Nouvelle histoire de Paris: La Restauration, 1815–1830* (Paris: Hachette, 1977); Philip Mansel, *Paris between Empires: Monarchy and Revolution, 1814–1852,* 2nd ed. (New York: St. Martin's, 2003); Christophe Leribault, *Les Anglais à Paris au 19e siècle* (Paris: Musée Carnavelet, 1994); and Mansel, "La France de la Restauration." Quotation from *Gazette de France,* translated in the *Times* of London, 10 July 1816, as cited by Athanassoglou-Kallmyer, *Eugène Delacroix,* 24.
27. "The English at Valenciennes in 1816."
28. Special police commissioner in Pas-de-Calais to minister of police regarding Englishwomen disembarking in department, 27 Feb. 1816, and related correspondence between prefecture and ministry of police, AN, F7/9811. On the influx of British women, most of whom were wives of noncommissioned officers and soldiers, arriving in French ports, see also correspondence between the French minister of war, the Duc de Feltre, the British secretary of war, the Earl of Bathurst, and the Duke of Wellington, Dec. 1815, BNA, WO 1/208; French ambassador in London, Osmond, to British foreign minister Castlereagh, 12 Mar. 1817, regarding his order to deny passports to such women, BNA, WO 1/214; French minister of war to military headquarters in Calais, France, 5 Nov. 1815, requesting that these women not be allowed to disembark, BNA, WO 28/17; administrative police responsible for department of Nord to prefect of Nord, 21 Oct. 1815, regarding order by Wellington to British commanders not to let these women disembark, AD Nord, 8R/10.
29. Véra Miltchina, ed., *Les Russes découvrent la France au XVIIIe et au XIXe s.* (Paris/Moscow: Globe-Paris/Progrès-Moscou, 1990); chargé d'affaires in Berlin, Cte. Pierre de Vaudreuil, to Talleyrand, Berlin, 7 Aug. 1815, CAD,

83PO/A242 (Berlin: Légation: Correspondance politique avec le Département des Affaires étrangères, 1811–1816).

30. Anon., *A Letter Addressed to an English Lady of Fashion at Paris* (London: J. Hatchard, Sept. 1815), 45; the *Times* of London, 20 July 1816, quoted in Athanassoglou-Kallmyer, *Eugène Delacroix,* 24; Anon., *Emigration; or England and Paris, A Poem* (London: Baldwin, Cradock and Joy, 1816).

31. William Jerdan, *Six Weeks in Paris, or a Cure for the Gallomania* (London: J. Johnson, 1817).

32. *Reminiscences and Recollections of Captain Gronow,* 79.

33. "Les mémoires du général-baron V. I. Loewenstern," 4; Vivant Denon to Bettine, Paris, 2 May 1817, in Vivant Denon, *Lettres à Bettine* (Arles: Actes Sud, 1999), 580–581; *Life, Letters, and Journals of George Ticknor* (Boston: James R. Osgood, 1876), 1:128; Victorine de Chastenay, *Deux révolutions pour une seule vie: Mémoires, 1771–1855* (Paris: Tallandier, 2009), 723.

34. AN, F7/6699.

35. Giles Barber, "Galignani's and the Publication of English Books in France from 1800 to 1852," *The Library* 16, no. 5 (1961): 267–286.

36. Mansel, *Paris between Empires,* 149; Ch.-A. Scheffer, *Tableau politique de l'Allemagne* (Paris: Plancher et Delaunay; Brussels: Chez Lecharlier; Warsaw: Chez Glucksberg, 1816); Thomas Moore, *The Fudge Family in Paris,* in *Poetical Works* (Leipzig: Bernh. Tauchnitz, 1842), 4:57–121.

37. Peter Hervé, *How to Enjoy Paris: Being a Guide to the Visitor of the French Metropolis in Two Volumes* (London: Egerton; Hoitt; Sherwood, Neely & Jones, 1816). For other examples, see: *Le guide du voyageur à Paris,* new ed. with figures (Paris: Théodore Dabo, 1814); F.-M. Marchant, *Le nouveau conducteur de l'étranger à Paris en 1824,* 11th ed. (Paris: J. Moronval, 1824); Étienne-François Bazot, *Nouveau guide, ou Conducteur des étrangers dans Paris, depuis la Restauration* (Paris: Chez Lécrivain, Libraire, 1817); *Itinéraire du voyageur à Paris, ou Description de tous ses monumens et de toutes ses curiosités* (Paris: Vallardi; London: Colnaghi, 1819); J.-A. Dulaure, *Panorama de la ville de Paris et guide de l'étranger à Paris; présentant l'origine, l'histoire, et l'accroissement de cette ville, la description de ses monumens, et ses établissements publics* (Heidelberg: J. Engelmann, 1820); Abel Goujon, *Histoire de la ville de St-Germain-en-Laye . . . ; ouvrage utile aux habitans et aux étrangers* (Paris: Ledoyen, 1829). On such guides, see also Hantraye, *Les Cosaques,* 192.

38. Mary and P. B. Shelley, *History of a Six Weeks' Tour, 1817* (Oxford: Woodstock Books, 1989), 86–87. On the reactions of tourists, especially British, see Victoria Thompson, "Foreign Bodies."

39. Tagebuch von Johann Michael Antlsperger, Hauptmann im k. b. 2. Infant. Reg. "Kronprinz," 1797–1818: Abschrift der Kriegstagebücher in der Hdschr. Slg. III Kriegs-& Heeresgeschicte im Allgemeinen No. 56 [typed ms.], Bay. HStA Kriegsarchiv, HS 442/2.

40. Seth William Stevenson, *Journal of a Tour through Part of France, Flanders, and Holland; Including a Visit to Paris, and a Walk on the Field of Waterloo:*

Made in the Summer of 1816 (Norwich: Stevenson, Matchett, and Stevenson, 1817), 157; Ch.-André Guibal, "Journal de ce que j'ai vu ou fait de plus remarquable depuis l'âge de six ans et demi," *Pays lorrain: Revue régionale mensuelle illustrée* 17, no. 222 (1925): 294; Cavalié Mercier, *Journal,* 2:32.

41. Quinet, *Histoire,* 91–92; Helen Maria Williams, *A Narrative of the Events Which Have Taken Place in France from the Landing of Napoleon Bonaparte on the First of March, 1815, till the Restoration of Louis XVIII, with an Account of the State of Society and Public Opinion at that Period* (London: J. Murray, 1815), 175.

42. Saxon authority to mayor of Tourcoing, 12 Aug. 1816, AM Tourcoing, 5H/28; Hantraye, *Les Cosaques,* 169–179.

43. See, for example, announcement of a "Cours élémentaire complet de la langue anglaise par prof. Poppleton, natif de Londres, et A. Boniface, sec. de la société grammaticale de Paris" in *JP,* 12 Aug. 1816; F. V. Nerland, "Danske fredsbevardende tropper I Frankrig, 1815–1818," *Krigshistorisk Tidsskrift* 39, no. 1 (2003): 23 (summarized for me in English by Willem Osuch).

44. On Barrois, see AN, F18/174 (Librairie étrangère, 1814–1830). Christian Gottfried Heinrich Geissler, *Hand und Hülfsbuch für Deutsche und Russen, um sich gegen seitig verständlich zu machen, welches alle nöthige Redensarten und ein Rußisch-Deutsches und Deutsch-Rußisches Worterbuch nebst bengefügter Aussprache enthält* (Leipzig: In Commission bei J. C. Hinrichs, 1813); *Vocabulaire français, allemand et russe, précédé d'un dialogue à l'usage des militaires français* (Paris: Koenig, 1815), advertised in *JP,* 15 Sept. 1815; G. Harmonière, *Le nouveau guide de la conversation, en anglais et en français, en trois parties: Vocabulaire; Dialogues; Idiotismes, expressions familières et proverbes* (Paris: Crapelet & Barrois, 1815), advertised in *Bibliographie de la France;* J. Martinet, *Dialogues nouveaux anglais-français* (Paris: Louis, 1815); *Élémens de la langue anglaise, par Siret, avec lettres de commerce*, new ed. (Paris: Brunot Labbé, 1815); Wm. Cobbett, *Le maître d'anglais,* and Poppleton and Boniface, *Cours élémentaire complet de la langue anglaise,* both advertised in *JP,* 30 July and 12 Aug. 1816; A. Sparrow, professeur d'anglais à Rouen, *Examen d'un ouvrage ayant pour titre: Méthode anglaise simplifiée, contenant des règles faciles de prononciation, et indiquant une marche nouvelle et certaine pour apprendre, sans maître et en peu de jours, plusieurs milliers de mots anglais, par M. E.-M.-J. Lepan, et Exposition des faux principes et erreurs qui y sont contenus* (Rouen: Baudry, 1819); M. Denys de Montfort, *Petit vocabulaire à l'usage des Français et des Alliés renfermant les noms d'une partie des choses les plus essentielles à la vie, en plusieurs langues; savoir: Français, Latin, Hébreu, Belge, Hollandais, Allemand, Prussien, Hanovrien, Badois, Hessois, Tyrolien, Suisse, Anglais, Écossais, Irlandais, Espagnol, Italien, Vénitien, Romain, etc.* (Paris: Chez Plancher, 1815).

45. A. Deloffre, *Landrecies de 1814 à 1818: Fragments d'histoire locale suivis de notes biographiques et historiques sur le Maréchal Clarke, duc de Feltre, né à Landrecies, 1765–1818* (Lille: Danel, 1910), 94; Cavalié Mercier, *Journal,* employs "mounting Cossack" throughout.

46. *Le drapeau blanc,* 11 June 1826, cited in P. Lévy, *La langue allemande en France* (Lyon: IAL, 1950), 276, quoted in Hantraye, *Les Cosaques,* 176.
47. Anne-Marie Rosset, ed., *La Restauration et les Cent-Jours*, vol. 5 of *Un siècle d'histoire de France par l'estampe, 1770–1871, Collection de Vinck—Inventaire analytique,* ed. François-Louis Bruel (Paris: Imprimerie Nationale, 1938), 88–89, and BNF Estampes, Tf 60–Pt Fol. (Caricatures sur les Anglais, 1816–1819).
48. "Les mémoires du général-baron V. I. Loewenstern," 12.
49. François Cochet, ed., *Les occupations en Champagne-Ardenne, 1814–1944* (Reims: Presses Universitaires de Reims, 1996), conc.; "Les mémoires du général-baron V. I. Loewenstern," 12; M. Symon, *L'Anglomanie, ou l'Anti-Français: Poème* (Paris: Delaunay, 1823), 8.
50. *C'est fini, ils ne tâteront plus des restaurans du Palais-Royal; car nous sommes-là!* (Paris: Aubry, n.d.), 3; *Le guide des dîneurs, ou Statistique des principaux restaurans de Paris: Ouvrage indispensable aux étrangers, nécessaire aux personnes qui ne tiennent pas ménage, utile à tous les gens de goût. . . .* (Paris: Chez les marchands de nouveautés, 1814); *The Letters of Private Wheeler,* ed. B. H. Liddell Hart (Witney, UK: Windrush Press, 1994), 181–182; Moore, *Fudge Family,* Letters III and VIII. On the history of the restaurant, see Rebecca L. Spang, *The Invention of the Restaurant: Paris and Modern Gastronomic Culture* (Cambridge, MA: Harvard University Press, 2000).
51. Paul Gaffarel, *La Seconde Restauration et la seconde occupation autrichienne à Dijon (juin-décembre 1815)* (Dijon: Darantière, 1896), 79; *Mémoires du Gén.-Major russe Baron de Loewenstern (1776–1858), d'après le manuscrit originel et annotés par M.-H. Weil* (Paris: Albert Fontemoing, 1903), 2:462. On the rise of French cuisine as the international standard, see Susan Pinkard, *A Revolution in Taste: The Rise of French Cuisine, 1650–1800* (Cambridge: Cambridge University Press, 2009); Jean-Louis Flandrin, "La diversité des goûts et des pratiques alimentaires en Europe du XVIe au XVIIIe siècle," *Revue d'histoire moderne et contemporaine* 30, no. 1 (1983): 66–83; and Alison Smith, *Recipes for Russia: Food and Nationhood under the Tsars* (Dekalb: Northern Illinois University Press, 2008).
52. *The Reminiscences and Recollections of Captain Gronow,* 44; Éléonore-Adèle d'Osmond, Comtesse de Boigne, *Mémoires de la Comtesse de Boigne, née d'Osmond: Récits d'une tante,* ed. Jean-Claude Berchet, vol. 1, *Du règne de Louis XVI à 1820* (Paris: Mercure de France, 1999), 566; "Les mémoires du général-baron V. I. Loewenstern," 5–6; François-Simon Cazin, *Les Russes en France: Souvenirs des années 1815, 1816, 1817* (Avranches: J. Durand, 1880), 17; Ozaneaux, *La vie à Colmar,* 67.
53. *Journal de la Marne,* no. 408, 26 July 1815, quoted in Georges Clause, "Les Russes dans la Marne en 1814 et de 1815 à 1818," in Cochet, ed., *Les occupations en Champagne-Ardenne,* 50.
54. "Les mémoires du général-baron V. I. Loewenstern," 10; *Le conservateur impartial* (St. Petersburg), 8/20 Aug. 1816.

55. *Extract of the Journals and Correspondence of Miss Berry,* 3:18–19.
56. De Chastenay, *Deux révolutions,* 662; *JP,* 11 Sept. 1815, 1 July 1816, and 11 Sept. 1815.
57. *JP,* 12 and 30 July 1815; *Journal des dames et des modes,* 15 Mar. 1818; Ozaneaux, *La vie à Colmar,* 67; *Journal des dames et des modes,* 10 Nov. 1818. On the foreign influences on French fashions in this period, see Susan Hiner, *Accessories to Modernity: Fashion and the Feminine in Nineteenth-Century France* (Philadelphia: University of Pennsylvania Press, 2010).
58. De Chastenay, *Deux révolutions,* 723; *Letters of Harriet Countess Granville,* 60; Moore, *Fudge Family,* 4:75; Roger Boutet de Monvel, *Les Anglais à Paris, 1800–1850,* 2nd ed. (Paris: Plon, 1911), 125. On LeRoy, see Fiona Foulkes, "'Quality Always Distinguishes Itself': Louis Hippolyte LeRoy and the Luxury Clothing Industry in Early Nineteenth-Century Paris," in *Consumers and Luxury: Consumer Culture in Europe, 1650–1850,* ed. Maxine Berg and Helen Clifford (Manchester: Manchester University Press, 1999), 183–205.
59. *Letters of Harriet Countess Granville,* 98.
60. In addition to James Chandler's *England in 1819,* see, for instance, Katie Trumpener, *The Romantic Novel and the British Empire* (Princeton, NJ: Princeton University Press, 1997).
61. Elizabeth Della Zazzera, "Romanticism in Print: Periodicals and the Politics of Aesthetics in Restoration Paris, 1814–1830" (PhD diss., University of Pennsylvania, 2016).
62. Tim Blanning, *The Romantic Revolution: A History* (New York: Modern Library, 2011); Michael Marriman, *Romantic Paris: Histories of a Cultural Landscape, 1800–1850* (Stanford, CA: Stanford University Press, 2009); Susan Crane, *Collecting and Historical Consciousness in Early Nineteenth-Century Germany* (Ithaca, NY: Cornell University Press, 2000).
63. *Cogitations of a Vagabond, by Authority of the King's Commission, during the Occupation of Paris, and Subsequently* (London: Thomas and William Boone, 1838), 189–190; Barber, "Galignani's"; Diana Cooper-Richet, "Les imprimés en langue anglaise en France au XIXe siècle: Rayonnement intellectuel, circulation et modes de pénétration," in *Repenser la Restauration,* ed. Jean-Yves Mollier, Martine Reid, and Jean-Claude Yon (Paris: Nouveau Monde, 2005), 122–140; Elkington, *Les relations de société,* ch. 8, "Rapprochement littéraire"; André Ratchinski, "Les contacts idéologiques et culturels entre la France et la Russie, 1800–1820" (PhD diss., Université Paris III, 1996), 401; Jean-Yves Mollier, "Conclusion" to *Repenser la Restauration,* 364. For data on editions and printings of various authors in this period, see Martyn Lyons, *Le triomphe du livre: Une histoire sociologique de la lecture dans la France du XIXe siècle* (Paris: Promodis; Cercle de la Librairie, 1987), and William St. Clair, *The Reading Nation in the Romantic Period* (Cambridge: Cambridge University Press, 2007).
64. "Le bon Français (mai 1814): Chanson chantée devant des aides de camp de l'empereur Alexandre," in *Oeuvres complètes de Béranger* (Paris: Perrotin, 1851), 1:86–89; *Le nain vert,* 7 Aug. 1815.

65. *Anglaisiana, ou Les Anglais, les Écossais et les Irlandais à Londres et à Paris; Les Anglaises pour rire, ou La table et le logement, comédie en un acte,* by Sewrin and Dumerson, Variétés, 26 Dec. 1814 (pub. Mme. Masson); Philip Henry, 5th Earl Stanhope, *Notes of Conversations with the Duke of Wellington, 1831–1851* (New York: Da Capo Press, 1973), 217. For examples of other plays caricaturing the British produced between 1814 and 1818, see Brazier, Moreau, and J.-B. Dubois, *La bouquetière anglaise*; Moreau, Lafortelle, and Dumersan, *Le boxeur français, ou Une heure à Londres*; Désaugiers, d'Allarde, and Simonnin, *Les deux boxeurs, ou Les Anglais de Falaise et de Nanterre*; Bourlin, *Une gageure anglaise, rue Louvois*; Merville, *Les deux Anglais*; all cited in Charles Beaumont Wicks, *The Parisian Stage: Alphabetical Indexes of Plays and Authors*, Part I, *1800–1815*, and Part II, *1816–1830* (Birmingham: University of Alabama Press, 1950 and 1953). On the use of caricature to counteract Anglomania, see Jean Guiffan, *Histoire de l'anglophobie en France de Jeanne d'Arc à la vache folle* (Rennes: Terre de Brume Éditions, 2004), esp. 112–113.
66. This description of the *montagnes russes* is based on Edouard de Keyser, "Un thème d'imagerie parisienne sous la Restauration: Le combat des montagnes et la guerre des calicots" (Paris: Le Vieux Papier, 1964); Robert Cartmell, *The Incredible Scream Machine: A History of the Roller Coaster* (Bowling Green, OH: Amusement Park Books/Bowling Green State University Popular Press, 1987); and Gaston Tissandier, "Les montagnes russes," *La nature* 693 (1886): 225–227, and "Les montagnes russes à Paris," *Revue des sciences et de leurs applications aux arts et à l'industrie* 16 (1888): 343–346. More recently, the *montagnes* have been analyzed by scholars in the fields of literary studies, art history, and urban studies, as cases of new practices of consumer culture and uses of public space for health and hygiene, especially for women, in the first half of the nineteenth century. See especially Sun-Young Park, *Ideals of the Body: Architecture, Urbanism, and Hygiene in Postrevolutionary Paris* (Pittsburgh, PA: University of Pittsburgh Press, 2018), and Peggy Davis, "La folie des 'montagnes russes' à Paris sous la Restauration: Un moment intermédial dans la culture de l'imprimé" (paper presented at Society for French Historical Studies, April 2017, forthcoming in *Réflexions historiques/Historical Reflections).*
67. Marquise de Montcalm, *Mon journal,* 198.
68. AN, F12/1027A and F12/1026/A.
69. Henri d'Almeras, *La vie parisienne sous la Restauration* (Paris: Albin Michel, 1965), note p. 61; Gustave Pessard, *Nouveau dictionnaire historique de Paris* (Paris: Eugène Rey, 1904); Lagier de Vaugelas, *Soixante vues des plus beaux palais, monuments et églises de Paris . . . , gravées par Couché fils* (Paris: Vilquin, Palais-Royal, n.d. [1818]); J.-A. Dulaure, *Panorama de la ville de Paris*.
70. *JD*, 14 July 1817.
71. [F.-F. Cotterel], *Promenades aériennes, considérées sous le rapport de l'agrément et de la santé, ed. revue et augmentée*, 2nd ed. (Paris: Belin, 1821), esp. 46 and 53–54.

72. Cotterel, *Promenades aériennes,* 9. On the role of these mountains in remaking Paris as a capital of pleasure, see Jonathan Conlin, ed., *The Pleasure Garden: From Vauxhall to Coney Island* (Philadelphia: University of Pennsylvania Press, 2013), 10.
73. Pellizzone, *Souvenirs,* 2:410–411 and fig. 22a.
74. *JP,* 22 July 1817; de Keyser, "Un thème d'imagerie parisienne."
75. MM. *** [Delestre-Poirson & Dupin, according to the *Annuaire dramatique* of 1817], *Les montagnes russes, ou Le Temple de la Mode, Vaudeville en un acte,* performed for the first time at the Théatre du Vaudeville, 31 October 1816 (Paris: Fages, 1816); Moreau et al., *Les montagnes russes, à propos épisodique mêlé de couplets,* received by censor 17 Oct. 1816, performed 29 Oct. 1816, AN, F18/625 (Censure: Théâtre des Variétés).
76. *La Folie Beaujon, ou Une heure avant l'ouverture,* performed 10 July 1817 [no publishing information], ms. in AN, F18 / 627; *La Folie Beaujon, ou Les promenades aériennes: Vaudeville en un acte,* performed 10 July 1817, also in AN, F18 / 627; *Les folies parisiennes, ou la Revue des trois montagnes russe, suisse, et de la folie Beaujon, suivi du vaudeville de Fanfan l'malin* ([Paris]: Imprimerie De Laurens, n.d. [1817]); *Les montagnes en Vaudevilles* ([Paris]: Imprimerie de Nicolas-Vaucluse, n.d.); [Claude Simplet and Corda], *Adieux d'un Champenois à la Folie Beaujon, également connue sous le nom de montagnes françaises, au sortir de la fête extraordinaire annoncée le 25 septembre dernier* (Châlons: Boniez-Lambert, n.d.); *Petit imbroglio sur le jeu des montagnes russes, dites de santé* [no publishing information], annexed to Cotterel, *Promenades aériennes.*
77. *JF,* 13 July 1817.
78. [Delestre-Poirson & Dupin], *Les montagnes russes, ou Le Temple de la Mode.*
79. Ibid.; [Simplet and Corda], *Adieux d'un Champenois,* 12.
80. Moreau et al., *Les montagnes russes, à propos episodique,* AN, F18/625; [Delestre-Poirson & Dupin], *Les montagnes russes, ou Le Temple de la Mode,* 20–21.
81. [Scribe et Delestre], *Le combat des montagnes, ou La Folie Beaujon.* Report by censorship administration 18 June 1817, AN, F18/633.
82. *Chronique parisienne,* Aug. 1817, p. 171; police reports from sections around theater in Paris in late July 1817, AN, F7/6844; *Grand combat du combat des montagnes, ou La campagne des calicots; pot-pourri, par Jérôme le Pacifique* (Paris: Mlle Huet-Masson, 1817); "Caricatures historiques: Calicots—1817," BNF Estampes, Tf 48, and "M. Calicot" (collection in which there are four prints regarding the "Combat des montagnes" in 1817), Bibliothèque de l'Arsenal, GD 49950; *JD,* 7 Aug. 1817; *JF,* 10 Aug. 1817; De Keyser, "Un thème d'imagerie parisienne," 6–9.
83. Eugène Scribe, with Henri Dupin, *Le Café des Variétés: Épilogue en vaudevilles,* first performed at the Théâtre des Variétés, 5 Aug. 1817 (Paris: Mlle. Huet-Masson, 1817); Peggy Davis, "Entre la physiognomonie et les Physiologies: Le

Calicot, figure du panorama parisien sous la Restauration," *Études françaises* 49, no. 3 (2013): 63–85.

84. Lagier de Vaugelas, *Soixante vues.*
85. Denise Z. Davidson, *France after Revolution: Urban Life, Gender, and the New Social Order* (Cambridge, MA: Harvard University Press, 2007).
86. On these accidents and the demise of the *montagnes russes,* see *Chronique parisienne,* Nov. 1817; D'Almeras, *La vie parisienne,* 62–63; Tissandier, "Les montagnes russes"; and Keyser, "Un thème d'imagerie parisienne."

CHAPTER SEVEN ✣ RECONSTRUCTION

1. *Oeuvres complètes de P. J. de Béranger,* new ed. (Paris: Perrotin, 1851), 1:194–195.
2. On this point, see Arthur Louis Dunham, *The Industrial Revolution in France, 1815–1848* (New York: Exposition Press, 1955), esp. 225.
3. Jeff Horn, *The Path Not Taken: French Industrialization in the Age of Revolution, 1750–1830* (Cambridge, MA: MIT Press, 2006), esp. 3.
4. Pierre Branda, *Le prix de la gloire: Napoléon et l'argent* (Paris: Fayard, 2007).
5. Branda, *Le prix de la gloire,* 488–492. On the handling of the financial crisis of 1814, see also Jacques-Joseph, Comte de Corbière, *Souvenirs de la Restauration,* ed. Bernard Heudré (Rennes: Presses Universitaires de Rennes, 2012). On the opposition to indirect taxes, see AN, F1a/588–589 (Perception des droits réunis: Détails relatifs aux désordres occasionnés par la reprise des Exercices dans les Dépts: Allier-Vosges).
6. Baron Louis quoted in A. Calmon, *Histoire parlementaire des finances de la Restauration* (Paris: Michel Lévy frères, 1868), 1:125–126; Branda, *Le prix de la gloire,* 495–496; Roger André, *L'occupation de la France par les Alliés en 1815 (juillet-novembre)* (Paris: Boccard, 1924), 162.
7. André Nicolle, "The Problem of Reparations after the Hundred Days," *Journal of Modern History* 25, no. 4 (1953): 343; Thomas Dwight Veve, *The Duke of Wellington and the British Army of Occupation in France, 1815–1818* (Westport, CT: Greenwood Press, 1992), 22; Eugene White, "Making the French Pay: The Costs and Consequences of the Napoleonic Reparations," *European Review of Economic History* 5, no. 3 (2001): 341.
8. Branda, *Le prix de la gloire,* esp. 503; and White, "Making the French Pay," 344. On Ouvrard, see Jacques Wolff, *Le financier Ouvrard: L'argent et la politique* (Paris: Tallandier, 1992).
9. Thomas Gauchet, "Restaurer le régime, restaurer la confiance: Les charges de guerre, leur processus de liquidation et de remboursement dans le Haut-Rhin, 1815-années 1820" (master's thesis, Institut d'Études Politiques, Paris, 2015), 148.
10. Gauchet, "Restaurer le régime," 86–89; Emmanuel Boudot, "L'occupation alliée de 1815–1818 dans le département de la Moselle" (master's thesis, Université de Metz, 1995), 17, AD Moselle; correspondence between ministry of inte-

rior and prefect of Nord, as well as between prefect and subprefect of Avesnes, ca. June 1816, AD Nord, 8R/17.

11. *AP,* vols. 16 (8 Jan.–31 Mar.) and 17 (1 Apr.–30 Dec. 1816).
12. André, *L'occupation,* 158–161; Gauchet, "Restaurer le régime," 118–127. For the original text of the law, see *Bulletin des lois,* vol. 81 (1816).
13. See, for instance, *JP,* 3 Jan. 1816, as well as Jacques Hantraye, *Les Cosaques aux Champs-Elysées: L'occupation de la France après la chute de Napoléon* (Paris: Belin, 2005), 142.
14. Petition from "Marchand de bas F. Webber," May 1816, BMV, H7/33.
15. André, *L'occupation,* 161.
16. White, "Making the French Pay," 342; CAC, F5/I/353 (Correspondance et liquidation, 1815); "Loi relative à la fixation du Budget des Dépenses et des Recettes de 1823, 17 août 1822," *Bulletin des lois,* 1822, no. 549; Boudot, "L'occupation alliée," 43; Henri Contamine, *Les conséquences financières des invasions de 1814 et de 1815 dans les départements de la Moselle et de la Meurthe* (Metz: Les Arts Graphiques, 1932), 92.
17. Hantraye, *Les Cosaques,* 141–145; Boudot, "L'occupation alliée," 44, based on Contamine, *Les conséquences financières,* 63.
18. Gauchet, "Restaurer le régime," 193. On the fiscal policy of the Restoration, the classic works are Calmon, *Histoire parlementaire,* and M. Marion, *Histoire financière de la France depuis 1715,* vol. 4, *1797–1818* (Paris: Arthur Rousseau, 1927). See also the memoir by the deputy who presented the report of the legislative committee charged with examining the proposed budget of 1816, Corbière, *Souvenirs.*
19. Calmon, *Histoire parlementaire,* 1:iii.
20. White, "Making the French Pay," 339. This account of the reparations required by the treaty of November 20, 1815, draws also on Nicolle, "Problem of Reparations," 343–354; Kim Oosterlinck, Loredana Ureche-Rangau, and Jacques-Marie Vaslin, "Waterloo: A Godsend for French Public Finances?" (Working Paper in Economic History 41, European Historical Economics Society, July 2013); V. A. Nigohosian, *La libération du territoire français après Waterloo, 1815–1818* (Paris: E. de Boccard, 1929); and Calmon, *Histoire parlementaire.*
21. Second Treaty of Paris, Convention on Pecuniary Indemnity, in *British and Foreign State Papers,* vol. 3, *1815–1816* (London: Great Britain Foreign and Commonwealth Office, 1838), 292.
22. White, "Making the French Pay," 344–346, and Nicolle, "Problem of Reparations," 344–346.
23. Nicolle, "Problem of Reparations," 348.
24. White, "Making the French Pay," 347.
25. Ibid., 337–338.
26. Oosterlinck, Ureche-Rangau, and Vaslin, "Waterloo," 3; André Nicolle, *Comment la France a payé après Waterloo* (Paris: Boccard, 1929), 7, quoted in Branda, *Le prix de la gloire,* 501; and Marion, *Histoire financière,* 4:418 and 432–433.

27. White, "Making the French Pay," 348 and 351.
28. Ibid., 361.
29. This account of the subsistence crisis of 1816–1817 is based on John D. Post, *The Last Great Subsistence Crisis in the Western World* (Baltimore, MD: Johns Hopkins University Press, 1977); Nicolas Bourguinat, *Les grains du désordre: L'État face aux violences frumentaires dans la première moitié du XIXe siècle* (Paris: L'École des Hautes Études en Sciences Sociales, 2002); Bourguinat, "La ville, la haute police et la peur: Lyon entre le complot des subsistances et les manoeuvres politiques en 1816–1817," *Société française d'histoire urbaine* 2, no. 2 (2002): 131–147; Bourguinat, "De Napoléon aux Restaurations: Les pouvoirs face aux crises frumentaires dans le Midi français et le Nord de Italie (1811–1817)," *SOURCE(S): Cahiers de l'équipe de recherche ARCHE,* no. 1 (2012): 55–71; and Robert Margolin, "Troubles provoquées par la disette de 1817," *Revue d'histoire moderne* 8, no. 10 (1933): 423–460. More recently, Gillen D'Arcy Wood has written a wonderful account of the artistic and environmental effects of the eruption of Tambora around the world, *Tambora: The Eruption That Changed the World* (Princeton, NJ: Princeton University Press, 2015).
30. Bourguinat, *Les grains du désordre,* 154.
31. Margolin, "Troubles," 424; Bourguinat, *Les grains du désordre,* 155; Post, *Last Great Subsistence Crisis,* 36–43.
32. Leuilliot, *L'Alsace au début du XIXe siècle: Essais d'histoire politique, économique et religieuse, 1815–1830,* vol. 2, *Les transformations économiques* (Paris: SEVPEN, 1959), 170.
33. "Soutz-sous-Forêts: Les événements de 1815–1817 relatés par le Pasteur Weissmann," *L'Outre-Forêt: Revue du Cercle d'histoire et d'archéologie de l'Alsace du nord* 122 (2003): 15–18; Bourguinat, *Les grains du désordre,* 65.
34. Post, *Last Great Subsistence Crisis,* 99; Daniel Peter, "Les demandes de passeport dans l'arrondissement de Wissembourg durant le premier semestre de 1817," *L'Outre-Forêt: Revue du Cercle d'histoire et d'archéologie de l'Alsace du nord* 55 (1986): 48–52.
35. Report from Caen, departing 2 May 1816, AN, F7/3825. For similar reports of unrest as a result of the grain shortage, see AN, F7/3826 (June 1816–Dec. 1817).
36. Minutes of the first meeting of the Commission des Subsistances, 6 Sept. 1815, AN, F11/3056. On the organization and purview of the commission, see the registers of its correspondence in AN, F11/51–57. On the long-term history of the state's approach to the grain trade, see Judith A. Miller, *Mastering the Market: The State and the Grain Trade in Northern France, 1700–1860* (Cambridge: Cambridge University Press, 1999).
37. Bourguinat, "De Napoléon aux Restaurations," 70–71.
38. Commission des Subsistances to minister of interior, Paris, 3 Apr. 1817, AN, F11/53.
39. Boudot, "L'occupation alliée," 45.
40. Bourguinat, "De Napoléon aux Restaurations," 66.
41. Leuilliot, *L'Alsace,* 2:161; decree from mayor of Valenciennes, 19 Mar. 1817, regarding "tax" on meat, BMV, D2/84; *Histoire de Strasbourg des origines à*

nos jours, vol. 4, *Strasbourg de 1815 à nos jours,* ed. Georges Livet and Francis Rapp (Strasbourg: Dernières Nouvelles d'Alsace, 1982), 53; Commission des Subsistances, bulletin of 22 Apr. 1816, with report from prefect in Arras, AN, F11/444; report from Dijon, 10 Nov. 1816, AN, F11/724.

42. Leuilliot, *L'Alsace,* 2:167–168; *Histoire de Strasbourg,* 4:53.
43. Minutes of municipal council of Pont-à Mousson, 1816–1818, AM Pont-à-Mousson, 1D/13 and 14.
44. List of householders in communes of canton of Charleville with right to distribution of bread, AD Ardennes, EDEPOT/Charleville/5H / 5; population statistic from AN, F20/408/1.
45. Post, *Last Great Subsistence Crisis,* 95. On these courts, see Jean Vidalenc, "La cour prévôtale de Seine-Inférieure, 1816–1818," *Revue d'histoire moderne et contemporaine* 19 (1972): 533–556.
46. Bourguinat, "La ville," 142–143; Bourguinat, *Les grains du désordre,* 403 and 406; and Margolin, "Troubles," esp. 447–451.
47. Report from Lille, departing 29 Aug. 1815, AN, F7/3824.
48. Petition from municipal council to minister of interior, 21 Nov. 1815, cited in *Courrier des Ardennes,* 13 July 1881, provided to me by Élise Nicolas, Médiathèque Voyelles, Charleville-Mézières.
49. See, for example, reports in AN, F7/9903 (Pas-de-Calais); AD Nord, 8R/12; and Chamber of Commerce of Paris to minister of interior, Feb. 1816, Archives de Paris, 2ETP1/2/50 (Correspondence de la Chambre de Commerce). On the long-standing tradition of cross-Channel commerce, see Renaud Morieux, *Un mer pour deux royaumes: La Manche, frontière franco-anglaise, XVIIe–XVIIIe siècle* (Rennes: Presses Universitaires de Rennes, 2008).
50. André Sacrez, "Les russes en 'Ardenne wallonne' (1814–1818) (suite et fin)," *Ardenne wallonne* 98 (2004): 10–17.
51. AD Bas-Rhin, RP/1247. On the negative economic effects of the Restoration in Alsace, see Leuilliot, *L'Alsace,* vol. 2.
52. Report from Calais, departing 25 Dec. 1815, AN, F7/3825.
53. Report from Feydeau section, 12 Nov. 1817, AN, F7/3838.
54. AN, BB18/972, no. 3229.
55. Report from Montmartre, 30 Dec. 1815, AN, F7/3838.
56. Report from Caen, 15 Dec. 1817, AN, F7/3826.
57. *JP,* 2 June 1816.
58. AN, F7/9902.
59. BMV, D1/58 (Registre de Correspondance, 2e Bureau, Feb.–July 1817).
60. Note from Feb. 1817, BMV, D4/119.
61. "Lettre circulaire du Sous-Préfet de l'arrondissement d'Avesnes, Prissette, aux Maires des communes de son ressort," 1 July 1817, AD Nord, 8R/12.
62. Table of debts of Allies, 1816–1818, AM Tourcoing, 5H/32.
63. For a sense of public opinion regarding the economy, see reports for these years from stagecoach drivers in provinces to ministry of police, in AN, F7/3824–3826.
64. Boudot, "L'occupation alliée," 32–34.

65. Jacques Hantraye, "Rebâtir après les défaites napoléoniennes: Les enjeux de la reconstruction immobilière dans la France du Nord et de l'Est, 1814–1860," *Annales historiques de la révolution française* 2 (2007): 185–198.
66. Guillaume de Bertier de Sauvigny, *Nouvelle histoire de Paris: La Restauration, 1815–1830* (Paris: Hachette, 1977).
67. Arnaud Gabet and Christianne Lepie, "La présence britannique à Cambrai de 1815 à 1848," *Cambrésis terre d'histoire* 7 (1993): 23.
68. Mayor of Charleville, 17 Sept. 1816, in AD Ardennes, EDEPOT/Charleville/5H/4. On the practices of the Russians, see John L. H. Keep, *Soldiers of the Tsar: Army and Society in Russia, 1462–1874* (Oxford: Clarendon, 1985), ch. 8, "The Struggle for Survival." On the Saxons, extract from a dispatch to Mr. d'Üchtritz, Paris, 8 Dec. 1815, regarding sums destined for salary and equipment of army corps, HStA Dresden, Bestand 11339 (Generalstab: Generaloberkommando), Nr. 338 (Militärkonvention für die Okkupationsarmee in Frankreich).
69. Commanding colonel of Prussian lancers to mayor of Charleville, 22 and 23 Mar. 1816, AD Ardennes, EDEPOT/Charleville, 5H/4; prefect of Bas-Rhin to command of Württemberger contingent, 3 Oct. 1816, HStA Stuttgart, E 289 a/Bü 283 (Bezeichnung des Bestands: Mobile Kommandobehörden I: Korrespondenz mit der Präfektur Strasβburg, Nov. 1815–Nov. 1818).
70. *JP,* 28 Apr. 1816.
71. AN, F7/9903.
72. "The English at Valenciennes in 1816, by the author of 'Waterloo,'" *The United Service Journal and Naval and Military Magazine* 1829: 324.
73. AN, F7/9903.
74. Report from Sedan, departing 17 Dec. 1818, AN, F7/3827.
75. *JP,* 13 June 1816.
76. Georges Clause, "Les Russes dans la Marne en 1814 et de 1815 à 1818," in *Les occupations en Champagne-Ardenne, 1814–1944,* ed. François Cochet (Reims: Presses Universitaires de Reims, 1996), 38.
77. Report from Sedan, departing 26 June 1816, AN, F7/3826. See also report departing 11 May 1816, AN, F7 /3825.
78. AN, F7/9889/2.
79. Odette Hardy-Hémery, "Valenciennes de 1815 à 1914: Une ville paisible dans une région en expansion économique soutenue," in *Histoire de Valenciennes,* ed. Henri Platelle (Lille: Presses Universitaires de Lille, 1982), ch. 11.
80. Jean-Louis Boithias, "Un siècle d'histoire de la brasserie en Livradois, 1814–1914," *Bulletin historique et scientifique de l'Auvergne* 44, no. 698 (1988): 117–154.
81. Gabet and Lepie, "La présence britannique," 28–29.
82. Philip Mansel, *Paris between Empires, 1814–1852: Monarchy and Revolution,* 2nd ed. (New York: Phoenix, 2003), 143–144, and Horn, *Path Not Taken,* 245–246.
83. Jean Lambert-Dansette, *Genèse du patronat, 1780–1880* (Paris: Hachette, 1991). For evidence of the surveillance of English workers in the northeast, see police reports in AN, F7/9901 (Nord) and 9903 (Pas-de-Calais).

84. Report to minister of interior from 2e Division, Bureau des Communes, 30 July 1816, and ministry of interior to prefect of Meuse, 31 July 1816, in CAC, F6/I/23.
85. J.-B. Say, *De l'Angleterre et des Anglais* (Paris: Arthus Bertrand, 1816); J.-A. Chaptal, *De l'industrie française,* 2 vols. (Paris: Antoine-Augustin Renouard, 1819). See also Ch. Dupin, *Voyages dans la Grande-Bretagne, entrepris relatif aux services publics . . . depuis 1816,* 6 vols. (Paris: Bachelier, 1825–1826); Cl. A. Costaz, *Mémoire sur les moyens qui ont amené le grand développement que l'industrie française a pris depuis vingt ans; suivi de la législation relative aux fabriques, aux ateliers, aux ouvriers et aux découvertes dans les arts* (Paris: Firmin Didot, 1816); Alexandre Maurice Blanc de Lanautte, Comte D'Hauterive, *Éléments d'économie politique* (Paris: Fantin, 1817); J. C. L. de Sismondi, *Nouveaux principes d'économie politique,* 2 vols. (Paris: Delaunay, 1819).
86. See, for instance, J.-R. Armonville, *Le guide des artistes, ou Répertoire des arts et manufactures* (Paris: Chaignieau aîné, 1818), and Léopold, *Dictionnaire universel-portatif du commerce . . .* (Paris: Pillet aîné, 1819). For periodicals, see *Bulletin de la Société d'encouragement; Annales des arts et manufactures; Archives des découvertes et inventions;* and the short-lived *Journal du commerce, de politique et de littérature* (March–Sept. 1815). For petitions from 1814–1820, see AN, C//2737–2740.
87. See, for example, Anon., *Moyen très equitable de réparer une grande partie des désastres de la France* ([Paris]: Lottin de Saint-Germain, n.d.); M. A. de M., *Considérations sur la situation de la France sous le rapport des finances* (Paris: Firmin Didot, Dec. 1816); J. A. Brosson, propriétaire cultivateur, *Moyens de remédier aux maux de la France, et de la rendre florissante par l'agriculture* (n.p.: Feugueray, n.d.); M. R. Deladériere, ancien régisseur et directeur des Fermes d'Artois, à Amiens, *Moyens de solder toutes les dettes de l'État sans recourir aux emprunts ni aux impôts rejetés à la dernière session des chambres, ou Supplément au mémoire ayant pour titre: Mode de suppression des impôts indirects existants, remis au Roi et aux Chambres au mois d'octobre 1815* (Amiens: Ledien-Canda, 1816), all in AN, CC//2738–2740.
88. Among many other such petitions, see M. Charles Tempier, *Essai sur les avantages qui résulteroient pour la France de la liberté absolue du commerce* (Paris: Le Normant, 1816), and André-Gabriel Langlois, *De l'industrie nationale au moment où nous sommes* (Paris: L. G. Michaud, 1817), in AN, C//2738–2740.
89. On the development of this liberal-protectionist political economy in the interest of the nation, see Francis Démier, "Nation, marché et développement dans la France de la Restauration" (PhD diss., Université de Paris X-Nanterre, 1991), and David Todd, *L'identité économique de la France: Libre-échange et protectionnisme, 1814–1851* (Paris: Bernard Grasset, 2008).
90. Horn, *Path Not Taken,* 14.
91. Speech by Cornet d'Incourt, 16 Apr. 1816, *AP,* 17:261.

92. Horn, *Path Not Taken,* 241, and Todd, *L'identité économique,* ch. 3, "La guerre des douanes (1814–1824)," esp. 55–56. The tariffs promulgated by the finance law of April 28, 1816, filled pages of the *Bulletin des lois,* no. 81 (1816).
93. Chaptal, *De l'industrie française,* 2:205. On the state's encouragement of industry in the early years of the Restoration, see Horn, *Path Not Taken,* esp. ch. 7, "Facing Up to English Industrial Dominance: Industrial Policy from the Empire to the July Revolution, 1805–1830."
94. Horn, *Path Not Taken,* 248.
95. Ibid.
96. Arthur Chandler, "Expositions of the Restoration: Paris: 1819, 1823, 1827," at http://www.arthurchandler.comexpositions-of-the-restoration-1819–1823–1837; L. Costaz, *Rapport du Jury central sur les produits de l'industrie française, présenté à S. E. M. le Comte Decazes, Pair de France, Ministre Secrétaire d'état de l'intérieur; rédigé par M. L. Costaz, Membre de l'Institut d'Egypte, et Rapporteur du Jury central* (Paris: Imprimerie Royale, 1819); *Exposition publique des produits de l'industrie française au Palais du Louvre, année 1819: Catalogue indiquant le nom des fabricans, celui de leur domicile et département, avec la désignation sommaire des produits de leur industrie* (Paris: Imprimerie Royale, 1819). The records of the organization of this exposition are in AN, F12/985.
97. Costaz, *Rapport du Jury central,* xxiv.
98. Wm. C. Somerville, *Letters from Paris, On the Causes and Consequences of the French Revolution* (Baltimore, MD: Edward J. Coale, 1822), 297–298.

CHAPTER EIGHT ✣ RECUPERATION

1. For a description of this porcelain platter, see Kimberly A. Jones, "Henri IV and the Decorative Arts of the Bourbon Restoration, 1814–1830: A Study in Politics and Popular Taste," *Studies in the Decorative Arts* 1, no. 1 (1993): 2–21.
2. This spike in references to Henri IV and Joan of Arc is evidenced by Google Ngram, as well as the official French publishing journal, the *Bibliographie de la France.* On Henry IV as a "tutelary figure" of the Restoration, see Emmanuel de Waresquiel, *C'est la Révolution qui continue! La Restauration, 1814–1830* (Paris: Tallandier, 2015). On the use of Joan of Arc as a political symbol through the end of the nineteenth century, see Venita Datta, *Heroes and Legends of Fin-de-Siècle France: Gender, Politics, and National Identity* (Cambridge: Cambridge University Press, 2011).
3. *Jeanne d'Arc aux jeunes françaises, ou Appel aux femmes courageuses de la capitale, par la Pucelle d'Orléans* (Paris: Imprimerie d'Abel Lanoe, n.d. [1815]). For other examples from this period, see: "Les soucis de Jeanne d'Arc," poem heard in Dijon, Apr. 1814, AN, F1a/583; J. G. A. Cuvelier, *La Pucelle d'Orléans: Pantomime historique et chevaleresque en trois actes, à grand spectacle; précédée du Songe de Jeanne d'Arc, et terminée par son Apothéose (avec musique), représentée, pour la première fois, à Paris, au*

Cirque Olympique, le 10 novembre 1813 (Paris: Barba, 1814); J. Avril (Grenoble), ex-inspecteur du Service des subsistances militaires aux Armées, Leipzig, 30 mars 1814, *Le triomphe des lis: Jeanne d'Arc ou la Pucelle d'Orléans, drame en cinq actes et en vers, imité de la tragédie allemande de Schiller,* trans, M. C. F. Cramer, ed. M. L. S. Mercier (Paris: Chez Bacot, 1814); F. Schiller, *Jeanne d'Arc: Tragédie romanesque,* trans. J. B. Daulnoy, bilingual ed. (Dusseldorf: J. C. Daenzer, 1815). On the use of such rhetoric about women to legitimize the newly restored monarchy, see Jennifer Heuer, "'No More Fears, No More Tears'?: Gender, Emotion and the Aftermath of the Napoleonic Wars in France," *Gender and History* 28, no. 2 (2016): 438–460.

4. *Serment des Amazones françaises* (Paris: Genty, 1815), BNF.
5. For examples, see: Comtesse de Genlis, *Jeanne de France: Nouvelle historique* (Paris: Fain, 1816); *Jeanne d'Arc, ou la Pucelle d'Orléans, fait historique de l'histoire de France, sous le règne de Charles VII* (Paris: Montaudon, 1815); Philippe Alexandre Lebrun de Charmettes, *Histoire de Jeanne d'Arc, surnommée la Pucelle d'Orléans,* 4 vols. (Paris: Bertrand, 1817); Abbé Bernet, "Panégyrique de Jeanne d'Arc prononcé le 8 mai 1817, dans l'église cathédrale d'Orléans" (Orléans: Rouzeau-Montaut, 1817); M. de Rougemont, *La maison de Jeanne d'Arc, Anecdote-vaudeville en un acte,* first performed at Théâtre du Vaudeville, 3 Oct. 1818 (Paris: Fages, 1818); and two fabric swatches for furnishings, "Vie de Jeanne d'Arc," designed by Ch. A. Chasselat and printed by roll on cotton by Hartmann et Fils, Munster, 1820, Musée de l'Impression sur Étoffes (Mulhouse), Inv. 858.88.1–967.12.1.
6. MM. Maréchalle, Ch. Hubert and ***, *L'épée de Jeanne d'Arc, ou les cinq . . . demoiselles: À-propos burlesque et grivois, en un acte, à spectacle, mêlé de couplets, . . . représenté pour la première fois, sur le Théâtre de la Porte Saint-Martin, le 1er juin 1819,* 3rd ed. (Paris: Quoy et J.-N. Barba, 1819).
7. Adèle d'Osmond, Comtesse de Boigne, *Mémoires de la Comtesse de Boigne, née d'Osmond: Récits d'une tante,* ed. Jean-Claude Berchet, vol. 1, *Du règne de Louis XVI à 1820* (Paris: Mercure de France, 1999), 230; engraving of "Statue Équestre de Henry IV, replacée sur le Pont Neuf le Premier Mai M.DCCC.XIV" (Paris: Chez Remoissenet, 1814), BNF.
8. N. B. de Rougemont, *Le souper d'Henri IV, ou la dinde en pal, comédie en un acte, en prose et en vaudevilles représentée, pour la première fois à Paris, sur le Théâtre des Variétés, le 23 avril 1814* (Paris: Au Théâtre; Hocquet, 1814); M. Maréchalle and Gombault, *Le soldat de Henri IV: Pièce en un acte, mêlée de vaudevilles, représentée, pour la première fois, à Paris, sur le Théâtre de la Gaîté, le 6 août 1816* (Paris: Barba, 1816). For evidence of the reception of these plays in the provinces, see report from Finistère on performance of "The Hunting Party of Henry IV," 4 Dec. 1815, AN, F7/3823, and J.-E. Raclet, *Précis historique des événemens qui se sont passés à Valenciennes, depuis le retour de Buonaparte, jusqu'au rétablissement de Louis XVIII* (Lille: V. Leleux, 1816).
9. For examples, see: *Le retour du lys et de la paix: Étrennes française, badine, joyeuse et épigrammatique, à l'usage de tous les Français; pour l'an 1816, 21ème*

règne de Louis XVIII (Lille: Vanckere, n.d. [1816]); *Henri IV, peint par lui-même,* 3rd ed. (Paris: CLF Panckoucke, 1815); Hyacinthe Foissey, *Caractère et vertus d'Henri IV roi de France et de Navarre* (Paris: Mme. Ve. H. Perronneau, 1817); and *Abrégé de la vie d'Henri IV, depuis sa naissance jusqu'à sa mort, Avec l'explication de la statue équestre de ce Grand Monarque* (Paris: Laurens, 1817).

10. On this statue, see *Description ancienne et nouvelle de la statue d'Henri IV, ou Grand détail historique sur la font, l'érection et l'inauguration de la statue équestre de Henri IV, et sur la pose de la première pierre de ce monument, par S M Louis XVIII, le 28 oct. 1817* (Paris: Chez Aubry, [1817]); Philip Mansel, *Paris between Empires, 1814–1852: Monarchy and Revolution*, 2nd ed. (London: Phoenix Press, 2003), 115–116; Albert Boime, *Art in an Age of Counterrevolution, 1815–1848* (Chicago, IL: University of Chicago Press, 2004), 16–17; and especially Victoria Thompson, "The Creation, Destruction and Recreation of Henri IV: Seeing Popular Sovereignty in the Statue of a King," *History and Memory* 24, no. 2 (2012): 5–40. Regarding the prints, see Anne-Marie Rosset, ed., *La Restauration et les Cent Jours,* vol. 5 of *Un siècle d'histoire de France par l'estampe, 1770–1871: Collection de Vinck—Inventaire analytique*, ed. François-Louis Bruel (Paris: Imprimerie nationale, 1938).

11. Sheryl Kroen, *Politics and Theater: The Crisis of Legitimacy in Restoration France, 1815–1830* (Berkeley: University of California Press, 2000); Bettina Frederking, "'Il ne faut pas être le roi de deux peuples': Strategies of National Reconciliation in Restoration France," *French History* 22, no. 4 (2008): 446–468; Matthijs M. Lok, "'Un oubli total du passé'? The Political and Social Construction of Silence in Restoration Europe (1813–1830)," *History and Memory* 26, no. 2 (2014): 40–75; and Emmanuel Fureix, "L'iconoclasme politique: Un combat pour la souveraineté (1814–1816)," in *Révolutions et mythes identitaires: Mots, violences, mémoire,* ed. Annie Duprat (Paris: Nouveau Monde, 2009), 173–193.

12. Étienne de Jouy, *Guillaume le Franc Parleur, ou Observations sur les moeurs et les usages parisiens au commencement du XIXe siècle* (Paris: Pillet, 1816–1817), vol. 2, no. 49, quoted in Pierre Rain, *L'Europe et la Restauration des Bourbons, 1814–1818* (Paris: Perrin, 1908), 182; Emmanuel de Waresquiel and Benoît Yvert, *Histoire de la Restauration, 1814–1830: Naissance de la France moderne* (Paris: Perrin, 1996); Francis Démier, *La France de la Restauration, 1814–1830: L'impossible retour du passé* (Paris: Gallimard, 2012); Pierre Rosanvallon, *La monarchie impossible: Les Chartes de 1814 et de 1830* (Paris: Fayard, 1994); Jean-Yves Mollier, Martine Reid, and Jean-Claude Yon, eds., *Repenser la Restauration* (Paris: Nouveau Monde, 2005); Denise Z. Davidson, *France after Revolution: Urban Life, Gender, and the New Social Order* (Cambridge, MA: Harvard University Press, 2007); Maximilian Owre, "United in Division: The Polarized French Nation, 1814–1830" (PhD diss., University of North Carolina, Chapel Hill, 2008).

13. This argument was first formulated by Paul Schroeder, *The Transformation of European Politics, 1763–1848* (Oxford: Clarendon, 1994). More recent studies of the Congress of Vienna include David King, *Vienna, 1814: How the Conquerors of Napoleon Made Love, War, and Peace at the Congress of Vienna* (New York: Broadway Books, 2009); Mark Jarrett, *The Congress of Vienna and Its Legacy: War and Great Power Diplomacy after Napoleon* (London: I. B. Tauris, 2013); and Brian E. Vick, *The Congress of Vienna: Power and Politics after Napoleon* (Cambridge, MA: Harvard University Press, 2014). The institutions and practices of international security in this period are now being reexamined by Beatrice de Graaf. See, in particular, her essay "The Allied Machine: The Conference of Ministers in Paris and the Management of Security, 1815–1818," in *Securing Europe after Napoleon: 1815 and the New European Security Culture*, ed. Beatrice de Graaf, Ido de Haan, and Brian Vick (Cambridge: Cambridge University Press, forthcoming in 2018).
14. The term comes from Schroeder, who labels this period the "Age of Recuperation," in *Transformation*, 586.
15. Emmanuel de Waresquiel, *Cent Jours: La tentation de l'impossible, mars-juillet 1815* (Paris: Fayard, 2008), 11; Pierre Serna, *La République des girouettes, 1789–1815 . . . et au-delà: Une anomalie politique: La France de l'extrême centre* (Seyssel: Champ Vallon, 2005), esp. ch. 5, "La girouette: Quand le *Nain jaune* et sa cohorte tiennent la girouette sur les fonts baptismaux."
16. On the strategy of *oubli,* see Kroen, *Politics and Theater,* esp. ch. 1, "The 'Counterrevolutionary' State and the Politics of *Oubli* (Forgetting)"; Lok, "'Un oubli total'?"; and Fureix, "L'iconoclasme politique."
17. For evidence of the shift back and forth from imperial to royalist symbols throughout the period 1814–1816, see authorizations and reports in AN, F1a/581, F7/4222, F7/6788a, and F7/3823 and 3824.
18. Register of deliberations of municipal council of Valenciennes, 19 July 1815, vol. 12, Oct. 1813–Dec. 1818, BMV, D1/22.
19. AD Meurthe-et-Moselle, 1M/627 (Politique générale: Premier Empire et Restauration).
20. Paul Leuilliot, *L'Alsace au début du XIXe siècle: Essais d'histoire politique, économique et religieuse*, vol. 1, *La vie politique* (Paris: SEVPEN, 1959), 125.
21. Claude Bailly, *Journal d'un artisan tourangeau, 1789–1830*, ed. Luc Boisnard (Chinon: Office du Tourisme, 1989).
22. Kroen, *Politics and Theater,* 49.
23. Leuilliot, *L'Alsace,* 1:125.
24. Max Bruchet, "L'invasion et l'occupation du département du Nord par les Alliés, 1814–1818," *Revue du Nord* 6 (1920): 298–299.
25. Subprefect of Lunéville to prefect, 2 July 1816, AD Meurthe-et-Moselle, 1M/627.
26. *JP,* 4 Jan. 1816. On a similar *mise-en-place* in Reims, see *MU,* 8 Jan. 1816.
27. Letter signed E. B. accompanying report of minister of interior Fouché on state of France, Paris, 7 Aug. 1815, *WSD* 11:108.

28. AD Bas-Rhin, 3M/18 (Police générale: Contrôle de l'esprit public, Seconde Restauration: Evénéments locaux, 1815–1819).
29. Kroen, *Politics and Theater,* ch. 1, "The 'Counterrevolutionary' State and the Politics of *Oubli* (Forgetting)." On the violet as a symbol of Napoleon, see David Andress, *The Savage Storm* (London: Little, Brown, 2012), 356–357.
30. Emmanuel Fureix, *La France des larmes: Deuils politiques à l'âge romantique, 1814–1840* (Seyssel: Champ Vallon, 2009); Frederking, "'Il ne faut pas être le roi'"; and Kroen, *Politics and Theater.*
31. See, for example, account of funerary service for Marie Antoinette, Strasbourg, Oct. 1816, AVES, 282MW/42 (Fêtes); report from St. Petersburg, 23 Jan. 1817, *MU,* 24 Feb. 1817; Fureix, *La France des larmes,* 169; Frederking, "'Il ne faut pas être le roi'," 460–461.
32. Report on festival of Saint Louis, Aug. 1815, AVES, 282MW/32 (Fêtes).
33. Orlov to Vorontsov, Paris, 10 July 1817, in Mikhail Semenovich Vorontsov, *Papiers,* vol. 27 (Moscow: n.p., 1883).
34. Fureix, *La France des larmes,* esp. ch. 3, "Une tradition revisitée," and ch. 6, "L'espace des expiations."
35. Rain, *L'Europe et la Restauration des Bourbons.*
36. Mansel, *Paris between Empires,* 98 and 105; Pierre de la Gorce, *La Restauration: Louis XVIII* (Paris: Plon, 1926), 92.
37. The Protocols of the "Conférence des Ministres des quatres Cours alliées," or Council of Allied Ambassadors, from Aug. 1815 to Dec. 1818 are in BNA, FO 146/1–30 and 41. Before the recent work of Beatrice de Graaf, the best source on the council was Rain, *L'Europe et la Restauration des Bourbons,* esp. ch. 6, "L'Europe et la Chambre Introuvable: La Grande Conférence."
38. Quoted in Emmanuel de Waresquiel, *Le Duc de Richelieu, 1766–1822* (Paris: Perrin, 1990), 262.
39. Protocol of the Council of Allied Ambassadors, 28 Feb. 1816, including letter of same date (in French) from Duke of Wellington to king of France, Paris (later printed in *WSD* 11:309–310), and Protocol of 6 Mar. 1816, BNA, FO 146/6; Ernest Daudet, *Louis XVIII et le duc Decazes, 1815–1820, d'après des documents inédits* (Paris: Plon, 1899), 122–123 and 131.
40. General Pozzo di Borgo to Comte de Nesselrode, Paris, 2/14 Apr. 1816 (No. 423), and Comte de Noailles to Duc de Richelieu, St. Petersburg, 7 May 1816, regarding conversation with Emperor Alexander I (No. 435), both in *Correspondance diplomatique des ambassadeurs et ministres de Russie en France et de France en Russie, de 1814 à 1830,* vol. 1, *1814–1816* (St. Petersburg: La Société impériale d'histoire de Russie, 1902).
41. Richelieu to Osmond, Paris, 15 Aug. 1816, in *Lettres du Duc de Richelieu au Marquis d'Osmond, 1816–1818,* ed. Sébastien Charléty, 7th ed. (Paris: Gallimard, 1939).
42. Sébastian Charléty, *La Restauration* (Paris: Hachette, 1921), 76; Waresquiel and Yvert, *Histoire de la Restauration,* 190–195; Philip Mansel, *Louis XVIII* (London: Blond and Briggs, 1981), 339.

43. Protocol of 8 Sept. 1816, BNA, FO 146/6; reports on Wellington's visits to localities in Bas-Rhin, Sept. 1816, AN, F7/9904; report from police commissioner in Moselle to minister of police, Decazes, Metz, 19 Sept. 1816, AN, F7/9900.
44. Report from police commissioner in Moselle to minister of police, Decazes, Metz, 19 Sept. 1816, AN, F7/9900; [Narcisse-Achille de Salvandy], *La Coalition et la France* (Paris: Delaunay, 1817). For a later example, see also *De l'intervention des étrangers dans le gouvernement de la France* (Paris: P. Mongie l'aîné, 1819).
45. Démier, *La France de la Restauration,* 243; Rain, *L'Europe et la Restauration des Bourbons,* ii and 477.
46. This argument was made in the wake of World War II by Paul Bastid, in *Les institutions politiques de la monarchie parlementaire française, 1814–1848* (Paris: Recueil Sirey, 1954), and has been revived in more recent work, including Rosanvallon, *La monarchie impossible,* 74. On these three laws, see André Jardin and André-Jean Tudesq, *Restoration and Reaction, 1815–1848,* trans. Elborg Forster (Cambridge: Cambridge University Press, 1983), 35–38; Démier, *La France de la Restauration,* ch. 4, "Le pouvoir selon la Charte, 1816–1820"; Thomas Dwight Veve, *The Duke of Wellington and the British Army of Occupation in France, 1815–1818* (Westport, CT: Greenwood Press, 1992), ch. 9, "French Internal Reforms"; and Mansel, *Louis XVIII,* ch. 14, "Liberal Years."
47. Quoted in Waresquiel and Yvert, *Histoire de la Restauration,* 208.
48. Ibid., 216–217.
49. Ibid., 219–222; Démier, *La France de la Restauration,* 259–263.
50. Baptiste Capefigue, *Histoire de la Restauration et des causes qui ont amené la chute de la branche aînée des Bourbons, par un homme d'état* (Paris: Duféy et Vezard, 1832), 5:309; Rudolf von Thadden, *La centralisation contestée,* trans. Hélène Cusa and Patrick Charbonneau (Arles: Actes Sud, 1989), esp. 53–55, and Pierre Karila-Cohen, *L'État des esprits: L'invention de l'enquête politique en France, 1814–1848* (Rennes: Presses Universitaires de Rennes, 2008). On the politicization of the public sphere during the Restoration, see also the work of Sheryl Kroen, Denise Davidson, and Max Owre cited above.
51. François Ploux, *De bouche à oreille: Naissance et propagation des rumeurs dans la France du XIXe siècle* (Paris: Aubier, 2003), esp. 12 and 138.
52. Commandant, Arras gendarmes, to minister of war, 2 Jan. 1816, SHD 3D/18, quoted in Veve, *Duke of Wellington,* 84.
53. Reports from Seine on students in Paris, AN, F7/6693; report from Préfecture des Bouches-du-Rhône: Bureau militaire et de police to minister of police, Marseille, 13 Mar. 1818, AN, F7/6692.
54. Démier, *La France de la Restauration,* 265.
55. Vicomte de Chateaubriand, *De la monarchie selon la Charte* (Paris: Le Normant, 1816), discussed in Waresquiel and Yvert, *Histoire de la Restauration,* 193.
56. Quote from Charléty, *La Restauration,* 125, cited in Démier, *La France de la Restauration,* 265.

57. In addition to the Protocols of the Council of Allied Ambassadors, BNA, FO 146/6, 14, 15, 22, 23, and 30, see Serna, *La République des girouettes,* esp. ch. 5, "La girouette: Quand le *Nain jaune* et sa cohorte tiennent la girouette sur les fonts baptismaux." On the relative liberty of the press in the Netherlands in this period, see David Todd Caraway, "Retreat from Liberalism: William I, Freedom of the Press, Political Asylum, and the Foreign Relations of the United Kingdom of the Netherlands, 1814–1818" (PhD diss., University of Delaware, 2003).
58. Report on "metamorphosis" of *Nain jaune* in *JP,* 31 July 1815, and Serna, *La République des girouettes,* 203.
59. *Les trois nains littéraires, Ou les bâtards du Nain jaune, se disputant ses dépouilles,* watercolor engraving by Pierre Adam and Eugène Delacroix (Paris: Martinet, 1815), BNF.
60. *Le nain vert,* esp. 7 Aug. 1815; *Le géant noir* (published by Delaunay, Sept.–Oct. 1815), 1 Oct. 1815.
61. AN, F18/40 (Censure); report from Mons, 13 June 1816, AN, F7/3826; Louis Viel-Castel, *Histoire de la Restauration* (Paris: Lévy frères, 1861), 4:455–456; Jean Breuillard, "L'occupation russe en France, 1816–1818," Part I, typescript ms. for *Revue des études slaves,* AD Ardennes, 1J/486; Stuart Semmel, *Napoleon and the British* (New Haven, CT: Yale University Press, 2004), esp. ch. 6, "Radicals, 'Legitimacy,' and History."
62. Richelieu to Osmond, Paris, 11 Feb. 1818, in *Lettres du Duc de Richelieu,* 155–156.
63. Report on investigation of fire at Wellington's hôtel in Paris, June–Aug. 1816, and report on "bruits publics," 1 Nov. 1817, both in AN, F7/6929.
64. Wellington to Bathurst, Paris, 12 Feb. 1818, in *WSD* 12: 271–273.
65. Report on the Bourse, 11 Feb. 1818, APP, AA 342 (Affaire Duc de Wellington, 1818); report from bureau at Porte Saint-Denis, 12 Feb. 1818, AN, F7/3839; reports from stagecoach drivers in provinces in Feb. 1818, esp. from Nantes, departing 26 Feb., AN, F7/3827.
66. Prince regent to Wellington, Carlton House, 14 Feb. 1818; Bathurst to Wellington, Downing Street, 21 Feb. 1818; Wellington to Bathurst, Paris, 25 Feb. 1818, all in *WSD,* vol. 12.
67. Wellington to Bathurst, Paris, 16 Feb., in *WSD,* vol. 12; Richelieu to Osmond, 19 Feb. 1818, *Lettres du Duc de Richelieu.*
68. Richelieu to Osmond, Paris, 23 Feb. 1818, in *Lettres du Duc de Richelieu;* APP, AA 342 (Affaire Duc de Wellington, 1818).
69. Kinnaird to Murray, Brussels, 30 Jan. 1818, enclosed with letter from Wellington to Bathurst, Paris, 12 Feb. 1818, in *WSD,* 12:273–275.
70. Wellington to Earl of Clancarty, Paris, 12 Feb. 1818, and Earl of Clancarty to Wellington, The Hague, 19 Feb. 1818, in *WSD,* 12:275 and 308–309.
71. Earl of Clancarty to Wellington, The Hague, 25 Feb. 1818, in *WSD* 12:336–337; Philip Henry, 5th Earl Stanhope, *Notes of Conversations with the Duke of Wellington, 1831–1851* (New York: Da Capo Press, 1973), 75–76; and *Le nouvel homme gris: Ephémérides politiques constitutionnels* 1, no. 1 (1818):

43. For a summary of the investigation, see also Decazes to Wellington, Etiole [Étiolles], 16 Aug. 1818, in *WSD* 12:640–641.
72. Wellington to Earl of Clancarty, Cambrai, 17 July 1818, in *WSD* 12:601–602.
73. Lord Kinnaird to Chamber of Peers, Paris, 15 Apr. 1818, with accompanying "Mémoire" regarding the case, in *WSD* 12:472–478.
74. *Mémoire pour Marie-André-Nicolas Cantillon, accusé d'avoir tiré un coup de pistolet sur la voiture du duc de Wellington; par Claveau, avocat et docteur en droit* (Paris, 3 Nov. 1818), AN, F7/6674.
75. Exposé by avocat-général Colomb, Cour d'Assises de Paris, 10 May 1819, transcribed in supplement to *Journal des débats,* 13 May 1819, AN, F7/6675.
76. Codicil of testament of Napoleon, quoted in obituary of Cantillon, from unnamed newspaper based on report in *Indépendance belge* [1869], which misdates assassination attempt to 1815 not 1818, in APP, AA 418; response of Wellington, quoted in Baptiste Capefigue, *Les diplomates européens* (Paris: Comptoir des Imprimeurs-Unis, 1843), 235–236.
77. Robert S. Alexander, *Bonapartism and Revolutionary Tradition in France: The Fédérés of 1815* (Cambridge: Cambridge University Press, 1991), 14. On Bonapartism, see also Sudhir Hazareesingh, *The Legend of Napoleon* (London: Granta Books, 2004), and Hazareesingh, *The Saint-Napoleon: Celebrations of Sovereignty in Nineteenth-Century France* (Cambridge, MA: Harvard University Press, 2004); Bernard Ménager, *Les Napoléon du peuple* (Paris: Aubier, 1988); and J. Lucas-Dubreton, *Le culte de Napoléon, 1815–1848* (Paris: Albin Michel, 1960).
78. Reports from Chalon-sur-Saône, AN, F7/3826 and 3827; Georges Livet, ed., *Histoire de Colmar* (Toulouse: Editions Privat, 1983), 137; report on division of Palais-Royal, 7 Feb. 1818, AN, F7/3839; Ploux, *De bouche à oreille,* 12.
79. Report from Strasbourg, departing 19 Jan. 1818, AN, F7/3827; report from Toulouse, departing 3 Oct. 1818, AN, F7/3827. On the material culture of Bonapartism, see, Hazareesingh, *Legend of Napoleon,* and Ménager, *Les Napoléon du people.*
80. Alexander, *Bonapartism,* 257, and André and Tudesq, *Restoration and Reaction,* 288–290.
81. Ploux, *De bouche à oreille,* 417; Hazareesingh, *Legend of Napoleon,* esp. ch. 6, "The Prince of Liberal Ideas."
82. Semmel, *Napoleon and the British,* 226–227; Alan Sked, *Metternich and Austria: An Evaluation* (New York: Palgrave Macmillan, 2008), 9.
83. Maximilien Lamarque to female friend, Amsterdam, 27 Dec. 1817 (Letter XVIII), in *Mémoires et souvenirs du Général Maximien Lamarque, publiés par sa famille,* (Paris: H. Fournier Jeune, 1836), 3:319–320.
84. Protocols of the Council of Allied Ambassadors, 9 Nov. 1817, BNA, FO 146/22.
85. Wellington to Bathurst, Paris, 8 Mar. 1818, *WSD* 12:380–381.
86. Démier, *La France de la Restauration,* 315–316.

CHAPTER NINE ✢ LIBERATION

1. This conference is discussed briefly in Paul Schroeder, *The Transformation of European Politics, 1763–1848* (Oxford: Clarendon, 1994), 592–593. Otherwise, histories of the conference are very dated: J. H. Creux, *La libération du territoire en 1818* (Paris: Didier et Cie., 1875); V. A. Nigohosian, *La libération du territoire français après Waterloo, 1815–1818,* (Paris: E. de Boccard, 1929); Charles Lacretelle, *Histoire de France depuis la Restauration,* 4 vols. (Paris: Delaunay, 1829–1835); Baptiste Capefigue, *Histoire de la Restauration et des causes qui ont amené la chute de la branche aînée des Bourbons,* vol. 5 (Paris: Dufév et Vézard, 1832); Albert Maurin, *Histoire de la chute des Bourbons: Grandeur et décadence de la bourgeoisie, 1815–1830–1848,* vol. 1 (Paris: Bureaux de la Société des Travailleurs réunis, 1849); Ernest Daudet, *Histoire de la Restauration, 1814–1830* (Paris: Hachette, 1882). Glenda Sluga reexamines the role of bankers in this and other post-Napoleonic congresses in forging the modern liberal international order, in "'Who Holds the Balance of the World?' Bankers at the Congress of Vienna, and in International History," *American Historical Review* 122, no. 5 (2017): 1401–1430.
2. [Narcisse-Achille de Salvandy], *La Coalition et la France* (Paris: Delaunay, 1817).
3. The above discussion of the troop reduction of 1817 is based on Thomas Dwight Veve, *The Duke of Wellington and the British Army of Occupation, 1815–1818* (Westport, CT: Greenwood Press, 1992), ch. 8, "The Troop Reduction of 1817," plus Appendix C, "Note of 10 Feb. 1817," as well Guillaume de Bertier de Sauvigny, *The Bourbon Restoration,* trans. Lynn M. Case (Philadelphia: University of Pennsylvania Press, 1966), 153–154. A "Memorandum of the Note on the Reduction of the Army of Occupation" was drafted by Wellington in a letter to the British ambassador to France, Sir Charles Stuart, on 9 Jan. 1817, in *WSD* 11:589–594. For additional detail, see AAE, Fonds France, vols. 694, 699, 709, and 710. On the financial arrangements, see also Nigohosian, *La libération*; S. Charléty, *La Restauration, 1815–1830,* vol. 4 of *Histoire de France contemporaine depuis la Révolution jusqu'à la paix de 1919,* ed. Ernest Lavisse (Paris: Hachette, 1921), 114; André Nicolle, "The Problem of Reparations after the Hundred Days," *Journal of Modern History* 25, no. 4 (1953): 343–354; and Eugene N. White, "Making the French Pay: The Costs and Consequences of the Napoleonic Reparations," *European Review of Economic History* 5 [2001]: 337–365.
4. Württemberger Marsch Plan, Apr. 1817, HStA Stuttgart, E 289 a/Bü 280 (Bezeichnung des Bestands : Mobile Kommandobehörden I: Verordnungen und Mitteilungen des Kriegsdepartements, des Chefs des Generalstabs des 8. Österreichischen Armeekorps une französischen Stellen an das Kommando des württembergischen Okkupationskorps im Elsaβ, 1816–1818); Nesselrode to chargé d'affaires of King of Saxony, St. Petersburg, 6/18 Oct. 1816, HstA Dresden, Bestand 10025 (Geheimes Konsilium), Loc. 6373/09 (Die Verpflegung

der kaiserlich österreichischen, kaiserlich russischen und königlich pruβischen und der mit ihnen verbündeten Truppen in dem Kriege gegen Frankreich und die deshalb getroffenen Veranstaltungen, 1816–1819); J. Breuillard, "L'occupation russe à Givet de 1816 à 1818, d'après les mémoires du Gén.-Baron V. I. Loewenstern," *Revue historique ardennaise* 12 (1977): 65.

5. Minister of interior to prefect of Haut-Rhin, Paris, 21 Feb. 1817, AD Haut-Rhin, 8R/1174; report from subprefect of Meurthe to ministry of police, 7 Apr. 1817, AN, F7/9899; correspondence between Württemberger department of war, Sir George Murray, and Duke of Wellington, Apr. 1817, HStA Stuttgart, E 270 a/Bü472.
6. Minister of interior to prefect of Nord, Paris, 20 July 1818, regarding insult by a wagon driver that provoked Wellington to issue order requiring all wagons to bear signs indicating the name of their owner, AD Nord, 8R/12.
7. Lt. Col. Sir Henry Hardinge to Lt. Gen. Sir George Murray, Sedan, 16 Feb. 1818, in *WSD* 12:345–346; report from subprefect of Verdun, 5 Feb. 1818, AN, F7/9900.
8. Subprefect of Verdun to ministry of police, 12 Apr. 1818, AN, F7/9900.
9. Creux, *La libération,* 79, and Veve, *Duke of Wellington,* ch. 7, "Wellington and the Barrier Fortresses."
10. Bertier de Sauvigny, *Bourbon Restoration,* 154; Richelieu to Osmond, 10 Apr. 1817, in *Lettres du Duc de Richelieu au Marquis d'Osmond, 1816–1818,* ed. Sébastien Charlety, 7th ed. (Paris: Gallimard, 1939); Wellington to Castlereagh, Paris, 21 July 1817, in *WSD* 12:1–2.
11. On these negotiations, see *WSD,* vol. 12, esp. Gen. Walterstorff of Denmark to Wellington, 14 Feb. 1818; Wellington to Castlereagh, 16 and 19 Apr. 1818; and Wellington to Earl of Clancarty, 23 Apr. 1818.
12. *Minerve français* II (June 1818), 387, quoted in Nicolle, "Problem of Reparations," 350; see also Daudet, *Histoire de la Restauration,* 126, and White, "Making the French Pay," 347.
13. Creux, *La libération,* 208–210; Bertier de Sauvigny, *Bourbon Restoration,* 154–155.
14. Earl Stanhope, Address on the Prince Regent's Speech at the Opening of the Session, 27 Jan. 1818, *Hansard's,* vol. 37, cc. 5–17.
15. Commissaire général at Cambrai, to minister of police, Valenciennes, 8 Feb. 1818, AN, F7/9901; Duke of Wellington to Earl of Liverpool, Paris, 4 Feb. 1818, in *WSD* 12:249.
16. *Chronique parisienne,* no. 14 (1818), 187, as well as nos. 12 and 13; *Réponse au discours de Milord Stanhope, sur l'occupation de la France par l'armée étrangère,* 2nd ed. (Paris: L'Huillier et Delaunay, 1818), esp. 24. Other responses to the Allied opposition to evacuation include [Narcisse-Achille de Salvandy], *Lettre au Lord Duc de Wellington, sur l'événement du 10 au 11 février; par l'auteur de la Coalition et la France* (Paris: Plancher, 1818), and Gén. Baron Jubé, *Lettre d'un Français à Lord Stanhope et Réflexions sur l'événement arrivé à Lord Wellington, dans la nuit du 10 au 11 février* (Paris: Plancher, 1818).

The French reaction is also evident in police records, e.g., in reports from stagecoach drivers departing from Valenciennes, 24 and 29 Mar. 1818, AN, F7/3827.

17. Richelieu to Osmond, 12 and 16 Mar. 1818, in *Lettres du Duc de Richelieu.*
18. Éléonore-Adèle d'Osmond, Comtesse de Boigne, *Mémoires de la Comtesse de Boigne, née d'Osmond: Récits d'une tante*, ed. Jean-Claude Berchet, vol. 1, *Du règne de Louis XVI à 1820* (Paris: Plon-Nourrit, 1907), 695; *Note secrète exposant les prétextes et le but de la dernière conspiration,* 2nd ed. (Paris: Foulon; Delaunay et Pélicier; Eymery, 1818); *De l'intervention des étrangers dans le gouvernement de la France* (Paris: P. Mongie l'ainé, 1819); Castlereagh quoted in Veve, *Duke of Wellington,* 149.
19. Veve, *Duke of Wellington,* 149, and Bertier de Sauvigny, *Bourbon Restoration,* 151–153.
20. For evidence of such "noises," see *Le nouvel homme gris: Ephémérides politiques constitutionnelles* 1 (1818): 42; reports from Strasbourg, 30 June, and Mulhouse, 1 July 1818, as well as numerous other reports from around France on rumors the congress was delayed and the evacuation would not occur, AN, F7/3827; note "Politique et faits," London, 9 Sept. 1818, AN, F7/6667; report from Besançon, departing 30 Sept. 1818, AN, F7/3839.
21. Report from Sedan, departing 8 July 1818, AN, F7/3827; report from Baron Delcambre, maréchal de camp, Châlons-sur-Marne, to ministry of war, 15 July 1818, SHD, 3D/54; commissaire général in Moselle to ministry of police, Metz, 24 June 1818, AN, F7/9900.
22. *MU,* 22 Aug. 1818.
23. Requests for passports to travel to Aix-la-Chapelle in 1818, AN, F7/12121; [Villemarest], *L'Observateur au Congrès . . .* (Paris: A. Eymery, 1818); *MU,* 17 Oct. 1818.
24. Lt. Col. Sir Henry Hardinge to Lt. Gen. Sir George Murray, Sedan, 11 Aug. 1818, in *WSD* 12:640; *MU,* 3 Oct. 1818, article from "Prusse. Aix-la-Chapelle."
25. Veve, *Duke of Wellington,* 155.
26. Emmanuel Waresquiel, *Le Duc de Richelieu, 1766–1822* (Paris: Perrin, 1990), 340; *MU,* 16 and 17 Oct. 1818; [Villemarest], *L'Observateur au Congrès,* 61.
27. *Lettres sur le Congrès d'Aix-la-Chapelle* (Paris: J.-L. Chanson, 1818), 91; *Le nouvel homme gris* 1, no. 2 (1818): 93–94.
28. Richelieu to Decazes, 28 Sept. 1818, in Ernest Daudet, ed., "Le Duc de Richelieu au Congrès d'Aix-la-Chapelle, 1818: Correspondance inédite," *La nouvelle revue* 114 (1898): 206.
29. Creux, *La libération,* 245–246.
30. Maurin, *Histoire,* 446; Bertier de Sauvigny, *Bourbon Restoration,* 156; and Creux, *La libération,* 255.
31. Metternich, quoted in Alan Sked, *Metternich and Austria: An Evaluation* (New York: Palgrave Macmillan, 2008), 74; Creux, *La libération,* 255. See also Schroeder, *Transformation of European Politics,* 592–593.
32. Reports from stagecoach drivers to ministry of police in AN, F7/3827 (July–Dec. 1818).

33. Comtesse de Boigne, *Mémoires,* 1:715; police report on English leaving hotels in Paris, section of Palais-Royal, 19 Oct. 1818, AN, F7/3839.
34. *MU,* 15 and 28 Oct. 1818.
35. Letter from Cambrai, 16 Oct. 1818, Rev. Stonestreet Papers, BL, Add. Ms. 61805; Jean-Louis Renteux, "Les Anglais à Valenciennes," *Valentiana* 49 (2012): 11; BMV, D1/58 (Registre de Correspondence, 2e Bureau), esp. letter to prefect, 8 Oct. 1818, and letter to subprefect, 30 Dec. 1818, regarding expenses for illumination and decoration of public edifices; reports from Valenciennes, 14 and 24 Oct., AN, F7/3827; reports from Cambrai and Valenciennes, Oct. 1818, AN, F7/3839 and 6667.
36. Report from Sedan, departing 12 Oct. 1818, AN, F7/3827; report to ministry of war on Count von Zieten order to mixed commission, 27 July 1818, SHD 3D/54; [Von] Löwenfeld to mayor of Sedan, 15 Nov. 1818, AD Ardennes, 1J/17.
37. Daudet, "Le Duc de Richelieu," 193–213.
38. Wellington, secret memorandum for the quartermaster general, the commissary general, and the commanding officer of artillery, Cambrai, 18 May 1818, and Wellington to Earl of Clancarty, Aix-la-Chapelle, 13 Oct. 1818, *WSD* 12:517 and 768; report from Valenciennes, departing 15 Oct. 1818, AN, F7/3827.
39. Poster and correspondence regarding public sale of Prussian artillery equipment, Sedan, Oct. 1818, SHD, 3D/56; report from Mulhouse, departing 15 Oct. 1818, AN, F7/3827; AM Tourcoing, 5H/16 (Mobiliers mis à disposition des alliés dans les logements: Inventaires, 1817–1818), 5H/23 (Construction d'un hangar pour l'armée saxonne: Réclamations des propriétaires: Correspondance, 1818–1819), and 5H/26 (Vente par adjudication des écuries ayant servies au logement des troupes saxonnes: Délibération du conseil municipal, ordonnance royale, correspondence, 1816–1822); AD Haut-Rhin, 8R/1124–1125 (Extrait du Registre des déclarations préalables aux ventes de meubles du Bureau de Ribeauvillé), 24 Dec. 1818, no. 408; Gustave Groeber, "L'occupation d'Oberbronn par des troupes würtembergeoises de 1816 à 1818," *Bulletin de la Société niederbronnoise d'histoire et d'archéologie* 8 (1960): 204–205.
40. Correspondence from commissaire général, Cambrai, Aug.–Nov. 1818, AN, F7/9902; report from Valenciennes, departing 17 Oct. 1818, AN, F7 /3827; Arnaud Gabet and Christianne Lepie, "La présence britannique à Cambrai de 1815 à 1848," *Cambrésis terre d'histoire* 7, Sept. 1993, 26.
41. Report on Russians near Maubeuge, early Nov. 1818, SHD, 3D/57; special commissioner to minister of police, Sedan, 28 Nov. 1818, AN, F7/9899; printed circular to mayors regarding departure of Bavarian army, Sarreguemines, 2 Nov. 1818, AM Sarreguemines, Section II, 9H57–10H7, no. 72 (Ende der Okkupation durch die Alliirten); minister of police to prefect of Meuse, 20 Oct. 1818, AD Meuse, 8R/35.
42. Plans for the evacuation of 1818 in Sir George Murray Papers, NLS, 46.7.12 and 13. For details on the numbers, routes, and requisitions of evacuating

German troops, see HStA Stuttgart, E 289 a/Bü 280 (Bezeichnung des Bestands: Mobile Kommandobehörden I: Verordnungen und Mitteilungen des Kriegsdepartements, des Chefs des Generalstabs des 8. Österreichischen Armeekorps une franzosischen Stellen an das Kommando des württembergischen Okkupationskorps im Elsaβ, 1816–1818); Bay. HStA Kriegsarchiv, B, 601 (Krieg gegen Frankreich, 1813/15: Occupationstruppen 1815/18: Ruckmarsch, Dislocirung im Rheinkreis, Durchmarsch fremder Truppen), and B, 607d (Krieg gegen Frankreich, 1813–1815: Kriegskosten Entschädigung Russland); and HStA Dresden, Bestand 11339 (Generalstab: Generaloberkommando), Num. 302 (Beiträge zur Kenntnis der gegenwärtigen Etappenstraβe für die in Frankreich stehenden sächsischen Truppen vom Hauptquartier Tourcoing, 1818); Bestand 11339, Num. 303 (Rückmarsch des mobilen Truppenkorps aus Frankreich und dessen Demobilisierung und Delogierung im Land und die damit verbundenen Auflösung der Depots des Husaren-Regiments und der leichten Infanterie sowie die Reduzierung der Mannschaft der Liniendepotbataillone, Octbre./Novbr./Decbr. 1818 und Januar 1819); Bestand 10025 (Geheimes Konsilium), Loc. 6373/09 (Die Verpflegung der kaiserlich österreichischen, kaiserlich russischen und königlich pruβischen und der mit ihnen verbündeten Truppen in dem Kriege gegen Frankreich und die deshalb getroffenen Veranstaltungen, 1816–1819); and Bestand 10026 (Geheimes Kabinett), Loc. 30041/2 (Die wegen der Verpflegung des aus Frankreich durch Sachsen zurückmarshierenden kaiserlich russischen Okkupationskorps geflogenen Verhandlungen, 1816–1818).

43. French lieutenant, quoted in Veve, *Duke of Wellington,* 162. On the organization of the evacuation, see Veve, *Duke of Wellington,* 158–161; Creux, *La libération,* 259–260; Natacha Naoumova, "Le corps d'armée russe en France, 1815–1818," in *Les occupations en Champagne-Ardenne, 1814–1944,* ed. François Cochet (Reims: Presses Universitaires de Reims, 1996), 22; and Anthony L. H. Rhinelander, *Prince Michael Vorontsov: Viceroy to the Tsar* (Montreal: McGill-Queen's University Press, 1990), 43, based on report by Vorontsov at end of occupation, 20 Dec. 1818, in Russian Archives, St. Petersburg, LOII, f. 36, op. 2, d. 58; Jules Duvivier, "La ville de Bouchain et l'Ostrevant de 1814 à 1818: L'occupation danoise," *Bulletin de la Commission historique du Nord,* vol. 34 (1933): 334; reports on Allied troop movements in SHD, 3D/56, 57, and 58; intendant militaire, member of the "commission mixte" with the Russian army to prefect of Meuse, 2 Nov. 1818, AD Meuse, 8R/35; reports from Calais, departing 27 and 28 Oct. and 7 Nov. 1818, AN, F7/3827; report from Calais, 1 Dec. 1818, AN, F7/9903.

44. Intendant militaire at Sedan, to minister of war, 10 and 11 Nov. 1818, SHD, 3D/57; Jean-Baptiste Lépine, *Histoire de la ville de Rocroi, depuis son origine jusqu'en 1850* (Rocroi: Mme. Veuve Lenoir, 1860), 245.

45. Mayor and deputies of Valenciennes to Col. Arbuthnot, Lt. Col. Blair, and Capt. Hay, Valenciennes, 9 Nov. 1818, BMV, H7/38 (Départ des troupes d'occupation); commissaire général at Cambrai to minister of police, 6

Nov. 1818, AN, F7/9901; local authority in Wissembourg to Gen. de Scheler, 3 Nov. 1818, HStA Stuttgart, E 289 a/Bü 283; Duvivier, "La ville de Bouchain," 336.

46. A. Deloffre, *Landrecies de 1814 à 1818: Fragments d'histoire locale suivis de notes biographiques et historiques sur le Maréchal Clarke, duc de Feltre, né à Landrecies (1765–1818)* (Lille: L. Danel, 1910), 192; André Sacrez, "Les russes en 'Ardenne wallonne' (1814–1818) (suite et fin)," *Ardenne wallonne* 98 (2004): 14; H. Vincent, *Histoire de la ville de Vouziers* (Reims: Matot, 1902), 274–275.
47. Georges Ozaneaux to mother, 24 Aug. 1818, in *La vie à Colmar sous la Restauration: Lettres de 1817 à 1820,* ed. Jules Joachim (Colmar: Paul Hartmann, 1929); Francis Lichtle, "L'occupation autrichienne à Colmar de 1815 à 1818," *Mémoire colmarienne: Bulletin trimestriel de liaison de la Société d'histoire et d'archéologie de Colmar* 123 (2011): 7.
48. Correspondence between Duc de Richelieu and Marquis de Latour Maubourg, with names of officers from Saxon army, 28 Dec. 1818, and between representative of king of Saxony and Latour Maubourg, 8 Feb. 1819, CAD, 206 PO/1/28 (Dresden Legation), no. 6, dossier F.
49. Deloffre, *Landrecies,* 92; Lichtle, "L'occupation autrichienne," 8; von Löwenfeld to mayor of Sedan, 15 and 16 Nov. 1818, AD Ardennes, 1J/17 (Copie des délibérations du Conseil municipal); report from commissaire of Ardennes on appearance by von Zieten before mayor and municipal council of Sedan, Mézières, 21 Nov. 1818, AN, F7/9899.
50. Veve, *Duke of Wellington,* 160–161.
51. Sr. Jacques, propriétaire at Consenvoye (Meuse) to ministry of war, 1 Dec. 1818, SHD, 3D/58. For other reports of such disorders, see SHD, 3D/57.
52. Reports on repossession of fortresses, SHD, VN 44 and 45; report from Metz, departing 29 Oct. 1818, AN, F7/3827; Georges Livet, ed., *Histoire de Colmar* (Toulouse: Editions Privat, 1983), 139; J. Breuillard, "L'occupation russe à Givet de 1816 à 1818, d'après les mémoires du Gén.-Baron V. I. Loewenstern," *Revue historique ardennaise* 12 (1977): 74.
53. Prefect of Haut-Rhin to ministry of war, Colmar, 14 Nov. 1818, SHD, 3D/56.
54. Protocol of 5 Dec. 1818, BNA, FO 146/30.
55. Philip Mansel, "Wellington et la Restauration," *Revue de la Société d'histoire de la Restauration* 2 (1988): 51; Julius Bryant, *Apsley House: The Wellington Collection* (London: English Heritage, 2005).
56. Lt.-Col. J. Leach, C. B., *Rough Sketches of the Life of an Old Soldier: During a Service in the West Indies; at the Siege of Copenhagen in 1807; in the Peninsula and the South of France in the Campaigns of 1808 to 1814, with the Light Division; in the Netherlands in 1815; including the Battles of Quatre Bras and Waterloo; with a Slight Sketch of the Three Years Passed by the Army of Occupation in France, &c., &c., &c.* (London: Longman, Rees, Orme, Brown and Green, 1831), 406; Catriona Kennedy, *Narratives of the Revolutionary and Napoleonic Wars: Military and Civilian Experience in Britain and Ireland*

(New York: Palgrave Macmillan, 2013), esp. "Conclusion"; Christine Wright, *Wellington's Men in Australia: Peninsular War Veterans and the Making of Empire, c. 1820–40* (New York: Palgrave Macmillan, 2011); Olivier Podevins, "L'occupation de Tourcoing par les troupes saxonnes entre 1816 et 1818: Un épisode peu connu de l'histoire de la ville" (article for research group on French-Saxon relations, Technical University, Dresden), 14–15, AM Tourcoing; Lichtle, "L'occupation autrichienne," 8; Rhinelander, *Prince Michael Vorontsov,* ch. 5, "The Territory," and p. 28.

57. Marc Blancpain, *La vie quotidienne dans la France du Nord sous les occupations, 1814–1944* (Paris: Hachette, 1983), 95.
58. Reports from Calais, 15 Oct. and 22 Nov. 1818, AN, F7/9903.
59. [John Gordon Smith], *The English Army in France: Being the Personal Narrative of an Officer* (London: Henry Colburn and Richard Bentley, 1830), 2:185–187.
60. Leach, *Rough Sketches,* 405–406.
61. See, for instance, Lépine, *Histoire,* 245, as well as reports on the duc's visits to various towns, to ministry of war, SHD, 3D/56.
62. *MU,* 23 Nov. 1818; *Le nouvel homme gris* 2, no. 1 (1818): 40 and 45.
63. Quoted in *Le nouvel homme gris* 2, no. 1 (1818): 45.
64. D. P. E., *Vrais et incroyables regrets, en forme de complainte, sur le départ des Alliés* (Paris: Brasseur, 1819). See also P.-A. Ducis, *Ode sur le départ des troupes étrangères* (Paris: P. Didot, 1818), and D. F. D*** [Decors], *Le neuf octobre mil huit cent dix-huit, ou le départ des troupes alliées* (Paris: Alexis Eymery, 1818).
65. Print *Départ des Prussiens,* in Armand Dayot, ed., *La Restauration (Louis XVIII-Charles X) d'après l'image du temps* (Paris: Revue Blanche, 1900), 62.
66. Jean-Baptiste Dubois et Brazier, *Une heure sur la frontière: À-propos en un acte, mêlé de couplets représenté pour la première fois à Paris, sur le Théatre de la Gaîté, le 24 nov. 1818* (Paris: J.-N. Barba, 1819); *Galignani's Messenger,* 27 Nov. 1818.
67. Armand Gouffé and Belle aîné, *Le retour à Valenciennes, ou Rentrons chez nous, Vaudeville en un acte, représenté, pour la première fois, à Paris, sur le Théatre de la Porte-Saint-Martin, le 1er Déc. 1818* (Paris: Barba, 1818); *Galignani's Messenger,* 1 Dec. 1818.
68. *La route d'Aix-la-Chapelle, Tableau-Vaudeville, en un acte,* first performed at Théatre du Vaudeville, 9 Nov. 1818 (Paris: Mme Huet-Masson, 1818).
69. Revised conventions, Nigohosian, *La libération,* Appendices XI–XVI; Nicolle, "Problem of Reparations," 353; Creux, *La libération,* ch. 4, "Crise financière"; A. Calmon, *Histoire parlementaire des finances de la Restauration* (Paris: Michel Lévy Frères, 1868), vol. 1, chs. 3, "Traités de 1815 et conditions imposées à la France," and 4, "Situation des partis dans la chambre de 1819."
70. Report from Calais, departing 27 Dec. 1818, and other reports from around France in Dec. 1818, AN, F7/3827; extract of telegraph from Uichtritz to Saxon minister, Paris, 16 Nov. 1818, HStA Dresden, Bestand 10026 (Geheimes

Kabinett), Loc. 2521/5 (Die bei der Krone Frankreich zu liquidierenden Forderungen, 1818).

71. Emmanuel de Waresquiel and Benoît Yvert, *Histoire de la Restauration, 1814–1830: Naissance de la France moderne* (Paris: Perrin, 1996), 243–253; Waresquiel, *Le Duc de Richelieu,* 349–351.
72. Christopher Hibbert, *Wellington: A Personal History* (Boston: Da Capo Press, 1997).
73. *Dépêches inédites du Chevalier de Gentz aux Hospodars de Valachie pour servir à l'histoire de la politique européene, 1813 à 1828,* ed. Comte Prokesch-Osten fils (Paris: Plon, 1876), 1:416–419.
74. Reports from stagecoach drivers to ministry of police, ca. Dec. 1818, AN, F7/3827; diary of Countess Malmesbury, Dec. 1818, Sir Lowry Cole Papers, BNA, PRO 30/43/38; and report from general secretary of prefecture of police, Hôtel de Ville, Paris, 28 Dec. 1818, AN, F7/3839.
75. George S. Williamson, "What Killed August von Kotzebue? The Temptations of Virtue and the Political Theology of German Nationalism, 1789–1819," *The Journal of Modern History* 72:4 (2000): 890–943; John D. Post, *The Last Great Subsistence Crisis in the Western World* (Baltimore, MD: Johns Hopkins University Press, 1977), esp. 171–172; Richard Stites, *The Four Horsemen: Riding to Liberty in Post-Napoleonic Europe* (Oxford: Oxford University Press, 2014); Joseph L. Wieczynski, "The Mutiny of the Semenovsky Regiment in 1820," *The Russian Review* 29, no. 2 (1970): 167–180; Marie-Pierre Rey, *Le dilemme russe: La Russie et l'Europe occidentale d'Ivan le Terrible à Boris Eltsine* (Paris: Flammarion, 2002), 147.
76. Nick Mansfeld, "Military Radicals and the Making of Class, 1790–1860," in *Soldiering in Britain and Ireland, 1750–1850: Men of Arms,* ed. Catriona Kennedy and Matthew McCormack (New York: Palgrave Macmillan, 2013), 66, and Jenny Uglow, *In These Times: Living in Britain through Napoleon's Wars, 1793–1815* (New York: Farrar, Strauss & Giroux, 2014), 638.
77. Post, *The Last Great Subsistence Crisis*, ch. 6, "The Political Epilogue."
78. H. Lebert, Foulard "Le Départ des Alliés en 1818" and relevant catalog entry and dossier, Musée de l'Impression sur Étoffes, Mulhouse; manuscript journal of H. Lebert, Bibliothèque des Dominicains, Colmar, esp. entries from Feb. 1816 and Oct. 1818 (vol. 3, pp. 6 and 91), generously provided to me by Fabienne Montchaud.

CONCLUSION

1. Finn Valentin Nerland, "Danske fredsbevarende tropper i Frankrig, 1815–1818," *Krigshistorisk Tidsskrift* 39, no. 1 (2003): 25–26 (translated by Willem Osuch).
2. *The Autobiography of Lieutenant-General Sir Harry Smith, Baronet of Aliwal on the Sutlej, G. C. B.,* ed. G. C. Moore Smith, M.A. (London: John Murray, 1903), 315.

3. On the outpouring of memoirs in the wake of these wars, see Catriona Kennedy, *Narratives of the Revolutionary and Napoleonic Wars: Military and Civilian Experience in Britain and Ireland* (New York: Palgrave Macmillan, 2013), and Leighton James, *Witnessing the Revolutionary and Napoleonic Wars in German Central Europe* (New York: Palgrave Macmillan, 2013).
4. Cited (in English translation) in Glynn Barratt, *The Rebel on the Bridge: A Life of the Decembrist Baron Andrey Rozen, 1800–84* (Athens: Ohio University Press, 1975), 37–38.
5. Carl Friedrich von Blumen, *Von Jena bis Neiße: Militär- und Kulturgeschictliche Bilder aus den Jahren 1806–1819,* ed. C. M. von Unruh (Leipzig: Georg Wigand, 1904), 211.
6. *Autobiography of Lieutenant-General Sir Harry Smith,* 308 and 334.
7. Barratt, *Rebel on the Bridge,* 37–38; Marie-Pierre Rey, *1814: Un Tsar à Paris* (Paris: Flammarion, 2014), 243.
8. On the role of the wars in the development of British nationalism see, in addition to the classic work by Linda Colley, *Britons: Forging the Nation, 1707–1837* (New Haven, CT: Yale University Press, 1992), which overlooks the occupation, Gerald Newman, *The Rise of English Nationalism: A Cultural History, 1740–1830* (London: St. Martin's, 1987), and Kennedy, *Narratives,* esp. 111–112.
9. In addition to James, *Witnessing the Revolutionary and Napoleonic Wars,* see Ute Planert, "From Collaboration to Resistance: Politics, Experience, and Memory of the Revolutionary and Napoleonic Wars in Southern Germany," *Central European History* 39 (2006): 676–705, and Katherine Aaslestad, "Remembering and Forgetting: The Local and the Nation in Hamburg's Commemorations of the Wars of Liberation," *Central European History* 38, no. 3: 384–416.
10. Karen Hagemann, "Occupation, Mobilization and Politics: The Anti-Napoleonic Wars in Prussian Experience, Memory, and Historiography," *Central European History* 39, no. 4 (2006): 609. On this point, see also Hagemann, *Revisiting Prussia's Wars against Napoleon: History, Culture and Memory,* trans. Pamela Selwyn (Cambridge: Cambridge University Press, 2015), and Volker Wacker, *Die allierte Besetzung Frankreichs in den Jahren 1814 bis 1818* (Hamburg: Dr. Kovač, 1999).
11. British officer to mayor of Valenciennes, 6 Nov. 1818, BMV, H7/38; Jean-Louis Rentaux, "Les Anglais à Valenciennes, 1815–1818," *Valentiana* 49 (2012): 7.
12. R. Wauthier, "Les Russes à Givet, 1816–1818," *Revue historique ardennaise* 19 (1912): 155–161; André Sacrez, "Les russes en 'Ardenne wallonne' (1814–1818)," *Ardenne wallonne* 97 (2004): 2–11, and Sacrez, "Les russes en 'Ardenne wallonne' (1814–1818) (suite et fin)," *Ardenne wallonne* 98 (2004): 10–17; Lt.-Col. Lesage, "Communication sur l'état actuel des bornes de distances russes du département des Ardennes," *Revue historique des Ardennes* 15 (1980): 88–92; J. Breuillard, "L'occupation russe à Givet de 1816 à 1818, d'après les mémoires du Gén.-Baron V. I. Loewenstern," *Revue historique ardennaise* 12 (1977): 66.

13. Jacques Hantraye, "Rebâtir après les défaites napoléoniennes: Les enjeux de la reconstruction immobilière dans la France du Nord et de l'Est (1814–1860)," *Annales historiques de la Révolution française* 2 (2007): 188; Hantraye, "Questions autour de la mort et de la sépulture des militaires en Lorraine lors des ocupations de la fin du Premier Empire et du début de la Restauration (1813–1817)," *Empreinte militaire en Lorraine,* August 2013, https://lorexplor.istex.fr/Wicri/Europe/France/Lorraine/fr/index.php?title=Empreinte_militaire_en_Lorraine_(08-2013)_Jacques_Hantraye&oldid=7661; and Bernadette Retournard and Marie-Agnès Sonrier, "Chaumont au contact de l'occupant, 1814–1815," in *Les occupations en Champagne-Ardenne: 1814–1944,* ed. François Cochet (Reims: Presses Universitaires de Reims, 1996), 51–75.
14. H. Vincent, *Histoire de la ville de Vouziers* (Reims: Matot, 1902), 273, courtesy of librarian at Bibliothèque Municipale de Vouziers. On this rebuilding effort, see Hantraye, "Rebâtir."
15. Jacques Hantraye, *Les Cosaques aux Champs-Élysées: L'occupation de la France après la chute de Napoléon* (Paris: Belin, 2005), 142.
16. Ibid., 144.
17. Petition from Jacques Elloy, garde-champêtre at Mansieullen, commune d'Anoux (Moselle), to Emperor Louis Napoleon, 16 Dec. 1852, AN, F2I/1696 (Ministère de l'Intérieur: Administration départementale: Réclamations de particuliers, 1814–1815/1852–1855).
18. Marie-Cécile Thoral, *From Valmy to Waterloo: France at War, 1792–1815,* trans. Godfrey Rogers (New York: Palgrave Macmillan, 2011), 214–215; David Hopkin, "Legends of the Allied Invasions and Occupations of Eastern France, 1792–1815," in *The Bee and the Eagle: Napoleonic France and the End of the Holy Roman Empire, 1806,* ed. Alan Forrest and Peter H. Wilson (New York: Palgrave Macmillan, 2009), 214–233; Ernest Denormandie, *Notes et souvenirs,* 2nd ed. (Paris: Société anonyme de publications périodiques, 1896), 195.
19. Marc Blancpain, *La vie quotidienne dans la France du Nord sous les occupations, 1814–1944* (Paris: Hachette, 1983), 387–388.
20. For examples, see: F.-E. Pougiat, *1814–1815: Invasion des armées étrangères, dans le Département de l'Aube* (Troyes: Bourquot; Laloy, 1833); A. Deloffre, *Landrecies de 1814 à 1818: Fragments d'histoire locale suivis de notes biographiques et historiques sur le Maréchal Clarke, duc de Feltre, né à Landrecies (1765–1818)* (Lille: L. Danel, 1910); Wauthier, "Les Russes à Givet," 155–161; Octave Beuve, ed., *L'invasion de 1814–1815 en Champagne: Souvenirs inédits* (Nancy: Berger-Levrault, 1914); Max Bruchet, "L'invasion et l'occupation du Nord par les alliés, 1814–1818," *Revue du Nord* 6 (1920): 261–299; Bruchet, "L'invasion et l'occupation du Nord par les alliés, 1814–1818 (suite)," *Revue du Nord* 7 (1921): 30–61; and Paul Leuilliot, "L'occupation alliée à Colmar et dans le Haut-Rhin, 1815–1818," *Annuaire de Colmar* 3 (1937): 157–164.
21. On the erasure of the memory of the occupation, see Christine Haynes, "Remembering and Forgetting the First Modern Occupations of France," *Journal of Modern History* 88, no. 3 (2016): 535–571.

22. See, for instance, Comte d'Haussonville, *Ma jeunesse, 1814–1830: Souvenirs* (Paris: Michel Lévy Frères, 1885); *Mémoires et souvenirs du Baron Hyde de Neuville,* ed. Vicomtesse de Bardonnet, 3 vols. (Paris: Plon, Nourrit et Cie., 1888–1892); Chancelier Pasquier, *Mémoires,* ed. Duc d'Audifret-Pasquier, 4 vols., 3rd ed. (Paris: Plon, Nourrit et Cie., 1893–1895); and Henry Houssaye, *1815,* 3 vols. (Paris: 1893–1895).
23. Roger André, *L'occupation de la France par les Alliés en 1815 (juillet-novembre)* (Paris: Boccard, 1924), esp. 164; Blancpain, *La vie quotidienne.* The one notable exception is Hantraye, *Les Cosaques.*
24. Mark Jarrett, *The Congress of Vienna and Its Legacy: War and Great Power Diplomacy after Napoleon* (London: I. B. Tauris, 2013), 369–371; Robert Gerwarth, *The Vanquished: Why the First World War Failed to End* (New York: Farrar, Strauss and Giroux, 2016), 171.
25. Henry Kissinger, *A World Restored: Metternich, Castlereagh and the Problems of Peace, 1812–1822* (Boston: Houghton Mifflin, 1957). On the settlement of World War II, see Michael Neiberg, *Potsdam: The End of World War II and the Remaking of Europe* (New York: Basic Books, 2015), and Susan Caruthers, *The Good Occupation: American Soldiers and the Hazards of Peace* (Cambridge, MA: Harvard University Press, 2016), esp. ch. 1, "Preparing to Occupy."
26. See, for example, David M. Edelstein, *Occupational Hazards: Success and Failure in Military Occupation* (Ithaca, NY: Cornell University Press, 2008), and Frederick Herman, "The Victors and the Vanquished: The Quest for Security as Illustrated by the Three Allied Occupations of Territory of the Defeated Power—France, 1815–1818; Germany, 1919–1929; and Germany, 1945" (PhD diss., Fletcher School of Law and Diplomacy, Tufts and Harvard University, 1954).
27. Thomas Dwight Veve, *The Duke of Wellington and the British Army of Occupation in France, 1815–1818* (Westport, CT: Greenwood Press, 1992), 167.
28. In *Songs of Béranger Done into English Verse,* trans. William Young, new ed. (Edinburgh: William Blackwood and Sons, 1878). On the context of this song, see Sophie-Anne Leterrier, *Béranger: Des chansons pour un peuple citoyen* (Rennes: Presses Universitaires de Rennes, 2013).
29. Description of color lithograph vignette accompanying a text of the song, "Chansons Politique de Béranger: La Sainte Alliance des Peuples" (Brussels: Tencé frères, n.d.), with reference to *Le nouvel homme gris,* no. 20, 1819, in Anne-Marie Rosset, ed., *La Restauration et les Cent Jours,* vol. 5 of *Un siècle d'histoire de France par l'estampe, 1770–1871: Collection de Vinck—Inventaire analytique,* ed. François-Louis Bruel (Paris: Imprimerie nationale, 1938), 429.
30. Jean Touchard, *La gloire de Béranger* (Paris: Armand Colin, 1968), 2:223.

Acknowledgments

THIS BOOK HAS gifted me with far more adventures than I ever expected when I set out to research it. One of the nicest surprises has been the many friends I have made along the way. First, I must thank Nicolas Bourguinat, who (without ever having met me) graciously agreed to host me at the Université de Strasbourg for a Fulbright Research Fellowship sponsored by the Conseil Régional d'Alsace in 2013–2014. In addition to endorsing my application for that fellowship and helping me with the paperwork required for my stay, Nicolas provided me with extensive suggestions on an early book proposal. He also invited me to present some of my preliminary research to a small conference on the collapse of the Napoleonic Empire and in two journals at the Université de Strasbourg, *SOURCE(S)* and *Revue d'Allemagne et des pays de langue allemande*. For recommending me for a Fulbright, I am thankful to Lloyd Kramer and Sheryl Kroen. Without the year in France funded by the Fulbright, the archival research for this book would not have been possible—or would have taken much longer. I thus gratefully acknowledge the Fulbright program as well as the Franco-American Commission in Paris, especially Arnaud Roujou de Boubée, Patricia Janin, and Emily Resnier, who facilitated and enriched my year in France. The Commission also generously awarded me a small travel grant to visit the Centre des Archives Diplomatiques in Nantes. At the Université de Strasbourg, Marie Deroche kindly assisted my family with visas. The extended stay in France afforded my family an opportunity to get to know the country and language better, make new friends, and travel widely in Europe. It was a transformative experience for all of us, for which I cannot thank the Fulbright program enough.

My research was also funded by a Franklin Research Grant from the American Philosophical Society; a Faculty Research Visit Grant from the Deutscher Akademischer Auftauschdienst (DAAD); a Cotlow Fellowship from the Department of History at the University of North Carolina at Charlotte; and three Faculty Research Grants from UNC-Charlotte. I thank these sponsors for their support. Much of the writing was supported by a Re-Assignment of Duties Leave from the College of Liberal Arts and Sciences at the University of North Carolina at Charlotte. For this, as well as for two small grants toward research travel and image fees, I thank Dean

Nancy Gutierrez. At UNC-Charlotte, Joël Gallegos in the Office of International Programs also generously provided financial assistance for international research and conference travel on several occasions.

In Europe, I benefited from the expertise of librarians and archivists at the following institutions: Archives Nationales (Pierrefitte-sur-Seine); Archives des Affaires Étrangères (Courneuve); Archives de la Préfecture de Police (Paris); Archives du Département des Ardennes (Charleville-Mézières); Archives du Département du Bas-Rhin (Strasbourg); Archives du Département du Haut-Rhin (Colmar); Archives du Département de la Meurthe-et-Moselle (Nancy); Archives du Département de la Meuse (Bar-le-Duc); Archives du Département de la Moselle (St.-Julien-lès-Metz); Archives du Département du Nord (Lille); Archives du Département de la Seine (Paris); Archives Municipales de Colmar; Archives Municipales de Pont-à-Mousson; Archives Municipales de Sarreguemines; Archives Municipales de Tourcoing; Archives Municipales de Wissembourg; Archives de la Ville et de l'Eurométropole de Strasbourg; Bayerisches Hauptstaatsarchiv Kriegsarchiv (Munich); Bibliothèque Médiathèque de Valenciennes; Bibliothèque Nationale de France (Paris); Bibliothèque Historique de la Ville de Paris; Bibliothèque de l'Hôtel de Ville (Paris); Bibliothèque Paul Marmottan (Boulogne-Billancourt); Bibliothèque Nationale et Universitaire (Strasbourg); Bibliothèque Thiers (Paris); Centre des Archives Contemporaines (Fontainebleau); Centre des Archives Diplomatiques (Nantes); Service Historique de la Défense (Vincennes); British National Archives (Kew); British Library; Hauptstaatsarchiv Baden-Württemberg (Stuttgart); Sächisches Staatsarchiv (Dresden); Library of Congress; Musée de l'Impression sur Étoffes (Mulhouse); National Army Museum (London); Scottish National Library (Edinburgh). While the individuals who helped me are too numerous to list here, special thanks go to Didier Hemmert at the Archives Municipales in Sarreguemines; Robert Itucci in the municipality of Givet; Michèle Lannoy in the municipality of Maubeuge; Fabienne Montchaud at the Bibliothèque des Dominicains in Colmar; Élise Nicolas of the Médiathèque Voyelles in Rocroi; Patrice Petit in the municipality of Rocroi; Denise Tatinclaux in the municipality of Vouziers; and Bernard Weigel at the Archives Municipales in Wissembourg—all of whom generously sent me reproductions or translations of materials from their collections. Thanks also to Bernard Metz in Strasbourg, who helped me to decipher some documents in old German script.

In France, I was repeatedly touched by the enthusiasm and generosity of colleagues, many of whom I met for the first time as a result of this project. In addition to Nicolas Bourguinat, I am grateful to Bettina Severin-Barboutie, Diana Cooper-Richet, Clotilde Druelle-Korn, Beatrice de Graaf, Jean-Marc Largeaud, Thomas Gauchet, Viera Rebolledo-Dhuin, Volker Wacker, and, especially, Jacques Hantraye. Although I was an outsider, they were all incredibly helpful and encouraging, sharing source ideas and unpublished works, orienting me to new archives, commenting on drafts, and discussing topics of mutual interest with me. Getting to know them has been one of the pleasures of my career.

In both Europe and the United States, I appreciated opportunities to discuss this research with colleagues and students. I am particularly grateful to the following for invitations to present my work: Stéphane Gerson, at the Institute for French Studies at New York University; Karen Hagemann, at the conference "War, Demobilization, and Memory: The Legacy of War in the Era of Atlantic Revolutions" at King's College, London; Daniel Whittingham, at the conference "Waterloo: The Battle That Forged a Century," also at King's College, London; Gabriele Clemens, at the Universität des Saarlandes (Saarbrücken, Germany); Phil Slaby, at Guilford College (Greensboro, NC); Jim Winders and Ellen Welch, at the Triangle Area French Studies Seminar (Chapel Hill, NC); and Alex Mikaberidze, to give the keynote address at the Consortium on the Revolutionary Era in Shreveport, Louisiana, in February 2016. I have also benefited enormously from discussions with co-panelists and participants at various meetings of the Western Society for French History; the Society for French Historical Studies; the Society for Military History; Nineteenth-Century French Studies; and the Consortium on the Revolutionary Era.

In the United States, numerous colleagues have assisted my work by commenting on conference papers or draft chapters, discussing ideas, and/or providing references, including Katherine Aaslestad, Rafe Blaufarb, Denise Davidson, Mary Dudziak, Karen Hagemann, Carol Harrison, Jennifer Heuer, Jeff Horn, Lloyd Kramer, Alex Martin, Michael McGuire, Michael Neiberg, Scott Reynolds Nelson, Joelle Neulander, Rick Schneid, Victoria Thompson, Trish Tilburg, and Ellen Welch. I am particularly grateful to Jeff Horn, for his close reading of the chapter on economic reconstruction, and Jennifer Heuer, for her helpful suggestions regarding the chapter on politics under occupation, as well as the Introduction and Conclusion. Special thanks also go to Carol Harrison and Sheryl Kroen, who first pushed me to undertake this project, giving me the courage to attempt an ambitious second book. As I ventured into the topic of the transition between Empire and Restoration, Denise Davidson and Jennifer Heuer have been wonderful interlocutors, collaborators, and friends. Thomas Veve generously shared his expertise on the British contingent in the occupation of 1815–1818. Denise Davidson and Dena Goodman passed along archival finds regarding the occupations of 1814 and 1815. In North Carolina, I have appreciated the camaraderie of the members of the Charlotte Area French Studies Workshop, which has sustained me with a little taste of Paris on the Catawba, especially Michèle Bissière, Carol Harrison, Allison Stedman, and Trish Tilburg.

Some aspects of the general discussion in Chapter 1 and Conclusion are informed by my preliminary examination in "Making Peace: The Allied Occupation of France, 1815–1818," in *War, Demobilization and Memory: The Legacy of War in the Era of Atlantic Revolutions*, ed. Alan Forrest, Karen Hagemann, and Michael Rowe (Palgrave Macmillan, 2016), 51–67, and "Remembering and Forgetting the First Modern Occupations of France," *Journal of Modern History* 88:3 (Sept. 2016), 535–571, respectively. I am grateful to the publishers for the initial opportunity to explore these subjects.

At UNC-Charlotte, I would like to thank my department chairs, Dan Dupre and Jürgen Buchenau, for their support. I am especially grateful to Jürgen for permitting me to take a leave from my term as Director of Graduate Studies in History, on two occasions, to complete the book. In addition, I thank Leigh Robbins, Gloria Davenport, and Linda Smith in the History Department Office for their help and patience over the years. I would also like to acknowledge the faculty and students in the Department of History. In addition to providing me with a wonderful community, many of them have taken the time to comment on portions of this work. For their suggestions, I thank in particular Karen Cox, Dan Dupre, Cheryl Hicks, Jim Hogue, Lyman Johnson, Heather Perry, Jill Massino, Gregory Mixon, Amanda Pipkin, Ritika Prasad, Aaron Shapiro, John Smail, John David Smith, and Mark Wilson. Two of my students at UNC-Charlotte helped me with research: Chris Kinley, in British and German sources; and Willem Osuch, in Danish ones. Warm thanks to both of them. For his assistance in creating the maps, I am grateful to Patrick Jones, cartographer in the Department of Geography and Earth Science.

For shepherding my manuscript into print, I thank the staff of Harvard University Press. I am indebted to my editor, Kathleen McDermott, for taking on this project and helping me to wrangle it into a manageable length. Her editorial assistants, Mihaela Pacurar and Esther Blanco-Benmaman, were consistently responsive and helpful. I am grateful to Daniel Sentance for his expert copy editing. I also thank the two outside readers, one anonymous and the other Rachel Chrastil. Their very thoughtful suggestions made this a much better book.

One of the greatest joys of the year I spent in Strasbourg was the new friends our family made. For making our family feel at home and giving us so many great memories, I am grateful to the teachers and families at the international École Élémentaire Conseil des XV and especially to the families of our dear friends Gillian and Jean-Charles Cante; Karima and Stefan Horvak; Rachael and Irek Kondak; and Nicole Schall and André Schmitt. Nicole and André deserve a special shout-out for taking me to Mulhouse to see the "Liberation" scarf at the Musée de l'Impression sur Étoffes in summer 2016.

Closer to home, I thank friends Veronica DeVita, Russ DeVita, Jana Hartenstine, Dan Hartenstine, Angie Willis, Tomas Gimenez-Elliaeson, Laurel Holtzapple, and David Blanton for their support and companionship. While you have all been fantastic friends, I have to give extra thanks to Veronica for sharing summer childcare with me at a critical early point in the project.

Most of all, I am grateful for my family. My parents, David and Marilyn, and brothers, Douglas and Ryan, have all encouraged my work, while also keeping me from taking it too seriously. My parents-in-law, Gary and Diane Wilson, have also been unfailingly supportive.

My husband, Mark Wilson, has always given me a room of my own, literal as well as figurative, as well as many good reasons to leave it at the end of the day. He also bravely and enthusiastically embarked on a year abroad with me, arranging a teaching position for himself in Germany, without ever having set foot in the country. And he took time from his own work to comment on various pieces of this project. Mark, I am so thankful to have you as my *compagnon de route,* every step of the way.

My biggest thanks go to my two sons, Oliver and Simon. During the years I was working on this project, they have grown from small children into young men, whose curiosity, creativity, sweetness, and humor amaze me. The two of them have endured regular discussions of French history with good cheer; accompanied me numerous times to France, including the year in Strasbourg; and even made a pilgrimage to Waterloo with me on a blustery day in fall 2013. I am beyond grateful to them for their openness to experiencing foreign schools, camps, foods, and languages. Oliver and Simon, you have made this project—and everything else—so much more interesting and meaningful.

Index

Page numbers in italics refer to figures and maps.